THE NEW ASIAN WAY

Rebuilding Asia through Self-reliance

Foong Wai Fong

THE NEW ASIAN WAY

Rebuilding Asia through Self-reliance

Pelanduk
Publications
www.pelanduk.com

Published by
Pelanduk Publications (M) Sdn Bhd
(Co. No. 113307-W)
12 Jalan SS13/3E, Subang Jaya Industrial Estate
47500 Subang Jaya, Selangor Darul Ehsan
Malaysia

Address all correspondence to
Pelanduk Publications (M) Sdn Bhd
P.O. Box 8265, 46785 Kelana Jaya
Selangor Darul Ehsan, Malaysia

Check out our website at *www.pelanduk.com*
e-mail: *pelpub@tm.net.my*

Perpustakaan Negara Malaysia   Cataloguing-in-Publication Data

Foong, Wai Fong
The new Asian way : rebuilding Asia through self-reliance /
Foong Wai Fong
Bibliography: p. 359
Includes index
ISBN 967-978-692-7
1. Asia—Economic conditions. 2. Asia—Politics and government. 3. Asia—Social conditions. I. Title.
330.95

Printed in Malaysia by
Swan Printing Sdn Bhd.

To the memory of my grandmother
Yie Zhuan Gui
who taught my family the value of self-reliance.

Do not dwell in the past,
Do not stay in the present.
Change with the trends,
Change with the times.

—GUAN ZHONG—
Chinese Scholar, Spring And Autumn Period

Foreword

Asia has to negotiate many hazards on its road to modernization. When the region's history, political background and economic and social systems are studied, it becomes clear that some new way—a new Asian way—must be found if it is to meet the challenges presented by today's changing world. Rapid growth, evolving institutions and the onslaught of global and technological forces are all factors that have damaged East Asia's economies in the recent past. However, these same factors can create opportunities for Asia. It is helpful to step back and put the experiences of the rest of the world into perspective—and learn something from them. This book is a *tour de force*, and in it, Foong Wai Fong, my partner in *Megatrends Asia*, has done that, brilliantly. Wai Fong is a third generation Chinese Malaysian who was educated in Malaysia and has worked and traveled widely in Asia and around the world. She is familiar with Asian culture and is conversant with its major languages. She has also witnessed at first hand the economic transformation of Asia in the last two decades.

Wai Fong has recognized that, throughout the world, changes must be made if personal, business and community success is to be achieved and maintained. An understanding of the big picture, of how Asia and the rest of the world are changing, is vital to ensure that the right changes are made. There will be new relationships, new leadership styles, new strategies and ways of organizing. It was this recognition that motivated Wai Fong to embark on this book.

The scope of the book is wide: it blends philosophy with economics, politics, sociology and history in a discussion of the future. Wai Fong has drawn on her knowledge and experiences to articulate a vision, a new global way, not only for Asia but also for the rest of the world. In her vision, the human attributes of spirit and attitude are universal, regardless of nationality, race, religion or culture. She discusses Asia in the context of the global business environment, outlines the cultural sensitivities and the conditions obtaining in the different countries of the region, and commends the attitudes that will put Asia back on the road to progress.

Since the 1980s, the global environment has undergone dramatic and unprecedented changes, making conventional approaches to problem-solving not only ineffective but inappropriate. Advances in science and technology, politics and economics have liberated us from physical, organizational, geographical and psychological restraints. Modern technology allows people to find quicker, more efficient, more pragmatic ways to achieve whatever they want to.

The most dramatic shift in the world today, however, is the shift of power from governments: the world is moving from being directed from the top down to being driven from the bottom up. The experiences of the 20th century seem to show that it is more effective and efficient to allow individuals to decide and achieve through their own efforts than through centralized state planning. It is now recognized that people must be allowed to participate in and enjoy the fruits of their labor and ingenuity. We can say that the dawn of the age of information and globalization completes the transfer of power from institutions (including governments and nation states) to individuals and their networks. We have come to the end of ideologically driven economies

This shift restructures the world, from one that was once dominated by mainframes (government to government) to one driven by a network of individuals. Geo-economics thus moves centre-stage and becomes the overriding consideration in global affairs, sidelining geopolitics. As we enter the 21st century, globalization is moving us towards a single world market. In the process, we are experiencing a rich paradox: while the global economy is of paramount importance, no-one knows how it works. I think that is the good news—if we don't know how it works, we can't fix it.

The global economy is self-organizing. Thus, the message for governments and societies is to dismantle any residual restraints that could limit the expression of their citizens' potential. This said, it must be pointed out that our global economy is still at a very primitive stage, and that the participants, having come from varying degrees of 'stateism' and liberal traditions, are only slowly adjusting to the complex workings of global capitalism. Even in the United States, at the centre of modern capitalism and with the strongest economy in history, much work still needs to be done to refine the workings of free enterprise. The US needs to continue to deregulate, reduce taxes, reduce welfare and downsize government. Europe's high unemployment is a result of its refusal to face the reality of the global economy. Europe is hampered by stubborn attitudes which oppose incentives, penalize business and protect labor. Britain's economy, however, has bounced back because restrictions have been removed and much of the power has been transferred from the state to the private sector. The financial crisis that began in Asia in July 1997 can be looked upon as the final call to governments to step aside in the economic realm. The crippling government structures in Japan and South Korea send a timely message to China as it carries out the largest economic restructuring in its history.

There is increasing certainty that people can achieve peace and physical well-being from the democratic process, the rule of law and the workings of the free market. Physical well-being—access to adequate food, shelter, health care and other comforts—results when individuals are allowed to seek a livelihood without undue interference from an oppressive elite. It has been achieved by millions in the world's developing economies. Today, there is abundant evidence that freedom is on the rise. Freedom House, an international body that surveys the status of political rights and civil liberties, reports that there are far more free countries now than in 1972, when surveys began. *The Index of Economic Freedom*, published jointly by the Heritage Foundation and *The Wall Street Journal*, confirmed the correlation between economic freedom and prosperity. Seventy-two of 150 countries were classified as free or mostly free in 1997, up from 65 the year before. Even though it is clear that freedom is essential for economic prosperity, politicians in many countries still cling to the advantages they gain from maintaining a nation state, even at the expense of their citizens' welfare and at the risk of lagging behind in the global economy.

In tandem with the free market, however, governments must promote and develop the rule of law or face the consequences of 'cowboy' or 'gangster' capitalism, as seen in Russia and some of the new economies of Eastern Europe. In the newly developing economies in Asia, the great infusion of investment funds resulting from the openness of the global system have contributed to the formation of asset bubbles, where opportunities to productively use these funds have been limited. The result is the destabilizing period of financial restructuring that Asia is experiencing as it approaches the new century.

Governments, overwhelmed by the power of the market, are reluctant to accept the reality of their loss of control. All the evidence shows that the market is far more effective than the state in allocating resources and creating well-being for the citizens. The free market system must therefore continue to develop. Governments and citizens must trust the process and allow the global system to evolve without interference, playing to a set of rules observed by everyone. Markets are self-correcting, and democratic. Bad economic policies are soon punished, in the same way that the market rejects poor-performing companies. There is nothing governments can do to control the free market, or to change it, except to ensure that their economic house is always kept in order. Governments must embrace this new reality and redefine their role, becoming, for example, enforcers of the law and defenders of security, and ceasing to be active economic players, even in the field of monetary policy.

It is now clear that those economies that recognize the new realities, and develop and refine the attributes of capitalism in the 21st century, will have the best chance of enjoying continued prosperity and well-being. It is useful to bear in mind the following:

1. Openness, to the benefit of all—free trade and private direct investment, the free flow of information and openness to immigration. A high income does not mean much if the cost of living is equally high (such as in Japan), because free trade is curbed. Such economies fail to result in a high standard of living for their citizens, defeating the very purpose of economic growth. Countries may boost savings rates, but the returns on these savings in a protected environment are miserable (as many Asians have experienced). It is now clear that an open system works best for people: it ensures the most efficient allocation of resources and maximizes returns on investments, be it for current consumption, for their retirement, or for the accumulation of capital for development purposes. The fact that the American stock-markets remain robust illustrates the workings of the open system—money

chases value-generating stocks. In a world where competitiveness is decided by brainpower, initiative and entrepreneurial drive, openness to talent is vital if intellectual capital is to be built up. The United States has one of the most open immigration programs: every year, some one million people enter the United States as legal immigrants. Who are these people? For the most part, they are skilled, talented and entrepreneurial. People want to be where they can make the most of their talents.

2. Transparency and the elimination of corruption. Transparency in administration and management, both of governments and companies, is sought by international investors who make long-term commitments investing in businesses and economies. The world had not paid much attention to the issue of corruption until recently, when the World Bank began to make it an important consideration in making loans. Even among Western nations, only a third of the 27 member governments in the OECD forbid outright domestic tax deductions for foreign bribes paid by their companies (these include the United States, Canada, Britain and Japan). Now the OECD has begun the process of requiring all countries to prohibit tax deductions for foreign bribes. A world made transparent by telecommunication technologies and mobility encourages ethics and trust: an open system is also a competitive one.
3. Money and talent go and remain where they are treated well, and governments and businesses in the 21st century should realize this. Trade and investment are the driving forces of continuous economic prosperity. In the global economy, based on information and knowledge, where intellectual capital is the bedrock of wealth creation, talent will find and settle in places where opportunities can be maximized and quests for achievement fulfilled.
4. Everyone can be a capitalist, and can thus be involved in the creation of wealth. The traditional conflict between capital and labor will be resolved with the widespread adoption of the stock-market as a wealth-sharing vehicle. Everyone can have a stake in the global economy by investing in good companies that are well-managed. Employees, customers, suppliers, management and stockholders share a common destiny and interest in such enterprises. It is a partnership in which each advances the other's interest by adding more value to the whole. Flexible markets, employ-

ability, performance-based pay for managers, optimized value for shareholders and customer satisfaction, all combine to make a winning proposition. The United States, where the mutual fund industry is now larger than the banking system, is the first country to experience such an extraordinary shift in wealth creation.

5. Economic growth is fuelled by technological change and innovation. The globalization of the world is being driven by information technology. Telecommunications is simultaneously creating a huge global economy and empowering the components of that economy—individual people. Information technology is redefining how products and services are created and how business is done. Twenty years ago, there were almost no teleworkers: today there are about 20 million worldwide and by the year 2016, probably 200 million. We are learning how to do old things better and in a new way, manufacturing operations are automating and becoming lean, and traditional industries which are trying to reinvent themselves are creating a culture of 'first time right'.
6. Entrepreneurship should be encouraged to flourish. The United States' ability to create new jobs and industries is due to its dynamic entrepreneurial talent. In the last six years, America created 15 million new jobs; Europe, on the other hand, has lost two million jobs in the past 12 years. From among the many start-ups in the United States have emerged the smaller companies that have given the US economy its energy and new jobs. In addition to factors like lower taxes, ease of start-up, and an egalitarian and pro-enterprise climate, a vibrant stock-market serves as the prime reward for risk-taking and entrepreneurship. In a supportive entrepreneurial environment, failures are tolerated, people are encouraged to try and try again if they do not succeed the first time, and success is celebrated with recognition and financial rewards.

Investment money finds businesses with potential. In the US capital markets, money is automatically allocated to firms that seem likely to earn the highest returns. This contrasts with such practices as lending to friends or relying on established corporate relationships, as is common elsewhere (like in Japan and other East Asian economies). The United States' practice of funding businesses with potential is one of the reasons why America funds so many of its young people who are the most comfortable and creative with new technologies. America's capital markets put a premium on the future, not the past—they are eager to support the new, not the old. Hundreds of billions of dollars are channelled directly to the stock by investors or through their fund managers, rather than through the bank.

7. Education and training must be a major priority; they are the keys to maintaining competitiveness. Asia and America share a culture of learning. In the United States, for example, people tend to be psychologically and physically mobile. They continue to learn at their own expense or at their employer's expense. American companies invest some US$100b a year in the training of their employees; this is in addition to America having the largest and best graduate and undergraduate business schools in the world. In its early stages of industrialization, Asia invested in its future by making basic education available to the masses. The immediate priority, especially for the emerging Asian countries, is to develop education and training in order to move up the value chain.
8. Job mobility is a growing phenomenon needs to be recognized. Countries with rigid labor policies, such as most European countries, are having a hard time adjusting to a global labor market, where supply is abundant and wage rates are constantly being driven down by new entrants. For example, Indians in Bangalore are among the best software engineers, giving their western counterparts a run for their money. Very soon, their jobs may move on to Africa or China.
9. World-class quality products and worldwide competitive prices will be the mantra for producers. As most products are or will soon be available everywhere, they must be made to a standard that is acceptable and sold at a price that is competitive. We live in a world where products can easily be replicated: what makes a product stand out is innovation, its ability to create demand, and the value it offers for a competitive price.
10. The global economy is driven by trade and foreign investment. It experienced unprecedented growth in the 1990s. Growth in global trade is faster than growth in output, and foreign investment by private companies has become the most powerful engine of growth in the world. Collectively, developing Asia is one of the largest sources of FDI capital in the world.

11. There should be limited government interference in the commercial sphere; strategies that allow governments to 'pick winners' have outlived their time. Privatization should not simply mean a shift from public monopolies to private monopolies: there must be a link with competition. Countries need to approach the best providers in the world in order to obtain efficient and competitive services. Protection of industries has led to inefficiencies; competition is the best safeguard for innovation and efficiency. Furthermore, the complexity of the global economy increases the risk of failure of state-directed or guided industrial policy; the global marketplace has become almost too complex for governments to accumulate the required knowledge. Asian governments should also realize that bureaucrats are not good at picking winners, because they have limited information on and knowledge of market conditions. The market, although inherently unstable, can do a far more efficient and self-correcting job than the bureaucrats.
12. All politics will be global. The globalization of financial markets, environmental concerns, the drive for transparency and the need for job creation have enlarged the context for domestic politics, putting an end to the idea that politics is local. National governments must listen and adjust their policies to make conditions attractive to foreign investment. National competitiveness alone is insufficient to draw in the funds and retain talent. An attractive national character, fiscal policies, transparency, openness, cost of living, infrastructure and the vibrancy of the arts become more important than labor costs. Government accountability will receive greater scrutiny from a globalized media and the Internet. Protectionism and globalization will polarize government policies—it will be a choice between letting the free market pick the winners or leaving it to the intrusive, heavy hand of the state.
13. GDP as a measure of economic output is not only universally inaccurate but also increasingly irrelevant. People care about whether there are high-paying jobs provided by progressive companies in their community. Companies and individuals will relocate to places with the most attractive tax benefits and economic freedom, thereby loosening the bonds of nationality. National interest is best served when individual or corporate self-interest is maximized. Investment analysts care less about sovereign risks

and more about the competitiveness of companies and how well they are positioned for sustainable growth. Attention is now moving from the competitiveness of regions or countries (which are integrating rapidly) to the competitiveness of companies (which, with the right intellectual capital and global reach, can be more secure).

14. Networks made up of companies and individuals are becoming more important economically than states, due mostly to the revolution in telecommunications. The overseas Chinese network is the third largest economy in the world; the economic activity of networked non-resident Indians is greater than that of India itself. To ethnic networks add business networks, such as automobiles and fashion, and then add the machinery that makes them all interact, the Internet. Although networks may be replacing the economic importance of nation states, they do not subvert their cultural importance. The more we all become economically interdependent, the more we want to hold on to and celebrate our cultural identity. Contrary to what the Japanese believe, the more they integrate with the global economy, the more Japanese they will become.
15. The importance of small and medium-sized companies cannot be overemphasized. Indeed, they will dominate the global economy. The media all over the world focus on large, highly visible companies, for example, the Fortune 500 in the United States, in spite of the fact that the 500 largest companies in the country account for less than 10 per cent of the US economy. New, small and medium-sized companies are at the heart of 21st-century capitalism. Japan, South Korea and Singapore need to cultivate a culture of entrepreneurship by establishing an environment and an infrastructure in which small and medium-sized enterprises can thrive.
16. The rich are getting richer and almost everyone is doing better. Inequalities will remain, but on balance, everyone benefits from the expansion of the global economy. The vigorous, innovative US economy is the most unequal of all industrial countries in terms of wealth and income. When there is freedom, very talented individuals will do much better than others. When the rich grow richer, there are greater incentives to invest back into enter-

prise, and hence the economy, thereby creating more jobs that help those on the lower rungs of society to move up. Meritocracy must not be compromised. The free market system means equal access to opportunity, which has a better chance of creating sustainable growth and thus eliminating poverty. The way to eliminate poverty is by now well known: it is by expanding economic opportunities, not by giving hand-outs. In other words, as Wai Fong observes in this book, 'creative growth works better than redistribution'.

The story of 21st-century capitalism will not only start with market economies marching towards one single global economy. It will also relate the triumph of the individual over the state. Humankind has done much to create structures that have tried to deliver well-being and prosperity. Along the way, though, we seem to have lost sight of fundamental priorities and values. Without values, a society will inevitably flounder. This book has an unequivocal message: that a strong value system is essential for growth, whether a self-reliant individual striving for personal success and fulfilment is involved, or a community or nation trying to achieve or maintain prosperity. Globalization, rapid technological change and strong competition are adding to the pressure on world economies—especially Asia's young economies in transition. If the story of 21st-century capitalism is to end in success, we must remain as committed to a strong value system as we are to the pursuit of prosperity and personal well-being.

John Naisbitt

Contents

Acknowledgment

Behind every successful project there is a champion, and behind every writer there is a cheerleader. When I decided that I wanted to be the champion for the new Asian way, I was privileged to have John Naisbitt, my partner in *Megatrends Asia*, as my cheerleader. *The New Asian Way* could not have been written if it were not for the inspiration and support John has given me every step of the way. John is a great cheerleader and a kind and most gentle critic; I am grateful for all the help and time he has spent with me in the creation of this book. I have been particularly affected by John's ever-curious enthusiasm for the happenings in the world, his ability to focus and seek clarity, and his enthusiasm to learn. John is a wonderful human being, and his generosity and sense of equality have shown me what humanity truly means. For helping me to learn about the world and to come to appreciate it as a globalist, I owe John a great debt. Many other people have in one way or other helped in the creation of this book. I am grateful to all the distinguished individuals in Asia and other parts of the world who have spent their valuable time with me. To legislator Christine Loh, founder of the Citizens Party in Hong Kong, Professor Dr Ambrose King of the Chinese University of Hong Kong, Professor Dr Wang Guang Wu, Director of the East Asian Institute in Singapore, Professor Tseng Shih Chiang in Taipei, Professor Dr Tu Weimeng at Harvard, Sven Atterhed in Stockholm, Mr Mao Yushi of Unrule Institute in Beijing, Tadashi Yamamoto of the Japan Center for International Exchange, David Ho and Calvin Tsao in New York, Alan Chan in Hong Kong, and KenYeang in Kuala Lumpur, I give special thanks.

My English-language editor, Elizabeth Goodman in Sydney, in particular deserves a special word of thanks. Elizabeth is not only great with her work, she is truly a world-class professional. Elizabeth has done a fantastic job editing the English manuscript and helped me present the material and clarify my thoughts. Special thanks also to Mr Chan Dapeng of Beijing who heads the Chinese translation team and is the business champion in arranging for the publishing of the book in China, thus making it possible for *The New Asian Way* to be first published in Chinese in record time. I am also grateful for the help of my research assistants, Me Me, Yew Chong, Meng Choo and Shan Yuen; my intern, Shiang Ngoh, and former colleague at Cittabella, Liu Ching, for their invaluable contributions to this book. Lastly, I wish to thank my former colleagues in Transforma and Nanyang Group, especially my former executive assistant, Sok Kuen. Thanks to my lovely niece Ying Mun, the bits and bytes generation in Asia, who helped with the typesetting of the glossary of Chinese words, and the names of people and places. My family, especially my sister Fei Lan, deserves my grateful thanks. Her dedication to taking care of the family, in particular, looking after my ailing father, allowed me to focus on the book. Without her, I would have been unable to accomplish so much.

About the Author

Partner and collaborator with John Naisbitt for *Megatrends Asia*, an international bestseller and television documentary, Foong Wai Fong is a Chinese Malaysian writer, columnist and much sought-after speaker for global companies. Wai Fong holds an honours degree in economics from the University of Malaya. She was an executive with AIA prior to founding Transforma, a leading conference and publishing services company in Asia. Wai Fong launched CittaBella Malaysia, a leading Asian women's magazine. She currently also serves as the founding director of The Center of Global Entrepreneurship Studies at Yuan Ze University, Taiwan.

She was one of the emerging young leaders of ASEAN (Association of South-East Asian Nations) who represented Malaysia in the Japan-based International Association of Traffic and Safety Sciences (ITASS) and Honda Foundation's 19th Forum, She is the founding director of the New Asia Forum, The Asian Women Leadership Symposium and Asia Advisor to the International Women's Leadership Forum at Stockholm, an initiative of Washington-based Center for Strategic and International Studies.

Wai Fong is a recipient of Malaysia's Woman of Distinction Award 1996. She divides her time between Kuala Lumpur and global travel.

Wai Fong could be contacted at http://www.megatrendsasia.org.

Introduction

Why do some individuals prosper whilst others fail? Why do some economies flourish whilst others falter? These questions have intrigued and puzzled us throughout history. If success is determined solely by individual initiative, it is hard to explain why the diaspora almost always do better outside their native lands. For example, overseas Chinese and Indians living abroad share the same story as the many European immigrants who achieved great success in the New World. The evidence points to the fact that even if people work hard, continuously develop their skills and have a positive attitude towards life, their efforts are restrained by the institutional fabric of their societies. The renowned Harvard University economist, John Kenneth Galbraith, observed, 'Many wonder whether it is government policy or education that has contributed to the tremendous improvement in the economic well-being of the world's people. I think the greatest single factor accounting for this growth has been the removal of restraints that has enabled people to feel free to pursue their self-interest.'[1] Many other thinkers and economists advocate the dismantling of institutional restraints and a greater focus on creating the kind of conditions that allow individuals to achieve their full potential. While a person's attitude towards self and the world is fundamental to their own progress in life, it is becoming increasingly important that young people have a good grasp of the 'big picture' of their environment and understand what they can do to reshape it.

The New Asian Way aims to give that big picture. It attempts to create a framework to make sense of the political, economic and social landscapes in a rapidly changing Asia. It continues the debate on the ways of improving our communities and finding the right balance between meeting the needs of individuals and the community. It puts in sharp focus the attitude that individuals and communities should hold in the context of the global trends of the 21st century.

Asia has undergone tremendous change in the last 50 years—the euphoria of an Asia on the rise, the flying geese phenomenon of industrial and economic development, and the rapid opening-up of communities to the world. Increasing material abundance and technology have raised great hopes for the future. The most celebrated economic achievement of the modern age was the 'Asian miracle', which according to the World Bank, was unprecedented in human history. But, just as we are about to enter a new millennium, the triumphant music suddenly stops. The financial crisis which began in Thailand in mid-1997 sent shock waves which had a churning effect on the psyche of the region, throwing up fundamental questions regarding Asia's economic management, social structures and political systems. Serious soul-searching must begin—is the Asian model a mirage? How can governments, businesses and people maintain their stability in the avalanche of external forces and conflicting values that threaten them politically, economically and socially?

The financial crisis has led to many to question the social contracts between Asian governments and their citizens, which were once taboo. The tragic end of the Suharto regime in Indonesia is the most dramatic manifestation of this process. If Asians recognize the lessons of the financial crisis, then the ways in which Asian societies operate in the coming century could be forever changed. While the leadership must be accountable, every citizen must also take a hard look at whether their own actions have anything to do with the problems. When a large section of a society is consumed by greed, it is hard to have a clear perspective.

A further issue tossed up by the 1997 financial crisis centered on the question of whether large, top-down organizations are still viable—which in fact is a question also faced by organizations worldwide. Japan's k*eiretsu* and South Korea's *chaebols,* which were once the locomotives of rapid growth, have now turned out to be a burden on their own economies—debt-ridden, over-extended, and unprofitable. Responsible for massive bad loans in the banking system yet the source of employment for thousands of people, their present circumstances not only threaten the fundamental stability of their countries' economic systems, but also pose a threat to global economic stability. This also confirms the need for alternative and more flexible economic models that can meet the expectations of an integrated global economy. Japan and South Korea will be put to the test to produce a new social contract between the government/business and the people. In the meantime, Chinese capitalists would do well to pay attention to the pitfalls of the 'big is powerful' concept.

The urgent need to build businesses that can originate value-added economic activities for the global market puts pressure on the management skills of the Chinese family capitalists in particular, and Asian entrepreneurs in general. Used to enterprises such as banking and real estate, that are non-exportable and at best regional, Chinese-driven businesses in Asia will be challenged to come up with products and services that meet world standards in an efficient and profitable environment, with or without foreign partnerships. 'Cheap hands' will no longer be enough to carry Asia forward. The export-driven strategy made possible by cheap labor and devalued currencies is now proving to be dangerously precarious. In other words, the future will no longer be just about creating wealth with other people's money, technology or markets; the focus will shift towards building Asian global enterprises using greater creativity.

Growing more urgent each day is the issue of how Asia can successfully move towards sustainable growth anchored in strong domestic demand. The long-held traditional value of frugality has proved to be an obstacle for Asia to transform from an export-oriented region to a consumer-driven one. Frugality is different from prudence. Wealth must be allowed to circulate, frugality could lead to stagnation. It is ironic to find Asian economies depositing their hard-earned foreign reserves in Western banking systems and financing consumption in the West, while their own domestic economies cannot shake off dependence on foreign capital. Despite Japan's sustained economic success (at least right up to the end of the 80s), the character of the Japanese economy has not changed; it still remains a largely producer economy. What is wrong with this picture? Does the lesson of modern economic growth suggest frugality has a regressive nature? Does the consumer-driven economy in the United States hold lessons for Asia?

Crisis is useful, in a perverse way. It forces you to think hard, reassess your values and help you decide your direction for the future. Although the financial crisis has in some ways shaken our self-esteem, it is a tremendous opportunity for Asians to make the changes necessary to move forward. It has the effect of putting us back on the fulcrum, where we must find the correct balance. I hope that the search for the new Asian way will help us refocus, take a long, hard and honest look at our own needs and circumstances, expand our strengths and hardens our resolve to shed old habits.

Asians must bear in mind that modernization is an ongoing process. It has to be admitted that despite the impressive advances of the Asian economies in the past few decades, the reality of today is that the old formula no longer works. Asia must change—we have to say goodbye to the old ways of running the government, the economy and our social lives. We have to re-examine our centuries-old traditions and values, and let go of a lot of psychological baggage. The world at the dawn of the new century is indeed radically different from the one we grew up in. We need to update ourselves, nurture a new mind-set and have the courage to face radical change. Honest adjustments must be made to several aspects of Asian culture and attitude.

A revolution of culture has to take place. I urge my readers to look at this taboo word 'revolution' with a new mind-set. Regard it in a positive and liberating context—one of creative reconstruction—not the old blood-stained version of toppling the establishment or abandoning traditions. The new culture will be one which respects individuals, celebrates their potential and allows them the freedom to enrich society. Asians have to put down the baggage of colonialism and reject the superiority complex they assumed on the strength of a civilization now long gone. We have to focus on integrating the best values of our own heritage and those from around the world, bringing forth the potential within us.

The harsh realities of global capitalism also highlight the critical issue of efficiency of people and capital. Admittedly, the effect of global forces on Southeast Asian economies still in transition has been devastating. Economies must play the game according to modern global rules: more open and transparent governments and corporate governance, more efficient and profitable businesses, and more productive, creative and self-reliant people.

The emergence of the new Asian way will also put an end to the crossfire of the unproductive debate on East–West values, which has led to tension between Asia's moralistic traditions and the Western modern pop culture. While some Asian leaders constantly lash out at what they regard as the decadence of the West, Asia's own popular culture is increasingly influenced by Western technology and ideas, especially those from the United States. Some Asian leaders, who hang on to Asia's so-called superior values, unfortunately fail to spell out the specifics as to how they can assure quality of life for everyone, now and in the future. It troubles me that the mere promise of the American Dream can lure away Asia's most talented. Many condemn the West for excesses, but play down the help the West has long extended to Asia. Admittedly, the West has done Asia much injustice, but it must be recognized that in spite of its own enormous challenges, its achievements, especially in science and technology, and the management of profitable global enterprises, are ubiquitous.

It is time to reconcile the differences between East and West. There must be an end to all the unproductive rhetoric of 'Asia rising, West declining' or now the meaningless 'West triumphant, Asia wounded'. This is not how the world works—life is not a zero sum game. We need to seriously begin to learn about and from each other and build the common values for a truly rich global civilization. The best has no East or West distinction—it is simply the best. If equality and liberal values are a good driving force, everyone would do well to take them on. What is important is to have a good answer for our own people when they ask, 'Why are dreams only possible elsewhere? Why only the American Dream, why not the Asian Dream?' Nana Naisbitt, a young American artist, expressed her wish to see a balance between Eastern and Western values. 'It is the yin and the yang of the East and West that can produce a creative convergence of cultures,' she said. Global businesses have been at the forefront of this meaningful direction, and global economic integration will continue to promote this understanding. We have to seriously consider how to preserve the best parts of our values, and yet evolve to cope with the challenges ahead. If we can give our treasured values and traditions a new interpretation which is compatible with the physical and technological realities of the present world, we will have the foundation for a great Asian renaissance.

The role of government and the relationship between the governed and the governor should also be re-examined. Government will still remain an important institution as an enforcer of the law and defender against security threats. However, we will have to depend less on the state for our well-being and prosperity. As countries integrate in today's global economy, it is impossible for governments hampered by a lethargic bureaucracy to know enough to stay current and act fast enough to meet the challenges of that economy. Top-down, big government model has been inefficient in putting resources to work, compared with the market-place. The market-place is where the desires and ingenuity of millions of individuals meet, and it is their decisions that finally determine what is viable and what is not. As the economist Friedrich von Hayek once said, 'No-one knows how the global economy works'. It is for this reason, amongst others, that it is both futile and fatal to allow the power to make decisions to be confined to a few individuals at the top.

All achievements are bottom-up, voluntary efforts. Personal achievement stems from inner motivation; enterprises are built by people whose hearts respond to a challenge, not by formal structures imposed on them. Black markets provide a good example. Black market activities are illegal, yet they remain vibrant. In certain economies, they form a larger sector than the conventional economy. Attempts to control black markets have been futile. A more productive alternative might be to guide these activities in a positive way that encourages individual effort. It has become clearer that the organization that works is one that is self-organizing. Command-and-control regimes are a conceit. The former Soviet leader Mikhail Gorbachev made this confession, 'What we know now, what we can clearly see from the vantage of today, is that too often leadership in the 20th century realized its potential through force, deception or propaganda.'[2] The next question that arises is, what conditions must be created in order to nurture self-leadership, and to promote self-reliance, self-motivation and creativity? What values, attitudes and relationships do we need to nurture and preserve in an achieving society?

Individualism must be allowed to flourish. The Asian renaissance can only come about when opportunities are available for individuals to grow, otherwise everything is just hollow talk. In other words, making individuals feel free and safe is a fundamental condition for creativity. The new Asian culture must celebrate that. This means equalizing opportunities in each of Asia's systems, liberalizing and opening up to each other and to the world. The same applies to the corporation and to the family.

There is a widespread belief in Asia that Western-style individualism is negative and that the political, economic and social systems that allow individual rights to reign supreme are certainly not suitable for Asians. The Western preoccupation with economics and materialism is seen as immoral, and in conflict with the Confucian tradition of moral uprightness and sacrifice. On closer examination, it is in this perception that we find the answer to our own backwardness, especially if we go back to the time when China was ruled by mandarin scholars. The mandarin scholars indulged in the elevation of morals, and disdained merchants of any kind. The reality, however, is that people are driven to create wealth for their own well-being. So as not to attract criticism for being too fond of money, people were forced to lead hypocritical lives, far from the ideals of Confucian morality. An important distinction that Confucian scholars must not overlook is that the old economy based on agriculture and characterized by low productivity has disappeared, to be replaced by a high-tech environment, which allows people to create values and trade in a win-win situation. Asia needs a modern 'wealth creation culture' which embraces the underlying rationale for the creation of a value economy, a fundamental prerequisite for other aspects of modernization. We need to focus on legitimizing creative and productive wealth creation in the context of an accepted set of game rules.

It is also often believed in Asia that Western individualism is unfettered, and that people are given the freedom to run amok. There is no such thing as unfettered freedom: the boundaries of what is and what is not permissible are clearly defined by law and social behavioural codes. Problems arise when some individuals choose not to take responsibility for their actions and then blame the consequences on society. Individualism itself is not to be blamed. On the contrary, individualism makes for productive endeavors and high achievements. Productive individuals create wealth and make good consumers. A society that consumes lays the foundations for economic prosperity, as demand makes for a robust market and supply creates more employment.

The images of the West that Asians see on television and read about do not tell the full story of Western society. The last century has seen great progress in the economic, political, scientific and technological fields. Most advances were made in the West, especially in the

United States. On the social front, voluntarism and entrepreneurship are flourishing as never before. The problems in the West are not due to individualism, but the entitlement mentality. The West is just as concerned with the decline of the family unit. The turbulence of a globalized world will see a return to family values and a search for meaning world-wide. Generation X is already rethinking divorce and is contemplating the virtues of the traditional family. What we need to work on is reinventing the traditional family into a modern family.

Another widespread expectation in Asia is that everyone should make personal sacrifices to ensure that group welfare comes first, on the grounds that this ensures stability, which will bring about prosperity. Freedom is viewed in the context of responsibilities, not rights. We are also told that excessive individualism leads to selfish attitudes, which in turn cause instability and inefficiencies, something Asia cannot afford. But where is the logic in all this? There is no doubt that irresponsible individuals are a social menace. However, responsible and achieving people are assets to the community—they bring value to the community. If we do not encourage people to be individualistic and show off their talents, how can we expect to have people who want to be different, creative and outstanding in their chosen fields? *Perhaps we should not be asking what sacrifices people should make for the community, but what people should do to reach their full potential and how their best can give value to the community.*

Individual rights must come hand-in-hand with responsibilities. Rights without responsibilities is a recipe for disaster. When some Asian leaders proposed that the world review the Universal Declaration of Human Rights, they risked being labelled autocrats by Western liberals. Their intention, however, was for more consideration to be given to the balance between individual rights and responsibilities. While the concept of responsibility is not totally absent from the United Nations' declaration, there has been no systematic attempt to spell out all the responsibilities that go with human rights. The Inter Action Group, made up of former heads of government and assisted by a group of experts, on the 50th anniversary of the Declaration of Human Rights in December 1998, tabled a new Universal Declaration of Human Responsibilities.[3] This is an example of Asians shaping the values of the world. In its preamble, the draft declaration states, 'The exclusive insistence on rights can result in conflict, division and endless dispute, and the neglect of human responsibilities can lead to lawlessness and chaos. All people have the responsibility to foster a better social order, both at home and globally.'

This book, which consists of 12 chapters, aims to demonstrate how a New Asia can be built through the adoption of the new Asian way—a way which draws the best from the East and the West, which discards the weaknesses and pitfalls of the present system, and upon which a progressive New Asia could be rebuilt. The way for all is to find the right balance—to maintain the present consumption and at the same time invest for the long term; to preserve valuable traditions and at the same time change.

Lessons from the world

The New Asian Way begins by tracing challenges and the experiences of the world's modernization process. Over the last 500 years, Asia in general and the Chinese in particular have just been bystanders as the West led in a series of economic, political and technological achievements. Modern methods of wealth creation, governance, science and technology have all been created and refined through the efforts of the West. The modernization of Asia has indeed been Westernization. This chapter then goes on to scrutinize the valuable lessons that Asia could learn from the world.

Building the market economy

Discussion continues in chapter 2 on how Asia could build a comprehensive industrial and modern business culture with Asian characteristics. Asia has the opportunity to choose an appropriate capitalist strategy, drawing on the experiences of the Americans, Japanese and the Germans, as well as those of the Chinese family capitalists. Economic stability and sustainable long-term prosperity, however, rest on Asia's will to build a genuine free market system. So far, Asia has only established a trading culture. This chapter further explores questions such as: How Asia's capitalist system could encourage more entrepreneurs to build global enterprises? How could Asia develop a sustainable management system for wealth creation, at the same time reduce excessive speculative activities that have no real productive value? What has to be done to further empower citizens?

Towards an opportunity society

Chapter 3 reviews the progress of Asia's young economies towards an opportunity society—one where the socio-economic system promotes the growth of individuals and offers equality of opportunity. Is Asia coming to terms with a culture of a level playing field and free competition, a culture where the best person wins, the fittest survive and the most efficient companies prosper? This chapter examines the various cultures and communities of the region broadly called 'Asia', comprising Hong Kong, Singapore, Taiwan, the People's Republic of China, Malaysia, Indonesia, India, the Philippines, Thailand, Japan and South Korea.

From hand-outs to a way out

Extending credit to people and offering them the opportunity to be self-employed have proved a far more effective strategy to eradicate poverty than most forms of foreign aid. This chapter shows how the micro-credit approach is turning the traditional development model using foreign aid channelled through government agencies, and has given hope to millions of the world's poor for a way out of the poverty trap. Micro-credit will be the way the poorest of the poor of Asia can improve their lives.

From working class to middle class

In Chapter 5, it is advocated that the engine of growth of the future for Asia are small and medium-sized enterprises including those at the township and village level. For individuals, the way forward to the middle class would be through business or by being a key employee whose input generates value for the employer. Communities will prosper through a partnership between global and local small/medium companies, building on an efficient human scale, through out-sourcing, subcontracting, in-sourcing and niche specialization. The transformation of China's state-owned enterprises, Japanese *keiretsu*, and Korean *chaebols* is also examined.

From local business to global enterprise

For an organization to be able to stay competitive locally and globally in the 21st century, it needs to attract, retain and motivate talented employees. To achieve this, a new relationship must develop between the employee and employer—employees could be given ownership of the enterprise, making them, in effect, their own employers. In the end, it will be the organizations run by entrepreneurs and owner-managers that will win. Chapter 6 emphasizes the importance of the individual as a source of value, rather than someone who depends on the employer for lifetime employment. It also examines how Asia's unique brand of corporate family, such as a traditional Chinese family business will take on modern characteristics.

From hands to minds

Asia's future economic success will also depend on its ability to create innovative products and to provide quality services. Asia must also reverse the trade in cultural products with the West, from a deficit to a surplus. While labor-intensive manufacturing will still feed millions in Asia's emerging markets, serious efforts must be made now to accumulate and disseminate knowledge. Asians in general, and the Chinese in particular have no tradition of systematically sharing knowledge, although progress is seen in communities such as Taiwan and Singapore. This chapter points to the need for a cultural shift, a recognition that the knowledge capital must be developed and shared widely in Asia.

From powerful leaders to empowering leadership

Following the Second World War, Asia's leaders advocated 'strong leadership' as the foundation for the region's development. However, changing times call for new attitudes towards the style of government. Chapter 8 challenges the next generation of Asian leaders to experiment with ways whereby the people become more involved. The most important leadership task for Asia's future leaders is to nurture and empower an achieving people, not to put them under strict authority. The political cultures of South Korea and Japan have demonstrated that paternalistic leadership can inhibit adjustment to the realities of the world. Today, paternalism has turned out to be a burden. The belief that dissent is subversive and that stability can only exist in the absence of dissent must be dispelled. If we accept that a modern and dynamic society is one that will hold together through stressful times, and if we can accept that when people know their interests are guarded and that their national flag makes the realization of their dreams possible, order will prevail. Asian leaders must focus on building a new culture which offers stability and in which people are empowered.

From strong government to engaged citizenry

The search for the new Asian way continues in chapter 9 with investigations into the political systems of Asia. In today's decentralized and complicated world, it appears that democracy is the way to efficiency and accountability. The biggest obstacle for Asia towards democracy, however, is the paternalistic top-down culture, in which vertical communication between the government and the governed prevails. People must understand that democracy is a bottom-up system where they should take greater responsibility for their lives by getting involved in shaping public policies. Holding elections doesn't automatically mean democracy. In a democracy, horizontal communication and plurality replace paternalism. However, it must be said that a soft landing is preferred. Well-intentioned but impatient Western liberals may advocate an abrupt break with the past, but it must be acknowledged that a culture for liberal democracy takes many decades to build. Also, it is impractical to have one standard model of political system throughout Asia. Each country will find its own ways of balancing the demands of development and political idealism at their own pace. Before liberal democracy can be put to work effectively, the people of Asia will need to have a firm understanding of what they want to achieve. The respect for the rule of law, equality of individuals and guaranteed freedom of expression are the fundamental values that Asians have to incorporate into their daily lives before a system of government based on these principles can become a reality.

Winning values

The adoption of the new Asian way also means that Asians have to be honest and face up to the achievements of the rest of the world. While some rejoice that many products consumed in the West are made in Asia, they ignore the fact that they are made according to Western designs and technology. Chapter 10 calls for a revolution of culture in Asia, a rejection of archaic conservative values and a reinterpretation of valuable Asian traditional values. Confucian values are high moral values, theoretically sound but hard to achieve. Asia needs to transform its old treasured values into values that can be applied to everyday living and that will travel well. To transform the Asian region to one that is dynamic and creative, Asia needs to be open to the flow of information. When people learn to take responsibility for them, the free flow of information will only enrich and enhance their lives. It is this sort of stimulation that helps communities grow. Things American, or Americana, are popular not because the United States is politically or economically powerful, but because it represents the ideas and dreams of the people. Asian attitudes must change: we must move from closed to open societies; from a paternalistic hierarchy to a society where there is individual responsibility and creativity; from short-term thinking to long-term planning; from Asia-think to global-think; from making sacrifices to making creative contributions; and from always putting skills and technology first to considering values first.

From public institutions to self-support communities

Chapter 11 moves on to examine the self-supporting organizations that are emerging worldwide. The enormous pressures caused by environmental degradation and social change mean that everyone must become involved in the search for solutions. Such bottom-up involvement is the only effective way to integrate demands for improved well-being with the preservation of the physical. Governments can only do so much. Where inefficient government bureaucracies fail, non-government organizations intervene to address rising concerns, to educate the public and to encourage involvement. Their effectiveness in solving social and community problems is in no doubt; they will continue as a dominant force in driving social change.

The new Asian way—the search continues

If we accept that individualism, the free market and democracy form the foundations of a modern society, and that open and global attitudes must influence the values that will help us remain competitive in the world, what will the new Asian way look like? Does Hong Kong, with minimalist government intervention, cosmopolitan sophistication and a free-wheeling capitalist environment, provide the model for the rest of Asia? Or does highly disciplined, corruption-free and efficient Singapore, run by a professional civil service, show the way forward? Many have suggested that Singapore should be more like Hong Kong and that Hong Kong should be more like Singapore.

Taiwan, although chaotic and physically less attractive, has a tremendously successful, home-grown industrialization program, and its globally competitive firms are being noticed. Its entrepreneurial culture supports innovation and makes good use of a technologically sophisticated work-force. Increasingly democratic, Taiwan society is vibrant and motivated, providing favorable conditions for free-market capitalism to flourish.

A combination of the values of Singapore, Hong Kong and Taiwan, the three economically most successful and almost homogenous Chinese and Chinese-run communities, may offer an alternative model to the Anglo-Saxon or Japanese approach. Can the new Asian way take the best of each of these and craft them to produce the perfect model? The new Asian way will continue to learn and draw from the best of the East and the West, the best of old traditions and modern ways, and adapt them to balance the demands of the present with the idealism of the future. The new Asian way will always be a work-in-progress—that is where the excitement and opportunity lie.

Foong Wai Fong

Part I

Modernization

Chapter 1
Lessons From The World

"America was established not to create wealth
But to realize a vision, to realize an ideal—
to discover and maintain liberty among men."

—Woodrow Wilson (1856-1924)—

IN the collective consciousness of Asians in recent centuries, modernization has almost always been equated with westernization. The Western nations lead the world in material abundance, in scientific and technological capabilities, as well as in vibrant economic and political systems. It is evident that the lives of modern Asians display strong Western influences—they wear Western clothes, use the telephone and other telecommunication tools, watch Hollywood movies, and practise the capitalist system. Whilst acknowledging this fact, Asians kept reminding themselves of their glorious early civilization. Not only were they the original inventors of key technologies, they also enjoyed wealth and a far more advanced social, political and economic system than the Europeans. At the beginning of the millennium, 'Western' civilization was only a step above barbarism compared with its Chinese, Islamic, Indian or even Byzantine counterparts.

Scholars have long been perplexed by the stagnation of Asian societies. One explanation is that, as the centuries wore on, most of the governments of Asia calcified into top-heavy empires that were unable to bring about change. For example, even though the Chinese had invented some of the greatest tools of modern civilization, they did not continue their scientific research, while Europe and America began to experiment in areas ranging from politics and economics to the organization of community life. A sustained period of scientific and technological discoveries and advances has culminated in the West achieving a position of supremacy in most fields, including medical science, engineering, and space. This period has also, of course, brought the West great wealth. At the same time, the West has achieved dominance in international political and economic relations through its developed economic and political systems. The popular cultures of the West, led by America, have also spread far and wide—American movies, popular music and fast food, French couture and cognac, English literature and books are all accepted worldwide. By the end of the 20th century, the people of western Europe and America have become the richest and most technologically advanced in history. In 300 years, they have progressed from one of the least advanced societies to the most advanced.

Notwithstanding the fact that the Asians are now left behind, they are tremendously proud of their heritage. The Chief Minister of the State of Sabah in Malaysia, Yong Teck Lee, once observed that, 'America is a country, whereas the Chinese have a civilization'. While the truth of this is indisputable, this raises the epochal questions for Asians: in spite of our early start, how did the West catch up? What is it that enables and empowers the West, especially America to define the style and set the agenda for modern life? Today, at the beginning of the next millennium, it is us Asians that have to play catch up.

An Explosion of Ideas

Early civilizations in both the East and the West had a wealth of philosophical discourse on the affairs of man. The Greek and Chinese philosophers, for example, gave the world an enormous storehouse of ideas on government and on human nature. However, Eastern civilizations focused on the spiritual pursuit of the meaning of being, resulting in a meticulously crafted body of moral codes on the refinement of human behaviour. Sciences devoted to the logical and analytical were, unfortunately, completely ignored. As an illustration, even though the Chinese were the first to discover gunpowder, they never went beyond making firecrackers which were only used to frighten away barbarians. Westerners focused instead on the practical, gathering knowledge and building an understanding of science and technology. Perhaps the greatest contribution of the West to mankind has been its enthusiastic spirit of innovation and enterprise in putting ideas to practical use and in improving the comforts of daily living. The quest for adventure and a strong sense of curiosity helped spur further efforts. The 20th century has seen an explosion in the number of ideas and experiments, ranging from science and technology to different ways of governance and the organization of economic and social lives.

Inventions and Innovations

Great scientific discoveries of the modern age which have profound influence on mankind almost exclusively originated from the West. These include Isaac Newton's law of gravity, Charles Darwin's theory of evolution, Albert Einstein's theory of relativity, Madam Curie's discovery of radium, Alexander Fleming's penicillin, Guglielmo Marconi's radio, James Watson and Francis Crick's discovery of the structure of DNA, and Jonas Salk's vaccine. Other equally impressive contributions are, *inter alia*, Linus Pauling's discovery of the nature of chemical bond, Stephen Hawking's theory of the origin of the universe, Nikola Tesla's findings on practical use of alternating current, Michael Debakey's contribution to heart bypass surgery, and BF Skinner's studies on human behavior.

Waves of experiments proceeded in the political and economic realms, from Karl Marx's *Das Kapital,* which expounded the theory of class struggle and the economics of capitalism, John Maynard Keynes' theories, as well as Adam Smith, John Locke and John Stuart Mills' free market school, to such comparatively recent champions as Friedrich von Hayek and Milton Friedman. These philosophical dissertations had influenced the thinking of political leaders throughout the world, and have more or less divided the world into countries which practise capitalism or communism.

The great tradition of innovation and invention lives on. Alexis de Tocqueville wrote in *Democracy in America* as follows:

> I accost an American sailor and inquire why the ships of his country are built so as to last for only a short time. He answers without hesitation that the art of navigation is every day making such rapid progress that the fine vessel would become almost useless if it lasted beyond a few years.[1]

Newsweek writer Robert J Samuelson has this to say:

> The drive to discover, think and improve reflected an optimistic belief in progress and a rejection of traditional society where status and power were fixed by birth or custom ... Generally, Americans have done best by using science and technology practically and profitably. The great American inventors (from Thomas Edison and the light bulb, to Alexander Graham Bell and the phone, and the Wright brothers and the plane) make the point. So does Silicon Valley. Because everyone seeks to win and no-one knows exactly what theory, gadget or gimmick will work—there is constant experimentation and improvisation.[2]

Britain pioneered the Industrial Revolution, whilst the American entrepreneurs enabled the ordinary man-in-the-street to enjoy the fruits of their geniuses. The automobile age would not have occurred but for Henry Ford; commercial aviation took off due to Eddie Rickenbacker's effort; and the world of modern publishing has a lot to thank for William Randolph Hearst's ingenuity. Walt Disney even built a mega-industry out of daydreams. (The Japanese, learning from the West, embraced science and technology and went on to perfect many of the inventions of the West.) Man cannot live by discoveries alone, but must find a way to commercially exploit them, to create economic prosperity, and bring the resulting benefits to as many people as possible.

Today, the enterprising spirit and the culture of innovation are reaching new heights as America leads the world in the digital and information revolution. Bill Gates seems able to conquer the world with his software operating system, and Ted Turner's global Cable News Network (CNN) rewrites journalism and history by 'making the world a smaller place'. Meanwhile, at the threshold of the new millennium, *Time* magazine reminds us of how microchip has changed the world's economy by naming Andy Grove, co-founder of Intel, 'Man of the Year 1997'.[3]

Scientists are still at work, and from time to time, they come up with such breaking stories that grip the world—on the role of DNA and its implications for biotechnology; the successful cloning of the sheep, Dolly, and so on. Many of these extraordinary achievements have benefited the entire human race: they have given us knowledge that improves the lives of billions of people, not only in the West but throughout the world.

The Dark Side of Technology

On balance, sophisticated inventions and innovations have made the world a better place to live in. Household appliances help lighten domestic chores, modern medicine allows us to lead a healthier and longer life, and the internet enables countless individuals to connect with the rest of the world and to exchange ideas. Some even attribute Asia's economic take-off to the widespread use of air-conditioning.

On a negative note, some blame the evils of society on the advancement of science. American social writer, Francis Fukuyama, is of the view that birth-control pill, a scientific creation, has 'liberated' women, and eventually brings to the disintegration of the family. Others opine that promiscuous sexual behavior is rooted in the availability of effective contraceptives. This, coupled with greater mobility of the population, are said to have resulted in the spread of HIV. Many are also wary of the power inherent in computers and telecommunications. In fact, some think that the instantaneous flow of electronic information was partly to be blamed for the panic that resulted in the Asian financial crisis in 1997.

According to a famous Chinese writer, Lin Yutang, the reason why the Chinese did not further develop their discoveries such as paper and printing, gunpower and compass is because, the Chinese mind is not analytical:

> It is easy to see why the Chinese mind cannot develop a scientific method, for the scientific method, besides being analytical, always involves an amount of stupid drudgery, while the Chinese believe in flashes of commonsense and insight'.[4]

However, it seems to some that the advancement of technology was not pursued as the Chinese feared the potential catastrophes. Professor Tseng Shih Chiang, Professor of Chinese Management at the Xiao Tung University of Taiwan, said:

> The Chinese first made many scientific and technological discoveries, but gave up their inquiry and the positive application of these discoveries because they sensed the destructive forces of technology, hence they returned to the cultivation of morals and values. The Chinese are romantic, they only want to bring out the angel in human nature, and fail to pay attention to how to restrain the devil in us such as setting up a system of laws.

I have also heard this familiar argument:

> Perhaps the Chinese know that laws cannot restrain or regulate behaviour, hence, in order to avoid the catastrophe befalling mankind, it is better to completely stop the pursuit of science and technology, because ultimately man cannot control the destructive forces of technology when aligned with the evil nature of man.

While most Asians rejected science and technology, the West in the meantime achieved miraculous progress. However, with freer flow of information and technology after the Second World War, Asians have learnt the lessons and have since reversed the position. Paramount leader Deng Xiaoping worked hard to change the Chinese from skeptics to believers, emphasizing that science and technology formed one of the pillars of the 'Four Modernizations' in the creation of a New China. Throughout Asia, engineers and scientists enjoy an elevated status as Asia continues its modernization efforts.

Sharing of Knowledge

What is remarkable about Western societies is not only in their attitude towards the sharing of information and knowledge, but also in their capacity for systematically organizing knowledge in media that can be transmitted to and shared by millions of people. In America, 'How-To' books form a huge segment in publishing, from *How to be Happy in Eight Minutes* to *Making your First Million*. The production of illustrated manuals which lay out the processes of all sorts of operations to help learners acquire skills in a systematic way is standard practice in the West, whereas few traditional Chinese manufacturers think manuals are important.

The Chinese rely too much on their intuition and their teacher, in spite of their tradition of recording history in writing. A trip to the Palace Museum, Taipei or the Shanghai Museum cannot fail to impress a Westerner, for there is abundant evidence of the magnificent technologies of ancient Chinese. However, the Chinese masters were so territorial and so protective of their unique skills that they guarded them very closely. The Chinese saying, 'When the student learns the skill, there is no place left for the master' expresses their view of knowledge-sharing, that is, to retain leadership, the masters must retain their advantage. The Western experience has shown us that what is important is not how much knowledge a society possesses; but the dissemination of knowledge throughout the society which would in turn enables it to move forward. We must understand the difference, and realize how important it is for our children to acquire knowledge and to prepare them to become lifelong learners.

Another aspect relating to knowledge has to do with the protection afforded to the originators of ideas. Intellectual property rights and protection are absolutely vital. Unlike in America, where individuals profit greatly from their ideas, both financially and in terms of personal recognition, the Asians in general and the Chinese in particular are notorious for not respecting intellectual property, notwithstanding that they have a strict moral code and a tradition of holding teachers in high regard. This is a rather unattractive part of Asian culture, and if unchanged, will perpetuate the territorial nature of people and retard the growth of knowledge.

In contrast, countries with a liberal climate which encourages people to explore and to realize a dream, is certain to attract people with enterprising spirit from all over the world. The United States has about a million immigrants every year. A more specific example would be the Silicon Valley in the United States itself which has successfully attracted those with drive and initiative. It is of pivotal influence in the world today, not only for its eminence in the world of electronic technologies, but also for its ultra-modern lifestyle, reflecting how people would be living, working and learning in the 21st century. American analyst of the information industry and author Esther Dyson observed:

> Many foreign people and especially foreign governments visit Silicon Valley in the hope that some of the Valley's economic fecundity will rub off on them. Often they look at the wrong features, focusing just on the high-tech rather than on the culture that makes the companies thrive. What they are missing is the entrepreneurial spirit and the cross-fertilization as companies start, merge, break up, and unleash second and third-time entrepreneurs into the mix.[5]

Silicon Valley is unleashing a global revolution. Already, by the wealth it has created, it has surpassed the financial services of Wall Street and the automobile industries of Detroit.[6] What began as dreams is now powering the wonder that is Silicon Valley.

Stable Political System

The young leader of the British Labour Party, Tony Blair, took over from the Conservative Party leader, John Major, as Prime Minister of Great Britain immediately after his party's victory in the General Election of May 1997. Power was transferred swiftly and without a glitch, and government machinery went on without missing a beat. Many Americans have the same confidence. An American friend of mine told me, 'Nothing will happen to the government of the United States of America if something were to happen to the President; we just get a new president, and business will be as usual.' This aspect of the government system is one which impresses Asians: not only there is no doubt about a successor, but there are also men and women ready and able to take over the leadership, and the people are happy to give them a chance to try out their ideas. The contest for public office resembles a market-place for ideas. Accomplished individuals in business and academia often take a pay-cut in order to spend some time in public office, and the quality of government is enriched by the input of intelligence and dynamism from a broader society. There is a well-defined and structured system where the balance of power is between the independent judiciary, the legislature and the executive. Although this system cannot guarantee good government, at least it prevents the abuse of power or possible corruption by power. Asian writer Frank Ching has poignantly lamented the Asian autocratic system, 'The welfare of a nation cannot be totally dependent on one individual'.[7]

Another aspect of government in America is the decentralized nature of the Federation of the United States of America. The states in the union have autonomy over the majority of issues affecting the lives of their citizens and, by and large, the American people take ownership of their governance. Alexis de Tocqueville wrote in *Democracy in America* as follows:

> It is not the administrative, but the political effects of decentralization that I most admire in America. In the United States, the interests of the country are everywhere kept in view; they are an object of solicitude to the people of the whole Union, and every citizen is as warmly attached to them as if they were his own. He takes pride in the glory of his nation; he boasts of its success, to which he conceives himself to have contributed; and he rejoices in the prosperity by which he profits. The feeling he entertains towards the state is analo-

> gous to that which unites him to his family, and it is by a kind of selfishness that he interests himself in the welfare of his country.[8]

The Triumph of Capitalism

The free market, the maximization of individual liberty, economic freedom, and decentralized decision-making are all ideas that have their intellectual roots in the theories of such thinkers as John Locke, Adam Smith and John Stuart Mills (later, Friedrich von Hayek and Milton Friedman came centre-stage). These concepts have become the driving force of economic life in the West, and with globalization, the free market ways are increasingly adopted by the rest of the world. Perhaps the event that heralded the triumph of the free market was the fall of the Berlin Wall in 1989; an event that took place in an unexpectedly peaceful manner. Overnight, the free market expanded and capitalism was on the ascendancy. With the collapse of the Soviet Union in 1992, the world put Utopia and the altruism of central planning to rest.

Reviled as morally objectionable and appealing only to the greedy, capitalism has been vindicated and embraced. From the end of the Second World War until the oil crisis in the 1970s, the Western industrial world enjoyed three decades of prosperity and rising incomes. It was a time of unprecedented achievement. American author and Pulitzer prize-winner, Daniel Yergin, described it thus:

> The children of wartime and post-war rationing became adolescents of economic recovery and growth, and then the parents of the consumer society. Housing improved enormously, families bought their first and then their second car; they acquired appliances, television. They began to shop in supermarkets and department stores, they went on vacations and traveled to foreign countries, and they purchased products that had been turned into brand names and status symbols by advertising, and most of all, they had jobs.[9]

This prosperity was not confined to the Western world alone—trade and investment spread the wealth to the developing world. The opening of markets and increasing trade in the 19th and 20th centuries have led to the integration of the global economy, allowing capital, management know-how and ideas to flow from the developed to the developing world. Today, the Western industrialized countries are still economically dominant. Six out of the seven industrialized countries which form the Group of Seven (G7) are from the West (Japan being the exception). These countries, which include the United States, the United Kingdom, France, Germany, Canada and Italy, collectively produce some 60 per cent of the world's Gross Domestic Product (GDP) and enjoy the highest standard of living in the world.

In the last five years, a new economy based on Information and Technology (IT) has emerged in the United States. New products, new services and revolutionary ways of doing things have all been made possible because of the creation of a global information network. After close to a decade of re-engineering and restructuring, the US economy stands at close to US$8 trillion, and is believed to be at the forefront of a global boom. Unemployment and inflation in the United States are low, and government deficit has fallen to its lowest point in decades, from five per cent of GDP (US$290b) to 0.03 per cent of GDP (US$22.6b) in 1997. A government budget surplus is in sight for the US economy.

The Individual is Sovereign

It is instructive to examine how Western and Chinese names are constructed. Let us look at the names of US President, Bill Clinton and China's President, Jiang Zemin. In the former, the individual, Bill, comes first. But for a Chinese name, the family name (in this case, Jiang) always appears first, thus implying that the individual is subordinate to the family.

In the West, the interests of the individual are of utmost importance. The political systems are designed to protect and to confer supremacy to the rights of the individual. The principles of freedom and liberty, and equality of rights are cherished. No one is above the law, not even the President of the United States. All these allow individuals to freely engage in political, social and personal causes.

The American culture also encourages people not only to question everything and everyone, but to get involved in shaping the public agenda. As a result, alternative viewpoints are promoted by advocacy groups, foundations, non-profit organizations and community groups. Thousands of these civil organizations form the backbone of the American civil society, debating and influencing public policy issues that affect the well-being of their communities.

Be that as it may, it should be mentioned that there is a cost to be paid in return for personal freedom. Divorce rates in the Western societies are high, and the traditional family is weakening. Like societies elsewhere, American society is fragmented. According to a survey conducted by *The Wall Street Journal* and NBC News, the young people from Generation X (commonly taken to be those aged 18–29) believe that the government should do more to solve problems and help meet people's needs. This is a somewhat surprising finding, since this group of people has been raised on a steady diet of government-bashing, and might have been expected to be more self-reliant.[10] In contrast, the senior citizen group (age 65 and above) believe that the government '... does too many things that would better be left to businesses and individuals'.

Hollywood and television have created a dangerously distorted image of the ordinary, middle-class American family, playing up the dysfunctional rather than the positive aspects of American life. Series like *Dynasty* and *Lifestyles of the Rich and Famous* suggest that Americans lead a life of decadence and self-indulgence. The dynamic values of American culture, especially self-reliance and the entrepreneurial spirit, get relatively little exposure.

The American Tradition of Volunteering

Community life is highly reliant. There is a strong tradition in the United States of giving time and money to schools, colleges, universities, hospitals, libraries, churches, museums and the arts. More than 80 million Americans give time to voluntary causes. According to *Forbes,* in 1980, Americans contributed about US$65b (as measured in 1990 dollars) to charity.[11] By the end of the decade, they were giving more than US$100b annually, a real increase of 45 per cent. The average American, who gave US$340 to charity in 1980, raised his or her contribution to US$486 in 1990. Personal contributions further increased from US$880 in 1993 to US$1,017 in 1996. Many of these contributions are from middle-class Americans; in fact, as much as 80 per cent of the whopping amount of US$150b donated in 1996 came from individuals. No other country in the world has such a strong bottom-up involvement in community work and philanthropy.

The Life-force of a Dynamic Economy

American culture nurtures original thinking and supports pioneering research. Each year, more Nobel prizes are awarded to American scientists than any other nation. Of the 547 Nobel prizes awarded to recipients in the West, Americans received 230 of them. In fact, many Asian scientists achieve excellence because they are based in America. AIDS researcher and *Time* Magazine 'Man of the Year, 1996', David Ho, said, 'I wouldn't be able to do what I do if I was in Asia.' David Ho's research on HIV was funded by private philanthropy.[12]

No nation has welcomed so many immigrants and refugees as the United States. Every child, irrespective of ethnic origin or family circumstances, can aspire to the American Dream. Colin Powell, the retired Chief of Staff for the US military, and Andy Grove, the co-founder of chip-maker Intel, are examples of people whose dream came true. Those who seize the opportunity, take risks and work hard are rewarded.

Freedom and Government

In 1994, American Speaker of the House, Newt Gingrich, delivered to the American people what he called 'A Contract with America', an attempt to reaffirm government's accountability to them. This contract outlined five principles to describe the basic philosophy of American civilization: individual liberty, economic opportunity, limited government, personal responsibility, as well as security at home and abroad. At that time, public confidence in Congress and other government institutions was at its lowest point in 20 years. The feeling among voters was that elected officials were neither accountable for their actions nor could they understand people's frustrations with a political process that did not work for the electorate. The Contract with America was an attempt to address these frustrations and to repair the fundamental rift between citizens and their elected officials.

To understand the definition of freedom and government, we have to begin with the 'social contract' of Jean-Jacques Rousseau. Rousseau wrote in the opening statement of his contract, 'Man was born free, and he is everywhere in chains'. Austrian economist Friedrich von Hayek pointed out this misunderstanding of liberty:

> Wanting to free men from all 'artificial restraints' ... made what had been called the savage the virtual hero of progressive intellectuals, urged people to shake off the very restraints to which they owed their productivity and numbers, and produced a conception of liberty that became the greatest obstacle to its attainment.[13]

Liberty must be understood in the context of the community. Hayek clarified:

> Rousseau's ideas led people to forget that freedom as a political institution had arisen not by human beings 'striving for freedom' in the sense of release from restraints, but by their striving for the protection of a known secure individual domain. Rousseau led people to forget that rules of conduct necessarily constrain and that order is their product; and that these rules, precisely by limiting the range of means that each individual may use for his purposes, greatly extend the range of ends each can successfully pursue.

If liberty is so cherished, why so many in the West support the welfare state? Why do so many willing to surrender their destiny to a system that favors big government? These are the same individuals who cherished Protestant values and upheld the tradition of hard work, creativity and pioneering. Have they forgotten what Adam Smith wrote in *The Theory of Moral Sentiments*, that:

> The desire to help others was admirable, but people also had a moral duty to take care of themselves. Prudence the rational pursuit of one's own material well-being and happiness is a cardinal virtue.[14]

Let's take a deeper look at the evolution of the welfare state—an important pitfall Asians must avoid.

The Western Welfare State

From the frontier days of self-help, the governments in the West have today become the guarantor of social progress and prosperity. Margaret Thatcher set in motion a wave of reforms and privatization that brought back the enterprising spirit, and had successfully reduced the state's involvement in the economy. Tony Blair, in a speech in early 1998 on 'Building a Modern Welfare State', concluded that Britain's welfare system was not 'a pathway out of poverty, a route into work or a gateway to dignity in retirement. Rather, it is a dead end for too many people'.[15] Leaders throughout Europe are realizing (though not frankly admitting it, like Blair) that the welfare state, albeit established with the noblest of intentions, has turned into a security trap.

It is clear that the social problems in American and other Western societies today are rooted in the attitude some people have in not taking responsibility for their lives. Regrettably, this attitude has caused people to blame the society at large for all their problems. The egalitarian fervor to achieve equality through a fair distribution of the wealth of an economy has resulted in an over-generous state. The safety net has become a comfort zone. People seek security instead of opportunity. Personal qualities of self-esteem, self-reliance and responsibility have been abrogated by a welfare mentality. Politicians, focused on their re-election prospects, are all too painfully aware that any attempt to dismantle the massive welfare state is a political dynamite. Yet the hard decisions must be made so that people are able to realize their full potential and look beyond the welfare safety net. Governments need to reduce their interference in private enterprise in order to induce the right conditions for businesses to thrive and to create more job opportunities.

John Naisbitt, the author of *Megatrends* (see foreword) spoke of the Western experience as 'a noble experiment that has failed'. Citizens take the good life for granted, and governments are seen as responsible for delivering it. To achieve that, governments tax heavily and run huge budget deficits. In the end, the economy becomes overburdened, wages increase and businesses become globally uncompetitive. Some societies in Western Europe appear to be reluctant to face the realities of a globalizing world. Observed from a distance, the situation in Western Europe is reflected in the Chinese saying, 'Just consuming, even the mountain will collapse'. For example, France is stuck in an over-generous social welfare system and a high unemployment rate. Instead of pressing for reforms, she is blaming the capitalist system for her woes. *Business Week* reported:

> There is a growing sense, among intellectuals and working folks alike, that the Anglo-Saxon formula for global competitiveness runs counter to Europe's notion of a fair and prosperous society.

The report states that a recent French poll showed that 66 per cent of the respondents prefer France's rich benefits and high unemployment to America's low jobless rate and tattered safety net. 'Here [in France], social security and social solidarity weigh more than efficiency,' says Ernest-Antoine Seilliere, president of the French conglomerate CGIP.[16]

Elsewhere in Europe, the problem differs in size and urgency. As the statistics in Table 1.1 show, the role of the state has expanded tremendously over the last century, especially since the 1960s. One of the chief causes of this has been the growth in transfers and subsidies, including income support, benefits for the unemployed, the disabled and sole parents, and above all, pensions.[17]

Table 1.1: Government spending as a percentage of GDP

Country	1870	1913	1920	1937	1960	1980	1990	1996
Austria	–	–	14.7	15.2	35.7	48.1	48.6	51.7
Belgium	–	–	–	21.8	30.3	58.6	54.8	54.3
Canada	–	–	13.3	18.6	28.6	38.8	46.0	44.7
France	12.6	17.0	27.6	29.0	34.6	46.1	49.8	54.5
Germany	10.0	14.8	25.0	42.4	32.4	47.9	45.1	49.0
Italy	11.9	11.1	22.5	24.5	30.1	41.9	53.2	52.9
Japan	8.8	8.3	14.8	25.4	17.5	32.0	31.7	36.2
Netherland	9.1	9.0	13.5	19.0	33.7	55.2	54.0	49.9
Norway	3.7	8.3	13.7	–	29.9	37.5	53.8	45.5
Spain	–	8.3	9.3	18.4	18.8	32.2	42.0	43.3
Sweden	5.7	6.3	8.1	10.4	31.0	60.1	59.1	64.7
Switzerland	–	2.7	4.6	6.1	17.2	32.8	33.5	37.6
Britain	9.4	12.7	26.2	30.0	32.2	43.0	39.9	41.9
United States	3.9	1.8	7.0	8.6	27.0	31.8	33.3	33.3
Average	8.3	9.1	15.4	18.3	28.5	43.3	46.1	47.1
Australia	–	–	–	–	21.2	31.6	34.7	36.6
Ireland	–	–	–	–	28.0	48.9	41.2	37.6
New Zealand	–	–	–	–	26.9	38.1	41.3	47.1
Average	–	–	–	–	25.4	39.5	39.1	40.4
Total Average	8.3	9.1	15.4	20.4	27.9	42.6	44.8	45.9

In 1997, Japan, France, Germany, Austria, Portugal, Spain, Italy, Britain, Belgium, the Netherlands, Finland and Sweden, all ran budget deficits.[17] The general government debt of the developed countries was also very high, as illustrated in Table 1.2 below.

Table 1.2: General government debt as a percentage of GDP, 1997

Japan	88.8
Greece	107.6
France	62.3
Germany	57
Austria	125
Portugal	53.8
Spain	68.3
Italy	62.7
Britain	73.3
Belgium	130.4
Netherlands	82.1
Finland	76.4
Sweden	58
United States	67.3
Denmark	70.8
Ireland	73.5

Source: EIU, 31 January 1998, *The Economist*

The pay-as-you-go welfare state of the United States will, for example, reach crisis level by the year 2012, when social security payments exceed its revenue. The Social Security Trust Fund, which consists only of Federal IOUs, will have to be used to meet the revenue shortfall. Paul Craig Roberts, a distinguished fellow at the Cato Institute has also pointed out that, since Lyndon B Johnson's presidency, the United States has spent some US$5 trillion in combating poverty but 'with very little impact on the poverty rate' [18] Britain's welfare costs have grown over the past 50 years at twice the rate of growth of national income; the British social security budget costs every working person £15 every day.[19]

A generous France

In real GDP terms (as well as in the French psyche), the State plays an important part. Public spending is 55 per cent of GDP, a higher proportion than in any other big industrial country. In the early 90s, unemployment increased rapidly. By 1997, over 12 per cent of the work-force was without work. At the same time, the public sector deficit rose from below two per cent of GDP to six per cent. Unemployment and the budget deficit are intimately linked—more people out of work tends to mean more benefits and social welfare payments to be borne by the state, and fewer people are paying taxes.

Elsewhere, being out of work would bring not only a financial crisis but also a crisis in one's personal confidence. But not for a Frenchman. The unemployment scheme, for instance, pays anyone who loses their job almost 70 per cent (net) of their previous wage for nine months. This is then reduced in stages. At the end of 1994, the French Government was providing a guaranteed minimum income to 907,000 people, 60 per cent of whom were unemployed. On top of that admittedly modest sum (an average of less than US$340 a month), recipients could claim family allowances and housing benefits. The result is, a newly out-of-work person only has a modest incentive to look for another job.

Economists have warned that, if radical reforms are not carried out promptly, the prospects for solving France's long-term unemployment look grim. The social security burden on the employer is enormous. If a firm takes on an employee at, say, US$1,500 a month, US$500 of that goes to social security payments paid by the firm, and another US$205 paid by the worker, who also has to pay income tax (unless he or she is one of the close to 50 per cent of French households that do not pay any). In any event, US$700, almost half the gross wage goes towards social security.

Almost everyone in France can use an unusually indulgent health service. Before the scheme was curtailed in 1995, patients could go to one doctor after another, taking their treatment *la carte*, passing most of the bill to the government. It is no wonder that among Organization for Economic Cooperation and Development (OECD) countries in the 1980s, health-care spending in France rose the most. France has little in the way of pension funds. Pensions are paid by the State on a pay-as-you-go basis. The social security system was projected to run a deficit of US$11b in 1995. However, that was not considered as part of the budget; that year, the budget was expected to produce a deficit of US$55b. On the revenue side, social security contributions accounted for 21.6 per cent of GDP in 1995, whereas income tax generated a mere four per cent. High earners are hit disproportionately hard. The top marginal rate for income tax is 58.6 per cent; half the revenue raised by income tax is paid by just five per cent of taxpayers. Together, the revenue from income tax, VAT, wealth tax and corporation tax amounted to only 14.1 per cent of GDP in 1994. The tax system discourages both employment and high incomes. With VAT at a ferociously high rate of 20.6 per cent and a flat-rate social security levy of 20 per cent of income, the poor are taxed heavily. In effect, France has a welfare system to suit the poor and a tax system to suit the rich, both systems working against job creation and enterprise.

The French stock-market is tiny. Capitalization was US$520b at the end of July 1995, which was less than 10 per cent of the size of the US market.[20] Savings tend to go into property, and France is known to have the world's highest proportion of families with second homes. There are few young companies; banks are risk-averse, and most French people do not really want to be entrepreneurs. In a special survey, *The Economist* noted:

> France has to change. In a competitive world, it cannot continue to tax its citizens significantly more heavily than those of most other rich countries. Nor can it afford, even though it is rich, to spend so much on social welfare: either it must find jobs for the unemployed or it must be less generous to them.[21]

Such heavy burdens are hard to dismantle without high political and social costs. I recall many Asians emigrating to the West in the 1970s because they admired the humanity of Western societies. It is ironic that such humanitarian and compassionate intentions could have such disastrous consequences.

Sweden goes to extremes

Sweden was lauded as a socio-economic model that practised 'capitalism with a human face' or 'the third way'. It not only managed to stay out of the Second World War, but also profited from it. While the rest of Europe focused on post-war reconstruction, Sweden profited from the post-war export boom. For more than three decades, from 1945 to mid-1970s, Sweden experienced constant growth. The economy was buoyant enough to support welfare in triplicate. Companies generated high profits, and living standards improved year by year. The range of public welfare institutions, health care, senior citizen care, schooling, child care, social services and various welfare programs was continuously extended, financed through incremental taxes on private incomes and corporate revenues.

During the 44 years that the Social Democratic Party governed Sweden, the Swedish public sector expanded to become the world's largest in relative terms. The individual tax burden also grew to record levels; until recently, the marginal income tax rate exceeded 60 per cent for most middle-class families, and was over 80 per cent for many of them. During the 1970s and 1980s, Sweden introduced very generous retirement and health benefits, lengthy paid leave when workers became parents, and liberal rules on taking days off. The Swedish welfare state is the most extravagant in the West. Although reduced from 71 per cent of national income in 1993 to 65 per cent in 1996, it is still the highest in the world.[22] Gary Becker, who won the Nobel prize for economics in 1992, wrote:

> The good habits and deep respect for the work ethic slowly built up in Sweden during the previous century have gradually been eroded by the adverse effect on incentives of 25 years of expanded taxes and regulations.[23]

Sweden's growth in per capita income in the last 15 years has fallen below that of the OECD average. Political pressure had since caused a cut back in the generous welfare benefits, following the trend of other Western nations.

Why work at all ?

In a stunning report in January 1998, *Newsweek* wrote:

> If you closed your eyes and just listened, you would have sworn it was a labor protest. Marchers poured through the streets of Paris demanding a bonus, a minimum wage, a formal legal status in negotiations with the government, a guaranteed package of social benefits. They occupied offices; they were thrown out by the police. There was just one thing missing: these strikers didn't have any jobs. They were unemployed—the long-term unemployed—a class unto itself in today's Europe, and one that is sending a loud, clear message: it's here to stay.[24]

Europe is in the grip of record unemployment: roughly one person in ten is out of work, and half has been on the dole for more than a year. In contrast, both the UK and the US economies are at an all-time high. A culture of non-employment has also taken shape in some countries. In Italy, for example, people work a little to earn a pension that allows them not to work at all. A *Newsweek* report stated:

> Out of Italy's total population of 57.5m, 23m are now active in the work-force. Ten million more receive pension benefits of some sort and a substantial majority of them are well below 60, some are in their 40s. These youthful pensioners march regularly through the streets of Rome, protesting plans to cut back on their entitlements.[25]

Gary Becker further commented on the situation in Sweden:

> It has been reported that on a typical day, almost one in four employees in Sweden is absent from work because of reported illness, parental responsibilities, study leave, or any of the many other reasons that entitle a worker to stay away from work. Swedish women are much less likely than American women to work full time, and Swedish men work many fewer hours per year than American men. Why put in so much effort at work when it is possible to get paid for staying home, when better jobs don't have much higher wages, and when taxes absorb practically all of any increase in pay?[26]

For some, there is no doubt that living off welfare is an attractive proposition and the cause of a hard-core entitlement mentality. Generous welfare payments are also a disincentive to work. In the United States, a Cato Institute study showed that welfare pays more than a regular job. For many with limited career prospects, a welfare package, consisting of Aid to Families with Dependent Children, food stamps, Medicaid, and assistance to meet housing, nutrition and energy requirements, has proved more attractive than earned income. The study showed that in 28 states and the District of Columbia, this kind of welfare package is worth more than the starting salary for a secretary; in 46 states and the District of Columbia, it exceeds the earnings of a full-time janitor; in eight states and the District of Columbia, it exceeds the national average for a first-year teacher's salary; and in five states and the District of Columbia, it exceeds the national median wage for a computer programmer.[27] When dealing with unemployment and the fallout from the financial crisis, Asian public policy makers, governments and labour leaders would do well to remember this important lesson from the West.

The Differences between the Culture of the East and West

To develop the New Asian Way, apart from setting priorities, an understanding of the differences between the cultures of the present East and the modern West is useful. While there is no doubt that some differences are due to varying stages of the economic cycle, one important fundamental difference has to do with how Asians and Westerners view and deal with their past. Since no culture is perfect, we should let our guiding principle be to always seek the best, whether the values are from the East or the West.

Glory of the Past v. Promise of the Future

Here lies the most glaring difference. Asian societies are wrapped in traditions that influence their present-day behavior. Pride bars the way to an acceptance of ideas from another culture. Asian languages are still filled with homilies from an agricultural and feudal past. In contrast, the West, especially the United States, is ever forward-looking, celebrating youth, adventure, new discoveries and breakthroughs that defy convention. In reporting President Bill Clinton's visit to China, a CNN correspondent observed that the Chinese were keen to show the President the grandeur of their past (in Xian), while the President wanted to draw the Chinese into the promise of the future.

Tolerance v. Assertion

Remarking about hopeless relationships, an American friend of mine observed, 'Americans do not want to suffer. They are prepared to make a clean break and start all over again.' In contrast, Asians are a much more tolerant lot. The rhetoric on human rights issues suggests an extreme dichotomy between East and West. In the East, one finds an inclusive, accommodating approach that does not seek to interfere in the beliefs and values of others. Asians can tolerate ambiguity and differences. In the West, in general, it is either black or white. Westerners have historically striven to impose their will on others, and are assertive about their values and ideals. To Asians, the tone of the rhetoric from the West implies that the West is at the centre of the world, and is the focus of attention of all other countries. Indeed, some Westerners seem to have a superiority complex. Even though the West has declared the end of the Cold War, it seems to be re-enacting itself in another sphere. Asians are getting a strong message from the West that the only way to modernization is through the Western way. Anyone doing it differently must be brought in line with economic sanctions which perhaps involve the withdrawal of 'most-favoured nation' status. Speaking in relation to the disapproval of the US on Association of South East Asian Nations' (ASEAN) stand on Myanmar, Senior Minister Lee Kuan Yew of Singapore commented:

> If you [the United States] are just going to apply sanctions and hope that they will collapse, that there'll be a change of government and everything will be fine, I don't share that optimism. For a country that's been isolated from 1962, when Ne Win took over they will just go back into their shell. Now they are coming out, I think change will come gradually but inevitably because the people will change. They get tourists, they will begin to have an appetite for consumer goods, and a chain of events will be set off. I believe that's a more likely outcome, and a more desirable outcome.[28]

So far, the Asian way has been a non-interfering one. Asians do not make it their business to impose their will on others. Asians seek to engage each other constructively; to find commonality within diversity. In the Chinese mind, China is the Middle Kingdom and they would co-opt any other groups of people on their periphery through peaceful means as far as possible. Chinese history abounds with emperors sending out princesses to make peace with aggressive kings in distant lands in order to achieve *Tien Xia Da Tung*, ie the world as one. In addition, Confucius said, 'If our ways are different, let's each keep to ourselves'. However, the question is: will and can Asian countries continue to keep to themselves in the light of the serious ramifications brought by the financial crisis beginning in 1997?

The non-interference approach may be beginning to change, especially when younger leadership takes over the helm. For example, with the instability in Cambodia, ASEAN has learned that it cannot ignore developments in one country that could destabilize regional security. There needs to be greater regional effort to accommodate points of view and to solve problems that have regional implications. Jusuf Wanandi, a leading thinker from Indonesia said, 'ASEAN must make an exception to its principle of non-interference in the domestic affairs of nations'.[29]

Asians have become increasingly assertive in their approach to regional issues. Asia will resist pressure from the West on how it should conduct its affairs. While there seems to be less quarrel between East and West on economic matters, in the area of government and human rights, the differences are acute. Despite the material prosperity and technological advances of the West, Western ideals will take a long time to become accepted in the tradition-bound societies of Asia. Asians resent the idea that the West sees itself as master of the universe, and the Western notion that America rules not only because of its might but because it is right is causing increasing scepticism and resentment. President Woodrow Wilson's, 'We set this nation up to make men free, and we did not confine our conception and purpose to America' is viewed as interference.[30] As Joseph Chan of the University of Hong Kong puts it, 'The search for a political morality is ultimately a soul-searching exercise for Asians themselves; to clarify the values and aspirations and to develop social, political, and philosophical norms that best capture them'.

The State v. The Individual

The political vision and aspirations of the West are not so different from that of the East. The fundamental difference lies with Asia's deeply rooted traditions and cultural attitudes in regard to the state and the individual. The Western view of the state's primary duty is that it determines the scope of basic individual rights, passes laws to uphold those rights and enforces them, with certain limitations. Joseph Chan of University of Hong Kong, wrote:

> Specifically, the state may restrict individual rights only on grounds of preventing harm and offence to others. The state must remain neutral among competing conceptions of the good life—anti-perfectionism; it must not restrict an individual's liberty for his or her own good—anti-paternalism; and it must not enforce society's morals by means of the law—anti-moralism. In other words, the state excludes perfectionism, paternalism and moralism as grounds for intervention.[31]

Traditional Asian values, especially Confucian-based ones, are completely the opposite. Again, Joseph Chan wrote:

> The most fundamental element in Confucian political thought is that the primary task of the state is to help citizens develop virtues and achieve the good

> life. It is the duty of the state in East Asia to carry out this task with due concern to the ethical and cultural life of society and within the broad constraints of basic individual rights.

Additionally, Eastern traditions emphasize the primacy of group harmony while the West celebrates the individual. Joseph Chan observed:

> The rationale for an inclusive view of the tasks of the state is at the same time cultural, sociological and philosophical. We see in East Asian cultures, in particular, Confucian-based ones, a strong emphasis on intimate family relationships and respect for elders, for example. From the sociological point of view, the pursuit of virtues and good life is not an entirely personal matter but requires conditions that can only be provided by collective effort. Social institutions, culture, and traditions are collective constructs that provide the conditions for people to live the good life.[32]

While Confucianism is an anchor of morality and uprightness, it appears to be idealistic in today's world of intense competition. As a doctrine, it respects individualism. In fact, all efforts are directed to helping individuals develop themselves, so that they can progress to become a sage; the state's responsibility is to provide an environment and leadership to make that happen.

Openness v. Deference

Westerners delight in open debate and public policies are thrashed out in the limelight of the media. Generally, participants do not get personal; they focus on the issue, each expects and allows the other to have his or her say freely. In the process, the public is engaged and educated over a whole spectrum of viewpoints, and then decide for themselves which to believe. Openness and hence transparency is a very Western habit—look at American homes where there are often no fences and where glass is used abundantly as building material. Asian homes, especially Chinese homes, are enclosed and covered up; there is no way one can get a glimpse of the interior from the outside. Open debate releases healthy energy and encourages creativity as people are not afraid of authority and are free to express alternative points of view no matter how contrary and critical. This is the beauty of pluralism. It is no accident that this clash of energy produces great creativity in US society.

Asians practise a different kind of privacy: some are masters of pretence, while most are taught to honor deference above debate. The Chinese in particular are a people who do not speak a lot; not speaking their minds does not mean they are in agreement, however. The conditioning to suppress their individuality is so powerful that few feel strong enough to want to have their voices heard. The Associate Dean of Manila's Asian Institute of Management warned Asian students, 'If you don't raise your hand and talk, you won't get graded'.[33] Confucius taught that the truly wise are silent and only the stupid are verbose, so people prefer to keep their thoughts to themselves. Added to this is the traditional deference to authority and position. At best, some discussion may take place, but it is likely to be minimal; there must be absolutely no confrontation. To many in Asia, conflict is a prelude to violent clashes that will inevitably result in instability, which long-suffering Asians fear. Hence, there are only closed-door dialogues, no open debates. Traditionally, Asians are not comfortable with transparency. Again, if leaders are supposed to do good for the people, as traditional values assume, subjecting them to public scrutiny is disrespectful.

Bold Moves v. Baby Steps

Asians have learnt to live with ambiguities for most, if not all, of the time. However, to many Westerners, the world may be distinctly black or white. As they tend to perceive there is only one way of doing things, they are inclined to take the 'one size fits all' approach. This is reflected in the way they do business. I am reminded of Star TV's initial debut in Asia based on a top-down, one-size-fits-all, pan-Asian approach—the same program was scheduled throughout Asia!

Asia's diversity requires different models for different needs; this is also the reason why patience is more a necessity than a virtue. The attention span of many Westerners, especially Americans, tends to be much shorter; they prefer the shock treatment and an immediate solution to a problem. In Asia, three steps forward and two steps back may be better to 'feel the stones under the water'. Cultural change is achieved by making small steps. The Chinese have also tried handling matters with shock treatment: remember the Cultural Revolution and the Great Leap Forward? We have learnt from these incidents, hence the wisdom of the 'One Country, Two Systems' policy as the framework for transition, as in the case of the return of Hong Kong to mainland China.

Objectivity v. Principle

Throughout Chinese civilization, there have been swings in the pendulum between objectivity and pragmatism. At various times in Chinese history, there had been tremendous pragmatism in adopting new ideas and openness; there had also been other times when the leaders were deadly stubborn in undoing mistakes. The importance of maintaining 'face' and upholding principles is so strong that it acts as a brake on the advancement of society. Those of us familiar with the struggle to embrace modernity in China lamented the length of time it took before the debate on 'seeking truth from fact' was settled and the ideology of deferring to the leader was set aside. In contrast, the West today seems to be moving in the direction of personal accountability and social responsibility. It is common for the heads of large companies, national leaders, and respected men and women to publicly admit their mistakes. In this context, it is interesting to see how perceived mistakes are dealt with: the Chinese adhere to 'keeping face' and do not apologize; the Japanese when cornered commit suicide; the Americans apologize and move on.

Dependence v. Independence

Centuries of paternalistic rule and a moralistic culture have the effect of breeding a strong interdependence among people. This is not only true of the relationship between government and the people, but in all social and economic relationships: parents provide for the children; employers look after loyal employees for life; men look after women in return for their devotion to the family. In contrast, Westerners allow their children to fend for themselves at what may seem a very young age; independence is highly prized. The editor-in-chief of the Chinese edition of *Cosmopolitan* magazine in Beijing told me, 'It is tough to be a woman in the West. You have to fend for yourself and be totally independent, whereas the support system here in Chinese society is still very kind to women.'

Learning the Lessons

Sitting at the 52nd-floor New York Bar at the Park Hyatt hotel in Tokyo's Shinjuku area, one will be overwhelmed by the power of human ingenuity. This wonderful piece of architecture, which is art and science in seamless combination, is the work of world-renowned architect Kenzo Tange and interior designer John Morford. Viewing Tokyo from such a towering height and taking in the city lights is to be vividly reminded of modernity and progress. The Park Hyatt is a symbol of Western technology, systematic organization and the ultimate application of knowledge.

Asians have long been fascinated by Western progress. The Japanese started to imitate and improve on Western techniques to the extent that, as the world entered the last quarter of the 20th century, many thought Japan would dominate the world. Like any other young adult growing up in Asia after the Second World War, I, too, was fascinated by things Western. I marvelled at the technological inventions, the artistic expression, and the dynamics of open debate. Young Asians especially envy the freedom and liberating environment enjoyed by individuals in Western societies. They yearn to have a voice of their own.

The benefits of Western modernization have spread far and wide. Western efficiency, systematic organization and presentation of knowledge, innovations in science and technology, all have been adopted by Asians who are exposed to the West either through education, living there, or working for Western companies.

For those of us who have the privilege of knowing the two contrasting worlds of East and West, both geographically and culturally, there is a paradox. While we are awed by the technological progress of the West and the dynamism of its intellectual fervor, we have to acknowledge that the West is not in a picture-perfect situation, as far as its social and economic problems are concerned. News of persistent unemployment in Europe, agitation for ethnic, gender and minority rights, and a rising discontent with the failure of government and big business to assure equality in society troubles everyone. After five centuries of experiments in political, economic and social development, the West has yet to find all the answers. So, what are the lessons we could learn from them?

The prime lesson is in the organization of community life. The rule of law defines the parameters of freedom, and therefore assures everyone the freedom to certain unalienable rights. This is the greatest weakness of Eastern societies: we speak of community living, yet without a definitive rule-of-law culture, we are unable to protect the individual when violations occur, when malevolent leaders are in power. Relationships are no doubt an effective social glue, but they are deficient in this modern day of rationality and objectivity.

The second lesson is that the East should avoid the Western model of welfare state system which does more harm than good—government tends to take over a large part of the individual's responsibilities, which in turn causes the economy to lose some of its dynamism. The unemployment problems in the West today are structural. Labor costs in Europe are astronomical with social security payments, high taxes, endless regulations and an anti-private enterprise culture. Governments can do a lot to rectify the situation by creating favorable conditions under which private enterprise can thrive and thus create the jobs so desperately needed. Government's role is to facilitate, not obstruct.

The lessons from the Western experience are very clear: conditions that optimize individual achievements have led to great advancement in science, technology, business, government and the arts. However, the attitudes of entitlement and not taking responsibility for one's own life, have undermined progress in many Western societies. Many Western governments seem paralyzed in their inability to solve these problems.

All societies evolve: they make mistakes, recover, adjust and go on. Like any individual or community anywhere in the world, there is constant effort to achieve perfection. 'We don't have all the answers to our problems,' said Jeffrey E Garten, Dean of the Yale School of Management and US Under-Secretary of Commerce for International Trade (1993–1995). While we greatly admire and respect the West, Asians would do well to remember the lessons the Western experience has provided us.

Part II

Wealth Creation

Chapter 2
Building the Market Econony

"When the granaries are full,
people will appreciate manners.
When material needs are satisfied,
people will learn about honor and shame.
If rulers respect the law and the system,
there will be harmony among relatives.
Only when the values of civility, loyalty, honesty
and shame are upheld, will orderly rule prevail."

—Guan Zhong—
Chinese scholar, Spring and Autumn Period

With the discrediting of communism, the capitalist system of private ownership and free enterprise has been widely implemented. Economic freedom places the individual above the state, whether in the form advocated by Adam Smith in *The Wealth of Nations*, or by Guan Zhong, the ancient Chinese philosopher in the kingdom of Qi during the Spring and Autumn Period. Guan Zhong argued that material well-being of the people should be the first priority, and his policies brought tremendous prosperity to the Kingdom. Early Chinese free marketeers supported decentralization and privatization, 'Let the wealth stay with the people (*cang fu yu min*); [governments] should not compete with the people (*bu yu min zheng*)'. They believed that prices should be set by the market, ie by the forces of demand and supply, and private property rights, free trade between nations, and minimal government intervention.

Angus Maddison's study for the OECD on the global economy showed that from 1820 to 1992 (a period of 172 years), per capita income globally grew to US$5,145, whereas between 1500 and 1820, it only increased from US$565 to US$651.[1] Technological progress can be given the main credit, while the accumulation of physical capital, development of human capital and integration of individual economies also helped fuel growth. Growth in some Western European countries was accelerated by input from their overseas offshoots—the United States, Canada, Australia and New Zealand. In the foreword to *The Index of Economic Freedom*, Robert L Bartley, editor of *The Wall Street Journal*, made this poignant observation:

> If new freedoms started capitalist development, our century has witnessed a turning away. Starting about the turn of the century, there have been new concerns with making the [growth] process fair to the players and, in particular, with protecting those left behind. The development of the welfare state may have protected the legitimacy of the capitalist process, as Maddison suggests. But it has been carried to levels with, to take the extreme example, 65 per cent of GDP passing through government hands in Sweden that demonstrably impede economic growth.[2]

The Index of Economic Freedom also warns against interventionist governments, and goes on to say, 'Businesses must be free to produce the kinds of products they want, in the quantities they decide, and to sell those products at the prices they and the market deem appropriate'.[3]

The Asian Economic 'Miracle' in Perspective

The West has dominated the world for almost 500 years. In 1820, having 14 per cent of the world's population, Eastern Europe, the Anglo-Saxon empire of Great Britain and the United States accounted for 25 per cent of world's income. By 1950, after 100 years of industrialization, their income share shot to 56 per cent, though their share of population was only 17 per cent. Meanwhile, Asia, with 66 per cent of the world's population, had seen its income share declined from 58 per cent in 1820 to 19 per cent in 1950. However, beginning from the 1950s, one of the greatest transformations in modern history took place. By 1992, Asia's share of world income rose to 33 per cent.

By world economic standards, Asia's achievement was remarkable. So remarkable that the World Bank described it as a 'miracle'. Asians, however, know that their achievements were not a miracle but the result of decades of hard work and pragmatic policies. Asia grew at an unprecedented 6.5 per cent a year for the three decades from 1965, ahead of any other region in the world. The basics underlying this achievement included low inflation, high levels of domestic savings, heavy investment in education, good work ethics, pro-business public policies, political stability and openness to trade, technology and investment.

Following the 1997 financial crisis, the region reeled from the devastation of its assets and the volatility of its currencies. After almost a year full of very bad news, some Asians are starting to doubt the strength of their own economies. Western money managers, who just months earlier had been celebrating the 'miracle', now point to the underlying institutional weaknesses. Some give the impression that these inherent weaknesses were not there when they first invested in the region, but what happened was that structural imbalances in these economies and the poor quality of growth came under critical scrutiny by the international investment community. Sensing what was ahead, they rushed for the exit. The widespread panic sparked the exodus of funds from the region—first the foreigners' money and then the Asians'. For the Asians, the sky seems to have fallen in. A region that has grown accustomed to high growth has been stunned by the massive destruction of wealth. Opponents of globalization are now having a field-day, denouncing the destabilizing effect of global capitalism and its ruthless chase for profit at the expense of 'poor people and poor countries'.

However, judging by the enormous wealth created, the mass of people uplifted from poverty, the improving infrastructure and the stock of skilled workers in the last 50 years, there is no doubt that Asia got the first part of the formula right. Even mainland China, still ranked as an 'unfree economy', is slowly but surely moving in the direction of the modern free market system. However, the fact that the free market system creates wealth does not mean that the system by itself is perfect or that the ensuing results are similar everywhere. Some may have forgotten that Asia's move to the free market is still in progress—the foreign managers have certainly forgotten that. As Asian economies advance their market reforms, they also have to cope with a whole host of vulnerabilities in the system. Moreover, the conditions facilitating growth in Western nations are very different from those that Asia must deal with.

It also comes as no surprise that the free market, which is driven by collective decisions of private individuals fuelled by self-interest, is inherently unpredictable. Its behavior is often too complicated for government to fully understand or to respond fast enough to. However, if Asia accepts the free market as an efficient though imperfect mechanism for resource allocation, the question seems to be how far the respective governments are willing to accommodate its somewhat chaotic dynamics? To what extent are they prepared to refine their public policies and institutions in order to make the free market work? How can Asians realize the promise of the market economy ?

Asia as an export platform

Asian governments, benefiting from Japan's early experiences and learning from each other, have, since the 1960s, successfully created an economic environment for profitable, private investment, almost always with foreign partners, from within or outside Asia. This has happened despite serious shortcomings in the overall political and economic conditions in some of the domestic systems. Foreign investors reaped tremendous profits from their Asian operations, which often greatly enhanced their competitiveness in world markets.

Manufacturing led by foreign direct investment (FDI) made Asia an export platform. Then a phenomenon described in the 1930s by the Japanese economist, Kaname Akamatsu, as the 'flying geese' formation occurred—countries progress in technological development by following in the wake of countries just ahead of them. According to Akamatsu's theory, Korea and Taiwan assumed leadership in textiles and apparel after Japan moved into high technology. A decade or so later, Korea and Taiwan followed suit by upgrading to electronics and automobile components, while the textile and apparel industries move to Indonesia, Thailand and Vietnam.

It was electronics that got the economies in Asia started on the road to industrialization. By 1975, East Asia employed roughly 95 per cent of worldwide offshore electronics assembly workers.

Foreign investment

The economic fundamentals of Asian nations attracted great inflow of FDI; first from the West, and then the more developed Asian countries invested in the less developed Asian countries. While foreign investment to the region remained brisk in the 1990s, there was greater competition within Asia and against other regions in the world. The FDI to China soared between 1991 and 1996, whilst the rest of Asia's share declined sharply. In 1996, China accounted for US$42.3b, or 52 per cent, of Asia's FDI; Singapore was the second largest recipient of FDI, with a US$9.4b increase in 1996, up from US$6.9b a year earlier; and Indonesia almost doubled its take to US$8b from US$4.3b in 1995. Together, these three countries accounted for 79 per cent of the increase in FDI into Asia in 1996.[4]

Between 1990 and 1991, the Association of South-East Asian Nations (ASEAN) grabbed 61 per cent of FDI inflows into Asia. (Asia, excluding China, only received 29 per cent of FDI to developing countries in 1996, down from 40 per cent in 1991). The problem that in part caused the financial crisis was not capital inflow. The real problem was the short-term flows—hot money that went to fuel the speculation in stocks and real estates.

As shown by table below, the outflow of these short-term investments, in part caused by panic and loss of confidence, further drained confidence in the region's stock-markets and currencies.

Table 2.1: Private Capital Flows for South Korea, Indonesia, Thailand, Malaysia and the Philippines

	$billions			
	1994	1995	1996	1997*
Equity investment	12.1	15.4	18.7	2.1
direct investment	4.7	4.9	6.3	6.4
portfolio equity	7.4	10.5	12.4	-4.3
Private creditors	25.8	63.8	78.4	-14.0
commercial banks	23.4	49.9	55.7	-26.9
non-bank private creditors	2.4	13.8	22.7	12.9
Private flows, net	37.9	79.2	97.1	-11.9

*Source: estimate only, Institute of International Finance, *Far Eastern Economic Review*, 16 July 1998

Integrating with the global economy

Asian economies and their stock-markets are very young. In financial circles, they are often termed 'emerging markets'. These economies are making a gradual transition to the market mode of operation, and some are only just coming to terms with the concept of private ownership. In China, for example, the state sector still plays a huge role in the economy, state enterprises account for 1/3 of industrial output, 2/3 of urban employment and more than 1/2 of investment in fixed assets.[5] Only Hong Kong, Singapore and Taiwan are classified free (according to pages xxix–xxxii of the Heritage Foundation's *Index of Economic Freedom* 1998), meaning that the transition to the free market system is complete. Japan, South Korea, Malaysia, Thailand, the Philippines and Indonesia are considered as 'mostly free', while China and India have a lot more work to do.

The world has known this all along, hasn't it? Foreign investors knew they were taking risks in emerging markets with less than perfect capitalist conditions. These fledgling economies have not yet developed the controls to manage the complexities of the free market; for example, some do not yet have proper bankruptcy laws. Bureaucrats do not fully understand globalization, so when a crisis occurs, they are ill-prepared for a painfully hard landing. US Federal Reserve Chairman, Alan Greenspan, observed:

> The accelerated opening up in recent years of product and financial markets world-wide offers enormous benefits to all nations over the long run. However, it has also exposed more quickly and harshly the underlying rigidities of economic systems in which governments– or governments working with large industrial groups– exercise substantial influence over resource allocation. Such systems can produce vigorous growth for a time, when the gap between indigenous applied technologies and world standards is large, such as the Soviet Union in the 1960s and 1970s and Southeast Asia in the 1980s and 1990s. But, as the gap narrows, the ability of these systems to handle their increasingly sophisticated economies declines markedly.

In Western developed economies, in contrast, market forces have been allowed much freer rein to dictate production schedules. Rapid response by businesses to changes in free-market prices have muted much of the tendency for unsold goods to back up or unmet needs to produce shortages. Recent improvements in technology have significantly compressed business response times and enhanced the effectiveness of the market mechanism.[6]

To Get Rich Quick is More Glorious

Asia benefited from globalization. By and large, the flying geese formation has played out across the region. First Japan, then South Korea, Taiwan, Hong Kong and Singapore 'graduated' from labour-intensive manufacturing to higher technology and added-value industries. Japan, Hong Kong, Singapore and Taiwan have already derived more than 50 per cent of their GDP from the service sector; Malaysia, Thailand, and Indonesia are in different stages of transition; and the Philippines, China, India and Vietnam and countries in South Asia are still struggling to get a better grip on the free market system.

At different times over the last three decades, robust exports and strong foreign investment fuelled growth in Asia. A money-making obsession developed and gripped the region. Quick profit was the common new Asian language, spoken and understood from Shanghai to Singapore, and from Harbin to Hong Kong. Speculative activities in real estate and stock-markets diverted energy and resources away from building on foundations of a real economy. For many sections of society, the good old work ethics of earlier times were replaced with a 'get-rich-quick' mentality. Younger Asians in their early 30s, who had never known hardship, developed quite unrealistic expectations. Mergers, acquisitions, take-overs and public listings became the preferred strategy to multiply the worth of companies, and making deals was suddenly more attractive than building up the real business. The region's own bankers, with further loans from foreign bankers, fuelled this euphoria with more easy credit. For example, in 1996, Japanese banks had US$299b out in loans to borrowers in the 10 largest Asian countries and Hong Kong. It is both puzzling and hard to believe that bankers, foreign banks especially, could be so reckless in their lending practices, allowing private companies to become so grossly overgeared!

The inflow of short-term portfolio funds created and sustained a picture of prosperity never seen before. Sadly, the party came to an abrupt end in the summer of 1997 following a spate of speculative attacks on the currencies of the ASEAN-4 (Thailand, Malaysia, the Philippines and Indonesia). First, the Thai baht was forced to devalue, followed by the Indonesian rupiah, the Philippines peso and then the Malaysian ringgit. That long overdue economic and financial restructuring became starkly apparent in South Korea and Japan. With the whole region in financial turmoil, confidence evaporated overnight; a net US$12b flowed out of Asia in 1997, compared with an inflow of US$97b in 1996—'a swing of almost US$110b in one year suggests that decisions are not being made entirely on substance,' as an editorial in the *Far Eastern Economic Review* noted.[7] As the crisis deepened, the vulnerabilities and flaws of many of these evolving economic systems were exposed.

Blowing bubbles

Few economies anywhere escape the fate of bubble-making during periods of fast growth. Of the anguish when the bubbles burst, Ahmad Kamar, senior partner at Arthur Andersen in Kuala Lumpur, observed, 'We became victims of our own propaganda'.

While things were humming along nicely at the world's most enviable rates of growth, conspicuous consumption crept in and a building boom took off. In spite of high domestic savings, the Southeast Asian region still required huge amounts of foreign funds to supplement domestic investment needs (see Table 2.2).

Table 2.2: Carried away at mid-term

	Gross Domestic Investment as % of GNP				
	1981–90	1993	1994	1995	1996
China	33.3	43.4	40.0	41.2	39.6
Hong Kong	27.2	27.6	31.9	34.5	33.0
Taiwan	22.5	24.9	23.6	23.4	21.2
South Korea	31.4	35.3	36.3	37.4	36.5
Indonesia	30.4	34.5	33.7	34.8	37.7
Malaysia	32.4	39.8	42.5	45.4	45.1
Philippines	22.4	23.6	23.5	21.6	23.9
Singapore	41.8	38.0	32.3	33.0	34.8
Thailand	31.1	41.3	42.0	44.2	43.8
India	22.8	21.4	24.4	26.7	28.8

Source: J P Morgan, *Far Eastern Economic Review*, 25 September 1997

Many of these investments were not for productive purposes, but for speculative activities. Stock-market capitalization was wildly unrealistic: at their peaks, Malaysia and Hong Kong had stock-market capitalizations in excess of 300 per cent of their GDPs.

Developing real estate was another road to instant millions; it was difficult to persuade investors to put money into industries, which not only have longer gestation periods, smaller returns and greater competition, but also require much harder work. Some even questioned the intrinsic value of work the value of one's efforts was measured by how quick and how much return one could get. It was rumored that undergraduates in Hong Kong spent their time speculating on the stock-market or selling real estate, with the justification that their instant wealth would allow them to employ dozens of people with university degrees any time!

A timely wake-up call

In hindsight, we may be able to regard the events of the summer of 1997 as a wake-up call—a call to work towards a real economy built on solid foundations and proper values. It is timely to examine the kind of capitalist system that is being built and see if the values embodied in them are sustainable. Speculation and gambling is not confined to Wall Street: Asians have adopted the stock-market frenzy, and may even have outdone their counterparts in the West. While a robust stock-market provides the vitality to fuel growth, Asians must recognize the real purpose of the establishment of stock-markets and not be misled by corrupt practices. At the present stage of East Asia's economic development, what East Asia really needs are more builders who can create sustainable global businesses and fewer speculative traders.

The financial turmoil has also brought into sharp focus the viability of over-regulated big business. Collusion between big business and government sent the South Korean economy into a tailspin. It is also becoming apparent that Japan's seven-year economic slow-down and financial troubles are turning out to be the weakest link in the global economy—a source of instability for Asia and a threat to the entire world.

A mess in the banking system

The burden of bad loans is, to say the least, embarrassing for Asian economies. Under the International Monetary Fund's bail-out program, Thailand closed 58 finance companies, Indonesia 16, and many more went under in Japan and South Korea.

At the end of 1996, total outstanding loans from the global banking system to Asia stood at US$752b. One third of these loans was provided by Japanese banks and lending institutions—local banks were cashed up with personal savings and were also offered cheap credit by foreign banks. Growth in domestic loans was also high, especially in Malaysia; valuable domestic resources were channelled into privatization, and the real estate sector booms.

The quantum of non-performing loans is staggering. Bad loans of Thai banks could amount to 1/4 of total assets, which means that restructuring could take as much as 20 per cent of GDP. In South Korea, bad loans are estimated at US$27b, some 10 per cent of the country's GDP. Japanese banks already have some US$250b in bad loans left over from the bubble economy of the 1980s. China's banking system is also faltering: the People's Bank of China conservatively estimates that at least 25 per cent of the nation's loans are non-performing; these loans are worth more than US$200b, a tremendous sum in a US$1 trillion economy. Although the Asian financial crisis is the result of private-sector debt accumulation and not imprudent government fiscal policies, it does expose the extent of the involvement and influence of governments in the free market system. A study by SBC Warburg Dillon Read reveals that Asia needs over US$110b in new equity to get debt-to-equity ratios down to reasonable levels.

A whole new financial infrastructure is called for, and in this regard, local banks are a key element. Asia needs to build a regional capital market out of the current financial mess. This means tedious but important work on details such as a decent clearing system, strict regulations, stringent rules on disclosure, and changes in legal codes. The cure for Asia's ills may be even more traumatic than the disease. Ultimately, though, what the region needs isn't merely a bigger dose of capital: Asian governments must be determined to diligently supervise the new banking and financial infrastructure and to support the regulators they appoint to enforce the rules.

Table 2.3: Sources of External Commercial Bank debt to end-June 1997

	$billion	Japan	US	Britain	Rest of Europe	Other
Indonesia	58.7	39.4	7.8	7.4	30.9	14.5
Malaysia	28.8	36.4	8.3	7.0	37.0	11.3
Philippines	14.1	14.9	20.0	7.6	40.5	17.0
South Korea	103.4	22.9	9.6	5.9	29.3	32.3
Thailand	69.4	54.4	5.8	4.1	24.5	11.3
Total	274.5	33.6	10.3	6.4	32.4	17.3

Source: Bank for International Settlements, *Far Eastern Economic Review*, 23 July 1998

Table 2.4: Non-performing Loans and GDP

	US$billion	GDP 1996	Problem Loans as % of GDP
Japan	550	4,598	12
South Korea	90	485	19
Thailand	36	184	20
Indonesia	No estimate	227	na
Malaysia	25	99	25
China	200	816	25
Hong Kong	na	154	na
Singapore	na	94	na

Sources: *Businessweek*, 20 July 1998; Goldman Sachs & Co, *Asian Wall Street Journal*, 6 May 1998

Table 2.5: Outstanding Loans provided by Global Banking System, 1996 (US$ billion)

	Total	Loans provided by the Japanese	GDP 1995
Hong Kong	207	87.5	142
Singapore	189	58.8	80
South Korea	100	24.0	435
Thailand	70	37.5	160
Indonesia	55	22.0	190
Malaysia	22	8.2	78
Total	752	238	1,085

Source: *Megatrends Asia*. David Hale, economist, *Asian Wall Street Journal*, 5 September 1997.

Table 2.6: Recapitalization requirements (in US$ billion)

	Listed Bank	Top 50 Industrials (foreign debt level)	Top 50 Indutrials **	Adjustment (%)***	Total Equity required	% of market capitalisation
South Korea	15	43	60	50	45	63
Thailand	15	19	11	20	24	65
Indonesia	6	15	7	na	13	54
Malaysia	1	9	10	na	11	10
Philippines	0	5	2	na	2	6
India	0	6	4	na	4	3
Taiwan	1	4	0	na	1	<1
Hong Kong	0	25	5	na	5	1
Total for Asia	38	13	103	na	109	9

* Short-term recapitalization requirement
** Recapitalization needed if gearing = 100%
*** Double-counting factor

Source: SBC Warburg Dillon Read, *Asian Capital Markets*, Henry Sender, *Far Eastern Economic Review*, 23 July 1998.

Super powers or super markets

The extent of the power exerted by the market is dawning on Asian governments for the first time. By and large, the long-term growth prospects of Asian economies have not changed drastically, although massive adjustments and restructuring are needed. Globalization has meant that changes in other parts of the world could render what used to be regarded as attractive conditions at home to lose their lustre. Costs have gone up considerably in the ASEAN-4 and Hong Kong, and currencies are overvalued vis-à-vis the US dollar and the Japanese yen. Asian leaders must face the reality of the global market. While some critics denounced the International Monetary Fund's bail-out program on the grounds that it might hamper a smooth transition to the free market, Asian governments are divided on whether to bail out certain sectors, especially the banks. Daim Zainuddin, a successful bumiputra entrepreneur and Malaysia's finance minister and economic advisor to the government, urged:

> Cut expenditure and no bail-outs for any companies. This is business. If the markets decide it should be that way, they have to face the consequences. No-

> body owes us a living; if you want to survive in this world, there is no way other than hard work and efficiency.[8]

Skilled workers and managerial talent are in acute shortage throughout the region. Transitions of the flying geese type are starting to look precarious: Indonesia and the Philippines will have to compete very hard with the dynamic and aggressive export engine of China. The flying geese pattern may not reassert itself in Asia because globalization has melted away boundaries. Production costs may no longer be the sole determinant of the location of a manufacturing facility; speed and access to final markets could have a bigger influence on where goods will be produced. Singapore, Taiwan, Hong Kong, South Korea and Japan will be looking for links further afield (such as Eastern Europe, Mexico and Latin America) which will give them better market advantages. The global rush to produce cars and semiconductors has resulted in over-capacity in these industries; the rising industries of tomorrow are going to be radically different. Now the global context has changed, the dynamics of competition are different, and a different strategy is called for.

Globalization and the New Asia

Globalization is the phenomenon of the integration of markets world-wide into a single global economy and the ascendancy of private business. The world has changed and is still changing fast. It is no longer dominated by political influence but is increasingly driven by economic forces and considerations. Political ideology as an overriding global force ended with the Cold War, and the subsequent disintegration of the Soviet Union. Computers and telecommunications technology, the opening up of markets and lowering of tariffs, all combine to spread capital, ideas, technology and people, across borders, time zones and cultures.

A Single Global Economy

The global economy is not only stateless but sleepless. Money respects no borders. With clicks on the screen, investors trade some US$1.5 trillion worth of foreign currencies and US$15 trillion in stocks world-wide every day. While many Asian leaders think that movements of capital are primarily the work of Wall Street, evidence suggests that this is not so. I suspect that the massive flight of capital from Asia—from mainland China soon after China opened up and more recently from Southeast Asia—had more to do with ineffective and inadequate regulations on capital control. Capital flow has increased exponentially: in 1995, currency transactions amounted to US$1.2 trillion a day, that is, 50 times the value of world trade. Before financial markets were liberalized in the 1970s, currency transactions were only six times greater than the value of 'real' trade.[9] It is becoming clearer and clearer that money flows into and stays wherever it is best treated (see foreword).

The networked world allows any individual or businesses anywhere in the world to participate; foreign exchange dealers are linked by some 200,000 computer terminals, which are connected online, in real time, with information accessible to all. Manufacturers can carry out borderless manufacturing, source for components on the world wide web, design, produce, market and deliver without even coming into contact with the physical inventory of their product. Individuals and businesses can communicate through the global information network, bypassing sovereign authorities. The global economy is open: information is available and can no longer be controlled or repressed. Prompt disclosure and openness helps governments and companies to strengthen the confidence of the international investing community, as well as that of domestic investors.

Information standard for currencies

Currency values are influenced more by the 200,000 interlinked computer traders who watch the markets, rather than by governments or central banks. 'No matter what the politicians and the spin masters of the world say, the market will remain a giant voting machine that records in real time, real evaluations of the values of currencies. Increasingly, currency values reflect less the power and privileges of the sovereign as much as a discipline on the economic policies of an imprudent sovereign,' said former Citibank Chairman Walter Wriston. Strong currencies are reflected in strong economies with strong effective policies.

Liberalization and acceptance of FDI

The global economy experienced unprecedented growth in the 1990s, and FDI by private companies drove much of it. Over the 1990s, East and Southeast Asia grew fast, accounting for just 1/4 of world output but 1/2 of world growth and almost 2/3 of world capital spending.[10] Global FDI flow reached a record US$347b in 1996.[11] Among the developing regions, Asia is one of the largest sources of FDI capital in the world; in 1996, it invested twice as much abroad as did Japan (US$23.4b).[12]

Foreign investment leads to growth in world trade; the share of world trade in world output rose to a record 21.6 per cent in 1996, up from 18.6 per cent in 1990 and 17.9 per cent in 1985.[13] Between 1991 and 1996, FDI outflows increased by 12 per cent annually, reaching US$3.2 trillion in 1996. From this production base, more than 280,000 foreign affiliates now generate sales valued at over US$7 trillion world-wide, a figure that easily exceeds total global exports of goods and services.[14]

Earlier trade patterns were based on resources; the possession of natural resources was considered vital for a country's development. Today, countries without natural resources but with the right investment environment can attract foreign investment in the form of manufacturing operations. The setting-up of electronics factories in East Asia epitomizes this shift. Foreign direct investment is a key driver in the economic growth of a country because, with it, trade follows.

The best advantage

A more open trading and investment environment enables capital to find the highest and safest returns. Latin America, Eastern Europe, Mexico and regions within the United States and Continental Europe are deregulating fast and becoming competitive enough for multinationals to consider relocating there. Competition for both capital and markets is intensifying: Asian economies surviving on low-cost labor will encounter serious competition in the coming years. It is estimated that one billion workers earning between US$5 and US$10 a day will enter the global economy, and that with the diffusion of technology and the injection of Western or Japanese management techniques, these workers could be 85 per cent as efficient as workers in the West.[15]

Smarter and cheaper always win

The global race towards efficiency will see inefficient producers dropping out; communities whose productivity cannot keep up with rising costs will find their growth faltering. The Darwinian nature of the free market accelerates progress: the key to survival is efficiency, creativity and productivity. Overprotective governments and rigid labor markets will stifle competitiveness, and institutional weaknesses such as a deficient legal system, corruption, nepotism, populist policies and inadequate banking regulations must be rectified. Investors and consumers today have choices; their benchmark is a global standard of excellence. Paternalistic Asian public policy-makers must recognize that to continue to protect inefficient home industries and companies that can no longer compete, only perpetuates the misallocation of resources and drains the system of scarce resources. Liberalization based on meritocracy will help good domestic firms to learn from and be eventually strengthened by strong foreign competition, whereas firms that need protection are forever a drag on the economy.

Uniqueness

A unique and special niche, whether it be in inventing, producing or distributing, is the key to survival. The community that has a unique talent has security in the global economy. Emerging markets, including many in Asia, have been growing on semiconductors, electronics and assembly work, using cheap unskilled labor. With overproduction of these products, Asia needs to develop new industries as soon as possible. The search for Asia's own core competence is becoming more urgent.

An end to 'mind your own business'

When international investors pour billions of dollars into an economy, it puts pressure on the domestic politics of the host country. Host governments cannot ignore the perceptions the international investing community has of their policies, especially those concerned with finance and the functioning of the judiciary. International investors, especially (impatient) Westerners who are used to a culture of transparency and openness, will expect adherence to their standards. For example, in some Western countries, national economic information is legislated by law to be independent, and the government has no jurisdiction over it. Western media, businesses and the general public expect and demand proper government accountability as a right— contrast this attitude to the deference Asians show to their leaders. The value of a currency today will no longer be determined by its links with gold or to international agreements (as in Bretton Woods), but by the judgment of buyers and sellers who form an opinion on its value from the information they receive. It wasn't all that long ago that central banks were powerful enough to fix prices and influence market movements at will. That is history now. To avoid incorrect judgments being made, or situations arising where there is a loss of confidence, accurate information and prompt disclosure are the only safeguards. Asia's year-long financial crisis has produced one glaring lesson: punishment for bad economic policies will be sure, swift and even brutal; the free fall of the Japanese yen and Ryutaro Hashimoto's humiliating defeat at the polls bear testament. Public policies will increasingly be driven more by global economic considerations than by domestic circumstances.

Capitalism Evaluated

Having reached this point of development of the capitalist system, Asian economies need to rethink their set of guiding values and strategies. The two contrasting free-market systems, the Anglo-Saxon one from the Americans and the British, and the communitarian approach of the Japanese and South Koreans although rooted in a democratic political structure, display very different underlying values.

The interests of the individual or of the group?

The Anglo-Saxon system rewards the individual and strives to maximize profits. The Japanese and South Koreans put the interests of the group first—individuals are asked to make sacrifices for the good of the company and the country. In the United States, intense competition is encouraged, thus sparking vitality and energy; individual performance is preferred to seniority or loyalty and individual brilliance is generously rewarded. US firms hire and fire without attaching too much emotion to the task or to the employee. In Japanese companies, this is unthinkable. In return for the security of lifetime employment, Japanese employees must make sacrifices so that, among other things, their company can improve its market share. Belonging to the world's largest corporation is their ultimate satisfaction, even if the benefits are intangible.

The CEOs of Anglo-Saxon corporations make more money than their Japanese counterparts; some CEOs in the United States make as much as 119 times the average worker's wages, compared with 18 times for the Japanese CEO. The generous stock options of the Anglo-Saxon CEOs encourage them to maximize current earnings and drive up stock prices.

Although Japan has the second-largest economy and is one of the wealthiest nations in the world, its people are perhaps the poorest among the G-7. In order to maximize profits, Japanese consumer prices are held at a level far above what would prevail in a free market. Japan's protectionist trade policies mean that the average consumer product is 40 per cent higher in Tokyo than it is in the United States.

Shareholder or employee: Who first?

Japanese companies, including banks, are the largest in the world. In every industry they target, they want to achieve the largest market share. Returns on investment are secondary to market domination and the longevity of the company. In the United States, labor and machinery are interchangeable, an unthinkable attitude in Japan. 'In America, automation replaces labor and wages fall. In Japan, it is the reverse,' observed economist, Lester Thurow.[16]

Japanese companies pay low dividends. In 1990, not more than 30 per cent of profit was paid as dividends, whereas US companies pay out as much as 80 per cent. In 1989, the average Japanese shareholder could expect a dividend yield on their investments of only 0.43 per cent—about as close to zero as it is possible to get. After seven years of economic slow-down and a delayed recovery in the stock-market, the future for Japanese shareholders is bleak.

Greater profit or bigger market share?

American companies report on a quarterly basis, so quarters become the time-frame for maximizing return to the shareholders. Fund managers dislike investment in research and development that takes a long time to show a profit. So while the most profitable companies in the world are American and British; Japanese companies have the largest market share in their chosen industrial sectors. Wall Street created another level of value for shareholders in Anglo-Saxon capitalism: shares are not just proof of ownership, they are also commodities that can be traded for many times their intrinsic value. With a philosophy of 'At the right price, everything is for sale', managers and owners pursue high present value. In contrast, ownership of shares in Japan is mostly confined to big business: 78 per cent of the shares listed on the Tokyo Stock Exchange are owned by members of the *keiretsu*, the group of Japanese Big Business. With interlocking ownership, outsiders have little chance to disturb the status quo.

Long term or short term?

Japanese companies retain profits to invest and also use more debt relative to equity—a source of capital that does not depend on immediate profit. They are also very patient: Japanese car manufacturer, Nissan, declared that it did not expect any profits on its new car, the *Infiniti*, in the first five years. In contrast, 47 per cent of all American firms will not invest unless profits start flowing within the first three years. Only 10 per cent of Japanese firms set a similar target.[17] According to Lester Thurow, Japanese companies are willing to cut profit to stay competitive. Matsushita's profit as a percentage of sales dropped from over 12 per cent in the early 1970s to between seven and eight per cent at the end of the 1980s. Hitachi's profits fell in a similar manner.[18]

Western institutional funds, such as pension funds, foundations and mutual funds, own 60 to 70 per cent of most publicly listed companies. Collectively, they are majority shareholders, but individually they are minority shareholders, which means that they have no control and play no role in the management of the company, though they welcome mergers and acquisitions, corporate exercises that can multiply the value of their holdings instantly.

Lester Thurow observed:

> Too often, Adam Smith's 'invisible hand' became the hand of a pickpocket. Free unfettered markets had a habit of discovering very profitable but non-productive activities. Practical experience taught that profit maximizing did not necessarily lead to output maximizing.'[19]

A Free Market with Asian Characteristics

That the rule of law prevails and there is minimal government involvement in commerce are widely accepted as fundamental prerequisites for the operation of the free market. Private enterprise, however, must find appropriate guiding values. The Chinese preference for the mean, that is, taking the middle path and not extreme positions, may be an appropriate guide in choosing the right set of values. On the one hand, a strategy to make as much profit in as short a time as possible is too destructive and too destabilizing for the community, whereas, on the other, a long-term strategy aimed at achieving maximum market share and oriented towards community well-being is too burdensome and inflexible. Middle ground must be found between the American and Japanese models. One model could be based on the family as the basic operating unit; the interests of the family come first because the interests of every individual are bound up in the family unit. *The family, however, must be regarded in a wider context: it can extend to shareholders, employees and customers. The family goes beyond blood relationships; it makes its decisions on the basis of objectivity and rationality.*

Today, successful Asian economies have either a top-down system with the government and big business assuming a strong role, or a bottom-up system where individual family units provide the thrust. Japan, South Korea, and to a certain extent, Singapore, where leadership is provided by the government and big corporations wield strong influence, are top-down economies. Japan has its woes with a highly regulated economy, South Korea is experiencing difficulties with huge loss-making corporations funded by the government and the banking system, and Singapore works very hard to encourage people to be more entrepreneurial. Bottom-up efforts by millions of individual family units have created the dynamism that drives the fast-growing economies of Hong Kong, Taiwan, coastal mainland Chinese cities and the overseas Chinese communities of Southeast Asia. This bottom-up, community-wide approach, I call self-reliance capitalism, and it is this kind of approach that I believe will be the effective model for the future. In self-reliance capitalism, while an effective government is still important, it plays an indirect role and does not compete with the private sector. Low taxes encourage hard work, and the absence of welfare makes saving necessary. The closest example of self-reliance capitalism is Hong Kong—one must not forget the merits of Hong Kong's system in spite of the current pressure on its economy to reinvent its competitiveness.

Chinese businesses, perhaps with the exception of those in Hong Kong in recent decades, have never operated in favorable *laissez-faire* environments. Since the government was never viewed as constructive, Chinese capitalists perfected the art of not drawing attention to themselves. According to Professor Gordon Redding, a specialist in Chinese Management with the Hong Kong University, the ground rules for Chinese are:

- Trust the family, contribute to it and rely on it.
- Build a network of reliable friends and behave honourably towards them to maintain it.
- Enlist the help of those in authority who may influence the fate of your business
- Understand that if you behave as a Confucian father-figure (and occasionally a matriarch), you have the right to expect complete loyalty and diligence from your subordinates in exchange.[20]

In Chinese capitalism, trust and honor are as binding as the laws of the land. Business is conducted informally; there is a certain sense of family. As the Chinese have been historically forced to keep a low profile for fear of persecution by either the mandarins in China or hostile governments in their adopted countries, their accounting systems are designed not to tell the whole picture of their operations. Transparency in corporate affairs, as understood in the West, is alien.

Family networks

The family network in its traditional form will be challenged to meet the standards of the global economy. It is, however, important to view Asian family networks against the perspective of the political backdrop. Close cultural ties and a hostile political environment have resulted in a Chinese family business that is typically lean, flexible, fast in making decisions, open to outsiders being co-opted into the network, and possessed of a global, borderless mind-set. Many Western management experts thinks that this Chinese model could emerge as a viable alternative to the large and rigid hierarchical model because it has all the attributes needed to respond fast and to exploit the niches in today's global economy.

Chinese firms are small and practise a strong, centralized leadership style, which accounts for their fast decision-making abilities. However, this style is best suited to those businesses whose success depends on the personal acumen, skill and connections of the owner/manager. It would be immensely challenging to build a global operation, where close liaison between the chief executive and staff on the ground would be impossible. The fact that the richest Chinese businesses are in Southeast Asia, especially in Indonesia where they collaborate with the ruling family, and that few Chinese businesses are successful in the West, suggests that traditional Chinese capitalist way risks being a relic of the past, incapable of operating in a decentralized, open and transparent environment.

The second and third generations of Chinese entrepreneurs are now refining their traditional networks in order to benefit from the opportunities of the global economy. These companies, such as Li & Fung of Hong Kong and Acer of Taiwan, are transforming the closed family system to one of an open extended family system, sharing ownership, power and decision-making. For people with no blood relationship, a new bond is created by way of partnership. 'The values that built Asia's Chinese businesses of the last half century will never be lost. With the younger generation learning Western ways of organization and formalizing communications and agreements in contracts, a modern model of Chinese network firms will be developed,' said Professor Tseng Shih Chiang of Taiwan's Jiang Tung University. I will take up this discussion in detail in chapter 6.

The Hong Kong model

Hong Kong is a near-perfect example of self-reliance capitalism—it enjoys small government and an efficient civil service, smaller government-managed welfare, low taxes, economic freedom and opportunity, and the rule of law. In self-reliance capitalism, there must also be a high tolerance for failure, available family support and an acceptance that the community itself has moral force. There is always room and hope for anyone who aspires to a better life, and who is prepared and willing to work for it. The Chinese say it doesn't matter where the hero hails from (*Ying xiong bu wen chu shen di*).

Companies or business units need to find their optimal size: they must be small enough to be flexible, yet large enough to be economic and effective. Family units need to be linked into their own network of core competencies with which they enjoy a long-term community spirit and a willingness to cooperate. However, they also need to remain discrete entities in order to stay competitive. This model may represent a better structure to cope with the challenges of the 21st century, when Asia will be put to the test to build a brand of capitalism that can successfully compete locally, regionally and globally.

Work is meaningful

In any form of capitalism, hard work counts. It is productive hard work that creates the real value that helps communities to best withstand the vagaries of the global economy. In general, the work ethics of Asians have not declined to any alarming extent, although business people wish the old ethic of loyalty remained. Young Asians would do well to remember that hard work counts, whether in good times or bad times. Work is not a means to an end, it is an end in itself, because, through work, you realize your values. American philosopher, Ayn Rand, said that work is the process of achieving your values; your work is the purpose of your life. Many of us may think that Americans don't work hard. This is not true. Americans in general do not work less hard than Asians. It is difficult to imagine how the American economy could have made such a remarkable recovery if it were otherwise. For legislation against work, no-one can beat the French. The French parliament recently passed a law limiting the working week to 35 hours, effective in the year 2000.

East Asians work longer hours per year and enjoy fewer paid holidays than Europeans. Don't get the idea that this is exploitation in the sweat-shops. Many Asian millionaires still put in a 12–15 hour day, possibly 320 days a year, only taking time off during the lunar New Year holidays when most things shut down.

Table 2.7: Working Hours

Country	Working Hours Per Year	Paid Holidays (No of Days)
Seoul	2,302	7.8
Bangkok	2,272	8.8
Hong Kong	2,222	12.1
Taipei	2,136	17.0
Singapore	2,044	17.7
In comparison		
Copenhagen	1,669	25.0
Dusseldorf	1,682	30.5
Madrid	1,721	32.1
Frankfurt	1,725	31.2
London	1,880	22.1

Source: *Conflict and Cooperation: The United States and East Asia*, Dr Tommy TB Koh, Federal Publications (S) Pte Ltd, 1995.

The lower the tax, the harder you work

Low taxes stimulate hard work. Asian governments are beginning to recognize the significance of this, and the trend has been towards lower taxation.

In general, the maximum tax rates in Asia are lower than elsewhere in the world, and they often kick in at higher levels. When Mr Goh Chok Tong, the Prime Minister of Singapore, was Minister of Trade and Industry, he remarked that, 'Several advanced countries, like Britain, have been hypnotized by a sock-the-rich slogan, only to discover that by heavy taxes on personal incomes, they have stifled the drive to excel and succeed'. Dr Tommy Koh, the Director of the Institute of Policy Studies and Chairman of the National Arts Council in Singapore, has observed the following differences between the tax rates of the richest countries of the world and those of Asia's emerging economies.

Table 2.8: Tax Rates of Asian and Western Countries

Country	Maximum personal tax rate (%)	Level at which maximum rate applies (US$)
Hong Kong	13	51,000
Singapore	30	272,000
Malaysia	31	59,000
Indonesia	35	23,000
Philippines	34	20,000
Thailand	36	160,000
Taiwan	40	128,000
South Korea	48	80,000
Japan	62	206,000
Sri Lanka	33	1,468
Pakistan	38	98,000
India	39	3,200
New Zealand	31	19,000
US	39	250,000
Britain	39	39,000
Australia	45	37,000
France	55	54,000

Source: *Conflict and Cooperation: The United States and East Asia*, Dr Tommy T B Koh, Federal Publications (S) Pte Ltd, 1995.

The average tax burden in the G-7 countries, expressed as a percentage of GDP, is 36.2 per cent. The comparable figure for the four Newly Industrializing Economies (NIEs) is 17 per cent, and 17.3 per cent for the ASEAN-4. If tax and non-tax revenue are combined, the total revenue collected by governments in the G-7 is 41.3 per cent of GDP, compared to 21.6 per cent collected by the four NIEs, and 20.3 per cent for the ASEAN-4.

Governments rarely bring in the additional money they expect with higher taxes, as recent US treasury figures make clear. When President Bill Clinton jacked up taxes in 1993, his treasury team predicted an increase of US$19.3b additional revenue, but the actual amount collected was only US$8.8b, less than half of what was anticipated. Hong Kong's marginal rate of 15 per cent manages to generate three times the relative revenue from its richest 10 per cent of earners than Japan does, with a top marginal tax rate of 50 per cent.

The *Far Eastern Economic Review* noted in an editorial:

> For decades, bureaucrats have viewed taxes as a policy lever they can move up or down at will. Japan may boast a low ratio of tax revenue to GDP, but this is only because it has tax evasion on a scale that rivals Italy. Right now, Japan's big businesses are clamouring for a cut in corporate tax rates, among the highest in the world. Yet Japan's core dilemma, the lack of individual incentive, goes unaddressed: the more productive you are, the more you are punished.[21]

Table 2.9: Tax and Non-tax Revenue of Selected Countries

	Per cent of GDP		Total (tax and non-
Country	Tax revenue	Non-tax revenue	tax revenue)
G-7	36.2	5.1	41.3
Germany	40.1	6.3	46.3
France	41.5	4.6	46.2
Canada	34.9	6.1	41.0
Italy	38.0	2.1	40.1
United Kingdom	35.2	4.9	40.1
United States	27.7	6.4	34.2
Japan	30.5	na	na
NIEs	17.0	4.6	21.6
South Korea	20.6	4.3	24.9
Taiwan	17.2	6.5	23.7
Hong Kong	13.1	3.1	16.3
ASEAN-4	17.2	3.1	20.3
Malaysia	18.9	6.2	25.1
Indonesia	16.8	1.9	25.1
Thailand	16.8	1.9	18.7
Philippines	16.0	2.5	18.5
Singapore	17.7	4.4	22.1

Source: Conflict and Cooperation: The United States and East Asia, Dr Tommy TB Koh, Federal Publications (S) Pte Ltd, 1995.

Lifelong learning

There is a strong tradition of learning in Asia. The educational needs of children are paramount. The corporate learning culture is strongest in Taiwan and Singapore, where second degrees are becoming important and are common among executives who strive to maintain their competitiveness. This culture of learning augurs well for Asia as it restructures its economies, although the pace and spread of education throughout the population must be greatly accelerated, especially among the non-Chinese population outside Korea and Japan.

Savings, spending and investing

For Asians, saving for rainy days and old age is a cultural habit; many Chinese Asians almost have a siege mentality and they save the most. Low taxes also encourage savings. Singapore's rate of saving is 48 per cent of GDP, its foreign reserves just past US$67b. When Singapore discovered that the average net return from Singapore's Provident Fund was lacklustre, measures were taken to allow citizens to do their own investment.

Table 2.10: Gross Domestic Savings as a percentage of GDP

Country	1975	1993
Hong Kong	28	30
Taiwan	27	27
South Korea	18	33
Singapore	29	48
China	34	34
Indonesia	20	38
Malaysia	23	38
Philippines	27	14
Thailand	20	27
India	19	23
Nepal	19	19
Pakistan	7	12
Sri Lanka	9	15

Source:Conflict and Cooperation: The United States and East Asia, Dr Tommy T B Koh, Federal Publications (S) Pte Ltd, 1995.

The financial crisis exposed inefficiencies in the deployment of Asia's vast savings pool. Since their capital markets are immature, Asians are overly dependent upon the banking system as a means of increasing their hard-earned capital; for businesses, banks are their source of finance. The crisis exposed the inadequacies of the banking system: rates of interest on deposits were low (1–2 per cent in Japan), and in many of the affected economies, there was a large number of non-performing loans. Asia needs well-managed banks and capital markets which can distribute capital to those who can use it efficiently. A bond market is also long overdue; it needs to be established to channel Asia's savings into long-term investment in infrastructure development.In stark contrast with the frugality of Asians, American consumers are sinking into a black hole of debt. Overall, consumer debt, which has surged 39 per cent in the last five years and now totals more than a trillion dollars, could be a time-bomb for the US economy and its banks, according to a 1996 study.[22] The study found that nearly four per cent of credit card loans were written off in 1995, up from 3.8 per cent a year earlier. The consumption orientation is one of the bedrocks of a capitalist economy. While Americans generally were enjoying greater returns on their savings, thereby reducing the need to save more, they were also running up huge personal debts. While we recognize the inherent dangers of overconsumption and living beyond one's means, it is also important that we acknowledge that excessive frugality is not helpful to economic expansion either. While prudence remains the key strategy in personal and family finances, Asian public policies may need to take into account the sense of security and safety that citizens derive from their political and economic systems. Building up steady domestic demand is as important as Asia's ability to export; such demand can only occur if there is a high level of confidence in Asia's political and economic systems.

Government intervention

Strong government leadership, such as in Japan, South Korea, Singapore and Taiwan, has often been lauded as the driving force for Asia's economic gains, whether the gains have been through five-year plans, research and development, education, controls or industry rationalization. In examining the government's in the economy, we must always bear in mind the state of the domestic economy and the context of the global environment at that point in time. Developed Asia's growth strategies were undertaken in times quite different from today's, and strong government intervention was used to maximize the efficiency of scarce skills and limited resources. Although the international dynamics have changed, conditions in China, India and the ASEAN-4 are similar to those that prevailed in the 70s and 80s. To insist that the state not intervene in the economy in any way may be fatal for the economic development of some countries.

The key is for Asian governments to know when to do less. Neither Japan nor South Korea has made any moves in recognition of this, even though they have mature economies. Taiwan has made this transition well. At the beginning of Taiwan's economic boom, the government played an overwhelming role in the economy. Over time, it progressively withdrew its control, confining itself to macroeconomics and focusing on the basic fundamentals—low inflation, high savings, budget discipline, monetary restraint, sustained emphasis on education, upgrading of technology and skills, building links with the global economy and watching income and equity distribution. Taiwan's father of economic development, KT Li, observed:

> Countries with a Chinese cultural tradition are often perceived as having entrenched bureaucracies and central governments. This is not only historically true, but is still true for Taiwan. Nevertheless, what we as policy makers did in Taiwan was to help various parts of the economy first to stand and then to walk, and then we let go.[23]

Smaller government is a start, but not enough. Today's leaders need great navigation skills to ensure domestic prosperity stays afloat in the turbulence of the global economy. Those in government can be likened to a SWAT team: professional, highly competent and efficient in the critical role they have to play. Various arguments and studies support this trend. A study by V Tanzi and L Schuknecht, two economists at the International Monetary Fund, to gauge the benefits of government spending, made an intriguing finding: public spending may be subject to diminishing marginal returns, and beyond a certain level, it stops delivering measurable social benefits.

As a general rule, those economies with the lowest rise in public spending since 1960 seem to be more efficient and more innovative. They boast lower unemployment and a higher level of registered patents. Moreover, because they do not need to levy high taxes to pay for government largesse, they also tend to have the smallest underground economies, in which people work but do not pay tax. For instance, the underground economy averaged 11 per cent of GDP in countries where public spending exceeded 50 per cent of GDP in 1990, but only six per cent in countries where it was less than 40 per cent of GDP.[24]

The study tracked the increase in public spending in industrialized countries over the past 125 years. Government spending rose from an average of eight per cent of GDP in 1870 to 15 per cent in 1920, and to 21 per cent in 1937. The three decades following the Second World War saw the biggest increase in public spending, mainly reflecting the expansion of the welfare state. By 1980, public spending was over 30 per cent of GDP in the United States, while in smaller European countries, it breached 50 per cent. In Asia, average government spending does not exceed 30 per cent of GDP. As the democratic process takes hold in Asia, Asians would do well to ponder these statistics and reflect on their traditions of citizen self-reliance.

Politics: the shrinking profession

With the notable exception of Hong Kong and Singapore, Asian managers at all levels are usually more cosmopolitan in outlook and more tuned in to the world than their public sector counterparts are. The *Far Eastern Economic Review* made this observation of the Manila APEC summit:

> Nowhere was this chasm more apparent than in the disappointing APEC summit in Manila: while business advisers inside and outside the official APEC framework proposed bold initiatives to liberalize national economies and coordinate regulatory standards and practices, political leaders offered a tepid package of largely symbolic gestures.[25]

Washington SyCip, founder and chairman of the Manila-based SGV Group, observed that:

> Business and political leaders look at the same problems from different angles. When a businessman looks at his situation, he takes into account that he is not only competing against his neighbour but maybe the guy from Taiwan or Malaysia. Politicians do not have that sense.

The fact that politicians and bureaucrats lack the perspicacity of businessmen could be attributed to two factors: pay and education. With few exceptions, Asia's civil servants are miserably underpaid, a situation which means not only corruption but a second-rate civil service, unable to attract talent from the private sector. As for education, Washington SyCip recalled, 'In the 1960s, when Singapore was sending their people to Harvard, my friends at Pan Am would sit around and tell me that Singapore wouldn't last. Today, Pan Am is long gone, but Singapore is still here.'[26] Singapore is not only here; as of June 1997, Singapore's per capita income surpassed that of the United States, and the quality of life of Singaporeans is one of the highest in the world.[27]

Under the demands of the global economy, big government such as Japan Inc is showing up as less and less effective. The *Far Eastern Economic Review* noted:

> Fifty years ago, when Japan was just getting on its feet, this model of Japan Inc. may have helped transform Japan into a formidable industrial power. In the era of microchips, however, it elevates bureaucratic judgment over the marketplace and in so doing threatens Japan's competitiveness. It is no coincidence, for example, that despite Japan's importance as a financial center and its large reserves of domestic capital, Japanese banks are only about a fifth as profitable as their American counterparts.[28]

Why then do we need government? Throughout their history, the Chinese masses have had neither faith nor trust in government as their protector. Even today, few believe that government can help with their well-being, but does government believe it? One of the most paternalistic leaders in Asia, Senior Minister Lee Kuan Yew, has said:

> The government does not believe it. In the ultimate crisis, even in earthquakes and typhoons, it is your human relationships that will see you through...But the family and the way human relationships are structured, do increase the survival chances of its members. That has been tested over thousand of years in many different situations.[29]

Freedom is profitable

The worldwide movement towards deregulation and privatization seems to suggest that economic freedom is more effective than government intervention. According to a major study, economic freedom is essential for economic growth.[30] Seventeen categories were used to measure the degrees of freedom during the past 20 years in over 100 countries. The results of the study gave the most convincing evidence yet that nations are unlikely to continue to grow without appreciable economic freedom, and that openness to trade is very important. Many people attribute growth, such as in South Korea, Japan and, to some extent Taiwan, to strong government intervention. However, the study showed that despite government intervention:

> Asian economies have generally been much freer than those elsewhere. They hold many of the top rankings on the freedom scale : Hong Kong is No1; Singapore, No 3; and Japan, No10. Even Taiwan and South Korea appear to be *laissez-faire* compared with most countries, for at 16th and 20th respectively, they rank well above the world average.[31]

Although Asian economies have more freedom in comparison with Western nations, further liberalization is needed. South Korea, for example, still protects many companies from purchase by foreigners. In Malaysia and Thailand, banks are off-limits. Across the region, energy, agriculture, and property are all protected to some extent, although Asian economies have benefited from openness, especially direct foreign investment.

Winner takes all

Every individual begins life from a different vantage point. Although a university education generally gives a better start in life, it is not necessarily the only way to get ahead. Malaysia's Lim Kim Hong only had three years of formal education, yet he built a multi-million dollar business and sold it for US$120m at the height of the market, later buying back a substantial interest.[32]

In free market economies, the size of one's reward is a function of demand and supply. For example, in the United States, a major league player in baseball averages over a million dollars a year, and a chief executive can make 200 times the pay of the average worker. In 1995, a record 556 executives in corporate America earned a million dollars or more. The picture in Asia is similar: businessmen are ahead of everyone else in earnings. The only country in the world where the politicians are not left behind in executive compensation is Singapore where the Prime Minister makes $901,400 a year.[33]

While it is true that the rich are indeed getting richer, it must be pointed out that the poor all over the world are also doing better. Economic growth and globalization has had the effect of lifting millions out of poverty.

Economist Gary Becker said:

> Perhaps the widening gap is not a bad thing. The richer section of the community, after reaping in higher returns, have greater incentive to invest and commit more to research and development, thereby creating more opportunity for the poorer section of the community so that they could get up as well.[34]

One third of humanity has tried to be fair by creating equality with central planning: we are familiar with the outcome of that experiment. However, the enemy of capitalism is government policy that represses private enterprise. A free system creates opportunities that everyone can take advantage of. The government's role is to create the environment to make the pie, not to distribute it. One view is that capitalism is unfair and results in inequalities, but another is that, while capitalism cannot create equality of outcome, it can create equality of opportunity. In a *laissez-faire* economy, it is performance that counts. The free market rewards those who work effectively and productively, not just hard.

One of the most important aspects of any society is that it gives people the freedom to choose. A society cushioned by welfare does not work; welfare makes people dependent and stifles initiative and self-sufficiency. An effective system provides avenues to opportunity and an environment where people are inspired to create more and venture. Economically speaking, it is a question of incentives. Let the market-place decides who gets what and how much. One remarkable feature of American society is that it has never really been an egalitarian society. As Ronald Reagan used to say when he was president, America is a country of opportunity, not of guarantee. In Asia, we must make sure that the word 'guarantee' does not creep into our vocabulary.

The returns that individuals get for their efforts are clearly a function of the values they bring to their jobs. What can we do about the disparities that arise? If you say, 'So what if the boss has created jobs and provided opportunities for us; he is still driving a BMW while we have to take the bus', then you should also question why you are not the boss. Can you be as capable and work as hard? Nothing is wrong with a winner-takes-all society, but it would be very wrong if there is no equality of opportunity for everyone.

Towards Sustainable Growth

Asia was well on its way to achieving critical mass before the financial crisis strike the region. Asia's own developed economies were reaching saturation in growth, and were spreading their wings outside to the rest of the region. Asian economies have to make structural adjustments; in the type of growth industries, in the type of organization structure and in the type of foreign partners they should seek.

In Asia, sustained economic growth is not a vision but a political and social necessity. Czech President Vaclav Havel has said:

> The only economic system that works is a market economy in which everything belongs to someone which means that someone is responsible for everything. This is the only natural economy, the only kind that makes sense, the only one that can lead to prosperity, because it is the only one that reflects the nature of life itself.

Apart from learning from the West, Asia can also learn from her own ancient heritage; 'market taoism' existed as early as the Autumn and Spring Period. Accepting the free market is only a beginning—truly nurturing the free market culture and building the institutions to support it should be priorities for the emerging economies of East Asia. Sustainable economic growth calls for managing priorities and resources in a moving picture of global dynamics. Asia has done it before—it has been pragmatic, open to learning and willing to work with partners from all over the world. East Asia would do well to open wide its doors and invite the world, and the competition, to come in to help it move towards a free market culture of a world standard.

Chapter 3
Towards an Opportunity Society

"A trail is blazed by man.
Where the mountain creates a block, you make another road,
Sighting no road ahead, man makes a turn."

—Chinese Proverb—

The raison d'tre of a community is to create as much well-being for its members as its resources can command. Hence, one method of measuring the success of an economic system is by looking at how much opportunity it creates for its citizens to utilize their skills, expand them, and achieve their full potential. In other words, the encouragement of creative growth. It is essential that a situation be created whereby everyone can take advantage of opportunities in an open, competitive environment. Any element that could undermine free competition, be it corruption, cronyism or a lack of meritocracy, will obstruct individual enterprise and reduce the efficiency of the entire economic system. Too many societies have made the mistake of insisting on equality of outcome and sought to redistribute wealth, with the result that growth has been retarded, talent and capital have taken flight, and the growth of the community has been stunted both economically and socially.

Are Asian countries maximizing opportunities for their citizens? How efficient are Asian communities? The concept of efficiency can vary widely: whereas it may only take a phone call in Hong Kong and Singapore to resolve a small matter, elsewhere several personal trips may be required. Asia's developing economies still have much to catch up in this regard; man-made and policy-created inefficiencies abound. The question is, to what extent and when are these economies prepared to allow free competition to decide who gets what and how much, without interference from public policy?

In some cases, privatization transformed entities that were once public monopolies into private ones, owned by people connected with the ruling establishment. Other public monopolies the government earmarked to become national role models became local companies run by people with no experience. Economic decisions were influenced by political and nationalistic considerations, with no reference to efficient allocation of resources. If market forces had been allowed to prevail, the consumer could have enjoyed more competitive prices and better products. Resources were directed towards huge projects regardless of whether these industries gave any comparative advantage or were within the competencies and skills base of the work-force.

Many Asians are fearful of liberalization, fearing that it means surrendering control to foreign dominance. However, if we trust the evidence, competition produces higher quality growth and more efficient enterprises. If we believe that free trade brings greater benefits, since it allows everyone to do what they do the best, liberalization will only help Asian economies to accelerate their climb up the value chain. An Asian businessman expressed his attitude towards control thus, 'You can own a 100 per cent of something small and have total control, but 40 per cent of something bigger could be better and more resilient than the 100 per cent you control fully'.

National pride aside, there are other reasons that make liberalization difficult and slow in Asia. There are great complexities in the racial, religious and cultural make-up of the region. The vast inequalities in income and the pace of change that people can cope with make further reform a delicate balancing act. Although the economies of Asia have demonstrated great openness in the past, as we enter the 21st century, global forces and domestic circumstances will combine to accelerate the process. Moving to a system of free competition and meritocracy will be the key challenge for the leadership of the economies of Japan, South Korea, Taiwan, Malaysia, Indonesia, Thailand and China.

To understand the extent of the changes that have already taken place in moving from a government-controlled to a market-driven culture, it is useful to examine Asia's young economies. Because of Asia's great cultural diversity, one cannot generalize. However, the depth and implications of cultural and social forces can be appreciated by placing Asian communities into broad groups based on language, religion and culture.

Confucian East Asia

In Confucian East Asia, the challenge is to turn a system and culture designed to serve the emperor to one where everyone can aspire to become an 'emperor'. The communities of Confucian East Asia are those at the forefront of the economic upsurge of the New Asia. Confucian East Asia refers to the Chinese in mainland China and the overseas Chinese communities in Southeast Asia including those of Hong Kong, Macau, Taiwan, Singapore, Malaysia, Thailand, the Philippines, Indonesia, Vietnam and Indo-China. Disparities exist among them in economic levels, degrees of exposure to the world and sophistication. However, common among them is their pride of their Chinese heritage, the written language and Confucian traditions. Another bond between them which may only be true of the older generation is their wish to see China emerge to become a successful world player.

What is known today as the Han Chinese is a group made up of many ethnic groups originally residing in mainland China. Over thousands of years, various indigenous cultures, habits and customs were blended and mixed as the culture evolved. Of China's 1.2 billion people, over 800 million speak Mandarin. Mandarin, the common written language, unified China almost from the beginning of its recorded history and was the medium in which the Chinese culture flourished. Chinese rituals and traditions are largely Confucian in origin, and the majority of the people are Buddhist or Taoist, with a growing number practising the Christian faith.

The Chinese communities all exhibit distinctive characteristics of their own, reflecting differences of geographical region and the impact that Western influence has had on them. Few would disagree that Hong Kong is the most modern and sophisticated. Although it is very Western, culturally, it is very Chinese. Singapore is as sophisticated as any major metropolitan city. The Southeast Asian Chinese, having lived under colonial rule, are English-speaking and have a better appreciation of Western business practices and the rule of law, although they do not yet fully subscribe to the objectives and transparent culture of the West. Many of them know little of their Chinese culture, nor are they able to speak Mandarin or Chinese dialects or write their own Chinese names.

In spite of these differences, a modern pop culture is evolving and spreading fast among these communities. Many pop idols are known to the entire Chinese world. For example, teenagers in Taipei, Singapore, Penang or Shanghai all know about mainland Chinese singer Faye Wong's new baby, while most are proud that Malaysian-born Hong Kong kung-fu diva Michelle Yeoh is the new Bond girl in *Tomorrow Never Dies*.

The challenges of modernization are most acute in the newly opened societies, such as those of mainland China. Professor Tu Weimeng of Harvard University observed:

> In the collective memory of the Chinese, culturally the last 150 years is blank; they only remember humiliation and suffering. It looks as though there isn't a contemporary modern Chinese civilization. People talk and hold on to thousand-year-old glories.

That is true; most Chinese-speaking Chinese talk proudly of their 5000-year-old cultural heritage, and those English-speaking overseas Chinese return from visits to China beaming with confidence and pride, inspired by such historical grandeur as the Great Wall of China. Many Chinese worry that Chinese society, especially the younger generation, is vulnerable to Western influences and will end up copying the West.

If Asia as a region is culturally Chinese-driven, can the Chinese offer Asia a way forward in the 21st century? Has any Asian community already achieved the New Asian Way? For now, the answer is, 'not yet'. But Asia's transformation is in progress. One trend is certain as Asia globalizes—Asia will Asianize, and in the process, Chinese cultural influence will resurface and reassert itself. It will take a critical mass of economic prosperity and political stability to spur an Asian or Chinese renaissance.

Many in Asia may fear that Chinese culture will dominate them. These are unfounded fears, as no single culture will dominate in today's open and global society. In a world increasingly driven by voluntary participation and the market, a culture's attractiveness lies in the hearts and minds of its people.

Jup Sang Hong Kong

Hong Kong demonstrates how self-reliance can make the difference. In the same spirit as American philosopher, Ayn Rand, who celebrated the Manhattan skyline, the Hong Kong skyline could be an inspiration for China and perhaps the rest of Asia.

British Finance Secretary, Sir John Cowperwaithe, who arrived in 1961, established freewheeling capitalism as Hong Kong's official doctrine. As pointed out by *Newsweek*, 'While Britain continued to build a welfare state, Cowperwaithe was saying "no"—no export subsidies, no tariffs, no personal taxes higher than 15 per cent, red tape so thin a one-page form can launch a company'. *Apple Daily*'s publisher, Yeung Wai-hong, recently suggested erecting a stature of Cowperwaithe, lest anyone forget to give credit to the man who allowed Hong Kong to become the world's best customer for Rolls Royce.[1]

British rule, by default, gave the people a system of Western rule of law with minimal government interference in economic activities. Hong Kong was already a developed economy at the time of the handback to Chinese sovereignty. It is the world's freest economy; with the highest concentration of millionaires and a per capita gross domestic product (GDP) of close to US$24,000.[2] Hong Kong also boasts a foreign reserve ranked fifth highest in Asia and sixth highest in the world. Successful businessmen command great respect; they are the role models for the young. Education, hard work and savings are valued as the way to upward mobility and eventual wealth. Traditionally, there is little place for politics. The one defining characteristic of Hong Kong people is that they 'just do, don't talk'. However, Hong Kong is not without her imperfections. Income disparity is wide, with the richest 20 per cent of the population enjoying half of Hong Kong's income, while the poorest 10 per cent share just over one per cent.

According to a study by Lo Shiu-hing, while all are in favor of private property rights and capitalism, Hong Kong society is divided in its political orientations.[3] Roughly, the groupings are as follows:

- The local elite; professionals and businessmen, who are conservative; anti-democratic, and see politics as a means to achieve profits and to support private property rights.
- The local middle-class liberals who fully support Western values, such as human rights and democracy.

- The local middle-class nationalists who are critical of Western values and have a strong sense of belonging to China.
- The mainland Chinese business elite, who are profit-oriented, see politics as a means of protecting their interests and achieving profit.

Before the handback of 1997, people in Hong Kong were apolitical. Lo observed:

> To the local elite, the beneficiary of democratic reforms would be the working class which would receive 'free lunches' from the popularly elected middle-class liberals. The business community felt that 'democratization' should proceed slowly and gradually, for the liberals will sell their bread to voters at cheap prices. Clearly, the elite is deeply suspicious and distrustful of the middle class liberal democrats.[4]

Louis Cha, a well-known author and publisher in Hong Kong, said:

> If a system of one person, one vote, is followed in election, the government and councils thus elected will most probably be representatives of the interests of residents in housing estates, workers and low-salaried employees, as they form the majority among the population. An elected government is bound to introduce a large number of welfare schemes and interfere with the operation of banks, big enterprises and factories.[5]

Hong Kong's distinctive energy comes from its singular fixation on business and getting things done. The Cantonese term, *Jup Sang*, meaning to scramble for life or survival, symbolizes the Hong Kong spirit. On 1 July 1997, Hong Kong entered another phase of its evolution, and had to move from *Jup Sang* to *Chai Sang*, meaning reinvent a life. The year since the handback has seen a rising enthusiasm for democratic governance and the emergence of a new breed of younger and professional politicians in Hong Kong. The general public has also begun to take a stronger interest in politics as the special region's economy begins to feel the impact of the region's financial turmoil.

Hong Kong's challenge is its very own success. Because of the political decision to maintain the Hong Kong dollar's peg to the US dollar, with competitive devaluation across the region, Hong Kong suddenly became the most expensive city in the region. For an economy highly dependent on services and tourism, this had serious implications. The Hong Kong stock-market and real estate have both fallen dramatically, and tourism, which accounted for 8 per cent of the economy, contracted by 25 per cent, sending the retail industry and the hotel and restaurant business into a tailspin. At the time of the handback, the greatest challenge seemed to be Hong Kong's ability to persuade Beijing to leave the self-reliant community alone. After nearly a full year of economic instability, Hong Kong must prepare to make radical adjustments, bring down the cost of doing business and reassert its competitive edge. Hong Kong enterprises have to reinvent a niche for themselves in high-end, value-added, economic activities, and to steer away from the more speculative real estate and trading activities. There is a fear that the Special Administrative Region's government of Tung Chee Hwa may resort to a short-term pain-killer that could undermine the tradition of non-interference by the state in the economy.

The special handback issue of *Newsweek* stated:

> Some people will expect more generosity from a post-colonial government. But we shouldn't dole out too many benefits. We should care for the handicapped and the elderly, for example, but I'm not sure we should do too much for the unemployed. There is already an alarming trend in our welfare programs: if you're a family of four, you can bring in more money from government benefits than from the head of the family working for a modest wage. This is dangerous. Nothing must threaten Hong Kong's spirit of 'Jup Sang' its instinct for picking the right straw, for surviving and prospering.[6]

Hong Kong is unique in Asia in that it has a cluster of professional services; financial, design, engineering, legal, consulting, marketing, transportation and insurance which makes it a source of intellectual power for the rest of the region. Additional strength comes from a network of offshore manufacturing facilities; Hong Kong's real economy employs some five million workers in 50,000 factories in mainland China and elsewhere in the region. The Hong Kong stock-market is highly vulnerable, since the banking and property sectors are heavily represented.

The high cost of operating in Hong Kong has given rise to speculation on its competitiveness with the rest of the region, a situation further aggravated by devaluations that occurred during the financial crisis. Victor Fung, chairman of the Hong Kong Trade Development Council, thinks that cost is only one factor in achieving a competitive edge, and it is not necessarily the most important one. He said, 'The true essence of competitiveness of real, lasting competitiveness is uniqueness. It is the gap between your product and what others are offering. It is defined by the value, not the cost'. On the subject of the added value that Hong Kong offers to the rest of the region, he maintained:

> The reason is simply that nowhere else in Asia has Hong Kong's confluence of strengths. They make Hong Kong different from every other economy in the region and more comparable to the high value-added metropolitan economies of New York, London and Tokyo. The three primary assets which create this competitive advantage are Hong Kong's service economy, its value-added manufacturing network and its special connection to the Chinese mainland economy.[7]

Taiwan in Search of an Identity

Taiwan has shown the world that you neither have to be big in resources nor have a nation-state status to be successful. Strong ambition and tenacity have produced the Taiwan 'miracle' and its success has confounded the economic theory that resources are basic to wealth creation. However, local politics seem to have other priorities—political maneuvers at the expense of economic considerations. In the meantime, regardless of the heat on either side of the Taiwan Straits, the business community presses on. After close to four decades of continuous growth, the result has been spectacular. In 1992, Taiwan's per capita gross national product (GNP) was only US$162; by 1992, it was US$12,214. In 1995, Taiwan had foreign exchange reserves of US$82.5b, the largest in the world that year.

The Taiwanese find their edge in a well-educated work-force and a strong industrial base of small and medium-sized industries. They are also great networkers, funding hundreds of ventures in Silicon Valley as well as at home in their determination not to miss out in the golden era of cyberspace. Entrepreneurs, acknowledging that Taiwan's economic future is closely tied with the Mainland, are using their capital, skill and technology to establish production facilities there.

While much work remains to be done to reduce bureaucratic control, to clean up corruption, and in the allocation of resources, the most significant recent development has been democracy. In March 1996, Taiwan became the first Chinese community in China's 5,000 years of history where the people decided who was to be their leader—Lee Teng Hui won a presidential election with a resounding 54 per cent of the vote. This was a significant event in the transformation of Confucian East Asia's political system, despite the chaotic election process.

Participation in the island's democracy is very much community. Through various social organisations and professional associations, intellectuals, professionals and the owners of small and medium-sized businesses are making their voices heard. 'Horizontal communication was emerging, there was discourse between various community groups and the flowering of opinions. That is the first stage towards achieving democracy,' said Professor Tu Weimeng.[8] Whether Taiwan's democratization fulfils its promise as the true beginning of the 'people's choice' and proves that a Chinese society is capable of having liberal political institutions will depend on how democracy continues to evolve in this community of 22 million. The social unrest that has rocked Taiwan has alerted the Chinese to a new possibility—a departure from a Singapore-like *status quo* and law and order. Although this social disturbance is unsettling, Professor Tseng Shih Chiang, an expert in Chinese culture from Jiao Tung University of Taiwan, said:

> It is O.K. The community as a whole has to go through all these shocks; after that people will refocus. For example, with increasing crime, the rich can find no security, and they will question the meaning of all this crazy wealth creation. At the end of these churning disturbances, people will find what they really wanted and start to treasure the values they decided to keep'[9]

Rapid modernization has somewhat weakened the traditional family in Taiwan, but not to any great extent. The family serves as a strong social institution and also fulfils a welfare function. It provides social and economic support for the old and, in times of economic downturn, it supports family members who are temporarily unemployed. Taiwan has no government-run welfare system similar to those in the West; it is only recently that some form of compulsory insurance has been introduced. Many of Taiwan's professionals show gratitude to the family for having funded their higher education and training. They are committed to looking after their parents in their old age and to helping other relatives with their education.

Chinese familial traditions are strong among Taiwan's businesses. Over 98 per cent of Taiwan's commerce and industry is dominated by small and medium-sized family firms. Their adherence to Chinese family values may be explained by the fact that a considerable number of them flourished on family funds and low-priced, sometimes free, labor provided by siblings and relatives. Taiwan has a vibrant official as well as grey capital market; between 1994 and 1997, Taiwanese firms raised close to US$28b through rights issues and public offerings, making Taiwan the top capital market outside Japan.

The quest to remain competitive and to advance is never-ending. From the mid-1980s onwards, the demand for books on self-improvement has been steadily on the rise. Many part-time professional and skills-development programs are offered by public and private educational institutions.

Taiwan's relations with mainland China is the most important issue facing the Taiwanese leadership. Many prefer to maintain the status quo and let matters take their natural course, while others advocate a separate and independent entity for Taiwan. Taiwan's assertiveness is not all that bad as Professor Tseng Shih Chiang said:

> Look at it this way the strong voices, although discomforting, may help the entire Chinese community, including those on the Mainland, to move forward, to understand the reality of democratization. What we are seeing is self-determination; people want a voice to assert themselves politically, internationally and culturally. This is new, and the Chinese leadership has to learn and respect this.[10]

Kiasu Singapore

Singapore is a successful city-state, though rather unpopular with liberal-minded people. Not only Western liberals dislike Singapore's tight controls, most Asians find Singapore's benevolent paternalistic system stifling. Few, however, can deny Singapore's extraordinary economic achievements. Asia's richest country enjoys a per capita GDP of US$23,500, up from just US$2,825 in 1970; it is the only country in Asia that has a per capita GDP comparable to that of the United States. At US$24,417 per capita of population, Singapore has the highest foreign reserves of any Asian nation.[11] Ninety per cent of people own their own homes as compared with an average of 50–60 per cent in other developed countries. The city is safe, impeccably clean and green, and traffic flows smoothly.

Unlike Hong Kong and Taiwan, Singapore's success owes more to the able hands of its leaders than to the entrepreneurial efforts of its citizens. Much of Singapore's success over the last three decades can be attributed to an export-oriented industrial strategy. The economy was first built by multinational corporations. Over 4,000 foreign multinationals employ Singaporeans, and together account for 75 to 80 per cent of the republic's investment in manufacturing.[12] Subsequently, the government-linked corporations (GLCs) became central to Singapore's regionalization efforts. Whether building a mini-Singapore in Suzhou in mainland China or a high-tech park in Bangalore, India, the GLCs are opening up opportunities for the Singapore private sector in and around the region. Singapore's investment in the Asia region more than doubled between 1981 and 1990. One estimate puts the dominance of Singapore government and government-linked corporations at close to 60% of the GDP of the island republic. Realizing that overseas expansion was hard if not impossible for most of Singapore's 80,000 small businesses to achieve, whether in manufacturing, commerce or the service sector, the government acted in the mid-1980s. The Association of Small and Medium Enterprises was established, and in 1989, the government committed itself to an SME Master Plan to foster local enterprise.

Singapore is '80 per cent middle class,' according to Senior Minister Lee Kuan Yew in 1987. Although there are some young risk-taking entrepreneurs, the major employer for the middle class is the Singapore government. However, Singapore's GLCs are different from state-owned enterprises elsewhere in the world: they are skewed towards profit-making and are doing a great job.

Although government expenditure represents about 1/5 of Singapore's total GDP, social security and social welfare spending is small. In 1988, for example, welfare spending amounted to 2.01 per cent of total budget expenditure compared with a Western average of 30 per cent.[13] Senior Minister Lee Kuan Yew has made it clear that the aim of the Singapore system is maximum efficiency: the most needed and the most talented are highly remunerated, exactly how the market system would have decided it.

There is great emphasis on formal education, and parents also arrange private tutoring for their children. One survey estimated that approximately 1/3 of all students from kindergarten to university make use of private tutors. This alone involves a total monthly expenditure of US$14m.[14] On the one hand, a government which has been in power since 1959 enforces discipline and constantly reminds its citizens of the need to stay competitive, while on the other, it admits that its biggest challenge is nurturing creative and risk-taking people. Gary Rodan had this to say about Singaporeans:

> Increasingly, they seek greater autonomy from the People's Action Party (PAP) state in an attempt to take some direct control over their lives. But to a large extent this involves autonomy as consumers, especially of cultural products, rather than autonomy as challenging the distribution of social and political power in Singapore society.[15]

The world is familiar with Singapore's low tolerance of opposition. One prominent businessman in Malaysia observed:

> Just as in business, competition is good in politics too. Perhaps the Singapore government can create its own two parties system. The chance for a strong opposition to evolve in Singapore is almost zero, so why not the government makes it happen?

His advice is for the PAP to split into two teams, while one forms the government, the other becomes the opposition to provide the checks and balances. 'After all, looking at the election manifestos of the 1997 election in Great Britain, there are really very few differences between the two contesting parties,' he observed.

Not a bad idea but will Singapore take the risk? Singapore's way of doing things has produced what the locals call a 'Kiasu', an 'afraid-to-lose' mentality. This mentality is everywhere: housewives shop feverishly at big sales; Mercedes and Jaguar-driving executives collect free textbooks from school for their children, are the first in line at the National Library to borrow the latest management bestseller, and reverse charges when calling overseas clients!

However, different stages of development require different approaches, and ever pragmatic, Singapore is heeding the call of the market. Many worry that all the things that make Singapore successful, particularly its ability to draw the best talents into government may make it unsuccessful in the 21st century. Following the financial crisis of the summer of 1997, Senior Minister Lee Kuan Yew commented that Singapore needed more of the 'buzz' of Hong Kong. Brigadier General Lee Hsien Loong, the deputy Prime Minister, who heads a committee on the reform and liberalization of Singapore's financial sector, said:

> We need to rethink our fundamentals and chart new directions. It is said that in Hong Kong anything not expressly forbidden is permitted, whereas in Singapore anything not expressly permitted is forbidden. This exaggeration captures an important difference in the two systems.[16]

Malaysian Chinese or Chinese Malaysian

Malaysians of Chinese origin operate in a much more complicated environment. To make a living in Malaysia's multiracial and multicultural setting, they focus on business and leave the responsibility of governance to the Malays. So long as the Chinese are left alone to make money, they care little about politics, and at most, watch from the side as spectators. Some in the business community are disdainful of Chinese politicians for their inability to grasp issues affecting the economic and social well-being of the community.

The *Business Times* of Singapore carried out a study in 1995 on the holdings of the richest men on the Kuala Lumpur Stock Exchange. The results were revealing: of the top ten, the first seven names were ethnic Chinese. The biggest player, Chinese gambling magnate, Tan Sri Lim Goh Tong, was estimated to be worth US$5.2b more than the combined total wealth of the country's three richest people of Malay origin, an amount of some US$1.7b jointly owned by Tan Sri Halim Saad of Renong, Tan Sri Rashid Hussain of the Rashid Hussain Group, and Tan Sri Tajuddin Ramli of Malaysian Airlines.[17] While it is true that Malaysia's affirmative action program for the Malays sidelined the Chinese, many second-generation Malaysian Chinese benefited from Malaysian Inc, a program whereby private Chinese businesses were invited to collaborate with the government and other Malay partners in a variety of privatized infrastructure and real estate development projects. However, the bulk of Chinese businesses in Malaysia excel in trading, real estate, finance and banking sectors that have shorter gestation periods, need less reinvestment and place greater reliance on the business acumen of owner/managers. This short-term and speculative orientation of Chinese business activities has partly to do with a discriminatory policy introduced in the 1970s to correct the economic imbalance among the major races. Many Chinese felt disenfranchised and insecure.

Many Chinese Malaysian accepted that the social and economic re-engineering efforts that began after the bloody race riots of 1969 were necessary to contain a potentially explosive situation. Privileges in education, business and employment were given to the Malays, referred to as *bumiputras*, meaning 'sons of the soil'. The government hoped to create an asset-owning Malay class, a middle class that would eventually control 30 per cent of the country's wealth. In spite of limited opportunities, the entrepreneurial Malaysian Chinese have managed to survive, and even thrive, under the system.

'The Chinese always kept moving up the ladder of comparative advantage,' said an economist at the National University of Malaysia. In the 1970s and early 1980s, most truck-drivers are Chinese, but most of them are Indians today. 'You seldom see a Chinese as a security guard, a chauffeur or an office boy; they much prefer their own small businesses.' Entrepreneurs are almost invariably Chinese: more than 90 per cent of the 130-odd companies listed on the second board of the Kuala Lumpur Stock Exchange are Chinese-controlled.

The Chinese mentality of making quick gains is partly cultural and partly influenced by a certain degree of political disenfranchisement. Such short-term orientation is now proving to have serious implications for the long-term competitiveness of Malaysia and will serve no-one's interests—Chinese or Malay. Many Chinese are reluctant to upgrade their industrial base through research and development, or through investment in human resources. Keenly aware of this threat to national competitiveness, Prime Minister Mahathir Mohamad has made known his intention to create a level playing field for all Malaysians (the pace may have to quicken as a result of the impact of globalization on Malaysia's competitiveness). In the meantime, Dr Mahathir has called upon the Chinese community to change its attitude in keeping with changing times.

The Chinese in Southeast Asia

Ethnic Chinese in Southeast Asia fear for their safety. Because of their economic dominance, they are worried about a backlash of resentment from the local population. 'Today's good fortune can become tomorrow's nightmare,' said Anto, an ethnic Chinese merchant in Indonesia.[18] 'We will be targeted, because Chinese wealth is associated with the government; people think we are getting rich through Golkar, the ruling party of President Suharto.' Some worried that the fate of the Chinese community had become too closely tied to that of the ageing Suharto, and those fears were not unfounded. While the politicians were looking for someone to blame for the financial crisis, the Chinese were once again targeted by violent mobs. Rape and other atrocities were committed during the riots of May 1998; the victims were innocent Chinese. The riots, which overthrew the Suharto regime, caused many thousands of Chinese to flee Indonesia. This resulted in total paralysis of the retail sector concerned with the distribution of food and groceries, since this sector had always been run by middle-class Chinese in Indonesia. According to Dewi Fortuna Anwar, a *pribumi* who is a political scientist at the Indonesian Institute of Sciences:

> For the Chinese to enjoy long-term security, they must open up their society and side with the Indonesian middle class. The Chinese who aren't doing business, like the badminton stars, are very much accepted. It is only when they become crony capitalists they are hated.[19]

Michael Backman, a Jakarta business consultant who has studied the Indonesian conglomerates, estimates that, of the 140 major business conglomerates that account for the bulk of Indonesia's gross national product, 110 of them are controlled by ethnic Chinese families.[20] It is no surprise that the resentment ran deep, because the Chinese monopoly embraces all kind of daily essentials, which Indonesians must pay for from their meagre earnings.

For overseas Chinese, wealth does not bring security. However, with the rise of a new rich indigenous class, who are also connected with the ruling regime, the race issue could subside, and over time, take on a class dimension. All is well during times of prosperity. Better times do seem to be ahead: Malaysia looks set to turn the corner, and Chinese Malaysians hope that one day racial lines will blur. In times of economic difficulties, there is a much greater need for strong leadership and honest communication so that racial integration can proceed. How Malaysia manages its race relations in its first recession in a decade is a true test of how successful its racial integration has been.

In the meantime, to be globally competitive, the goal must be greater economic efficiency, which can be partly achieved by creating equal opportunities for all races and all social groups. Two changes must take place: affirmative action for the *bumiputras* must focus on building self-reliance and encouraging them to help themselves, rather than depend on hand-outs. The economic inequalities in Malaysia and Indonesia will not go away unless a strong indigenous entrepreneurial class is developed. That will take time and great effort, as even the Chinese are not all born traders nor are all of them entrepreneurs. They have a long history of learning how to succeed from many failures and hardship.

Some critics say that the slow transition to transparency, the rule of law and free competition in Indonesia has been due to the close partnership between Chinese big business and the government. This is an aspect of development that needs to undergo radical reform under the new government of Indonesia, and perhaps, to a lesser extent, in Malaysia. The allegiance of businesses to their local community is a sensitive area. However, while the government can ask them to be patriotic and create opportunities for their countrymen by staying at home, globalization and the need to maintain global competitiveness also place demands on them. Only when the local community emerges strong and competitive can it hope to retain the capital of Chinese companies. In framing their national development policies, Southeast Asian governments cannot ignore the element of competitiveness in the race issue.

For a whole raft of reasons, the reality of race must be squarely confronted by honest public policy and candid communications between all groups. Global competition has led to competition not only between the Chinese and the Malays or *pribumis*, but, more importantly, between Malaysians and Indonesians and the world. Education, dialogue and joint ventures between the races will help. Politicians would do well to remember that exploiting the race issue to win votes only puts the future of the community and the country at peril.

If the Chinese continue to feel insecure, they will continue their short-term speculative activities which do not benefit the host economy. If public policy does not address the issue of belonging, recognition and security; Southeast Asian Chinese will never be able to build competitive industries that are solid, global and sustainable.

China's Agenda for Change

The modernization of China could be the biggest unknown in the world. If all goes well, and many Asians believe it will, China will make the world richer; but if it fails, instability in China could create a situation with the potential to destabilize the entire world. Although this would be a disaster, there is a higher risk of this happening than China becoming a great military hegemony, as some may have worried.

China is the world's largest emerging market; it faces the twin challenges of reforming its economy and its social and political systems. The last 20 years of reforms have produced outstanding results. China has successfully lifted some 300 million people out of poverty according to the World Bank, the biggest such shift in history. With the help of foreign investment, in less than two decades, China went from an unknown to one of the world's 10 biggest exporters of manufactured goods. *The Economist* reported that, 'Twelve years ago, exports from foreign ventures made up only one per cent of all China's exports. Today, the figure is about 30 per cent and growing voraciously.'[21]

Both the Chinese and the world are convinced of the irreversible direction of the reforms, to the extent that instead of continuing to 'feel the stones underneath the water', the pace of reform is likely to accelerate, especially following the devastating results of the financial crisis that has swept Southeast Asia. The down-to-earth sayings of paramount leader Deng Xiaoping, 'The colour of the cat doesn't matter so long as it catches mice', 'To get rich is glorious' and 'It's okay for some to get rich quicker than others,' became powerful guiding values (although the ideological conversion was not without a long and hard struggle). The Chinese economy grew at an average rate of about nine per cent a year from 1978 to 1991, and then at official rates of about 13 per cent between 1992 and 1994, and nine per cent between 1995 and 1997.[22]

The most enriching of China's reforms so far are those that allowed farmers to work for themselves rather than for the collective; as well as the granting of ownership to the people. The dramatic transformation of the countryside is truly one of the miracles of the 20th century. Farmers who cultivate their own land now produce enough grain to feed an entire village, and have a surplus to sell to the State. This has completely reversed the situation where, year in and year out, the State had to subsidize local needs for grain. These measures show the way for the future—that growth comes not because central government says so, but because central government acknowledges the natural inclinations of its people and gives them the opportunity to do their best and keep the fruits of their labors.

The economic boom created new middle classes. For the first time, people are enjoying economic freedom, a taste of material well-being, and have hope for a better future. The hype and the boom of the early reforms prompted macro-economic controls to guide the economy along a more sustainable path to growth. The sobering effects of the financial crisis of 1997 means China now has to work even harder to bring about solid internal organization and reform the management culture, especially where the State-owned enterprises (SOEs) are concerned.

The Communist party presides over a complex system with seven levels of government and a vast bureaucracy separating the people from their leaders. The country is made up of 31 provinces, 160 prefectures, 2,500 counties and cities, nearly 100,000 townships and urban wards, and over a million rural villages. Population pressure puts a lot of strain on resources; for example, Chinese agriculture must feed five times the population of the United States with 60 per cent of its cultivated area. Other challenges for the 21st century include :

- addressing the problems of some 310 million people still living in poverty;
- creating employment opportunities for some 15 million new entrants to the job market annually;

- redeploying some 30 million workers from the ailing SOEs with skills that may not be relevant in new industries; and
- recapitalizing and modernizing the banking system and making banks 'real' banks.

The SOEs account for 40 per cent of output at present, and take up as much as 70 per cent of the banking credit. Although most of them are loss-making, credit flows where the State's credit plans dictate, not to where the highest return can be earned. The Chinese leadership has pledged to weed out such inefficiencies in the next three years, but to do that, it has had to admit that the 'iron rice bowl', the unbreakable cradle to grave care and feeding of its citizens, is no longer secure. Employees of the State are provided with almost everything including housing, medical treatment and pensions but all these benefits are no longer secure. Privatization and mergers are inevitable, and without a social security safety net, society, especially the elderly and the unemployed, must be braced for adverse social consequences.

Further reforms in China are no longer straightforward. Far-reaching changes are needed in management philosophy, and better incentives and methods of rationalizing industry are needed. Furthermore, local custom barriers and protectionist attitudes between its fragmented and over-regulated domestic markets must be broken down. 'We had central planning in the past. It really was about developing regional economies. The same products are found everywhere,' said Wu Cheecheng, a member of the Lioniang Province Committee on trade and economics. This explains why there were over 100 production lines all over China making televisions. Additionally, the combined production of 34 automobile factories was still less than the output of one single Japanese factory.[23] China has 120 automobile makers and 2,000 companies making automobile parts. Mao's legacy of central planning and self-reliance scattered heavy industries arbitrarily about the country, far from markets, which means goods have to be shipped from one end of the country to the other, despite infrastructure problems. According to *China News Analysis*, a newsletter run by European Jesuits, in 1994, some 34 per cent of the freight carried on China's railways was shipped between regions. (In comparison, Japan's inter-regional traffic adds up to only 15 per cent of the total.)[24] Economic considerations will see further integration of the provinces of China, not political disintegration as a result of the weakening of the central government, as some in the West have predicted. The rationalization of regulations between provinces will give industry the opportunity to achieve economies of scale.

China has also been quietly reforming its political system. Premier Zhu Rongji has vowed to cut back on bureaucracy and downsize government. President Jiang Zemin looks set to allow greater openness in public discussion on issues related to China's growth and development; he also appears willing to improve relations with other countries, especially the West. A refreshing breeze of openness is being felt in China; on the political, economic and social fronts, an ambitious agenda of change is contemplated. The collapse of the Suharto regime in Indonesia and the rapid destruction of the Indonesian economy, an economy built on 30 years of development, must have strengthened the resolve of the Chinese leadership to establish a solid, enduring political and legal system that will ensure sustainable economic growth. The televised debate between President Jiang Zemin and President Bill Clinton during the American President's visit to China in June 1998 stunned many China-watchers; some have begun to hope that finally the ancient civilization of China is serious about democratization.

Islam in Asia

The second emerging group of Asians is the Muslims. Asia has over 500 million Muslims, concentrated in Indonesia, Pakistan and Bangladesh, with smaller groups in Malaysia and mainland China. Abdurrahman Wahid, who heads Indonesia's largest Muslim organization, *Nahdlatul Ulama*, best sums up Asia's challenge:

> Currently, other ancient civilizations are faced with grave challenges that will decide their future. Civilizations based on faith, such as Islam, Buddhism and Confucianism, are beset with problems in coping with the excesses of materialism and the secular way of life. Their morality is being tested severely by the emergence of hedonistic tendencies and increasingly value-free orientations. The basic underlying situation is the problem of adjustment to the modernity imposed by Western civilization, which is mainly based on acquiring advanced technology and sciences geared towards industrialization and international trade.[25]

Malaysia Boleh

The Malay Muslim community in Malaysia has achieved great progress under the aggressive and determined leadership of Prime Minister Dr Mahathir Mohamed. Prime Minister for some 18 years, Dr Mahathir personifies the competitive and global Malaysian Muslim. He is inspiring Malaysia to evolve a development model that is uniquely Malaysian.[26] The aim is to achieve economic progress and political plurality while building a 'Bangsa Malaysia', a Malaysian race.

So how is Malaysia doing? The Malaysian economy has been growing at over nine percent for almost a decade; with increased income, people generally feel satisfied. The most discernible change is the enhanced morale of the Malays or *bumiputras*. With education, exposure to Western ideas and technology, and uninterrupted economic growth, the Malays have been transformed. In particular, a select group of Malays, referred to as the 'New Malays' by the media, has emerged; self-confident, assertive and eager players in Malaysia's economy. Prime Minister Dr Mahathir, himself a New Malay, is promoting the spirit of 'Malaysia Boleh' (Malaysia Can).

There was no middle-class Malay at the start of the New Economic Policy (NEP), a 1970s program aimed at narrowing the gap between the economically active Chinese and the indigenous people. (The NEP is the only affirmative program for the majority in the world—the Malays make up the majority of Malaysia's population.) Although the NEP is already over a quarter of a century old, self-reliance is still weak. Harun Hashim, former senior director at the Economic Planning Unit of the Prime Minister's Department said:

> Having created a group of middle-class income earners does not mean that their earning capacities have also grown up fast enough over time. This is where the problem lies for the bumiputra middle class ... a salaried/wage earning class who are rather restrictive in their utilization of their actual potential for a number of reasons ranging from a culture of complacency, societal outlook, lack of encouragement, family influence, risk-averse mentality, and so on. What is required more today is those middle class who are entrepreneurial in nature and attitude, thus opening up their outlook of becoming risk-takers in their search of better income and wealth creation.[27]

The former general manager of the Kuala Lumpur Stock Exchange, Salleh Majid, a *bumiputra*, wrote:

> Without an existing high quality middle class, the bumiputra cannot hope for creating a strong upcoming future middle class from the bottom groups. Furthermore, without consistent support from the top class the successful entrepreneur and the Government it is difficult to push the current middle class up the brackets. The basic problems therefore are that the bumiputra have a layer of middle class but only a small portion is willing to take up the challenge of wealth creation leading to the top.[28]

Indonesia's Tragic Return to the 1960s

Modern Indonesia is very much a creation of President Suharto but, in the end, he brought about the destruction of the fruit of 30 years of development. In a country of 200 million people spread across 6,000 islands, there was impressive economic activity for over 30 years, with an annual average growth rate of seven per cent. The average per capita income increased to US$1,023, and the percentage of Indonesians living below the poverty line plummeted from 58 per cent as recently as 1972 to just over 11 per cent. This is quite a feat in a country so diverse and spread out.

The internal structure of the economy was transformed. Agriculture as a percentage of GDP declined from 53.9 per cent in 1960 to 19.5 per cent in 1991, while over the same period, manufacturing climbed from 8.4 per cent to 21.3 per cent. By 1995, manufacturing accounted for 1/4 of GDP. Indonesia moved towards an outward-looking export economy of low-cost manufactured goods.

Interests linked to the State and the leadership dominated the economy. For example, the Chinese-controlled conglomerates and the Suharto family dominated the key sectors, such as wheat, sugar and rice. The poor citizens had to live with monopolies on staples; for example, they had to pay a price that was 58 per cent above the world price for sugar.[29] The Suharto children's business activities blanketed everything from cars, telecommunications, petrochemicals and toll roads, to power plants, television, shipping, airlines, taxi cabs and even birds' nests. The dominance of the family moved Richard Robinson to pose the question, '... whether they represent a metamorphosis of the politico-bureaucrat into capitalist or whether they are simply rent-seekers in a transitory phase of booty capitalism'.[30]

President Suharto himself recognized the tensions in the economic inequality; but did not address the issue to any great extent. It is unthinkable that, in 30 years of development, such imbalances were not genuinely addressed. In 1995, Suharto proposed that Indonesian firms or individuals who reported more than 100 million rupiah (US$42,000) in income or profit, should donate two per cent to a fund to help the poor. In December 1996, he further suggested that wealthy Indonesians who did not contribute would have their houses marked to shame them into action. Leading Chinese businessman, Sofyan Wanandi, observed:

> We (the business community) left it to the government—it was nothing to do with us. But today, business must take the initiative. Indonesia's future development depends on more than simply improving the lot of ordinary Indonesians. It requires persuading them that the system which creates this new wealth is itself legitimate.[31]

The *Far Eastern Economic Review* echoed this concern:

> We doubt that the social equation will be squared by turning the poor on the rich. If the economy were instead opened up, smaller Indonesian firms would find their markets readily enough (and without the dependency inherent in an affirmative-action program). As for Mr Suharto's two per cent surcharge on the wealthy, the cultivation of envy is not likely to produce either the harmony or wealth. On the contrary, what Indonesia needs most is a system where people can hit it rich without the patronage of government.[32]

Overall, the State continues to be the fountain of social and economic power, and success depends upon gaining access to it.[33] Those who wield State power and bureaucratic authority continue to be the pivotal group. There is no genuine move towards deregulation; the bureaucracy is resistant to change. Many feel that the Ministry of Trade and Industry, for example, shouldn't be handing out licences. In a country where regulations allow civil servants to supplement their incomes, it is not surprising that even cabinet ministers are divided over reforms. Corruption distorts everything and remains hard to wipe out. With decentralization has come a growth in local fiefdoms, in which officials have become adept at creating new sources of revenue. In two localities in South Sumatra and Kalimantan, a land tax has been slapped on fishing boats. 'The further you go from Jakarta, the more the local governments intervene,' says a researcher. 'In some cases, the government doesn't have full knowledge of what's going on. In other cases, it's a way of keeping allegiance.'[34]

Difficulties brought about by the devaluation of the rupiah and overleveraged Indonesian private firms caused an implosion within the economy in May 1998. Students demanded the resignation of their long-time ruler, President Suharto, and demanded economic and political reforms. Bowing to intense pressure, President Suharto resigned, putting in place his protege, the unpopular spendthrift Vice-President BJ Habibie. For a nation that has been suppressed for over three decades, and in the absence of any mechanism or culture of democratic governance, the road to reform will be a long and winding one.

The challenges of rebuilding are enormous. How best to rebuild an economy that can contain the fall-out of the financial crisis as well as rapidly reform the stubborn political machinery left over from the past? Just like other countries in the region that are governed by strong leaders, sidelining legitimacy in the name of stability and economic growth can no longer continue. Sofyan Wanandi, Chairman of the Gemala Group, maintains that, in a society as fractured as Indonesia, it is imperative '... to have one party who can keep stability'.[35] A strong government, a ruling party riddled with nepotism, and big business heavily influenced by politics are all factors militating against the creation of a society that offers opportunity. Far-reaching changes will have to take place if the average Indonesian man and woman are to ever enjoy equality of opportunity.

Liberal Democracies in Asia.

There is large group of English-speaking Asians in Asia. They are the political elite, civil servants, professionals and merchants, found in Hong Kong, Singapore, Kuala Lumpur, Jakarta, Manila, Bangkok, Bombay, New Delhi and other major cities. They and their children were trained in schools in the West or followed a Westernized curriculum. English is their common tongue; many of them speak no indigenous dialects. They are called 'bananas' (yellow outside and white inside) by fellow Asians. They are among the most affluent in Asia, and in their cultural habits, are not so different from each other or their peers in the West. They tune in to CNN, read *The Asian Wall*

Street Journal and *The Economist*, surf the Internet and can tell the difference between Chablis and Chardonnay.

Many 'bananas' are the leaders of the New Asia the current generation of Asian family business empires, the new entrepreneurs, leaders in government and multinational companies, intellectuals, and academics. They are the most global and open-minded of Asians. Many of them, while hard-core Anglophiles, like Hong Kong-based entrepreneur David Tang, have taken to promoting the culture of their roots. David Tang's 'Chinoseries', the China Club in Hong Kong and Beijing, and his line of Shanghai Tang ready-to-wear Chinese fashion, are signs of changing times returning to one's cultural roots is in!

India: Priorities Going Backwards

Frequent polls, fragile coalition government and diehard conservatism continue to plague Indian public life, obstruct economic liberalization and weaken India's political and economic structure. Even though the long-reigning Congress Party, which governed India for 45 of its 50 years of independence, has relinquished power, there is still no sign that India is maintaining unity in order to make a fresh start.

India's immediate priorities are stabilizing both the process and the institution of government and freeing up a state choking on its own regulations. After four prime ministers in two years and a weak coalition government, even India's 600 million voters are getting weary. In spite of a meagre per capita income of about US$400, the new government chose to promote national pride with a nuclear bomb program, rather than demonstrate commitment to economic reforms. Seventy per cent of Indians still live in rural areas—mostly without electricity, safe drinking water or sanitation. It is hard to imagine how a nuclear bomb can be more meaningful than getting these people out of poverty. The Indian economy is at no point integrated with the wider world economy; its share of world trade is a pathetic fraction of 1 per cent, and the total capital inflows from overseas amount to a mere 1.5 per cent of the gross national product.[36] The government still sings the praises of *swadeshi* (economic nationalism), and welcomes the chips that go into computers rather than those found in fast-food outlets. Meanwhile, the economic reforms that began in 1991 go on at a snail's pace. The Congress Party, which has ruled India for all but five years since independence, and Delhi, the centre of power, are losing their dominant positions. Power has been moving from the upper to the lower castes, and from the centre (Delhi) to the regions. In the last election, the Congress Party lost ground to regional, caste and other smaller parties; its share of the vote sank to an historic low of less than 30 percent. Cynicism about the ability of Congress to deliver has spurred the growth of smaller, regional parties.

India's economic reforms come some 20 years later than China's. Since independence in 1947, a succession of governments has made India a centrally directed socialist state that erected barriers to foreign trade and investment. The bureaucracy regulates every aspect of private sector operations. While some observers admire India's democratic practices and her comprehensive system of rules in comparison with China's lack of either, in practice, all the red tape makes China look like an express lane. In spite of reforms, India's central and state governments remain hugely over-extended, and steps to loosen controls are slow in coming. Meanwhile, the business sector is impatient. 'We no longer have the time to contemplate world events and react at leisure. Speed as well as quality of response is the crying need,' Deepak Parekh, head of HFDC, a fast-growing and diversified finance company based in Mumbai, said of the bureaucratic paralysis.[37]

India's economic reforms have included cutting taxes and tariffs and simplifying procedures for foreign investors. Forty-year-old controls on consumer imports are being phased out, new aviation and broadcast policies introduced, financial sector reforms pushed through, and plans to deregulate India's oil and gas industry unveiled. Deregulation is India's key to creating a more equitable and conducive environment for private enterprise. The pressure to continue to open up the economy, however, is also coming from an army of Indian consumers.

One good example is in telecommunications. Foreign companies are offering Indian consumers the chance to make telephone calls to the United States via the Internet, charged at the rate of 10 cents a minute, as compared with US$2.20 a minute charged by the state-owned monopoly Videsh Sanchar Nigam Ltd. Instead of heeding the call of the market for more competitive pricing, VSN is blocking the Internet sites and threatening consumers that it will cancel their current services. Technicians and consumers are undeterred: they are finding ways to get around the blocks and keep talking on the Internet. Unlike telecommunications companies elsewhere in the world, which are deregulating and not fighting new technology, VSN, while losing millions of dollars in revenue, is still determined to weed out the 'unscrupulous elements'!

The middle class, estimated at upwards of 200 million, is eagerly buying televisions and electronic gadgetry. Seven straight years of good monsoon rains, the lifeblood of the country's rural economy, have enabled farmers to reap bountiful harvests. The Indian middle class is seen as a positive, even dynamic force that wants, '...politicians and bureaucrats out of economic life; they want India to open up and join the world. Their most striking characteristic is their drive. These people are making things happen,' according to Das, an Indian writer.[38] India boasts the most vibrant democracy in Asia, yet its economic development lags behind that of all her East Asian neighbours. The scale and scope of reforms required are enormous. India still has a large rural population, some 328 million people still live below the poverty line, and over half of India's adults are illiterate. The transformation that India needs is to change Nehru's vision of socialist self-reliance to that of empowerment of the people.

The Philippines is Slowly Bouncing Back

In defending the liberal democratic traditions of the 1960s, the Filipinos are not trying to show their richer neighbors practising Confucian models that they have an alternative, but are simply repairing the damage done to the economy by the Marcos dictatorship.

In the early 1960s, the Philippines had one of the most industrialized economies in Southeast Asia, with a rising class of manufacturing entrepreneurs, a substantial salaried middle class, a growing working class, a high level of formal education and a political system organized around electoral democracy. However, the economy was dominated by the elite. It is generally agreed that the country's economic stagnation is largely a consequence of an entrenched oligarchy whose practices were rooted in a background of landed privilege and who controlled the economy by holding monopolies.

In the period before the imposition of martial law in 1972, three major events took place within the wealthy and property-owning class. First, there was shift towards the investment of capital as the basis of private wealth; second, it was expanded through recruitment from the ethnic Chinese trading community and professional middle class; and third, wealth was increasingly concentrated in the hands of a small number of family conglomerates. One estimate was that 'The top 10 per cent of stockholding families at this time controlled almost 78 per cent of corporate assets'.[39]

President Corazon Aquino began and President Fidel Ramos continued the process of dismantling 'crony capitalism' and created a more liberal economic environment. Old business interests have been able to re-establish themselves, and new capitalists have risen to prominence, notably from among the ethnic Chinese and in the regions outside Manila. Relative political stability has returned. Both the Aquino and Ramos governments demonstrated a greater commitment to the idea of free-market capitalism than did their predecessors. Economic growth has been pursued through policies that favor privatization and the deregulation of trade and investment; Ramos, especially, has promoted competition. Through the breaking up of private monopolies, higher levels of production and service are being achieved, particularly in areas that had suffered from a lack of investment and technological change.

In spite of the fact that businesses in the Philippines are dominated by the old moneyed mestizos and the Chinese, new business entrepreneurs have emerged, and a number have started to form their own large conglomerates. Between 1975 and 1985, an average of 4,600 corporations were formed annually; from 1986 to 1990, the figure increased to 6,000. The younger and more gutsy upstarts found themselves popular with foreign investors, including Japanese manufacturing investors, who tend to favor these innovative entrepreneurs.

We can expect the middle class to become increasingly active in political discourse. This is due in part to the increased social power that capitalist development and the State have concentrated in the hands of formally educated administrators, managers and professionals, and to the proliferation of non-government organizations over the past decade. In the short term, it is highly unlikely that rapid progress can be made in completely eliminating every aspect of 'crony capitalism'. The advances made so far have resulted in an accumulation of wealth not only among sections of the old elite, but also among those who have risen to become part of the country's expanding middle class. As links form and strengthen with regional and global labor markets, prosperity could reach all levels of society.

Japan's Paradise Lost

While Japan's political and corporate leaders are trying to figure out how to get the economy out of financial chaos and avert a serious recession, the people of Japan are finding solace in a hit movie—*Paradise Lost*. It is the story of an affair between a Japanese housewife and a salaryman, the two categories of people who feel the most 'trapped' in Japan. Frustrated with a long economic slowdown and bypassed for promotion, the salaryman found true love with an equally unfulfilled housewife. Unwilling both to end their affair and to hurt their families, the only way out was death. They committed suicide together, dying in each other's arms. *Paradise Lost* struck a chord among the Japanese: within two weeks of its release, over a million people had seen it.

The long downward slide of Japan Inc that John Naisbitt and I wrote about in 1995 is now official.[40] Tokyo has confirmed that its economy is in recession, a contraction of 5 per cent on an annual rate. Unemployment in Japan is at an all-time high, while consumption is at an all-time low.

Japan's glorious rise in the 1980s made it the only Asian economy to rival the might of the West. But now, it is experiencing a long, drawn-out economic decline that shows no signs of subsiding. Will it soon become the land of the setting sun? The West once feared Japan for the strength of its economy. Now it is the reverse— the West fears Japan because of the weakness of its economy, a weakness that could have a disastrous effect on the rest of the world.

Cultural barriers to reform

Visitors to Japan never fail to be impressed by its modern, clean, well-laid out streets, efficient public transport systems, well-mannered people, refined cuisine, and advanced technology. But while the Japanese society presents a modern exterior, deep inside, it is still very conservative—it is firmly based on hierarchical structures, is risk-averse, and adheres to conventional concepts. The oral contraceptive pill for women was legalized only two years ago—almost 40 years after it became available in the United States, and Japanese companies are weighed down by conservative accounting and reporting standards. In general, the Japanese are unwilling to integrate with the outside world. Even now, the observation is often made that, for such a sophisticated economy, there are very few who speak English. In a meeting in Kyoto recently, John Naisbitt observed that, 'Foreign investment has been higher in Cambodia than in Japan.'

Then there is the all-too familiar 'denial' characteristic of the Japanese—their refusal to admit failure and to deal with shame is deeply embedded in their psyche. The Japanese have been extremely reluctant to acknowledge the more shameful aspects of their involvement in the Second World War, and more recently, have sought to deny their behavior in the Nanjing Massacre. The way in which officials caught up in the Ministry of Finance scandals have made their exit would suggest that suicide is preferable to taking responsibility or making reforms

An economy in recession

To the world's dismay, the same denial syndrome is occurring in the economic realm. Since the bubble economy burst in the 1980s, Tokyo's economic policy has been little more than substantive denial. Rather than acting swiftly to contain the economic haemorrhaging, Japanese politicians resorted to self-serving rhetoric. Public money has been wasted on non-essential, sometimes dubious projects favored by the politicians. Since 1992, a series of fiscal packages supposed to stimulate the economy has been released, totalling over 75 trillion yen (US$563b). However, these measures have been largely cosmetic; grand gestures that look good in the headlines but which have done nothing to relieve the stagnation in domestic demand.

Japan is suffering a massive crisis of confidence. It is deep pessimism and uncertainty about the future that have caused the considerable contraction in domestic demand. Consumers are holding on to their purse strings and refusing to spend. Two factors—unemployment and concern about future finances—exacerbate this situation.

A younger leadership

Another unfortunate result of the strict hierarchies and closed, insular minds in Japanese society is that it does not encourage the rise of younger people to positions of leadership. The Senior Minister of Singapore, Lee Kuan Yew, said recently in a discussion on Asia's challenges, 'Asia needs a change to younger leadership'.[41] Indeed, Japan's 'ageing' leaders, are reluctant to face up to the new realities of the world and lack the initiative to act boldly. Risk-taking, letting go and trusting in the process are qualities that are not in the style of the older Japanese leadership. There is an urgent need for younger leaders to move in and deal with the new realities.

Funding the age pension

Growing public alarm about the pension system is spreading, and although less tangible, may be another factor that is encouraging older consumers to save rather than spend. The OECD estimates that social security spending on pensions as a proportion of GDP will rise to 10.2 per cent in 2035, double the current level. Japan isn't an old country yet: only 16 per cent of its people are over 65, in line with other OECD countries. With a declining birth-rate and rising life expectancy, the government estimates that by 2035 or so, more than 30 per cent of Japanese will be 65 years of age or older. Middle-aged Japanese are extremely worried by this, and have inevitably become conservative both in outlook and politics as they strive to keep their financial assets. One study, by economists David Asher and Andrew Smithers, pointed out that the pension schemes of the 25 companies which file US accounts are underfunded by 40 per cent or more; the situation for smaller domestic companies is believed to be even worse. These same economists also released a study recently in which they noted that if the Fiscal and Investment Loan Program (FILP) is included, Japan's true public sector debt could climb to 150 per cent of GDP—higher than that of Italy or Belgium.[42] (FILP is dubbed the second budget, which is 2/3 the size of the national budget and operates like a cross between a development bank and a pension fund.) Furthermore, if International Monetary Fund estimates of unfunded state pension liabilities are included, Asher and Smithers estimate that the total obligations of the public sector towards its debtors and pensioners probably exceed 250 per cent of GDP.

In 1997, 14 corporate pension schemes failed, a sharp rise from the year before.[43] The Rice Dealers' Association's two pension schemes failed recently, leaving the equivalent of US$21m in unpaid liabilities and affecting some 3,000 rice farmers. Even worse, the Association asked pensioners to return part of their pensions, in some cases, up to 1.4m yen. This has provoked anger and panic among the rice farmers, particularly in the Osaka area.[44] Although this is the first failure of an industry association, many fear it will not be the last. Another scheme, managed by Yasuda Trust Bank, used to pay returns of around 7 per cent on investments before 1995; by 1998, the return had fallen to around 2.5 per cent (and a mere 1.4 per cent after operating expenses). Consequently, the scheme now has 7.3b yen in liabilities but only 4.7b yen in recorded assets. With this kind of news assailing the Japanese, it is not surprising they are concerned and that consumer spending continues to slump. Poor returns and the inability of the pension fund schemes to pay may extend the retirement age of workers—and reduce benefits. Peter Taker of Dresdner Kleinwort Benson in Tokyo pointed out that a retirement package, even one from a blue-chip employer in Japan, now amounts to no more than the amount a teenager can earn in a fast-food outlet.[45]

The penalties of protectionism

Another problem for the Japanese economy is protectionism. Agriculture is just one industry which is subsidized and protected from foreign competition. Japanese consumers have for a long time been paying higher prices than the citizens of other G-7 countries for the same commodities. The reluctance of the Japanese to open their markets has Western business executives and political leaders throwing their hands in the air with exasperation. If Japan opens up to allow foreign companies to compete with domestic enterprises, this measure, along with other reforms, could reinvigorate the Japanese economy. A report from the Japan Center for Economic Research projected in 1995 that an overall deregulation program would completely eliminate the differential between Japanese and foreign prices, and increase GDP by 18.7 per cent.[46]

A shaky financial system

Bearing in mind that protectionism has resulted in the Japanese becoming poor people in a rich country, the liberalization of Japan's securities market (and hopefully other markets soon) will ultimately benefit Japanese investors and consumers. Japanese companies know only too well that if they are to survive the increased competition resulting from financial reform, they must improve their return on investment and profitability. As the fund management industry grows and returns improve, smaller investors will have the influence to force management to be more responsive to their needs, as in the United States. Currently, Japanese investors put 60 per cent of their savings into low-interest bank deposits (earning between 0.5 per cent and 2 per cent); Americans invest 60 per cent of their savings in the stock-market. The Japanese, unfortunately, don't have much option—until quite recently, they could only invest inside Japan, and inadequate monitoring of corporate affairs and poor profitability of companies made bank saving the only viable way of saving, even with the current banking debacle. There is sad irony in the fact that the banks, once considered absolutely secure, are losing customers' savings through inept lending to unprofitable and badly managed companies.

The value of bad loans is estimated at 80 trillion yen (US$600b) or 12 per cent of GDP. (In absolute numbers, it is still smaller than the US$1 trillion involved in the Savings & Loans crisis in the United States in 1989).

Opening up to the outside world

Foreigners in Japan, or *gaijin*, have for a long time been kept at arm's length, not to be allowed to enter mainstream Japanese society. However, Nikko Securities' joint venture deal with Travelers Group Inc of the United States marks a significant reversal of this anti-*gaijin* attitude. The chairman of Nikko Securities said, after announcing the joint venture, 'We on our own are hard to change. With this joint venture, we hope to operate closer to global standards'. The positive response from the market suggests that the Japanese are saying yes to an 'American-style management and shareholder culture', and welcoming the 'Anglo invasion'. New York-based Travelers Group will effectively take over the investment banking and international securities operations of Nikko Securities Co, one of Japan's 'Big Four' brokerages. Nikko, seemingly the weakest of the surviving Big Four, has suffered losses in five of the last seven years, including a US$500m loss in the year to March 1998. Under the terms of the joint venture agreement, Nikko will maintain control of 51 per cent of the company, although the joint venture will, by all accounts, be run by Salomon. Nikko President Masashi Kaneko, responding to criticism of foreign takeovers of Japanese companies, said, 'That is old-styled thinking; this is a global business'. He has since been quoted as saying, 'This joint venture company will run according to the Salomon Smith Barney style, the American style'.[47]

Some of the financial reforms of the Big Bang have been successful, however, in that they are finally opening up a grossly overprotected financial industry that has kept Japanese investors out of lucrative international markets. In April 1998, for the first time, stock funds managed by foreign firms incorporated in Japan took in more assets than did their Japanese counterparts. Foreign help in asset management may provide some rays of hope to the hapless Japanese investor who has been frustrated for well over a decade: from 1980 to 1995, the average return on pensions was a mere 2.5 per cent. Until and unless Japanese consumers see the yield on their savings show a sustained improvement, there is no hope that domestic demand will pick up.

Bitter medicine

The blame for the current inertia can be sheeted home to the politicians: securely backed by conservative supporters, they have no incentive to force through the painful restructuring that's needed to revive Japan's economy. One often wonders whether Japan's political leadership has fully grasped the size of the challenge—it may have, but then found itself paralyzed by a powerful bureaucracy. The direction that Japan must take to regain paradise is clear: it must show a will of steel in restructuring the economy and it must engage the help of the *gaijin*. Both prescriptions will be hard to take: the resistance of many Japanese to change, particularly the conservative elderly, is one of the reasons Japan has found it difficult to restructure.

There must be firm action in the area of taxation, such as a large but temporary cut in consumption tax to encourage spending, and interim cuts in income tax as an incentive to maximize earnings. Most of all, the cleaning-up of the banking system must proceed without any further delay: confidence in the banking system will not be restored until insolvent banks are closed without penalty to bank customers. Overall, the government must commit itself to pursuing expansionary fiscal policy until the economy has fully recovered; only then can it safely proceed with structural reform.

While the economic malaise in Japan is not yet terminal, the patient must take the medicine fast. By international standards, the conditions in Japan can be turned around, though not easily. When compared with the experiences of Germany and France, the challenges are not insurmountable; Germany and France are now enjoying brisk growth after a prolonged period of stagnation.

Reinventing Japan

In the 21st century, innovation will be a new source of wealth creation. The environment in which innovation prospers requires motivated individuals, dynamic small companies and flexible corporations. Japan must evolve from a system that emphasizes production into one that recognizes the importance of creativity; it needs to draft a new social contract based on the value of the individual; and it must ensure that the rewards are commensurate with merit and ability rather than seniority. American companies went through a painful restructuring process in the 1980s, in which old structures were set aside and structures far more suited to the 1990s were created. Success, as history has shown us, is not a static state—we have to constantly reinvent the means to achieve it.

Japan's external position is arguably the world's strongest. Its net foreign assets are vast in absolute terms and, at nearly 25 per cent of GDP, far exceed those of any other large economy. Its foreign reserves stand at US$200b and it possesses 1/3 of all the world's savings. Every year, Japan's large and rising current account surpluses add substantially to its position.[48] Japan also looks fine on the supply side. Potential output (what the economy could produce if its capacity were fully employed) is still growing, although it has slowed down compared with the 1980s.[49] A revival of the productive sector implies cutting taxes on income and on property transactions, encouraging banks to dispose of their non-performing loans, and deregulation. 'Lowering the marginal tax rate is more important than one more public works program that would throw yet another bridge over the same channel, dig another tunnel to a remote village or renovate a port in an area where fishermen no longer work,' said Takatoshi Ito, Professor of Economics at Hitotsubashi University in Tokyo.[50]

Throughout history, Japan has prospered through its uncanny ability to reinvent itself, as displayed in the Meiji Restoration and the reconstruction following the Second World War. If Japan is to remain a responsible world economic power; it has to do nothing less than reinvent itself, again. 'To succeed, it must carry out widespread structural reform immediately—creative destruction of the structural barriers that continue to impede the economic growth that is needed for a recovery in Japan, as well as in the region. This is not because it is an easy way out, but because it is the only way out,' urge Professor Robert Edelstein and Jean Michael Paul.[51]

East Asia is important to Japan and Japan's recovery is pivotal to East Asia rebounding, at least, for the decade ahead, before China can achieve the critical mass to lead the region. Japan's exports to America and Germany comprise only 2.4 per cent of GDP, whereas East Asia receives some 2/5 of Japanese exports.

The Other Asia

Many indigenous Asian communities are, either through isolation or political strife, largely oblivious to what is going on in the world. While Vietnam is trying to get to grips with economic reforms, Laos, Cambodia, Burma and the indigenous communities in the highlands and mountains of tropical Asia are cut off from mainstream Asia's cultural influences. This situation may not continue much as longer education, telecommunications and satellite television could change things very rapidly.

Thailand: Getting Rich Too Quickly

At different times in Thailand's history, there has been a different but distinct class of capitalist. First, under an absolute monarchy, were those from the royal family and the aristocracy. Chinese and European traders, as well as those (mostly Chinese) who worked as tax agents for the administration, and benefited from the wealth of the economy. After the Second World War, the Chinese and Sino-Thai tycoons emerged from the ranks of petty traders and the laboring class to take control of the country's economy. There are many Chinatown rags-to-riches stories about these capitalists moving into agriculture, trading, finance and then manufacturing. Much of their initial wealth came from finance, their heyday being the 1960s and 1970s. Sino-Thai conglomerates were established, often based around a bank, to service the expanding manufacturing sector, especially import-substitution industries. This remains powerful, controlling the giant commercial banks and having substantial stakes in agro-industries and manufacturing. In the late 1970s, a new generation of capitalist arose. This group is well-educated, its members are often from business families and increasingly identify themselves as Thai. They are national and international in orientation, obtaining their wealth from Thailand's economic growth and investment in technology.

Thailand, the only Asian country which has never been colonized, has registered impressive economic growth. Like elsewhere in Asia, the results have been opportunity and prosperity for many. The professional and technical, administrative, executive and managerial, clerical, services and sales categories of the Thai middle class have expanded from about 10 per cent of the population in 1960 to 21 per cent in 1986. Tertiary education expanded at a remarkable rate during the 1960s. By 1990, there were more than 360,000 students enrolled in some 30 to 40 state and private universities. The number of graduates in the work-force increased from 185,000 in 1970 to about 1.8 million in 1991.[52]

In spite of frequent changes of government, Thailand has weathered 22 prime ministers, 17 coups, and 16 constitutional revisions since it became a constitutional monarchy in 1932. The Thai economy roared on, fuelled by foreign investment and credit from foreign banks. The business of building a sound foundation for a lasting economy got side-tracked into blowing huge bubbles in real estate and conspicuous consumption. Following the devaluation of the Thai baht and an International Monetary Fund bail-out, 58 of its 94 financial institutions were closed. Ahead of the Thais is a painful period of adjustment while the economy is restructured; there will be slow growth and at least two million unemployed. There needs to be a very fundamental change, not only in the way the Thais do business and run their politics, but in their very mentality.

The Thai economy needs to refocus, strengthen its weak industrial base and cut back on consumption. Mass consumerism rejected the value of restraint, as expounded by Buddhism, a relic of the past. A new lifestyle, heavily influenced by the West, swept through the country. Thais are also experiencing shocks in the form of cultural disintegration, the breakdown of the traditional family, illicit drug use, and other social ills.

On the political front, Thailand is crying out for a government that can act professionally and implement policy effectively. Conservative parliamentarians and the Thai army resisted the introduction of a new, more liberal Thai Constitution. However, the economic crisis of 1997 (and a nudge from the country's enlightened king) expedited matters and in September 1997, Parliament passed the new Constitution, with the support of the army. That Constitution, among other things, enshrines greater press freedom, guarantees education for every Thai up to 12th grade (instead of just to sixth) and demands greater accountability in government. 'The new Constitution was born out of the idea that to participate in the global economy, you have to have a well-managed country and [therefore] we need democracy and political reform to manage things better,' said Pana Janviroy, editor of Thailand's *The Nation* newspaper. 'This crisis has brought in a new government that is the most talented you could have here.'[53]

End of South Korea's Miracle

To a large extent, South Korea's economic challenge mirrors that of Japan. What was a backward agricultural economy has become the 11th largest industrialized economy in the world. With a combination of gritty industriousness and fierce pride, its 46 million people have achieved, over the last three decades, an annual growth rate of over eight per cent, and per capita income has risen from US$80 in 1960 to over US$10,000 in 1997, a 100-fold increase.[54]

South Korea's economic strategy has been anchored in a close collaboration between the government, big business (the *chaebols*) and the banks. South Korea's obsession with bigness, which led to the creation of a web of big companies that dabble in all kinds of activities, has proved fatal. *Chaebols* are in every business cars, steel, petrochemicals, shipbuilding and electronics, building bigger plants and conquering more markets. Excessive capacity built up and their mountain of debts required double-digit growth to sustain operations. Most of the *chaebols* are overstaffed and overleveraged, and seven of them have already collapsed or gone bankrupt. The banks have already suffered at least US$52b in bad debts due to *chaebols* defaulting some 17 per cent of their portfolios and it has been reported that as many as 1/2 the top 30 *chaebols*, with debts of more than five times equity, may be in danger of collapsing.[55]

The banks have borrowed heavily from abroad. According to the Central Bank of Korea's own estimates, non-performing loans and those at risk are now a sizeable 16 per cent of loans nationwide.[56] Although there are signs that the government is changing its attitude towards commerce, no real action has been taken to break the alliance between the *chaebols* and the government or to tell workers that the iron rice bowl is no longer guaranteed.

Wages in Korea have risen some five-fold in the past 12 years. To start being competitive again, workers may have to adjust to the end of lifetime employment and lower wages. A long period of prosperity has built up a substantial middle class in Korea, but not an entrepreneurial class. Rapid economic and social changes have eroded old social structures while altering expectations. At present, the State is confronting a dilemma: on the one hand, it stands to inherit a Confucian and thus moralistic idea of government, while on the other, it seeks to move to a less regulatory environment in which citizens have greater freedom.

Korean society is still emerging from its authoritarian and Confucian inheritance in politics and culture. The old values frequently conflict with contemporary aspirations for democracy and an open economy, resulting in the paradox that, while the new middle class frequently argue for democratic reforms and insist upon some measures of political and economic equality, their own behaviour often remains rooted in notions of hierarchy and the privileges that come from personal connections. Further contradictions arise in a situation where you have the Korean middle class adhering to the old Confucian elitism (for example, the status that comes from formal learning) and at the same time enthusiastically indulging in consumerism. It appears that a way of life and aspirations unique to the middle class have yet to develop.

Chapter 4
From Hand-outs to a Way Out

"There is a way to end poverty
by helping people help themselves
up the economic ladder."

–Mildred Leet—
Co-founder of the Trickle Up Program

Many of us tend to think that helping people means giving them what they need. Unfortunately, this well-intentioned philanthropy is misguided. Giving unconditionally only cultivates dependence; the act itself does the recipient injustice and takes away their dignity. People can only be helped to help themselves; in other words, the answer does not lie in redistribution, but in helping people to find a way out using their own abilities.

In spite of continuous economic growth over the last century, the fruits of development have not been shared equally. Far from it. Seventy-seven per cent of the world's population receive only 15 per cent of the world's income, while the income of the richest 20 per cent is seven times that of the poorest 20 per cent. The world's poor reside largely in the Southern Hemisphere, mainly in Africa, Latin America and Asia; others are in Eastern Europe and the former Soviet Russia. The average income for people residing in the Northern Hemisphere is US$12,000, nearly 17 times that of the average income in the Southern Hemisphere. There are 1.2 billion poor people in the developing countries and the number is growing. By the year 2000, there will be another 100 million. The governments of rich countries, faced with huge budget deficits, are no longer in a position or mood to provide aid. Even when aid was available, experience shows that only 1/3 reaches those needing aid; the rest goes in military and infrastructure expenses or corruption.[1]

Global Poverty

A recent study on global poverty by the World Bank showed that even though the incidence of poverty is declining, between 1987 to 1993, the number of people living on less than a dollar a day increased from 1.227 billion to 1.314 billion (see Table 4.1 below).[2]

Table 4.1: Population living below US$1 a day in developing and transitional economy 1987-1993*

Regions	Number of poor people (millions)			Headcount Index (%)**		
	1987	1990	1993	1987	1990	1993
East Asia & Pacific	464	468.2	445.8	28.2	28.5	56
EAP excluding China	109.2	89.3	73.5	23.2	17.6	13.7
Eastern Europe & Central Asia	2.2	na	14.5	0.6	na	3.5
Caribbean	91.2	101	109.6	22	23	23.5
Middle East & North	10.3	10.4	10.7	4.7	4.3	4.1
South Asia	479.9	480.4	514.7	45.4	43	43.1
Sub-Saharan Africa	176.9	201.2	218.6	38.5	39.3	39.1
Total	1,227.10	na	1,313.90	30.1	na	29.4
Total excluding ECA	1,224.90	1,261.20	1,299.30	33.3	32.9	31.8

Notes

*These estimates revise and update those in Implementing the World Bank's Strategy to Reduce Poverty (World Bank, 1993)

**The headcount index refers to the percentage of people living below the poverty line

Source: World Bank News Release 96/745, 22 March 1997

The effects of poverty are devastating. Every year, seven million people die from easily preventable diseases. About 1/2 million women die from maternity-related complications, and nearly eight million children die from diseases linked to contaminated water and air pollution. Fifty million children are mentally or physically impaired because of malnutrition, and 130 million children, 80 per cent of them girls, are denied an education.

The eradication of poverty is a major challenge for international bodies. The World Bank, for example, has for years tried to combat poverty by providing foreign aid; the US foreign aid program has tried to do the same. However, such programs, though well-intentioned, fail to achieve their purpose. Poverty is caused and perpetuated by deficiencies in the political and socio-economic systems.

The Failure of Foreign Aid

For years, US foreign affairs experts have stressed the importance of foreign aid to developing countries, particularly in reducing the number of poor in these countries. The US Agency for International Development (USAID), the main agency in charge of handing out most of America's US$12b foreign aid budget, argued that the economic prosperity achieved in the period following the Second World War was attributed to foreign aid programs such as the Marshall Plan in Europe. However, a recent study by the Heritage Foundation challenged this. The study concluded that not only did the US foreign aid program fail to promote economic growth in less developed countries but also many recipient countries are worse off because of it.[3] According to the study:

> Haiti has depended on US foreign aid for 52 years, yet it is one of the world's poorest countries. Over this period, Haiti has received almost US$1b in foreign aid. In 1994, the United States spent further money on its military operation to 'restore' democracy to Haiti. In 1965, Haiti's gross domestic product (GDP) per capita was US$360; by 1994, it had fallen to US$225.
>
> Peru has also received US foreign aid for 52 years, receiving almost US$2b. Its per capita GDP in 1965 was US$1,126; by 1994, it had fallen to US$1,103.
>
> Somalia has received almost US$1b in US foreign aid over the past 41 years. Its per capita GDP of US$123 in 1965 had shrunk to US$111 by 1987.
>
> Niger has received over US$500m in US foreign assistance over the last 37 years, but its per capita wealth shrank by over 60 per cent from 1965 to 1994, falling from US$617 to US$272.[4]

Defenders of foreign aid say that people around the world rely on it for survival, therefore it must be continued on humanitarian grounds. In reality, much of the aid does not reach the poor. As much as 70 per cent of US foreign aid is spent on financing US contractors and consultants, many of whom duplicate services provided by USAID. The *1997 Heritage Foundation Report* cited the following examples:

> A US company called Planning & Development Collaborative International contracted with USAID to sponsor a 1993 study tour to the United States for

> the Romanian Union of Architects. It was never explained how acquainting Romanians with American architecture would help build a prosperous free-market economy in Romania.
>
> In 1993, the Academy for Educational Development of Washington, DC, undertook a study for USAID to determine how Indonesian health workers could improve their interpersonal communication skills.
>
> Four organizations co-operated on a USAID contract worth over US$2m that culminated in a study of ecotourism in Central America. The study included a section on the 'cultural and socio-economic impacts of tourism' and a list that ranks the 'desirability of native fauna for the tourist industry by marketing value and observation satisfaction'.[5]

One of the most glaring examples of waste occurred in Bangladesh. The country has received US$27b in foreign assistance over the last 23 years. Of this, 75 per cent was spent in donor countries to pay for commodities, equipment, consultants, experts, and contractors. The remaining 25 per cent was spent in Bangladesh on local contractors, suppliers, consultants and bureaucracy.[6] Another example of waste is the World Health Organization (WHO), whose annual budget reaches almost US$1b. Of this, 2/3 is spent on salaries, rent and supplies in Geneva, rather than in implementing health programs in developing countries.[7] Contrary to what it is intended for, foreign aid has little or no impact on the lives of the poor. The reason is obvious: administration from distant, top-down institutions is ineffective. Rather than helping the poor, such aid tends to reinforce the *status quo*.

The consequences of poverty and unemployment are socially destabilizing and have threatened the economic systems of developing countries. An effective alternative to foreign aid must be found. Fortunately, an alternative model at the grassroots level is gaining popularity, as well as increasing attention from major lending institutions and governments.

Micro-credit as an Alternative Model

If people have the misfortune to be born in the slums of Calcutta or among the impoverished foothills of Tibet, they could be condemned to a life of destitution. Contrary to common belief, Ashok Gurung, a research officer with the Trickle Up Program (TUP) in New York City, is of the view that these people are worthy of assistance. In an interview with me in November 1996, he said, 'Let us be realistic, these poor are indeed very enterprising. They have a strong survival instinct. Think about this, the fact that they can survive with so little resources shows that they are very resourceful. There are lazy people, rich or poor, everywhere. But there are many poor people who are hard-working; they just need a break in their lives. They need opportunities.'

In recent years, micro-credit has attracted world-wide attention for its success in combating poverty. Essentially, it is the granting of small loans to poor people to help them become self-sufficient entrepreneurs. With the loans, they set up small businesses and also improve their standard of living. One of the better-known practitioners of micro-credit is the Grameen Bank, founded by Mohammed Yunus in Bangladesh in 1976.

The Grameen Bank

The rationale underlying the activities of the Grameen Bank is that the poor cannot escape poverty because they are denied access to credit with which they could start their own enterprises, for they could not provide collateral. However, the Grameen Bank took the view that, given the opportunity to purchase their own means of production, the poor could embark on income-generating projects that would allow them to break free of the vicious circle of 'low income, low savings, low investment, low income'. In other words, the banker's confidence rests in the will and capacity of the borrowers to succeed in their undertakings.[8] Yunus does not believe merely in creating employment; he believes that the only way to break the poverty trap is to make people asset-builders.

Community Responsibility

Grameen Bank's approach to providing credit for the poor is based on group responsibility and disciplined repayment methods. The bank's lending process starts with five people who collectively own less than 50 decimals of land and who agree to form a group where they guarantee and monitor each other. Once formed, the group is organized and trained in weekly meetings by bank staff. They learn the Grameen rules and regulations; how to keep financial records, both individually and as a group; and how to behave individually and as a group. This approach makes it relatively easy for the bank to monitor the activities of its borrowers. It essentially uses peer pressure to monitor and enforce contracts, provides an incentive structure for the borrowers to repay, and helps screen out potentially bad borrowers, all of which would not only be costly but also ineffective for the bank to try and do itself.[10]

The lending mechanism is quite transparent. Applications and approvals for loans are discussed by the members of the group at their mandatory weekly meetings, and decisions are made on a consensual basis. Keeping everything in the open makes corruption and embezzlement of funds extremely difficult to go undetected.[11]

The other important component of the Grameen Bank's credit system is savings. Savings provide the bank with the funds for lending. Each member of the five-person group is required to save two cents each week.[12] In addition, five per cent of the loan is levied for what is called the 'group fund', and for every US$23 above a loan greater than US$23, 12 cents is levied as an emergency fund contribution. The group fund is managed by the group and provides an additional source of loanable funds for the poor when mutually agreed. The emergency fund is managed by the Grameen Bank and is used as an insurance against default owing to death, disability or natural disaster. Apart from the savings, each member is required to purchase one Grameen Bank share worth US$2.30. In addition to a stake in the ownership of the bank, borrowers have representation on its board of directors.[13] Initially, the government owned 60 per cent of the bank and the rest belonged to the borrowers; today, the borrowers own 88 per cent.[14,15]

The administrative structure of the Grameen Bank also differs from that of conventional banks. Decision-making is decentralized: there are four tiers—the head office, zone offices, area offices and branches, each with distinct functions. The head office, located in Dhaka, is headed by the managing director, Mohammed Yunus. The zone offices, area offices and branches are field units.

The head office is involved in mobilizing resources from external sources and in providing training and major policy decisions. Zone offices have the autonomy to make their own administrative decisions. They supervise the branches (each zone office supervises between five and 10 branches) and are responsible for formal loan approvals, based on the recommendations of branch managers.

The branch is the most important unit in the Grameen Bank's operations, as it is the one in closest contact with its members. The branch is also the basic profit-making unit. A typical branch supervises 50–60 centres located in villages within walking distance, and is responsible for group formation, member training and loan supervision. A centre consists of six to eight groups, and each group, the lowest level in the management structure, is made up of five people.[16]

The Good Banker reported the following interesting case concerning a woman called Hajeera Begum:

> Hajeera Begum was born in a village not far from Dhaka. Her father, a farm laborer, could not feed his six daughters, and he married her off to a blind man simply because he demanded no dowry. Hajeera and her husband survived on what little she earned cleaning houses, but she was unable to feed her three children regularly. One day she asked her husband for permission to join Grameen, but he had heard it was a Christian front organization bent on destroying Islam. He threatened to divorce her if she joined.
>
> Without telling anyone, she traveled to a nearby village and attended some introductory sessions where Grameen workers explained the principles of the bank. The first time the members of the group she joined took the oral exam regarding the rules of Grameen, Hajeera was so nervous that she couldn't answer the questions. 'All my life I was told I was no good. I was told I brought only misery to my parents because I was a woman and my family could not pay for my dowry. Many times I heard my mother say she should have killed me at birth. I did not feel I was worthy of a loan, or that I could ever repay it.'
>
> She would have given up, but the other members of her group encouraged her, and she passed the exam. At last the day came when she mustered the strength to ask for a loan of 2,000 taka, the equivalent of US$46.30. When she received it, tears ran down her face. Her group persuaded her to use the loan to buy a calf for fattening and a share of the rice harvest to process and sell. When her father brought the calf to the house, her husband was so excited that he forgot his threat of divorce.
>
> Within a year, Hajeera had paid off her first loan, taken a second loan and used it to rent a piece of land, planted it with 70 banana seedlings, and used the balance to buy a second calf. Today, with a mortgage, she owns a rice field, and goats, ducks and chickens. 'We now enjoy three meals a day,' Hajeera said. 'We can even afford some meat once a week. I intend to send all my three of my children to school and college, and university. You ask what I think of Grameen? Grameen is like my mother. She has given me a new life.'

The Outstanding Work of Grameen Bank

How successful has the Grameen Bank been in providing loans to the poor? David Bornstein's *The Price of a Dream* reported that:

> For the past two decades, the Grameen Bank has extended loans in excess of US$1.5b for self-employment purposes to some of the poorest people in the world landless villagers in Bangladesh. It has lent half of that amount in the last two years. Today, through a network of more than 1,050 branch offices, the bank serves more than two million clients, 94 per cent of them women. Each month, it adds thousands more, with new loans totalling US$30 to US$40m. The proportion of its loans that are repaid, 97 per cent, is comparable to the repayment rate at Chase Manhattan Bank.[17]

Such figures inevitably attracted the attention of the World Bank, who did an in-depth study of the effectiveness of the Grameen Bank.[18] The study concluded that the bank has shown a phenomenal expansion as the following indicators illustrate.

Membership

During the period under study, the membership of the Grameen Bank increased 840 per cent, from 171,622 in 1985 to 1,614,673 in mid-1993.[19]

Lending volume and portfolio mix

According to the study, apart from membership, the growth of the bank was also reflected in average lending per branch, which grew from an average of US$43,056 in 1986 to US$145,139 in 1992.[20] The average loan outstanding for a branch increased from US$25,232 in 1986 to US$157,870 in June 1993, an increase of 526 per cent.[21]

Mobilization of savings

There was enormous growth in savings in the period of 1982 to 1992. Total savings increased by 2,920 per cent during this period, from US$2.66m in 1985 to almost US$81m in 1992. In the first six months of 1993, total savings had increased by 31 per cent to US$105m. The savings and deposits mobilized in the period under study were more than adequate for the Grameen Bank to continue its lending operations without any funds from external sources: the bank attained savings-lending equality in 1989. This was partly due to increases in members' savings and deposits. For comparison, it is interesting to note that the total savings mobilized by the Grameen Bank were four times larger than the combined savings records of five major commercial banks in Bangladesh.[22]

Social development

Besides its financial and training services, the bank has introduced the 'Sixteen Decisions', a comprehensive social development program. They are the guidelines for codes of conduct and activities aimed at improving the social and financial conditions of the rural poor. The bank also educates its members on health, nutrition and productivity. The implementation of the 'Sixteen Decisions' has resulted in an increase in marriages where there is no dowry. By June 1993, 18,616 such marriages had taken place, compared with 2,738 in 1985.

The bank also encourages its members to operate nurseries at the centres, which also double as day-care centres. As of June 1993, there were 16,169 centre-operated schools, up by 386 per cent from 3,326 such schools in 1985. Enrolment has increased by 543 per cent over the same period, from 71,467 in 1985 to 459,405 in mid-1993. The bank also organizes workshops on various topics such as operational procedures, livestock and poultry care, health and nutrition and other social issues. The total number of participants in these workshops has increased by 655 per cent over the 1985–1992 period.[23] The bank also distributes seeds and seedlings to promote kitchen gardens and tree-planting.

Sources of Funds

Since its inception, the bank has been able to finance its activities through resources made available at concessionary rates by various external and internal sources. As of June 1993, the proportion of foreign funds available to the bank amounted to 75 per cent of total resources; 43 per cent of total funds (some US$63m) were provided in the form of grants.[24]

Although the Grameen Bank has recorded phenomenal growth between 1985 and 1993, nonetheless, one question still remains: is it a viable alternative to foreign aid in alleviating poverty? In other words, can the Grameen Bank sustain its credit operations and other activities as a viable financial institution?

Borrower viability

The viability of the Grameen Bank ultimately depends on the ability of its borrowers to repay their loans. This can be assessed in terms of outcomes relevant to the economic and social welfare of the bank's members as well as the drop-out rate and loan repayment performance.

The formation of a Grameen Bank group and its viability depends on the decision of each member to continue within the group-based system, given the costs and benefits of program participation. Members may drop out of the program for a variety of reasons, including when they no longer require credit or other bank services.

The aggregate drop-out rate increased from about five per cent in 1985 to 15 per cent in 1991. The rate was higher for men: 22 per cent in 1991 compared to seven per cent in 1985. In contrast, the corresponding drop-out rates for women were 14 per cent in 1991 and four per cent in 1985. Overall, the drop-out rate increased annually by 17 per cent over the 1985–1991 period, while the average annual growth rate was 21 per cent for women and 18 per cent for men. This suggests that the benefits must have been great enough, otherwise the membership drop-out rates would have been higher.

The loan repayment record is another indicator of borrowers' viability. The proportion of defaulters (those who have not repaid after 52 weeks) was nil in 1985/1986. In the period of 1987 to 1989, about one per cent defaulted, and in 1990/1991, about two per cent defaulted. Given the large number of borrowers, nearly 1.6 million, and the volume of disbursements, the default rate is almost negligible, which indicates the long-term viability of the borrowers and their groups.

In 1994, a study by Shahid Khandker compared the wages in 25 'Grameen' villages with those of 72 villages not in the Grameen program.[25] [The wage at village level is the average of all categories of labor (formal, informal and agricultural) undertaken by men, women and children.] The study showed that the Grameen Bank has a positive effect, not only on rural wages, especially for male and child labor, but also on economic growth at the grassroots level.

The savings mobilized from each member are another indicator of borrower viability. Savings per member were US$8 in 1992, rising to US$15 in 1997. As the borrowers' drop-out rate is quite low and their loan repayment rate is high, this suggests that the Grameen Bank has generated substantial benefits and has been sufficiently sustained to keep its members enrolled in the program. The 40 per cent annual growth rate in savings from 1985 to 1992 can be regarded as an indirect measure of borrower liability and program sustainability. Given the extent of the benefits of the Grameen Bank, the social cost of such program intervention is small. In 1992, the Grameen Bank received about 11 per cent subsidy for each taka disbursed to its borrowers; this per-taka loan subsidy was 12 per cent in 1987 and gradually increased to 14 per cent in 1990. As the bank's activities are aimed at the rural poor, its members actually receive this subsidy in the form of training and organizational assistance to improve their means of production, rather than as a direct transfer. In this sense, in 1992, each member received support equivalent to US$10, compared with US$7 in 1987 (based on estimates using long-term deposit rates). Note, however, that the per-member savings mobilized far exceed the per-member subsidy. Thus, if making the poor save is a measure of social benefit, then the benefit exceeds the cost of such a program.[26]

The Poor are More Creditworthy

The Grameen Bank boasts an impressive 98 per cent repayment rate. Its default rate of only two per cent is an embarrassment for Bangladesh's commercial banks, in which default rates are deplorable, at about 70 per cent for agricultural loans and 90 per cent for industrial loans. According to Mohammed Yunus:

> The difference lies in the psychology of the borrowers. The rich can evade the consequences of non-payment; the poor cannot. They value access to credit so highly, and dislike the loan sharks so much. So they are only too grateful for a once-in-a-lifetime opportunity to improve themselves.

The real key to Grameen's high repayment rate, however, has more to do with gender than with class. By design, 92 per cent of its borrowers nation-wide are women. The bank targets them because it considers them more reliable than men. Children order their priorities, making them less likely to squander funds and more likely to use them for household capital improvements. As Yunus says, 'If being poor is tough, being a poor woman is toughest'.[27]

Can the Grameen Bank be replicated?

If the Grameen Bank model can be reproduced, it holds hope for millions of others in the world. Its success has brought about other micro-credit programs in countries as diverse as Malaysia, Kenya, India and even the United States. In 1985, micro-credit institutions had about one million customers world-wide; in 1995, it was estimated that the figure was approaching 10 million.[28] USAID has recently done a study on 11 micro-credit programs, and its key findings are significant.[29]

Outreach to the poor

Programs reach the very poor. Clients were typically very small businesses that would normally be excluded from banking services. Six of the 11 programs have outstanding loan balances averaging US$200–400, and some are even below that. Programs offering small loans tend to attract more women.

Micro-credit programs have achieved significant coverage. Several institutions, notably in Bangladesh and Indonesia, have achieved major coverage on a national scale. The Grameen Bank covers almost half the villages in Bangladesh, reaching over two million clients. In Indonesia, the Unit Desa system of the Bank Rakyat Indonesia (BRI) has more than two million borrowers and 12 million savers, and the Badan Kredit Desa (BKD) systems cover 20 per cent of villages in East Java with small loans. In Bolivia, Bancosol and another institution have reached 50,000 clients, about 10 per cent of the potential loan market. Most programs are growing rapidly and may soon be of national significance.

Micro-credit programs have also experienced rapid growth, at rates ranging from 25–100 per cent per year. The BRI program is only a decade old, and CorpoSol in Costa Rica increased from fewer than 7,000 clients in 1990 to 32,000 by 1993. The key to this rapid growth has been the ability to maintain financial viability controlling bad loans, holding administrative costs to manageable levels, and developing a rapidly growing base of financial resources.

High-quality services are provided under the programs. Dramatic annual growth in the number of borrowers, the loan portfolio, and in some cases, savings deposits, are all evidence of strong client demand and overall satisfaction with the services received. Clients were willing to pay interest rates significantly above the rate of inflation and to repay loans on time They emphasized short-term working capital loans and graduated lending, whereby initial loans were small, and loans were renewed and increased on the basis of the borrower's repayment record. Turnaround time for loans, the period from when the borrower made the loan application to the time the lending institution lent the money, was significantly less than two weeks, and lenders were located close to where the borrowers worked.

Operational efficiency and full self-sufficiency

Ten of the 11 institutions examined in the study were operationally efficient. They fully covered the cost of day-to-day operations, including salaries and other administrative costs, with program revenues from interest and fees. The programs operated from rural Bangladesh to urban Bolivia, with a range of clients, and with loans often as low as US$38. Five programs were fully profitable. Revenues covered both the non- financial 'operating costs' and the financial costs of obtaining funds to loan out. That these programs no longer rely on concessional funds or other subsidies is illustrated in Table 4.2 below.

In short, micro-credit programs are likely to become the most important tool to combat global poverty in the near future. Ismail Serageldin, the Vice President of the World Bank, noted that these programs have progressed from the fringes of charity work to become a commercially viable part of world-wide banking. Micro-credit is growing at an annual rate of 30 per cent and is likely to reach nearly US$12b by the end of 1997.[30]

Table 4.2: USAID Analysis of 11 micro-programs

	BKD	LPDs	Grameen	KREP	BRK	ADOPEM	FINCA	Corpsol
Basic Institutional Profile*								
Number of branch office	5345	651	1030	6	14	6	1	0
Number of employee	16035	4913	10452	60	34	47	19	355
Total assets (USD)	62.59	25.59	238.69	1.94	1.58	1.79	1.7	15.68
Average annual growth of assets (in percent)	2	34	30	116	69	99	39	131
Clients - women (in percent)	50	40	94	60	45	100	26	50
Profile of Credit Service*								
Number of loan	907451	145183	1586710	5303	8787	3500	5121	32022
Annual growth rate of loan portfolio (in percent)	0	25	35	213	65	92	36	134
Camel analysis - efficiency and financial self-sufficiency**	118	137	79	38	43	89	75	104

*Basis of 1993 US$, adjusted account

** Financial self-sufficiency = operating income/total adjusted cost

Note: The 11 institutions studied were Agence de Credit pour l'Enterprise Privee (ACEP) of Senegal; La Asociacion Dominicana para el Desarrollo de la Mujer (ADOPEM) of the Dominican Republic; Banco Solidario SA (BancoSol) of Bolivia; Badan Kredit Desa (BKD) of Indonesia; the Unit Desa System of the Bank Rakyat Indonesia (BRI); Bankin Raya Karkara of CARE (BRK) of Niger; Corporacion de Accion Solidario (CorpoSol) of Costa Rica; the Grameen Bank of Bangladesh; Kenya Rural Enterprise Programme (KO-REP); and Lembaga Perkreditan Desas (LPDs) of Indonesia.

Source: Table 1 of Maximizing the Outreach of Micro Enterprise Finance: The Emerging Lessons of Successful Programs

The Trickle Up Program

Another example of a successful micro-credit program is the Trickle Up Program (TUP), which was founded by former development workers Glen and Mildred Leet in 1979. Like the Grameen Bank, the TUP was founded to help the poor start or expand their businesses by providing them with access to credit. The TUP made the same assumption that poor people already have the capability to create viable enterprises. Other than providing basic business training and a conditional start-up grant, the TUP also emphasizes on the strengthening of business skills, so that entrepreneurs are better equipped to sustain and expand their businesses. The TUP businesses are based on products or services that people know how to make or do and for which there are local markets.

The programs are run by volunteer co-ordinators and staff, with input from development agencies that want to incorporate micro-enterprise development as a part of their services. An innovative database management system makes it possible to assist a large number of businesses with a high level of accountability and low administrative costs.[31] According to the TUP guidelines, groups must meet the following conditions in order to qualify for a grant:

- Ownership: they plan the business themselves.
- Local resources: they secure any necessary approvals or resources.
- Time/energy: they work a minimum of 1,000 hours within three months.
- Self-sufficiency: they anticipate a profit.
- Reinvestment: they reinvest at least 20 per cent of the profit in the enterprise.
- Growth: they anticipate a continuing and expanding levels of self-employment.
- Accountability: they report on their business and its results.

The program gives low-income people an opportunity to establish profitable businesses and increase their incomes, enabling them to meet their families' basic needs. In addition, they develop entrepreneurial and book-keeping skills, the ability to save and reinvest, and increased confidence in themselves and their future.[32]

There are thousands of stories on the success of the TUP; the following is just one.[33]

> Estel Garcia is a single mother who migrated to the city seeking a better life for her five children. She and her children live in a shack made of woven mats in the desert outside Trujillo, Peru. Unable to find steady work, Senora Garcia relied on the community soup kitchen to feed her family. There she learned about the TUP opportunity to create her own business. She joined two friends, Marili and Angelica Castro, who had a sewing machine, and started a TUP business producing men's shirts, using the seed capital to buy the fabric, sewing supplies and plastic bags.
>
> The three are now ambitious businesswomen who use their initiative to overcome obstacles. Since the city markets are swamped with clothes, Senora Garcia travels once a month to the Andean region to sell to rural people who don't have access to clothing stores. Her mother cares for the children while she is away. Senora Garcia explained proudly that, with her share of the business income, she now covers basic necessities, including clothes and school books.

The TUP work somewhat like the Grameen Bank model. The process begins by providing a family or group with business training material and a start-up loan in the form of a US$100 conditional grant. The first US$50 is given to a group which completes the business plan and agrees to invest 1,000 hours of work in three months, and to reinvest 20 per cent of their profit in the enterprise. The group receives the second US$50 when the business report shows that the conditions of the grant have been met. Training is designed to show people who have little or no education how to start and continue in business; it helps them estimate profitability and encourages saving, reinvesting and record-keeping. The program is delivered through co-ordinators, field-based professionals from development agencies who volunteer their services. Working in partnership with a world-wide network of co-ordinating agencies, the TUP can operate cost-effectively, with no overseas offices or staff, and the agencies can incorporate a self-employment program at the grassroots level.[34] Table 4.3 below indicates the impact that the TUP is having throughout the world. The TUP derives its income from a range of sources: from foundations, 41 per cent; from individuals, 37 per cent; from corporations, 11 per cent; from organizations, eight per cent; and from governments, three per cent.[35]

Table 4.3: Trickle Up Program Results by Region

Region	Number of Business in 1979	Number of business in 1995	Trained	%	Average Investment	Average Profit
Africa	18,068	3,654	15,694	61	38.89	146.48
Americas	14,539	2,635	10,163	60	130.56	278.32
Asia	18,945	3,037	11,946	54	55.72	119.23
Europe	394	33	138	64	81.81	199.07

Source: Trickle Up Program Annual Report

The TUP: A Case Study

Apart from its main focus of helping the poor, the TUP has proved that its methodology can also be used to help preserve the environment. Its involvement in the Caohai wetland project in China is a vivid illustration. The Caohai Nature Reserve in southern China is one of the most important wetland and wintering grounds for a variety of migratory birds, especially the endangered black-necked crane. It was completely drained in 1971 to create extra arable land, but later the soil was found to be unsuitable for farming. In 1982, the Guizhou Province Authority decided to restore the wetlands by flooding. As the flooded area expanded, the number of black-necked cranes, which had dwindled following drainage, rose dramatically.

However, the restoration of the wetlands created more problems. The Caohai Nature Reserve is located in Weining County, one of the poorest provinces in China. With a per capita income of under US$25 a year, most villagers rely on a diet of corn and potatoes, because rice, the basic staple, is too expensive. Such extreme poverty forced many farmers to harvest what they can from the wetlands, but their activities jeopardized the conservation efforts. The authorities found themselves caught in a dilemma: on the one hand, they wished to conserve the wetlands and the bird population, and on the other, they had to mitigate the effects of the conservation project on some 15,000 poor farmers. In 1992, the International Crane Foundation, based in the United States, the Environmental Protection Agency of Guizhou Province and Caohai Nature Reserve came together to make the TUP work for those affected by the conservation. The program was based on three key features.

Focus on the poor

The program targeted those families that were most affected and disadvantaged by the conservation of Caohai Nature Reserve.

Environmental awareness

A key component of the program was to create environmental awareness among the participants. Hence, the TUP supported the development of businesses that are environmentally sustainable. Beneficiary families planted five trees in an area of their choosing as a first step in alleviating the damage done to the wetlands by the farmers. Although tree-planting alone will not solve the problem, it was essential in order to raise awareness of the connection between the conservation needs of the reserve and the development of the community, as well as the responsibility the villagers share for managing and protecting their water resources.

Community trust fund

Those villagers who received a TUP grant were encouraged to save and invest their profits in their communities through savings programs called community trust funds (CTFs). Each TUP household agreed to invest US$25 in the fund, which attracted an additional US$100 grant from the International Crane Foundation and was further augmented by funds provided by the Environmental Protection Agency of Guizhou Province. The CTFs not only provide a way for the farmers to obtain more capital for business expansion, but they also get participants involved in the long-term development of their communities. Additionally, CTFs provide reserves that all villagers can draw upon, not just the beneficiaries of the TUP.

The story of the Miao family provides a glimpse of how the TUP works. The Miao family, clearly one of the poorest families in the region, was originally excluded from the list of families suggested by village leaders to receive TUP funds. They were eventually given funding after a visit by a field co-ordinator who determined their need for assistance and potential for creating a successful micro-enterprise. A few years ago, the Miaos had been forced to beg in the neighboring town in order to survive. Through participation in the program, the family is now able to use their labor and stove-making skills to support themselves. The funds provided by the TUP are used to purchase raw materials necessary for building stoves which can then be sold for a profit. They make the stoves from old oil barrels from the local town, where they draw an income outside the reserve by recycling waste products; in this way, they reduce the pressure on the reserve's limited resources.[36]

Micro-credit Shows the Way

Ever since Marx, capitalism has been criticized for its bias towards the rich and its victimization of the poor. Given its philosophy and way of doing things, the Grameen Bank, and in particular, the concept of micro-credit, is unconventional. According to Mohammed Yunus:

> Capitalism is recognized as the best principle to ensure the optimal use of resources. It tells you when you are going in the right direction in mixing inputs, when you are going in the wrong direction, and when you have just the right combination of resources. Free-market competition ensures that you are pushed out of any comfortable position when your competitor finds a better way of doing business. It is the driving force for all innovations, technology changes, and better management.[37]

What Yunus objects to is not capitalism as an economic system but rather the view of capitalism which says that greed is the main motivator of economic behavior. Yunus continued, 'The engine of the capitalist system is supposed to be fuelled by greed to keep the system moving. I feel that this is one wrong assumption that has led the world to a self-fulfilling prophesy.'[38] One problem associated with the 'greed alone' scenario of capitalism is the alleged damage it does to the poor. By denying them a chance to escape poverty, damage is also inflicted on the general economic system itself. There have been numerous examples of financial institutions suffering losses due to greed, the most glaring of which was the Baring Bank fiasco. The collapse of Barings was due to a group who let greed become their sole motivator in futures trading. As a result, the bank ran up a loss of US$1.3b which ultimately led to its collapse.[39]

Yunus argues for an alternative capitalist system:

> We must envisage a world which has not only greedy people, but also people with strong feelings for their fellow human beings. Also, between them, there

> are many people who are neither all greedy, nor all self-sacrificing. They can swing either way or spend their lives following a middle course with a careful mixture of selfish deeds and personal sacrifices for the community. In this alternative version of the capitalist world, instead of one motivating factor (greed) to keep it in motion, we can introduce social consciousness or social dreams as another motivating factor. Both types of people can be in the same market place, using the same tools and concepts of capitalism, but pursuing completely different goals.
>
> The alternative vision of the world under capitalism will not be as black as it turned out under the 'greed alone' scenario. This capitalist world can accommodate all shades: white, grey and black. I think this is the most realistic vision of the world under any framework, capitalist or non-capitalist.[40]

True entrepreneurs can never be driven by profit alone: a sense of social consciousness does not permit it. Although profit should be the bottom line of any enterprise, it should be one which takes into consideration the wider social implications of its enterprises. The Grameen Bank experiment in particular and the concept of micro-credit in general prove that such a possibility exists. In short, micro-credit is not only capitalist-friendly but it is capitalism with a human face.

In developing countries, micro-lending is big business. Some US$7b in loans is spread among 13 million borrowers, according to World Bank estimates. At the 1997 Micro-Summit of government aid agencies and micro-lenders in Washington DC, a target was set to raise US$8b from the commercial market by the year 2005.[41] 'We must build bridges that give the poorest access to the vast amount of money traded in the financial markets,' Mr Ismail Serageldin, a vice president of the World Bank, told a conference on aid hosted by the Asian Development Bank in Manila in June, 1997.[42] That is the point. The work of micro-credit is instructive. Those micro-loans, averaging a mere US$70, have so far helped 600,000 villagers out of poverty. In comparison, the US$1 trillion foreign aid that the United States government has given to poor nations since the Second World War has only produced justifications of why the programs did not work.[43] Glaring corruption puts humanity to shame. Zaire's late ruler, Mobutu Sese Seku, amassed a personal fortune close to US$2b during the period his country received US$8.5b from Western donors, including the International Monetary Fund and the World Bank.

Aid managers argue that assistance programs will only work in countries with good practices, functioning institutions and cohesive societies. In fact, in these communities, there is no need for aid. In East Asia, Botswana and Chile, there are governments that are accountable, predictable and transparent; they don't need assistance in the form of aid, they can find foreign investors. Today, private capital accounts for 80 per cent of long-term financial loans to developing states. More and more developing communities are learning to put their houses in order so as to attract foreign investors. An expansion of micro-credit programs and the transfer of skills at the grassroots level will make an immeasurable contribution to those ground down by poverty and limited opportunity.

Chapter 5
From Working Class to Middle Class

"There is no incentive necessary other than government support. Incentive means taking away government tax and giving it to the company and then calling it profit."

—Dr Mahathir Mohammed—
Prime Minister of Malaysia

Paid employment in traditional Asian companies rarely provides opportunities to build an asset base; often, the only way to financial independence is to be self-employed. This is why so many Chinese start their own businesses, no matter how humble it is at the outset. People running their own businesses experience a unique feeling of creativity that they could rarely have if they were to work for someone else: few companies provide their employees with a satisfying feeling of participation and financial ownership. The small business sector therefore provides an opportunity for upward mobility. 'Small and medium-sized business provided the route to middle class-dom for millions of people in Taiwan, Hong Kong and Malaysia,' observed Michael Wu Ming Yih, Associate Director of UOB Venture Management.[1] America is another good example of an economy that promotes the small business culture, and where angel investors (investors who provide funds to finance business start-ups) can be found. To keep the community robust with ideas and innovations, and to maintain competitive energy, society needs to encourage people to take this route. Small businesses are an effective route towards self-reliance; they also form an important breeding ground for new technologies, which over time develop into the new industries of tomorrow—Microsoft is a good example.

A World of Global and Local Partnerships

All over the world, the media gives big business a great deal of publicity. We read and hear about chief executive officers who pull down enviable pay and bonus packages, who achieve celebrity status and for whom governments lay out the red carpet. The power of global companies is formidable, their influence far exceeding that of politicians in terms of the benefits they can bring a community.

The power of global business

The turnovers of transnational companies can exceed the aggregate gross domestic product (GDP) of some national economies. The largest business in the world, General Motors, achieved sales of US$164b in 1996.[2] Also, in 1996, Ford's turnover of US$147b was larger than the GDP of Saudi Arabia; the Exxon Corporation's turnover was US$120b, and Norway's Philip Morris' was US$54b, more than the 1995 GDP of New Zealand. The sales turnover of Visa International, the credit card company, is expected to exceed US$1 trillion in 1997.

Transnational companies are not only borderless, but stateless. They constantly search for locations that offer the competencies they need to beat the competition. If the local community lags behind in skills and other essential competitive factors, they uproot themselves and move on.

For instance, by offering an environment where operating costs are far lower than in Singapore, Penang, a northern Malaysian island, has succeeded in attracting a lot of high-tech firms, such as Hewlett-Packard, Intel, and Siemens. However, before the financial crisis, firms were complaining that Penang was becoming too expensive.[3]

Many Asian economies, especially those of Malaysia and Singapore, have been built on the backs of multinationals, first American and European, and, starting in the 1980s, the Japanese, the Koreans and then the Taiwanese. Foreign direct investment from developed Asia has been responsible for most of the growth in developing Asia; in China, the principal foreign investors are overseas Chinese firms in Southeast Asia, especially Hong Kong and Taiwan. Singapore has been and still is the Asian headquarters of many multinationals. However, Singapore is aware that this dependence on foreign companies can make her economy vulnerable. In order to attract foreign companies to Singapore, the government offers a dollar-for-dollar training subsidy which also allows Singaporeans to gain valuable skills and technological know-how. At the same time, the government is acutely aware of the need to develop its own entrepreneurs. Building a stock of home-grown businesses able to compete abroad is critical to the continued prosperity of the community.[4]

In today's highly competitive global environment, it is not realistic to expect transnationals to swear allegiance to local communities with poor or deteriorating operating conditions, especially those communities that are too small to constitute a sizeable, final domestic market. These large companies are not anti-local: the reality is that the competitiveness of a community is a changing and moving picture. For example, when a labor-intensive shoe-making industry ceases to be viable in Taiwan, it relocates itself to the suburbs of Jakarta. Neither is globalization a bad thing for national economies. In fact, it is quite the opposite. Global companies bring many advantages to the local community. These include:

- the transfer of knowledge and technology;
- the setting-up of infrastructure, enabling the local community to leap-frog to the latest facilities, both in skills training and physical amenities;
- the opening of a gateway to world markets;
- diversity and a global perspective on standards world-wide; and
- a new management culture, setting different standards for efficiency and quality.

Building an effective global-local partnership is the key strategy to developing the business sector of a particular community. Incentives and efforts to attract foreign direct investment and multinationals only represent the initial steps. Subsequently, great effort is needed to develop and strengthen the small business sector so that it can take full advantage of the imported expertise. The aim is for local businesses to eventually develop an industrial cluster of their own to produce branded goods for world markets. In Asia, only Japan, South Korea and Taiwan have successfully nurtured sizeable domestic industrial clusters at the higher end of the value chain. Nurturing the local business sector will therefore be an urgent priority in the next decade. In the long run, local economies should be able to count on the expansion of the small business sector to provide the jobs and the exports to sustain their growth.

Commenting on Malaysia's evolving economy, authors M Salleh and L Rahim noted that:

> Our industrialization has made such great strides that we do not think any more in terms of 'import-substitution' or 'export-orientation', but rather how we could strengthen and diversify our industrial base through a concerted and accelerated development of small-medium industries (SMIs). And this, in conjunction with the ongoing investments by large-scale industries, will lead to a well-balanced, dynamic and competitive integrated industrial sector.[5]

It's a Small World

The transnational corporations are important, but not dominant. Small and medium enterprises (SMEs) and small and medium industries (SMIs) are the backbone of enterprise and employment. They make up no less than 96 per cent of all firms in the APEC region and employ over 1/2 of the total work-force on average. A study commissioned by the APEC countries showed that they account for 70 per cent of total employment in China, Japan, Taiwan, Thailand and Brunei. In some instances, SMEs generate up to 84 per cent of total employment. Ninety-nine per cent of Japan's 382,000 manufacturing enterprises are classified as 'small firms', which is to say they employ fewer than 300 employees and are capitalized at less than US$814,000. They account for 72 per cent of all manufacturing jobs.[6] In India, small-scale enterprises constitute an important segment of its industrial sector. This segment is a powerhouse of economic activity, encompassing a wide range of products, sophistication, technology and size. Over 75,000 products conforming to ISO 9000 are being manufactured.[7] SMEs are important in the developed economies too, and member countries of the Organization for Economic Co-operation and Development (OECD) give special attention to them.

In continental Europe, where entrepreneurship is not as valued as, say, in the United States, small companies are where the action is. Today, Europe's hot growth companies are showing a remarkable ability to take advantage of the growing trend towards deregulation, the nascent secondary stock-markets, and the rapid spread of the Internet, which connects companies with customers at minimal cost.[8] One outstanding example is TelePizza, a pizza delivery service started a decade ago with $80,000. Its work-force now numbers 6,000 and it boasts sales of $260m.

Every third enterprise in France is a small business. Two million people or nine per cent of the work-force work in the country's 823,000 small businesses.[9] In Germany, 99 per cent of its 2.6 million enterprises were SMEs in 1990. With a work-force of 27 million people, they employed 2/3 of the total German work-force.[10] Dr Walter Doring, Economic Minister and Deputy Chief Minister of the German province of Baden-Wurttemberg, stated, 'Our SMIs, with up to 500 employees each, form the main portion of the state's economic structure, employing about 1/2 of the total work-force and about 1/2 of the total gross national product in the state'.[11]

There are 22 million non-farm-related small businesses in the United States. Small businesses employ about 60 per cent of the private work-force and are more likely to hire women, younger and older workers. Ten million jobs were created in the last four years, 90 per cent of them by companies which employ 50 or fewer employees.[12] In fact, most Americans start their working lives in small businesses. Small firms are responsible for 54 per cent of all sales in the United States. Exports have accounted for almost 70 per cent of the growth in the US economy since 1989, and 50 per cent of them are from companies with fewer than 19 employees. In fact, the percentage of small businesses exporting has increased over the past four years. In 1992, only 11 per cent exported compared to 26 per cent in 1995.

Large and cumbersome; small and nimble

Many Asian business owners dream of building a kind of *keiretsu* (the group of big Japanese companies, 'Japan Inc') or *chaebol* (the Korean equivalent). China has expressed an ambition to nurture 1,000 of her State-Owned Enterprises (SOEs) into mega-sized conglomerates. However, big, centrally-controlled, top-down enterprises are has-beens (the financial crisis of 1997 testified to that). As John Naisbitt pointed out in a seminar to the Chinese community in Kuala Lumpur in 1996, a different kind of bigness needs to be created. The conventional mega-corporations of the industrial model are too rigid and too slow to respond to the speed at which the market changes today.

In 1996, it was expected that corporate mergers world-wide would be valued at US$1 trillion dollars, which would suggest that large-scale operations are needed to compete in the global economy.[13] The fact is, however, that when businesses become huge bureaucracies, the enterprise weakens. Professionals who manage according to numerical goals, and a top management with little knowledge of the business, especially in a diversified conglomerate, are bound to fail. The huge behemoths are unwieldy and slow, lacking the nimbleness so critical to today's competition. The only answer is that as businesses merge, they restructure their entire organization. The past decade has given salutary warning to some of the giants: Du Pont, Salomon Brothers, Westinghouse, General Motors, IBM and Sears. Rather than celebrating their size, big companies have taken to hiding it; they try to imitate the agility of their smaller rivals by shrinking their headquarters, slashing away layers of management and breaking themselves up into smaller units.

The need to deconstruct and reorganize into smaller units is driven by the need to focus on core competencies: the things that, as a company, you and you alone can do better than anyone else. JP Morgan, the investment bank, has constructed an index that measures the extent of a company's focus on a scale of one to a hundred. American companies that decided to 'clarify' their business by focusing on the one thing they did best outperformed the rest of the market by 11 per cent over the subsequent two years.

A Networked Approach to Efficiency

The need to focus on core competencies has led to various out-sourcing arrangements (subcontracting jobs out) and in-sourcing (bringing the consultant in-house). It is now routine for companies to have their catering, cleaning, building maintenance, security, computer systems and even their mail-rooms run by outside contractors. Many go even further. Nike designs and sells sports shoes without stitching a thread itself. Cirrus Logic, a semiconductor firm, has all its manufacturing done by subcontractors such as Taiwan's Semiconductor Manufacturing Corporation.

Many Asian business leaders are very uncomfortable with out-sourcing, citing loss of control as the major reason for dissatisfaction. It is true that major out-sourcing mistakes have occurred, and companies are now carefully looking at out-sourcing, deciding what is best kept in-house and what is more efficient to out-source. An effective out-sourcing strategy should be flexible and put you in the position to hire the best and most competitive contractor available. Competition also helps keep people honest and innovative.

A new kind of bigness

The ideal picture features large and extensive networks made up of small, independent companies that have the ability to respond quickly. Small companies cannot on their own benefit from economies of scale or undertake research and development, but they can organize themselves into loose networks or strategic alliances to benefit from a collective effort. In the United States, a popular consolidation strategy called 'roll-up' helps small companies maximize their potential. What roll-up does is to integrate small firms into a substantial company that can afford professional management and aggregate the business to achieve the returns needed to make a public listing possible. In Asia, it is harder to implement rollup because of the older generation's stubborn refusal to relinquish their independence.

In this age of globalization, big is indeed clumsy, and big companies have come to realize that they need to be as agile and as flexible as their smaller competitors. Technology often changes the context of doing business. By remaining small, companies can focus on what they do best and thus be able to outperform the competition. As companies retrench staff, they are, in many cases, handing jobs over to smaller firms. The statistics on the growth of jobs in small US companies is evidence. Downsizing in the big corporations therefore need not be a bad thing; it opens up opportunities for the smaller fellows to grow while the big corporations get to focus on their core competencies.

Even for higher-level skills and specific competencies, companies are resorting to 'in-sourcing'. Instead of putting additional people on the payroll, they contract specific jobs to outside experts who work in-house. Swedish financial giant, Skandia, uses a great deal of in-sourcing expertise in its expansion plans. Leif Evindson, Director of the Future Center, said to me, 'We build bridges, we leverage on our structural capital and build linkages with specific expertise that we require'.

The 21st century ought to be a golden age for small firms, especially those dealing with high technology. During the past decade, factories have increasingly focused on the high-tech markets, where barriers to entry tend to be low, rather than on the traditional heavy industries. Thanks to flexible manufacturing techniques and the relatively low cost of computing, economies of scale can now be realized by even the smallest businesses. In many cases, nimble small firms literally took over the work of big companies during the 1980s. By the end of the decade, on one estimate, more than half the production costs of some large firms was accounted for by their small subcontractors.

Continental Europe and Japan are out of place in this world of smallness. While management theorists are unanimous in their opinion that downsizing is bound to escalate, Western Europe and Japan still have hundreds of huge companies protected by the state against competition. Deregulation, when it inevitably comes, will make them shed jobs as savagely as AT&T did. Moreover, many European companies are still unfocused in comparison with their American competitors. Growing global competition will force these Europeans to choose between excelling in one business and cutting large numbers of jobs in the process or becoming also-rans in several. Getting rid of people will never be nice, nor is it always politically possible, but European and Japanese managers will have to learn to live with downsizing, if they ever hope to survive.[14]

The new global organization

Occupying a narrow niche but having the ability to operate globally, small companies are expected to have a hey-day. There will either be fewer large companies, or large companies will be redefined as a collection of small companies. Small companies will especially dominate in the knowledge/information economies where brain power determines success. We are not so much moving from manufacturing to service industries as we are from manual to knowledge-based functions. Many areas of what have traditionally been viewed as manufacturing processes are actually service functions, such as product development, research and development, product design, marketing and distribution. Talent and skills are best kept current in smaller units, and entrepreneurial abilities and initiative are needed as small companies set up their networks of competencies.

L Richardson wrote in *Asian Business*:

> The manager of tomorrow will find it necessary to concentrate on productivity as well as innovation. He must consider the number of hours needed to produce each unit of production, the cost of those hours and the capital invested for each unit. This may mean dividing production between several countries.

Today, an Asian marketer of leather gloves buys the cow hides in Wichita or Kansas City in the United States where the cattle are kept in small enclosures where they can't move much. This produces leather with no scratches. Next the skins are sent to Spain or Italy for tanning and a soft leather is produced. From there they go to China where cheap labor is available to cut and sew the fingers and other components together with a super-strong thread made in Delaware, USA. From there the gloves go to Hong Kong where the brand name is attached inside the gloves. They are sorted into pairs and put into cardboard cartons and placed on a container ship bound for the world's markets.[15]

Perhaps the most instructive example of corporate reconstruction is ABB, the world's largest power engineering group. ABB has transformed itself into 1,200 small companies, each with no more than 200 employees yet with combined sales of US$30b a year. In the future, giant companies will find it impossible to make profits at the same pace as smaller, speedier and more innovative groups. Lou Gerstner is turning IBM around by deconstructing the company into smaller, stronger units. In mid-1993, IBM announced it would devolve its UK operations into 30 separate businesses, each of which could fix prices and costs and be totally responsible to its own customers. Gerstner said at the time, 'The creation of a business federation will give more ownership and accountability to business managers, enabling the company to return to profit more quickly. Some of the separate companies will have only about 50 employees.' It must also be pointed out that IBM today is not only a manufacturing company; its consultancy division contributes substantially to the company's total revenues.

Restructuring the Giants

The large companies built on the industrial model are headed for extinction. Japan's low-profit *keiretsus*, South Korea's loss-making *chaebols* and even Singapore's competitive and profitable government-linked corporations feel the pressure to change. Perhaps the greatest challenges stem from the *chaebols*: some 49 of the largest ones made only $65m in net profit in 1996, with total sales accounting for some 95 per cent of the nation's GDP. This low profitability reflects inefficiencies in the deployment of capital. China has announced there is no time left to 'feel the stones underneath the water' and has declared that it will restructure the hundreds of loss-making State-owned enterprises (SOEs). Successful restructuring of these corporate behemoths will forever change the face of corporate Asia. Is size important? 'It depends on the industries. Scale is important for certain industries. Overall, it is dangerous to generalize; appropriate scale and balance is key,' said Professor Zhao Chunjun, Deputy Dean of the School of Economics and Management at Tsinghua University in Beijing.[16]

Can Japan become entrepreneurial?

Stories of the woes of Japanese companies are becoming too familiar. While the government drags its feet on deregulation, frustrated business leaders are getting impatient. They know their future lies in their ability to invent new businesses and break out of the over-regulated system, and they are starting to encourage employees to be entrepreneurial and to support them through joint ventures. Changes are slow in coming, but they are in motion.

One of the biggest developments Japan will see is the emergence of smaller companies that, despite their size, pack a mean wallop in technology and value-added services and are independent of the *keiretsu*. 'Too much wealth is concentrated in the hands of a few big companies,' says Abe Shuhei, investment guru and president of Sparx Asset Management Co in Tokyo. Instead of betting on blue-chip stocks, Abe turned to smaller businesses. He now manages a $250m fund for institutional investors ranging from Warburg Pincus Funds in the United States to Kuwait's finance ministry. His track record is good: Sparx's funds consistently outperform the JASDAQ index (the stock exchange index on which small, growing companies may be listed). Abe said his company focused on small companies '... because they represent the future of Japan'. As to the reason, Abe pointed to examples like Fuji Photo Film Co, which rules the Japanese photo industry. Fuji's film costs four times more in Japan than it does in the United States, an arrangement it has got away with by controlling a massive network of *keiretsu* retailers. But since the 1980s, a number of small distributors 'have sneaked through the cracks' by offering cheaper film, and consumers are catching on. 'If the big guys don't change,' Abe said, 'the small guys will take over'.[17]

In the past, a major barrier for small business has been a lack of financing, either from banks or venture capital partners. In Malaysia, to alleviate this problem, the government has established the Malaysian Exchange of Securities Dealing and Automated Quotation (MESDAQ)—a new market for the listing of small technology companies.

Even blue-chips companies are noticing the profit potential in small companies. Japan launched a new stock exchange in 1997, the Frontier Market, enabling small firms to sell shares to the public. This move is designed to enable fast-growing, small companies, which are shunned by big banks and brokerage houses, to raise funds and so nurture Japan's future industries. Many other Asian nations, such as Hong Kong and Singapore, are also starting to focus on funding small start-ups.

How to restructure the chaebols?

Powerful vision and a strong determination to grow drove the Korean *chaebols*, and indeed they provided the dynamism in the industrialization of South Korea and helped in the transformation of its economy. However, ambitious corporate goals are the reasons they find themselves in their current precarious position. As they fail to deliver profitability and satisfy their shareholders, the *chaebols* know that there is only one way out: restructure or perish. Kim Dae Jung's reformist administration still needs to convince the biggest groups, but everyone knows that further delays in the restructuring process will only mean a longer wait for the rebirth of the South Korean tiger economy.

The *chaebols* have lost focus and over-extended themselves, expanding from chips to ships, from Indonesia to Ireland. They grew fat on state-directed investment and a domestic market that was closed to foreigners. With the financial meltdown and South Korea on the brink of bankruptcy, they face a government that can no longer afford to be protective. Other countries with lower costs, such as China and India, now have the advantage, and are moving aggressively into more technological and higher value-added industries and services. Stephen Marvin, head of research at Ssangyang Investment & Securities, observed, 'Only the best Korean companies that become more focused and can compete with foreigners will survive'.[18]

Scaling-back has long been perceived by management as a retreat and a blow to corporate pride, but as Korea's economy slows down, some of the *chaebols* cannot hold out any longer. In 1996, the net income of Korea's 30 largest *chaebols* fell by 90 per cent compared with that recorded in the previous year, according to the Daeshin Economic Research Institute in Seoul. Other *chaebols* are trying to slim down by finding ways around the labor laws: a rigid labor market in South Korea, and strong unions, are standing in the way of corporate restructuring, making the reform process that much harder. Textile company, Sunkyong Industries Ltd, an affiliate of the Sunkyong Group, Korea's fifth largest *chaebol*, shed 924 white-collar employees in 1996, 25 per cent of its total work-force in a retirement program. Sceptics say they have heard the *chaebols* talk of reform before, but that it produced little action. The *chaebols* may have no alternative but to go through the pain.

The core problem in the management of *chaebols* is the efficient use of capital and productivity. The average gearing ratio of *chaebols* is 4–6 to one, debt to equity. The productivity of some of the bigger *chaebols* is horrendous. For example, although South Korea is the world's fifth-largest car-maker measured by the number of units manufactured, its leading car producer, Hyundai Motor, made only 27.9 cars per employee in 1996, compared with 44.7 cars by Toyota in 1974, when the Japanese industry was at a similar stage of its development.[19] Discipline is the new mantra for the *chaebols*. However, while the management of the *chaebols* reins in the organizations that for decades drove double-digit growth, Professor Sumatra Ghoshal and Donald Sull of the London Business School advise them not to lose their dreams and passion for growth, but keep them for after the restructuring. It is important that they do not repeat the fate of Western managers who preside over companies that have low running costs but no growth. 'Cutting costs was painful, but managers find it an order of magnitude more difficult to stimulate growth,' they warned.[20]

Korea's *chaebol*-first banking system has had a very serious impact: it stifles the entrepreneurial spirit of anyone with the gumption to start up a small or medium-sized business. To be sure, the country has thousands of such enterprises, but they are mainly suppliers for the industrial behemoths and, as such, beholden to them. (In Taiwan, in contrast, there are numerous medium-sized firms that set their own agenda and are sufficiently flexible to compete in the increasingly competitive world market.) A multitude of troubles confronts these corporate Davids among South Korea's Goliaths. The smaller the company, the poorer its access to such corporate nourishment as funds, people and technology. Lenders often charge small companies higher interest rates, top university graduates shun them and distributors don't trust their products. Even the government admits the present economic structure disproportionately favors the *chaebols*. Until that structure changes, critics say, most small and medium-sized firms will remain trapped, the first to go under each time the economy bogs down. In recent years, the government of South Korea has sought to encourage entrepreneurs by forcing the banks to allocate 40 per cent of what they lend to the smaller firms.[21]

According to the Korean Federation of Small Businesses, a record 13,992 of small and medium-sized firms went bankrupt in 1995, despite economic growth of around nine per cent. In the first seven months of 1996, a further 6,425 companies went out of business. Small companies will also be hit especially hard by foreign competition as South Korea opens its economy on joining the OECD.

Change is on its way and will be accelerated. In February 1996, in a demonstration of its resolve, the government established a new Small and Medium Business Administration. Also at that time, economists teamed up with the State-owned Korea Broadcasting System to launch a one-hour weekly program called 'Small and Medium-sized Companies TV Department Store', during which viewers can call in to buy featured items. Other recent measures include the development of common brands under which several small companies can market their goods, and an official seal of excellence, indicating a government guarantee of product quality.[22]

State-owned enterprises: China's burden

In China, a State-Owned Entreprise (SOE) is an enterprise owned by the government, whether assigned to the province, municipality or county for supervision and management. The central government is the ultimate authority. SOEs were first set up by the Communist Party. After the communist's victory over the Kuomintang in 1949, they emerged as the pillars of the socialist system, also dispensing social welfare. In the years since the birth of the People's Republic, these monsters of State enterprise have come to dominate both the economy and people's lives. About 340 million Chinese owe their livelihood to the SOEs. Efficiency, however, is an alien word to SOEs.

They tend to lose money, even when well-equipped with the latest technology. The reason is what Harvard economist, Janos Kornai, calls the 'soft-budget constraint', interpreted as the 'setting up of production without due regard to costs and prices or availability of raw materials'.[23]

They tend to be over-staffed—it is politically difficult to lay off workers, even if the firm is losing money. The bureaucrats and employees of the SOEs have a strong vested interest in perpetuating the State sector. State enterprises are miniature welfare states within welfare states.[24]

SOEs make things nobody wants. They churn out unwanted products resulting in huge stock inventories that cannot be sold. An editorial in *The Asian Wall Street Journal*, quoting a report in the Chinese newspaper, *Economic Daily*, on the seriousness of this problem, stated:

> Manufacturers, particularly makers of consumer goods, reported inventories of finished products totaling US$60b, or about eight per cent of GDP. That doesn't surprise analysts who have been watching the economy throughout the reform years. In 1989, the situation was even worse, with firms holding inventories worth 11 per cent of GDP. China's growth loses some of its luster when you consider how much of it, measured by official statistics, is mouldering away in warehouses.[25]

The Chinese leadership is confronting the SOE problem. There was no choice—the iron rice bowl had become a cracked clay pot offering little nourishment with even less security. Since 1978, a number of changes have been made to improve efficiency. After the adoption of the open-door policy in 1978, competition began between the SOEs and private enterprise. The contract responsibility system (CRS) was a major instrument introduced by the economic reforms. In the first stage of the CRS (1978-1984), the authority to allocate profits and the pricing policy were decentralized to production units, where managers were encouraged to maximize profits. The second stage (1985-1993) aimed at further decentralization of decision-making in the areas of production, pricing, market, wages and personnel management.[26] Under China's current Five-Year Plan (1996–2000), Beijing has committed itself to concentrating on a core 1,000 SOEs, while the others are to become candidates for bankruptcy, merger, divestiture, and management buy-outs. Almost 50 per cent of China's approximately 108,000 SOEs made losses in the first half of 1995, and since they received preferential treatment, including large subsidies, their poor performance has had a negative impact on the Chinese economy. In the first eight months of 1995, SOE industrial output rose only 8.3 per cent compared with a 13.7 per cent increase across the board. It has been estimated that, on average, non-SOEs require less than 1/3 as much investment as SOEs to achieve the equivalent industrial output. Although SOEs account for less than 50 per cent of gross industrial value output, they were responsible for almost 2/3 of the US$7.89b loss made by Chinese firms in the first nine months of 1995, an 18.8 per cent increase in State sector losses over the same period last year. Between 1978 and 1996, the contribution of the State sector to China's total industrial output shrank from 78 per cent to about 42 per cent; it has been forecasted by some economists to drop to 30 per cent by 2000.[27]

China grasps the nettle

The hardest task confronting China is to close down the worst-performing SOEs. A bankruptcy law was put in place in 1986, but has been little used owing to its inadequate nature and concern over the social implications of mass closures. However, a pilot project in 18 'pioneer' cities is currently under way. Some 474 SOEs have been identified as suitable candidates for bankruptcy or merger. Bankruptcy procedures have begun for 161 of them, but only 58 have actually been declared bankrupt. The bankrupt companies had combined debts of US$385m and assets of just US$225m. Opposition to bankruptcy does not only come from the managers and workers but also from banks and local governments, reflecting China's so-called triangular debt problem: the chain of unmet obligations that forms when A can't pay B, who therefore can't pay C. In some cases, Beijing tries to save firms through mergers, breaking them up into smaller management units, selling shares, transferring surplus labor to service industries and inviting foreign investment. Experience has shown that enterprises forced to live within budget constraints improve their performance.

Finally, and perhaps ultimately, there's the hidden cost of hindering job creation in the non-state sector. 'In any event,' said Harvard economist, Jeffrey Sachs, 'what happens finally in many countries is that governments are pushed to the wall'. Governments have no choice but to act more radically, and for China, the wall is looking closer.

Although Beijing has accepted the need for ownership reform in order to encourage market-oriented behavior among SOEs, it still has not resolved the issue of ownership, especially the concept of total privatization. An East European-style mass sell-off of State industry is not considered compatible with the development of a socialist market economy. Instead of privatization, Beijing has embraced the concept of corporatization. Many large and medium-sized enterprises are earmarked for transformation into joint-stock companies with public ownership spread across a variety of State institutions and enterprises. In this way, majority 'State' ownership is maintained, even though the central government has little or no direct role in running the company. Corporatization provides a mechanism for the formation of State sector conglomerates where cross-ownership in the style of the Japanese *keiretsu* can be developed. However, this strategy can only improve efficiency if subsidies are progressively withdrawn. Furthermore, conflicts of interest between shareholders and enterprises are likely as the former will frequently include the administrative and regulatory bodies of the former central planning apparatus. The radical reforms to be carried out by Chinese new premier Zhu Rongji aims to address this all-important issue. Basically, the State intends to sell its interests in small SOEs. There are some small and medium-sized SOEs that have become joint ventures with foreign interests; others have sold shares to employees. The State intends to only partially sell the large SOEs.

The managers of some of China's biggest SOEs are a new breed. In their late 40s, they tend to be resilient (many experienced the Cultural Revolution) and possess of an overseas education, often in market economics. In reforming the SOEs, they are extremely flexible. For example, in making it possible for employees to afford the cost of shares, they are highly disposed to compromise in the valuation of the enterprise. In April 1997, Dr Yang Mu, a former banker and economist-turned-entrepreneur, told me:

> First they take out the land value, which makes up the bulk of the value of the enterprise. Then they deduct all the debts and liabilities and, if necessary, they disregard the cost of pensions, housing and welfare paid to retired and existing workers. Once valuation has been arrived at, the workers can pay for their share prices from profit and bonus. The key is to transfer ownership and let the workers take responsibility.[28]

A number of SOEs have been listed on foreign and domestic stock exchanges and others are keen to be listed because of the benefits of injections of capital. Private and foreign participation is likely to be mainly restricted to minority shareholdings in the 'subsidiaries' of State-owned holding companies.[29] Although the healthier of China's SOEs will continue to play a major role in the national economy, the national blueprint insists that, by the year 2000, each company be wholly responsible for its profits and losses. Those failing will go bankrupt, and managers will be able to lay off redundant workers. The planners pin most of their hopes for soaking up the inevitable unemployment on the creation of new jobs. They calculate that with an annual growth rate of nine per cent, some 58 million new jobs will be created over the next five years.[30]

China had hoped that, with the growth of private industry, the State-owned chunk of the economy would cease to be a problem. That has not happened. Although private enterprise has bloomed, State-owned industry has scarcely withered away. In 1991, SOEs still employed 107 million people, compared with 75 million in 1978, and in 1992, they soaked up $90b in government subsidies.[31] Not only do these behemoths devour scarce resources that could be better used by China's dynamic private and collective companies, they owe $361b to China's four major banks. About 35 per cent to 40 per cent of the loans have turned sour.

Jiang's initiative for a competitive China

In a recent article in *Economics Daily*, the head of China's most powerful think-tank opposed privatization on the grounds that it denies 'the basis of socialism in China'. However, the ineffectiveness of the State sector has caused enormous wastage of valuable resources. Since the color of the cat shouldn't matter so long as it catches mice and the socialist cat hasn't caught many mice recently, SOEs should be allowed to privatize. Dr Yang Mu said:

> One must not over-react to what Chinese leaders say. In China, one must understand that, in view of the baggage of socialist ideology, three peculiarities exist in Chinese public statements. There are those things that can be said, but will not be done. There are those which cannot be said, but are well under way. There are also those that can be said and will also be carried out. In the case of privatization of state enterprises, the reality seems to be the second scenario.

In his first major policy initiative since Deng Xiaoping's death, President Jiang Zemin is set to take up the reform Mr Deng didn't tackle—privatization. No-one in China is calling it that, but it means exactly that. Government officials and economists have said that Mr Jiang and other top leaders have reached a consensus to allow the vast majority of State-run enterprises to diversify their ownership by taking on domestic institutional investors, issuing stock, or allowing foreigners to acquire stakes. With this change in policy, Mr Jiang would be dismantling one of the last ideological tenets still held by China's Communist Party. 'This is a breakthrough,' said Xiao Geng, a professor at the University of Hong Kong. 'State-run enterprises no longer have to live. They will eventually become private enterprises.'

Economists have predicted that the new policy will present opportunities for foreign investors, as well as for Mr Jiang. China could increase the speed with which it opens up sensitive sectors like energy, services and infrastructure to foreign participation, especially if it also gains entry to the World Trade Organization in the near future, as Chinese leaders hope. For the moment, mergers are China's preferred method for overcoming the State sector's woes. In Shanghai alone, some 600 mergers have already taken place, according to the official *Liberation Daily*, and not a day seems to go by when another isn't announced. A Chinese merger, though, doesn't bear much resemblance to a Wall Street one. Since the factories involved usually belong to the same government bureau, the shareholders don't change. 'It's really just a transfer of an entire company, staff and assets, to another company with the same owner,' explained Gao Peng, assistant to the general manager at Shanghai Vantone, a Chinese financial holding company.

With the mergers, it is hoped that the country's resources will be more efficiently allocated. In 1996, an article in the *Far Eastern Economic Review* said, 'There's a real need in Chinese industry to concentrate resources'.[32] Some analysts also speculate on how many companies that result from mergers will enjoy effective management. Mergers can work, if they have the right leadership. 'One problem is that most mergers do not have strong leaders,' said a Shanghai-based consultant. 'Often, they're just a change of name and a relocation of equipment.'

From Beijing to Hanoi to Delhi, governments have recognized that they cannot compete in a world economy if they do not revamp their state sector. Granting state-owned firms monopolies and unlimited access to scarce capital squeezes out would-be private competitors. Even a crude form of privatization restores a company's incentive for profit and relieves the government of the considerable burden of running it. Across Asia, governments deserve credit for recognizing that private cats are better at catching mice than public cats.[33] In the massive corporate restructuring that must take place in Asia following the financial crisis, governments must go one step further, that is, move aside completely—stop picking winners and deciding who should be on the 'death list' (as the South Koreans put it) —and let market forces take over.

Zhucheng, where workers are owners

When Zhucheng, in the backwaters of China's Shandong Province, was selected to be a guinea-pig for small and medium-sized State enterprise reform in 1992, it was not something that the city felt particularly proud of. But nobody ever imagined that it would turn out to be the spark that could transform the nation's industrial landscape. At a time when 'privatization' was a dirty word (it still is), a 36-year-old by the name of Chen Guang sold, within a mere 22-month period between September 1992 and July 1994, almost every single State and collectively owned enterprise that he could lay his hands on. The feat earned him the nickname 'Chen Mai Guang' (Chen Sells All). Altogether he sold 272 of the total 288 enterprises, or 95 per cent of them. Prior to the sell-out, Mr Chen had found, in an audit of 150 enterprises, that almost 69 per cent were losing money in line with the national average. Half-way reform measures proposed were overwhelmingly rejected by the workers. What followed the great fire sale became legendary: every single one of the 272 enterprises sold has turned a profit.

Statistics showed that, in 1994, the pre-tax profit of the city's enterprises rose a stunning 113 per cent, productivity surged 123 per cent and the city's fiscal revenue increased 50 per cent—all double the 1991 figures. In 1996, pre-tax profits rose 13 per cent, productivity was up 54 per cent and revenues went up 24 per cent. How did all this happen? Mostly because 77.2 per cent of the enterprises was restructured into 'co-operative joint stock' companies. Simply put, ownership was sold to the workers.

For Peng, a laboratory technician, when she walked out the accountant's office after paying for her shares in the Star Insulation Material Plant, 'All of a sudden, everything in the factory became precious'. She remembered to turn off a running tap which, five minutes before, she would hardly have noticed. Six months after Star's employees bought the company, pre-tax profits had quadrupled. At the same time, 85 per cent of similar, State-owned enterprises were wallowing in red ink.

A visit to Zhucheng by the then Vice Premier Zhu Rongji, in March 1996, affirmed the city's experiment in reforming small and medium-sized enterprises. According to Wang Qingxing, deputy secretary-general of Shandong Province, by mid-September 1996, out of a total of 44,000 enterprises, 29,000 had undergone restructuring. There were drawbacks, however, to Zhucheng's method of restructuring SOEs: one obvious defect is the growing income gap between old workers who hold more shares, and newcomers with fewer shares, and the non-transferability of shares to outsiders. However, these shortcomings are not serious. There is one basic feature that stands out: the cutting of the cord between the government and local enterprise.[34] Perhaps another level of reform should start for the successful enterprises.

Over the past 20 years or so, China has lifted some 200 million people out of poverty, the biggest such shift in history. Once it was the world champion of gradual reform process—the process Deng Xiaoping called 'fording the river by feeling for the stones'. In recent times, however, the leadership has recognized the urgency of the problem of the SOEs and aims to solve them over the next three years. The most enriching of China's reforms, and those with the most remarkable outcomes so far, are those that allowed farmers to work for themselves rather than for the collectives, and those that made township enterprises possible. Once the ownership issues are settled, these enterprises take off rapidly. They spread across the land like a bush-fire, not because the central government said they should, but because the government chose not to interfere with the entrepreneurial abilities of the farmers.

Private Cats Catch More Mice: TVEs

Up to the early 1990s, the Township and Village Enterprises (TVEs) were the heroes of the new Chinese economy. They are fast building wealth and are competing with the bigger SOEs in the extent of their contribution to industrial output and exports. The taxes paid by TVEs account for 1/5 of China's tax revenue.

The growth of the TVEs has been remarkable:

- The enterprises now employ some 125 million people more than those employed in the State sector, and equal to about 70 per cent of those employed in the cities.
- They provide jobs to 1/2 of the 400 million workers outside the cities.
- They account for over 30 per cent of farm households' income, up from 20.5 per cent in 1991.

In 1996, *The Economist* commented on their success:

> More than any other sector, the enterprises have been the beneficiaries of reform. They now number about 25 million and collectively account for about 1/4 of the economy. Indeed, by some accounts, they produce over 1/2 of its industrial output, surpassing the state sector. Less notice has been given to the part that rural enterprises have played in China's export success. In 1986, their share of total exports was 9.2 per cent. It is now more than 40 per cent, thanks largely to enterprises in the coastal provinces of Guangdong, Fujian and Jiangsu. In the clothing industry, the share is 90 per cent.[35]

Origins and growth

The historical roots of Chinese TVEs can be traced back to the Great Leap Forward (1958-1960). In an effort to carry out Mao's policy of self-sustenance and of self-reliance, millions of peasants, after having been organized into communes, were mobilized to set up small village workshops for the production of goods for local consumption. Though the Great Leap Forward turned out to be a disaster, the commune system continued, leaving behind a convenient administrative framework for organizing the pre-reform types of rural enterprise.[36] Throughout the 1960s and the early 1970s, the government pushed for the development of five small industries (cement, chemical fertilizer, machinery, power, iron and steel) in the rural areas as a key component of Mao's overall development strategy. The communes, which took over the town or township administration, were considered ideal for setting up a cellular type of self-reliant economy comprising agricultural, manufacturing and service activities. In 1984, these communes came to be known as TVEs.

Ownership and control

TVEs are profit-oriented business entities that exist within the confines of a town. While the town government holds certain institutional responsibilities towards its enterprises, it is only as an administrator or impartial regulator. Most TVEs operate very much on their own. A TVE must have a director, usually a local appointed by the town government or the village community which owns the enterprise. The director makes all the important decisions on what to produce and how to produce it right from the beginning.[37] This person organizes all the factors of production, ie, raises capital, purchases equipment, acquires the technology, hires the labor, procures the materials, and so on. Virtually all crucial business decisions concerning production and marketing are made by the TVE director, and it is the director, not the town government, who is responsible for the profits. Once the business has become profitable and the TVE has fulfilled its financial obligations to the town government, the director is more or less given a free hand to manage and develop the TVE as he or she sees fit.[38]

Production and business orientation

The TVEs are generally dynamic and growth-oriented. Despite their humble origins as rural enterprises, they soon transformed themselves into competitive businesses. The number of employees can range from a few hundred to over a thousand. The diversity of Chinese TVEs and their strong business orientation are neither found nor matched elsewhere. Rural enterprises are usually location-specific, taking advantage of local resources directly linked to agricultural production. But many Chinese TVEs are either not resource-based or have transcended their agricultural base. These behave more like an ordinary urban-based industry, depending on such factors as entrepreneurial abilities, technology and marketing. Hence the Chinese TVEs produce a wide range of consumer goods and intermediate products, not just for local markets nearby, but also for the national market and for export.[39]

Since they operate outside the State sector, TVEs usually have to bid for their production requirements in the open market. Unlike

SOEs, they have to earn their profits; to maximize their profits, and to optimize their resources.[40]

Incentive-based pay

The interests of TVEs parallel those of their town governments: if the TVEs thrive, prosperity immediately spills over into the entire town in terms of employment and income generation; the tax revenues increase, and eventually economic and social development spreads throughout the region. Unlike the SOEs, which have the financial support of the government, a TVE might not be able to pay its employees if it were in serious trouble—most TVEs are just too small to treat their workers as permanent employees on an egalitarian wage system.[41] So TVEs follow a kind of incentive-based pay system, which links wages directly to the individual as well as to the performance of the enterprise.[42]

Tight budgetary constraints

The contributions that town governments make to the success of their TVEs are more difficult to quantify. It is well-known that town governments usually provide a lot of assistance to TVEs in the beginning, such as supplying the initial capital, appointing the director, helping to recruit labor, providing administrative support, and securing loans from the local branches of the State banks. Town governments also help TVEs acquire land for their factories. However, while they cannot openly protect their TVEs as 'infant industries' against competing products from other regions, they can and do unofficially help or protect them in a number of ways. Most TVEs have budgetary constraints and they survive through efficiency and by maintaining their competitive edge.[43]

Challenge for the future

The rapid growth of the TVEs in the 1980s came as a surprise even to the Chinese leadership. In June 1987, the late Deng Xiaopeng commented that, 'The greatest achievement which we did not expect is the TVE's growth'. The TVEs are now a permanent feature of the new Chinese economy, and they will no doubt remain a vital sector. The Chinese economy grew by 13 per cent in 1992 and by another 13 per cent in 1993, when there was tremendous expansion in TVEs in terms of output, employment and exports. TVEs are not without their challenges. A number of problems not foreseen in the 1980s are emerging —capital, loans and technology are not easy or cheap to obtain any more. It has become increasingly difficult and expensive to recruit workers, in an increasingly competitive labor market; the new generation of TVE directors are also expecting to be paid market rates of remuneration.[44] Although the institutional and economic environments will become more difficult for them, TVEs will probably adapt by becoming more sophisticated in their operations as China moves towards the free market.

Judging by the outstanding performance of the TVEs, there is no doubt that any reform efforts need to encourage more entrepreneurs. The way to the future is to encourage more small fellows to 'plunge in'. When they start to make and keep wealth on their own, they will never want to return to the shelter under the big tree.

Chapter 6
From Local Business to Global Enterprise

"We have already missed the industrial revolution.
We must not miss the information revolution.
If we let go of such good opportunities, even heaven will not forgive us."

—Stan Shih—
CEO, Acer Group

Twenty-two-year-old Acer Group is a global operation in leading-edge computer technology. Founded in 1976 in Taiwan, it is the third largest microcomputer manufacturer in the world. In 1996, its revenues totalled US$5.8b in 1996.[1] Acer sells its own brand-name computers in over 100 countries and employs 16,000 employees in 36 countries. The seven founders of Acer were all born in Taiwan, have never gone abroad to study or work, and started with only US$40,000. Stan Shih, the 54-year-old founder and chief executive, said:

> It doesn't matter whether Acer is a Chinese company. What matters is Acer must be the first Chinese world-class international company. We were taught in school that the Chinese are the best people in the world. We have had many important inventions, but in the last 100 years, we have made the least contribution to mankind. It is time we do our part.

Stan Shih embodies the New Asian Dream: the spirit, knowledge, scope and attitude of the new global entrepreneur that will remake the social and business landscape of Asia in the new century. Although Stan Shih is perceived by some as a latter-day Don Quixote, his global company, only one generation old, has yet to prove its resilience in the choppy competition that prevails in the high-technology market-place. While Acer's achievements may not match some of the global giants, Stan Shih is determined to make Acer a top international brand. Acer's pioneering efforts have led to the widespread adoption of brand names by other Asian enterprises. Asia now perceives brand names as intellectual property and as being vital for its competitiveness.

Entrepreneurship is the Key to Progress

While entrepreneurial talent is not part of the economist's formula for economic growth, there is no denying that it is the hidden driving force behind family and national economic success everywhere in the world. Hong Kong, Taiwan and many Chinese communities in Southeast Asia were built by entrepreneurs. Few of them started with high ideals. Most began their business as a means of survival and took it from there. Government policies that brought stability and promoted free trade helped them build up the business. With world economic and technological forces intensifying their impact on the region, entrepreneurs who can develop new niches will be needed even more. Entrepreneurship helps to sustain economic growth and to create the much-needed jobs for Asia's millions; it is also critical for the modernization of Asia.

Lifting the Bamboo Curtain

The first generation of entrepreneurs in Asia were hard-working families who suffered hardships and scarcities in very difficult times. They were tough and resilient; the success of the post-war export drive can be attributed to them. For example, Chung Ju Yung, founder of the Hyundai Group of South Korea, is the son of a farmer, and only had a primary education. After toiling as a laborer and a rice vendor, Chung started an auto-repair shop with little more than a set of old tools. When he stepped down as chairman of Hyundai, the conglomerate was the country's largest shipyard and its first and biggest auto-maker.

In Hong Kong, Li Ka Shing's Cheung Kong Group today accounts for about 10 per cent of the total market capitalization of all publicly quoted companies. When he moved to Hong Kong at 12 years of age, he worked 16 hours per day selling plastic belts and watchbands to support his mother and two siblings. In 1950, aged 22, he started Cheung Kong, making plastic combs and soapboxes; in 1979, he bought control of the property and trading conglomerate

Hutchinson Whampoa from the Hongkong & Shanghai Bank. Li is now one of the richest men in the world.

Liem Sioe Liong, one of Southeast Asia richest Chinese, braved wars, rebellions and hardship to build his Salim Group into a globe-spanning empire. Born in Fujian Province in China, he left home to work in his brother's peanut oil firm in Java. Liem built up a marvelous network of connections, and through this gained control of much of the logging, clove, flour-milling and cement industries. His companies are now among Indonesia's largest, and his financial empire stretches from Hong Kong to the United States.

These are just three familiar names in Asian business circles, their lives exemplifying the era of conflict and hard struggle that followed the Second World War. These men succeeded in laying the foundations for economic development. To understand how modern capitalism works in Asia, it is necessary now to step back and examine the backgrounds of the Chinese merchants, from an historical and cultural perspective.

The Culture of Chinese Merchants

'It is not greed that drives the overseas Chinese,' said Simon Murray, a Westerner who used to run Li Ka Shing's empire in Hong Kong and who is now himself an entrepreneur. 'It is fear and the yearning for the protection that money will give you [that drove them].' According to Professor Wang Gung Wu, director of East Asian Studies at the University of Singapore and a noted authority on overseas Chinese:

> What is often forgotten is that modern Chinese entrepreneurs, like their counterparts in South Asia, the Middle East and the Mediterranean, have evolved from traditional merchants and they have been around for a very long time. As merchants, they have been active in East and Southeast Asia for much longer than the Japanese and the Koreans.

Professor Wang made the following analysis of the Chinese merchant culture, both in the Mainland and overseas.[2]

> In terms of social status, merchants were traditionally on the bottom rung of society, and until relatively recent times, they have stayed in that lowly position. Poverty and a lack of educational opportunities forced them to start in trade. Some say that only good luck, hard work, stoic endurance and the virtues of a family system approved of by the Confucian literati lifted them up

above others who started the same way.

Many Chinese had, and still have, a negative image of merchants. Merchants appear to them to be cunning, greedy and uncouth. Even the most successful merchants were often objects of pity or mirth, if not the targets of ridicule and literary satire. But no-one ever denied their usefulness: Confucius and other philosophers acknowledged their value to society as facilitators of trade. For their work, and the risks they were prepared to take, they deserved appropriate rewards. Provided they 'knew their place' and did not seek to change the approved social and political structures, they were allowed to ply their trade. Merchants operated under the most difficult conditions of any group in China, hence they quickly learned how to grasp opportunities.

Profit-seeking and risk-taking were, of course, regarded as typical merchant activities. The literati vigorously rejected the first because it challenged the public good and was therefore immoral. They also frowned on risk-taking because it was not only opportunistic but also endangered a family's fortune or reputation. For the merchants, however, such strategies were vital for the successful running of their business. Conscious of disapproval, the merchants did tone down the profit-seeking motive and warned about the foolishness of excessive risk-taking. However, they were fully aware that without high profits and the risks that had to be taken to get them, the chances of success would be slim. Without entrepreneurship and the successful commercial undertakings that would follow, the merchant class could never hope to rise above that of staid and respectable artisans. It was this deep understanding that motivated them to develop the entrepreneurial talent for which they later became famous. They saw wealth as the only way to gain respectability, and the way in which they used that wealth was an essential part of their strategy for upward social mobility.

Professor Wang has identified three dominant characteristics of the overseas Chinese merchant culture: the importance of the family as a primary unit of trade, the freedom from the control of the mandarins and the risk-taking features of their entrepreneurship.

Family networks

The family was vital to the merchant. Up until the 20th century, all successful overseas Chinese merchants, whether originally from a merchant family or not, started by working for a relative who had a business. If they were closely related, they were deemed more worthy of trust and were more likely to improve their position rapidly; otherwise, hard work, honesty, thrift, and some early signs of initiative and talent were essential if they were not to remain in menial positions all their lives.

Freedom from control of mandarin

For merchants trading overseas, freedom from control by the mandarins was a large bonus. However, there was always the danger of racial discrimination, instability and interference from Western powers, so it was inevitable that Chinese mercantile success depended on certain patterns of patronage (institutional protection such as that afforded by a just legal system was non-existent).The major difference, however, was that the Westerners were open and flexible, whereas dealing with the mandarins meant taking on an inflexible bureaucratic structure. The merchants found that these foreign officials were unlike Chinese mandarins in one very important respect: Westerners were dedicated to profit, and appreciated Chinese trading ingenuity, something the mandarins in China would find impossible.

Generations of entrepreneurs

What would have been a more significant achievement for the overseas Chinese merchants would have been the ability to produce succeeding generations of entrepreneurs to maintain the family fortunes. This brings us to the difficult question of what constitutes entrepreneurship. A dictionary would define an entrepreneur as one who manages, organizes and undertakes a commercial enterprise, including all the risks associated with it. At one level, Chinese merchants are renowned for their boldness in risk-taking. Taking risks is not blind gambling but part of a consistent and carefully calculated strategy to yield handsome profits over a period of time. Entrepreneurs are clearly not mere risk-takers; they are or can be industrious, shrewd, ruthless and driven to make a profit, and as such, they need considerable freedom in which to maneuver so as to take risks at the right time and place.

Chinese merchants overseas had this freedom because they were not held back by an agrarian bureaucratic state with orthodox Confucian mandarins intent on keeping society as little changed as possible. They learned to overcome discriminatory laws, to adapt to new methods of operation, to become more innovative themselves and to use the best parts of foreign cultures. Since the end of the Second World War, the new merchant class overseas has become more confident and articulate. Their status is equal to that of any successful professional. They have combined what they have learnt from the West with what they recognize as their cultural heritage. 'Chinese merchant culture has been significant as the most modernizing force among Chinese living overseas,' said Professor Wang.

The Characteristics of Chinese Capitalism

Much has been written about the ability of the Chinese to generate wealth, but little is known of their 'wealth-generating engines'. This in part reflects their capitalist culture, closed and opaque, and their enterprises, local and fragmented. The fact is there are very few Chinese global generators of wealth; Chinese capitalists tend to concentrate on local and regional markets, with the leading players dominating the real estate and financial sectors.

Favorable conditions

In the aftermath of the Second World War and the struggles for political power in Southeast Asia, the Chinese had the economy to themselves. As Western investors began coming to Asia looking for cheap production sites, many Chinese started as contract manufacturers for labor-intensive products such as toys, textiles and shoes. Many relied on technology bought, borrowed or even stolen. Small and medium-sized Chinese businesses all across Asia operate as licensees of Western franchises. For example, Walt Disney's 66 franchises in Malaysia are all Chinese-owned or managed; they peddle a wide range of goods bearing the 'Mickey Mouse' label. These overseas Chinese capitalists are 'stateless' in outlook and don't care too much about the long-term competitiveness of their businesses.

When their operating environment changes and profit margins start to decline, they move on. In Hong Kong, industries making wigs, plastic flowers and radios sprang up, made a profit and then disappeared. Only in Taiwan was any deliberate effort made to upgrade the industrial base and to move up the value chain. It is no exaggeration to say that, among Chinese-owned and run industries, Taiwanese industries lead in technology.

Minorities and refugees

Overseas Chinese in Asia still have what anthropologists call the 'minority syndrome' and the 'refugee mentality'. Those living in Southeast Asia are in a minority, including Singapore which, although it is majority Chinese, is surrounded by large Muslim communities. Anti-Chinese sentiment flares up every now and then. As Chinese culture discourages Chinese involvement in the military, the result is they are often left totally vulnerable, with neither political nor military protection. The only safety is in accumulating assets. Overseas Chinese in Taiwan and Hong Kong are different: they are not minorities, but refugees from communism. Many still regard their homes as only temporary; if something really goes wrong, they can take their wealth to some safe Western haven, such as Canada, the United States or Australia. For the time being, they are guests in transit (*kuok kek*).

Whatever their status, these people have a tremendous drive to succeed. They work extremely hard, live frugally, save a lot and are obsessed with their children's education. Ronnie Chan, chairman of Hang Lung Development in Hong Kong, said:

> The overwhelming need to succeed and succeed fast also makes the Chinese overseas businessmen extremely flexible. Time is never on their side. With the government and military not under their control, they must bend with the wind and grab whatever opportunities that come their way. What if an opportunity arises in an area where they have no expertise? Learn as you go! What if there are not the necessary resources? Find it, create it or make do! What if there are barriers in the way? Go over it or around it, but never right through, never confront.[3]

As success depended on who you knew, not what you knew, so the overseas Chinese cultivated connections. Such practices remain widespread today. An employee of a Chinese engineering company that failed to win a contract for a megaproject complained, 'We spent hundreds of thousands to come up with a new technology to do the job, but we lost to someone who later copied our technology. My friends said I was stupid, I should have invested in *guanxi* and not in R & D'.

Reluctance to invest long-term

Chinese capitalism developed a very short-term view of business and there was no strategic planning. When the economy took off, many businessmen switched to real estate development. Those who could get licences went into banking, finance or stockbroking. As business opportunities expanded, they went into more and more new areas, the result of which is today's massive conglomerate of unrelated businesses. Some of these conglomerates are so large and diversified that it defies belief that management can have the depth of expertise and the industry knowledge to manage them all.

Chinese enterprises in Malaysia and Hong Kong tended not to progress up the value chain; when conditions for business became unfavorable, they either quit labor-intensive production completely or relocated. Taiwan and Singapore are different in that they have a Chinese government that focuses on the long term. Taiwan especially has a strong domestic industrial base, partly due to the leadership provided by the Taiwanese government and partly because of the vision of many of Taiwan's leading industrialists. The inference that can be drawn is that Chinese capitalists within Chinese nation-states value long-term business strategies and reinvest to keep their competitive edge, whereas the 'stateless' overseas Chinese focus only on making money. It should be pointed out that the mind-set of the overseas Chinese is a reaction to political circumstances, not globalization.

Keeping it in the family

Chinese families traditionally keep to themselves. In family-owned public companies, they usually act as if they own the whole thing, though usually it is no more than 40 per cent. Board meetings are short and are often held informally over dinner; an agenda is a mere formality, seldom covered. Assets are brazenly shuffled between private and public companies; after a company has gone public, many owners cannot distinguish between what is theirs and what belongs to the company. Such attitudes will have to change radically: when Asian companies go to the market for capital, they will come under intense scrutiny from strict regulatory bodies and the demanding standards of institutional investors.

Another weakness of the family-owned Chinese company is its reluctance to trust 'outsiders'. As a result, few bright young managers want to work for an organization where they can never advance and are treated like a servant. Criticizing the boss is not only unacceptable, it is regarded as insubordination; try challenging a point of view and you will be labelled rebellious. The Chinese boss makes up his mind fast and changes it equally fast; managers are not consulted. One survey in Hong Kong found that Chinese professionals preferred to work for Western and Japanese managers. Anybody, in fact, who was not Chinese.[4]

Guanxi v. Expertise

Overseas Chinese have had relatively little success in building large businesses outside Asia, mostly because of the tremendous money-making opportunities at home. Since they are used to a strategy based on closed connections, can they function in a transparent, regulated environment? Some say it is no coincidence that the richest Chinese capitalist is in Indonesia and not the United States. The culture is different in the West; the overseas Chinese themselves complain about the rules and admit it is harder to operate.

Management? What management?

Critics say that Chinese businesses have no system of management. They don't believe in formally organizing functions and work processes. There appear to be a lot of people working on a task, but each is afraid of upsetting the others, and for the sake of harmony, remain polite and obedient. It is often said that deep-pocketed tycoons make snap decisions on investing millions of dollars on projects without undertaking proper feasibility studies or drawing up a business plan. This is probably due to the fact that the knowledge and connections of the business what management consultants would call its structural wealth remain with the owner-entrepreneur or the manager. The Chinese insist that there is 'order amidst the chaos' and pride themselves on their flexibility. Being a strategist counts more than being a good manager. Most overseas Chinese firms are efficient because the bosses are dictatorial; the head of the family makes nearly all the decisions. In the bigger conglomerates, the corporate purse is only to be entrusted to a family member or a member of the inner cabinet. This management style could help in businesses which involve properties. It also allows firms to change direction quickly; a company can be started without a feasibility study and closed overnight after a discussion with a few senior executives over dinner. Unlike the Japanese, when the Chinese see no prospect of making money in the short term, they close the business with no qualms about firing people.

How will the Chinese Capitalists Face the Future?

We must remember that Asia's economic growth is only a very recent phenomenon. Overseas Chinese companies and their construct are the product of their environment, and as that changes, so will they. In the absence of a large home market (however, this may change as China liberalizes), those operating in Southeast Asia were trying to eke out a living from the narrow cracks in the system (*chia fong li seng choon*). Asia's great diversity and narrow market segments do not allow economies of scale; globalization has only become a force within the last decade.

Virtually every large family group is now trying to adjust and modernize, and the question is how long it will take and in what form they will eventually emerge. Many pack their children off to Western business schools, hoping they will acquire the knowledge to transform the business. Unfortunately, many of them return with an enthusiasm for the Wall Street ethos, more interested in making deals than putting in hard work on the business. Some families are luckier. Young Jeffrey Koo of Taiwan's China Trust Commercial Bank returned to Taiwan with a business education from America's Wharton Business School. He is now in charge of an overseas venture. 'My father told me to come back to Taiwan because he thought there were going to be great opportunities here. He has the relationships and the capital, and our generation has the expertise to expand aggressively into new business areas in Asia,' Jeffrey said. His father has also assembled a core management team of young, Western-educated ethnic Chinese. All of them have worked for prominent Western investment banks in Asia.[5]

Strategies for the Future

The global economy has for the first time created a level playing field for entrepreneurs and the initiated. The economic advantages of the industrial era, such as natural resources, labor and capital, have ceased to be the determinants of success. Anyone with a good idea, a good technology or just good organizing abilities can create his or her own enterprise, anywhere in the world. The industries of the future will be those that provide products and services that fulfil the spiritual and cultural quests of the people, in other words, industries that have a high content of knowledge and/or culture. There will always be a demand for material things, but the excitement will be in the 'soft' businesses. For example, Bill Gates does not deal in steel or oil, but in ideas and software.

The traditional sectors of automobiles, electronics, pharmaceuticals and banking are already dominated by global giants, but opportunities do exist in these sectors if Asian entrepreneurs can offer alliances drawing on their strong local connections and knowledge of local markets. Greater excitement lies in the business opportunities created by the information revolution. The growth industries of the 21st century will be biotechnology, new materials, civil aviation, telecommunications, computer hardware and software, education, entertainment, and travel and tourism. In order to participate in these opportunities, Asian businesses need to make some fundamental paradigm shifts.

Paradigm shifts

The generational shift in leadership and paradigm shifts in business focus are already evident in Asian business. The first generation of entrepreneurs built empires through family connections and sheer hard work. The new generation has taken the best features of Chinese business speed, entrepreneurship and networking and adapted them to meet the needs of a meritocratic corporate system. These new entrepreneurs are intent on making products that, by global standards, are high in quality and low in price.

Developing a truly global mind-set

Quality and price knows no East-West distinction. To be able to sell throughout the world, it is important to view the whole world as a potential market as well as a resource centre from which to draw resources, whether they be materials, design input or manufacturing capabilities. The Giant Bicycle Company of Taiwan is one of the world's biggest bicycle companies; 93 per cent of its sales are made outside Taiwan. Giant employs resources from around the world. It has 65 designers and development engineers world-wide. Forty-five of the designers are in Taiwan; the designers in China and Japan concentrate on commuter bikes, the designer in the Netherlands contributes ideas based on the traditional European racing bike, and the designer in the United States works on mountain bikes. All this input goes into the design centre in Taiwan. Giant's designers use computer-aided design, swap ideas on computer and over the phone, and meet twice a year in Taiwan to review their work. The common language used is English.[6]

Concentrate on what you do best

To assume leadership in an industry, Asian businesses need to refocus and consolidate. With increased liberalization and opening up of markets, competition will force them to excel in their chosen field. An operation spread across many fields, especially unrelated businesses, does not have the in-depth knowledge needed to maintain a leading position in any of them. American giant Westinghouse sold all the businesses in which it considered it could not be the market leader in order to focus on broadcasting, where it intends to become the leading player. Achieving niche competence is the key to competitiveness. A unique product or service can only come from sharper focus.

New ways of doing old things

Entrepreneur Jimmy Lai correctly interpreted the desires of an increasingly affluent Hong Kong. Lai is the well-known founder of Giordano, one of Asia's most popular retail chains. Now a newspaper and magazine publisher, Lai represents a generation that is focusing more on the lifestyle market than on manufacturing. Lai entered

Hong Kong in 1961 hidden in a fishing boat. He began to work his way up from the floor of a glove factory, where he cleaned for $8.50 a month and a place to sleep. He also learned English by picking up what he could from overseas customers. With a partner, in 1975 he used money made on the Hong Kong stock-market to buy a textile factory. This was the foundation for Giordano, which brought a friendly approach to mass-market retailing. Lai next transferred the marketing techniques he learnt at Giordano to the world of publishing, a business in which he had no previous experience.[7]

Malaysia's bumiputra entrepreneur Rashid Hussain upset many in the establishment when he introduced independent research and analysis for the stocks listed on the Kuala Lumpur stock exchange. He is Malaysia's newest multimillionaire and represents the new generation of bumiputra entrepreneur: knowledgeable and professional. Having put together Malaysia's largest brokerage house, he went on to form his own banking group.

Tong Kooi Ong is a Malaysian finance wizard who rapidly built a bank. Widely acknowledged as Malaysia's best analyst, Tong is a driven and intensely competitive businessman. He tried to introduce commission-free stockbroking using the electronic infrastructure provided by the Internet, but industry pressure forced him to abandon the plan. Watch for his next move.

Moving up the value chain

Asia must upgrade its infrastructure and expertise so that it can move up the value-added chain in world trade. Self-reliance can only be achieved if value can be added; staying at the bottom of the manufacturing supply chain only perpetuates dependence and deepens vulnerabilities to global competition. There is, however, serious concern about the ability of Chinese enterprises to compete in the future liberalized markets of Asia, where global brands come to local markets with a different marketing and management strategy. Western firms have clearly defined management and career structures, better compensation, greater respect for the individual, more aggressive branding, marketing and promotion all of which could put Chinese firms at a serious disadvantage. Many Asian business leaders agree that the impediment to growth is not lack of technology.

As Stan Shih of Acer said:

> Technology can be acquired, at home and abroad. The real bottleneck lies with advertising and marketing ... We know how to make, we can make large quantities cheaply, we must know how to sell. In manufacturing, we can score 70 to 90 marks...but in advertising and international marketing, we can only get between 5 and 30 marks. Imagine our value if we strengthened our advertising and marketing.[8]

Asian businesses must have a sharper focus and concentrate on moving up the value chain, making things and providing services that the world wants and marketing them well. They need to also bear in mind that building a successful business is more than making money: global enterprises not only can improve the livelihoods of millions but allow consumers all over the world to have new experiences. People such as Kanosuke Matsushita, David Packard and William Hewlett, Henry Ford and Bill Gates have not just created wealth—they have improved people's lives.

Continuous learning and innovation.

Chinese businesses are weak in terms of nurturing and accumulating intellectual wealth. They are too impatient to innovate and instead resort to copying; even with brand names and trademarks—they steal Western ones. Unlike the Japanese, they lack the tenacity and the will to innovate. Many view research and development projects such as the Apollo space mission as costing too much and taking too long to bring a good return on the investment. Fortunately, this attitude is changing.

Building Modern Global Enterprises

Asia has many wealthy capitalists, but few powerful global enterprises. The Chinese are unlike the Japanese who, as a powerful and unified group, were driven to conquer market share around the world. Chinese economic power is scattered and disorganized at a time when Chinese business ambitions are just beginning. Diversified Asian conglomerates often cite the absence of a big domestic market on which they can focus to reap economies of scale. This is given as the reason for their not making it onto the list of big global companies. I think the explanation for this is more historical: it is because Asia is a latecomer in industrialization. As Asian economies continue to grow, it is only a matter of time. There is no doubt about the advantages of a large domestic market, but many excellent global Western companies originated in very small domestic markets.

There are two types of global company in the world today. The first type are multinationals that began their businesses in huge home market in countries such as the United States, Japan or Europe, and then developed their strength to go global. The second category of global companies consist of smaller companies from, for examples, the Scandinavian countries, Australia and Canada, where the domestic markets are also small, and they must develop overseas. The multinationals dominate international production in such industries as automobiles, consumer electronics, chemicals, pharmaceuticals and petroleum. They can achieve great economies of scale and build extensive distribution networks across national borders. Alan Rugman, a fellow of strategic management at Oxford University, observed, 'Although they are at the forefront of globalization, they remain firmly rooted in their native regions, particularly in the 'triad' blocs of North America, the European Union and Japan. 443 of the world's 500 multinational enterprises come from these areas.'[9]

Table 6.1: The World's 500 Largest Multinational Enterprises

Country/Bloc	Number of Multinational Enterprises in 1997
United States	175
European Union	155
Japan	112
Switzerland	12
South Korea	12
Canada	8
Brazil	5
Australia	7
China	9
Other	10

Source: Fortune Magazine, 'The Fortune Global 500', 3 August 1998

Table 6.2: The World's Leading Multinational Enterprises

Rank	Company name	Home country	Index of transnationality
1	Nestle	Switzerland	94.0
2	Thomson Corporation	Canada	93.3
3	Holderbank Financiere	Switzerland	92.1
4	Seagram Company	Canada	89.7
5	Solvay	Belgium	89.6
6	ABB Asea Brown Boveri	Switzerland	88.6
7	Electrolux	Sweden	88.3
8	Unilever	UK/Netherlands	87.1
9	Philip Electronics	Netherlands	85.4
10	Roche Holdings	Switzerland	85.1
11	SCA	Sweden	79.1
12	Northern Telecom	Canada	78.4
13	Glaxo Wellcome	UK	76.5
14	Cable and Wireless	UK	75.6
15	Volvo	Swede	73.8
16	News Corporation	Australia	73.5
17	Royal Dutch/Shell	UK/Netherlands	73.0
18	Grand Metropolitan	UK	72.4
19	Petrofina	Belgium	70.4
20	Saint-Gobai	France	69.7

UK (5), Switzerland (4), Netherlands (3), Canada (3), Sweden (3), Belgium (2), Australia (1), France (1).

Sources: World Investment Report 1997 UNCTAD, Data for 1995. 'Mastering Global Business'. Financial Times, 30 January 1997, Alan Rugman, Thames Water Fellow of Strategic Management at Templeton College, Oxford University.

These multinationals conduct over 2/3 of their activities outside their home country. Alan Rugman's 'Index of transnationality' provided in Table 6.2 above is a simple mean of the ratio of foreign to total activities for three indices: sales, assets and employees. These companies are just the opposite of the 'triad' blocs shown in Table 6.1. They are generally from smaller countries such as Switzerland or Canada and need foreign sales to achieve global status. For example, Canada has a small market, only 10 per cent of that of the United States, so Canadian companies such as Thomson have to make most of their sales overseas.

The common factors for both types of global giant are: they are the best in the industry, either regionally or globally; they have a strong brand; and they outsource and subcontract to benefit from the efficiency of manufacturers around the world. For Asian companies who operate in the diversified and smaller, fragmented domestic markets, the global strategies of the companies in Table 6.2 may be instructive.

The new extended family

Neoh Kuo Cheng, a senior executive of a Dutch consulting and services firm based in Singapore, spent most of his working life in the United States before returning to Asia. He said, 'There is this thing about the family-ness of Asian business which I don't find in American companies. You know who you are working for: as long as you stay long enough and are outstanding, you will somehow get a pat on the shoulder from the owner. In Western public companies, employees do not have a human figure to look up to in the owner; it is hard to imagine who we are working with or for.' Neoh advises Asian firms to work hard at preserving this culture of family-ness.

Dr Emilia Roxas of Asia World Development Group of Taiwan and the Philippines is the first woman CEO of a major Asian conglomerate. She favors keeping the family structure because, unlike Western professional management which works in time-frames from quarter to quarter, the family is long term. She adds that the Chinese have in fact perfected the art of defining relationships in a community framework: responsibilities and role-playing between father and son, husband and wife, brothers and sisters, are already established. There is a social arrangement that brings stability and order.[10]

Born as family concerns, Asian firms tend to have a single, dominant commander who is rarely challenged, often simply because leadership and ownership are the same. As these family businesses move into new areas and new markets, the 'family' must also move on. When ethnic Chinese entrepreneurs team up to take advantage of each other's strengths and connections, they must also create a new organizational structure to maximize their potential.

For the traditional overseas Chinese business, extending the family is a challenge. While they were good at patriarchal centralized structures and businesses that required just a few key decisions each year, such as shipping or property, now they are faced with business operations with thousands of people making millions of decisions at different locations. There is no choice but to trust foreigners and to delegate as the business expands.

The top-down organizational model is also being replaced by self-organizing enterprises on a more human scale. As Asian governments liberalize trade and free their domestic economies, and as business expands in scale and geography with the rising economic tide, the old model of *guanxi* may become harder to practice. A new kind of *guanxi* among employees, suppliers, customers and shareholders must be developed in order to build the cohesiveness that retains people, motivates performance and guarantees loyalty. People do not only work for money or glory; they also seek a sense of belonging.

A strong management structure

Strong leadership at the top often results in a group of weak and deferential middle managers. As the scale of operations becomes bigger, those local family firms with patriarchal management structures and a low to medium technology base are vulnerable. Management reforms are needed that focus on creating an effective structure for middle management.

A remarkable success story of personal talent and personality is that of writer Louis Cha. Perhaps it is no exaggeration to say that he is Asia's most successful writer both in terms of readership and the financial success he has achieved in publishing. Hong Kong-based Cha started by writing Chinese kung-fu novels that made him the most popular writer in the Chinese world. Following this success, he founded *Ming Pao*, which became Hong Kong's most respected Chinese daily newspaper. One of the reasons for its popularity was Louis Cha's regular columns and editorials, as well as the daily excerpts from his latest novel. Since Cha took *Ming Pao* public and sold his interest, it has lost some of its influence. Had Cha established an effective management system, things might have been different. In contrast, Jimmy Lai built a successful market for *Next* magazine and *Apple Daily* with lightning speed. Both publications were created by a management system supported by a strong editorial team. *Next* broke even after 18 months, and has since gone on to become a market leader. Similarly, after three years, *Apple Daily* has become Hong Kong's most popular daily. Although a somewhat controversial figure, Jimmy Lai deserves high marks for innovation and ingenuity.

It is unfortunate that the principles underlying Louis Cha's personal success could not be systematically organized and passed on to an equally outstanding successor. In Jimmy Lai's case, aggressiveness, creativity and determination built an outstanding management system. Employees can always fall back on the system to guide them, and managers can learn the traditions and repeat successful practices. It is this kind of employee and a solid management system that will help Asian businesses make the quantum leap in scale and regional reach.

Strategic alliances

To acquire the technology needed to compete internationally and to save time, Asian businesses can either buy into Western companies that are strong in technology and thereby tap into that technology, or they can forge strategic alliances with Western multinationals. In the latter case, the Western partner would supply the technology and marketing channels into the West, while the Asian partner would supply the local distribution networks and marketing expertise within Asia. An example of this kind of alliance is the Hong Kong-based New World Property Group which, while it owns many properties, leaves their management to an international hotel chain.

Most Chinese entrepreneurs know what they do best, and leave what they don't know to others. This does not mean they are complacent. Many realize that, at a certain point, they will have to do business in unfamiliar territory. City Development Hotels Group, owned by Singaporean Kwek Leng Beng, is acquiring major hotels all over the world, while at the same time building up its management arm. Some day, Kwek hopes his Millennium hotel chain, under his own management company, will be regarded like any other five-star Western hotel chain. Robert Kuok has already pioneered the very reputable Shangri-la hotel chain in Asia, which has helped considerably in developing local expertise in hotel management.

Professional management

When the founders of Asia's ethnic Chinese business groups retire, their successors often become embroiled in struggles over control and direction. Such instability raises questions about the staying power of these corporate empires. Additionally, many of them are now traded on regional stock-markets, so internal, generational problems have implications that go beyond family and even regional borders. One pressing issue is the creation of professional management structures in Asia. On the one hand, there is a shortage of experienced managers, and on the other, a culture that does not respect and value specialists.

The passing of the mantle frequently forces conglomerates to modernize by bringing in professional managers who introduce long-term strategies such as making investments in research and development. Although Asian family firms are increasingly turning to outside professional managers, they still have difficulty trusting them. Professionals often feel they will never have real authority. Some Asian tycoons treat their professional managers like servants rather than trusted associates; others simply can't let go of the reins and continue to interfere in company operations. Entrepreneurs who have trouble letting go may prefer to keep a small part of their business as their sole domain, and allow the rest to be run by outsiders. This strategy has been adopted by Indonesia's Salim family with their Hong Kong-based conglomerate, First Pacific Co. In addition to the Salim family, many Asian business families have found the right formula: Malaysian Chinese entrepreneur Robert Kuok and Hong Kong's Li Ka Shing both entrust large chunks of their global empires to hired professionals.

The relationship between employee and employer is changing, whether the enterprise is privately or publicly owned. A feeling of ownership in the enterprise is key. If the entrepreneurial talents of Asia's managers are combined with a sense of ownership and management responsibility, the enterprise will flourish. Talented employees do not want to waste their time in a job or work with people with whom they cannot identify. Many Asian entrepreneurs dismiss this as irrelevant, on the grounds that the success of their businesses has more to do with their own skills, acumen, connections and capital than with the talent of hired managers. While acknowledging that these entrepreneurs have been successful in their chosen industry sector, the experiences of successful global players seem to suggest that if Asian entrepreneurs want to develop a global business, where team-work and employees' contributions are critical to success, they will have to change their attitudes.

The catchword for successfully managing relationships between employee and employer, between manager and shareholder, is 'value'; each participant in the wealth creation exercise must be able to add value. If employees are to be viewed as 'value-generating' units in themselves, a radical change in attitude must take place.

A stake in the company

Should the goal of companies be the maximization of returns for the shareholders or should companies assume a wider purpose and broader obligations, including those towards employees, suppliers, customers and the general community? Should companies be more concerned with certain categories of stakeholder, especially those who help to make the business, rather than be preoccupied with increasing the wealth of their shareholders? What is the most effective way to generate wealth?

Lifetime employment, at least for a significant number of core workers, has been the hallmark of Japanese and German capitalism. It has been argued that this version of stakeholder capitalism, by guaranteeing jobs for life, gives employees a strong incentive to invest in acquiring skills valued by their firm. But opponents argue that, while the skills acquired may be valuable within the firm, they may have only limited value outside it. In recent times, such stakeholder capitalism has come under unprecedented strain; Japanese companies have already begun to end lifetime employment, the sacred pledge they made to their workers in exchange for their loyalty.

Stakeholding is supposed to produce higher investment. A look at the inventors of stakeholder capitalism, Japan and Germany, shows that their economies, most notably that of Japan, outperformed the shareholder economies in the first few decades after the war. The gap has narrowed significantly in the past 20 years or so, and in the past decade, the shareholder models have shown signs of overtaking the stakeholder ones. The downturn in the German and Japanese economies, and the fact that these economies are paying attention to shareholdings, should give pause for thought to those in the United States and Britain who advocate stakeholder capitalism. It would be ironic if the United States and Britain were to shift towards this model just as it was about to be abandoned by its inventors.

Human assets in the form of intellectual capital are the deciding factor in global competitiveness. To nurture this intellectual capital and to keep it in the company, organizations must create bonds of ownership in both implicit and explicit ways. The implicit way is to foster intellectual groups in areas that are central for the company to maintain its competitive edge, such as team and organizational training. The explicit way is to forge a bond between the company and the employee, that is, to treat employees as if they are capitalists. Today, in a number of companies, employees are also shareholders; some are employee, manager and shareholder combined. Employee ownership is a key way in which companies can protect their intellectual assets.

Microsoft was incorporated to create a vehicle to share ownership with its employees; since its inception, it has never needed other people's money. Perhaps it is no exaggeration to say that Microsoft is the most celebrated entrepreneurial enterprise of the late 20th century. One of America's most admired corporations, General Electric, has stock option plans that extend to 22,000 employees, compared with just 200 in the 1980s. Stock ownership isn't the only way in which a company can acknowledge the contribution its employees make. Some offer bonuses; they are, in effect, dividends the company pays its employees in recognition of the investment of human capital.

There are various types of equity participation and profit-sharing schemes. Some employee-ownership oriented companies share profits with their employees in innovative ways. For example, Intel announced in 1997 that it was paying its staff US$820m in bonuses; this worked out to be, on average, about 33 per cent of base salary. In giving incentives, Hong Kong's Li & Fung is 'more aggressive than even the Americans', claims Victor Fung. 'We make a point of saying we want to attract people whose alternative would be to run their own business. So we take a whole operation, split it into about 70 different profit centers, each run by a little John Wayne. He runs a business of maybe US$50m, with 50 people. He may get five or 10 per cent of the profits.' Japan's Softbank rewards its 6,000 employees with stock options. Owner Masayoshi Son plans to divide Softbank into 600 virtual companies with 10 members each. 'Each of these units can make quick, dynamic, authorized decisions,' said Son.

In Taiwan, Stan Shih has pioneered an unprecedented model by breaking his Acer Group, which has a market capitalization of US$2b, into 21 public companies, to open up the company for listing in local bourses. This will allow staff members, customers and suppliers to take up equity in the company. Acer's 21–21—Project 21 listed companies in the 21st century is the first step in making everyone a shareholder. Once that is achieved, the interests of both shareholders and company will be aligned, and the inherent conflict between the capitalist and the worker would have been resolved. It will be in everyone's interest to give of their best, since everyone will share in the result a healthy share price.

Loyalty and lifetime employment

Loyalty is a big issue between Chinese employers and their employees. Some employers expect too much. Malaysian entrepreneur Liu Wan Min said:

> We cannot ask people for their loyalty, we can only ask people to be responsible. Loyalty implies that the individual makes sacrifices to the organization at the expense of himself, which does not make sense, is not sustainable, and is not reasonable to ask of the workers. We can only ask people to be fair, and return the value in a reasonable and fair amount over what they have been remunerated for.

Companies just cannot tear up their contract with their workers, the unwritten contract which promised security and automatic promotion in return for loyalty. The burden of lifetime employment weighs heavily on many companies, and many are now switching to a notion of lifetime employability. This means warning workers that they may well lose their jobs if the company can no longer make effective use of them, when their skills are too expensive or have become irrelevant to the company's operations.

The best companies already understand that if they are to retain their own right to flexibility, they also need to make their workers flexible. Training costs money. While firms that train their employees risk losing them to rivals, they stand a better chance of being rewarded with not just less anxious employees but ones of high calibre. The best people queue to work for firms that offer not the illusion of security, but an opportunity to stay employable.

Chinese companies practise a kind of family togetherness. Formal contracts are not popular, neither is there an expectation that the company will undertake training. There seems to be a tacit understanding that employees must ensure that their abilities and capabilities can meet present and future challenges. Everyone must pull their weight; if they don't do their jobs properly, the boat sinks and everyone drowns.

Team-work

Culturally, Chinese are not great team players. However, the complexity of the world of tomorrow demands a sharing and collaborating culture, an acceptance that everyone in the organization is important for the prosperity of the business. Sumantra Ghosal , a professor at the London Business School, says that this consciousness of the employability of staff members also reflects a revolution in the organization of firms. Everyone must realize that they are responsible for enhancing the company's human capital and so improving its competitiveness. The chairman of Intel, Andy Grove, tells his 40,000 workers that it is not Intel that is competing, but every one of them, and that it is his task to give them the tools they need to do the job.

Members of organizations must collectively identify the skills they can develop together that competitors will find hard to duplicate; in other words, they must identify their core competencies. Andy Grove believes that to operate in a world shaped by globalization and the information revolution, there are only two options: adapt or die. The new environment is governed by two rules: first, everything happens faster; second, anything that can be done, will be done if not by you, then by someone else, somewhere.

As a general rule, you have to accept that no matter where you work, you are not an employee; you are in a business with one employee yourself. You are in competition with millions of similar businesses, millions of others all over the world, picking up the pace, capable of doing the same work that you can do and perhaps more eager. Thus, the key to survival is to learn to add more value today.[11]

Stan Shih of Acer has the last word. He likens managing a new business opportunity to:

> An ant having spotted a big bean that is too heavy to be carried home by itself. So it goes and fetches all its fellows. Together they happily carry the bean home. We need to build a strong cohesive team to exploit the opportunities together.[12]

A World-wide Entrepreneurial Drive

The traditional skills of entrepreneurship have moved from the corner store to some of the world's most prestigious institutions of learning— from Harvard in the United States to Oxford in the United Kingdom and Beida in China.[13] Relatively unrecognized some 25 years ago, entrepreneurship is now a subject taught at universities around the world, including some 400 in the United States alone. Not only are prestigious business schools starting to offer exciting programs on entrepreneurship and holding contests for the best business plans, students, professors and alumni are joining hands to create new businesses. The inspiration for these ventures comes from the success of many student start-ups, such as Netscape, Yahoo, and most visibly, Microsoft, the company that Harvard drop-out Bill Gates created and built into a multibillion dollar empire that has made Gates the richest man in the world.

The Massachusetts Institute of Technology's student-run business plan competition encourages students from engineering and other science disciplines to work with those in business to create new companies based on the technology of their discipline. The 1997 finals of the competition, now in its tenth year, brought together some 600 venture capitalists, angel investors, lawyers, accountants and students. Graduates and faculty members from MIT have founded 4,000 businesses which, in 1994 alone, generated some $232b in sales world-wide, according to a recent Bank of Boston study.[14]

In Asia, the entrepreneurial movement has also moved onto the campuses. Beijing's famous Beijing University and Tsinghua University both have extensive joint ventures with businesses. The Shanghai Finance and Accounting University also has a joint venture with global accounting firm—Price Waterhouse. Of all these activities, the most visible to date is Founder Group, Beijing University's high-tech venture that is developing the Chinese publishing system. In 1974, Professor Wang Xuan helped develop the publishing system at the University and later patented a method of accelerating the processing of Chinese characters, a key element in Founder's Chinese publishing system, which displaces the cumbersome manual Chinese typesetting operations. The Founder Group today is a publicly listed company on the Hong Kong stock exchange, with an extensive network of distributors and offices throughout China and the world.

Philanthropy and the Economy

While certain business entrepreneurs must work hard to dispel their negative, profit-seeking image, certain sections of the society must, for their part, discard the notions that profit is immoral and capitalism is bad. The world-wide drive to develop entrepreneurial talents is remaking industries and creating new jobs—thriving economies bear testament to the fact that entrepreneurs are entitled to the respect of the society. If philanthropy means a vibrant economy where opportunities abound for men and women willing and able to work, the businessmen and women who create enterprises are the philanthropists. Millions in tomorrow's Asia need to be able to pin their hopes on them. Asian entrepreneurs must raise their sights from moneymaking to enterprise building. As Stan Shih said, it is about time Asians contribute to the betterment of mankind.

Chapter 7
From Hands to Minds

"Each individual is responsible for
choosing one course of action over another.
It is the choice that gives value to the act,
and nothing that is not acted upon has value."

—Jean-Paul Sartre—

Durian, the king of fruit in Southeast Asia, can now be purchased over the Internet at the click of a mouse. It is a novel idea to buy durian, 'satisfaction guaranteed', in the comfort of one's own home, scrolling through the various grades of quality and price before making one's choice. This thorny and powerful-smelling fruit, loved by locals and adventurous foreigners alike, is usually sold by sweaty, half-naked roadside fruit sellers who speak no English. Durian is the first fruit to be sold in cyberspace, so the advertisements claim. Durian is now part of electronic commerce: the local entrepreneur runs a successful trade where buyers send in orders complete with credit card and delivery address details, and the fruit is then delivered by a distributor. This happens not in Palo Alto or Boston Route 128, but in Singapore. Before long, many commodities will be marketed like this.

Technology, globalization and advances in science are moving forward at an unprecedented rate, and are making a huge impact on our lives, changing the way we work, learn and live. The money and excitement in the production of goods and services in the next century are going to come from the application of knowledge in the creation, marketing and distribution of existing and new products and services. New and better materials will replace existing ones; new ways of providing service will save valuable time and add quality to our lives. The information age promises to make us more efficient and creative producers, and to increase consumer satisfaction.

While the impact of technology will be felt everywhere, living and doing business in Asia will become especially challenging. The acquisition of skills becomes particularly relevant. For example, just a decade ago, before knowledge jobs become mobile, highly educated Indian engineers and Filipino management graduates could not find jobs in their home countries. Now, editors in Manila and engineers in Bangalore are working for clients all over the world through telecommunications. While the advanced Asian economies will experience the same kind of changes as the West, including changing employment patterns as they restructure, developing Asian economies will be facing stiff competition from each other as they address the need to graduate up the value chain. So, in Asia, two types of economy will be in juxtaposition. These can be likened to the first curve and second curve economies which Dr Ian Morrison, President of the Institute of the Future in Santa Fe, described in his book *The Second Curve.*[1] Morrison makes a distinction between existing economies (which he terms first curve) and new ones (second curve). He suggests that businesses pay attention to the different characteristics of each curve to reach an understanding of them and to learn how to manage the transition involved.

Asian individuals and companies must know the status of their skills and their organizations: do they belong to the first curve or second curve? Are they about to exit the first curve and enter the second? What preparations are needed to make the transition? Except for Japan, South Korea, Taiwan and Singapore, most factories in Asia made labor-intensive products such as electronic parts and toys to the specifications of multinational companies, using imported technology and machinery under the management of expatriates. In other words, the working class in Asia formed the hired hands. Labor-intensive manufacturing now faces two possibilities: the multinationals will move closer to their final markets, or will move to where the production costs are lower.

For manufacturing workers in industrialized Asian communities, such as Singapore, Hong Kong, Taiwan and even Malaysia, the process of moving up the value chain from labor-intensive to high tech and high value will continue at varying rates. To achieve long-term sustainable growth, it is necessary for the companies in these economies to produce high-quality, world-class products. As the service sector expands due to increasing domestic consumer demand, the restructuring of economic activities will intensify. This all underlines the importance of an educated, knowledgeable workforce. If the battle of the next century is to be won by brainpower, it follows that the greater the store of knowledge a community possesses, the more competitive it will be. As Asia moves from hands to minds in its progress up the value chain, the single most important challenge facing individuals, companies and governments is the effective transformation of labor from a mere factor in production into a generator of value, a storehouse of intellectual capital.

Table 7.1: First and Second Curve Economies

First Curve		*Second Curve*
	Market	
Capital		Knowledge
Producer		Consumer
Atlantic		Pacific
Japan		China
International Trade		Electronic Commerce
Computer		Internet
Money		People
	Organization	
Mechanistic		Organic
Engineering		Ecology
Corporations		Individuals and Networks
Horizontal and Vertical Integration		Virtual Integration
Business Processes		Culture
	The Individual	
Hard Work		Hypereffectiveness
Security		Uncertainty
Current Career		Future Career
Faith		Hope
Loyalty		Courage

New Technologies

Engineers have always been problem solvers, and in the future, they will be the ones building the new infrastructure, the global information network, as well as the tools we need to access it. Technology is ubiquitous: it is where we work, where we learn and where we live. In the 21st century, the jobs in the new economies of urban Asia will require new skills. Being a latecomer is not always a disadvantage: in a world driven by rapid technological change, latecomers have the opportunity to move ahead, if they are aware of what is happening. As our young people leap-frog from labor-intensive to high-technology industries, they bypass one whole era of development. They move from the industrial era straight into a world of computers, networks and ideas. They also have the advantage of not having to unlearn the habits of the older workers.

There are two aspects here. First, we must closely examine the skills that the information age requires, and start now to build the institutions and the infrastructure that will deliver them. Second, we must now begin to abandon the old culture, framework and organization of the industrial era, which could become a burden on us in the future. As science and technology will increasingly play a central role in our lives, mastery of them is essential. The two main scientific areas are information technology and biotechnology: both will have a great impact on human lives in the coming century.

Information technology

It has been predicted that in the 21st century, we will spend most of our time in front of a screen of some kind: some go so far as to say that just surfing through hundreds of television channels and the Internet could take up to eight hours a day! The point is that information technology is already part of our daily lives. Any service that can be digitized and transmitted, such as electronic banking and electronic commerce, can be produced and marketed. The speed of data transmission increases daily, as a result of improved modems and communication networks. Internet usage continues to spiral upwards: some industry analysts forecast that, just after the turn of the century, some one billion people will have access. Countries are already linked through satellite systems that provide cellular, paging and wireless data transmission world-wide.

Whole new industries will spring from cheap communications, as services such as design, data processing and marketing are subcontracted around the world. The impact of the Internet is also being felt in the executive-search field. For certain categories of executive, electronic searches through the Internet are speeding up the pace of recruitment. 'It is now much easier, not just cheaper, to recruit trained computer operators and programmers in Bombay than it is in London,' said Dr Anne Julius, chief economist for British Airways.

The century of biology

The winner of the Nobel Prize for chemistry in 1996, Robert F. Curl of Rice University said that while the 20th century was the century of physics and chemistry, 'It is clear that the next century will be the century of biology'.[2] The 21st century came early. In February 1997, a 52 year-old Scottish embryologist, Ian Wilmut, stunned the world by announcing that he and his team at the Roslin Institute near Edinburgh in Scotland had created an exact copy, a clone, of an adult Dorset sheep, by the name of Dolly. Now a team at the University of Massachusetts hopes to produce offspring with altered genetic material, originally derived from a mature animal's cell. Eventually, this technology could produce healthier breeds of livestock, animal organs which can be used for transplants, and milk from cows which contains human hormones. Suddenly, mind-bending consequences become possible. Improvements in sheep and cattle farming would be only the beginning. If the cloning of humans ever becomes a reality, ethical questions aside, the possibilities can only be guessed at.

Dolly's entry into the world is only a tip of the iceberg in the field of biology. Science is on the brink of an explosion in its ability to understand and manipulate life. Until recently, researchers searched painstakingly for genes: it took 10 years to identify the cystic fibrosis gene, at a cost of over US$150m. Isolating one obesity gene took a decade. However, now gene sleuths are approaching from the other direction and are deciphering the entire genetic code (known as genome) of organisms. Scientists hope to be able to draw up complete blueprints of every living thing from nematodes and mustard plants to mice and men by the first decade of the 21st century all neatly catalogued in computer databases.

The effects of this ground-breaking research could go beyond biology. Some scientists believe that the century of biology will usher in a new era in electronics, and research is being conducted into the potential of gene splicing and genome engineering for computing. The lure of genes as the basis for computation is that the twisting helixes are jam-packed with information far more intensively than on the densest microchip. Chips can do only one thing at a time, whereas a DNA can theoretically do 100 million billion things at once. There is still a long way to go, however, before DNA replaces silicon. Companies working in the field of biotechnology are attracting a great deal of attention from both Wall Street and the large pharmaceutical companies. The latter are competing fiercely to be the first to identify the genes involved in such devastating diseases as diabetes, cancer, Alzheimer's disease and schizophrenia.

Although biotechnology is in its infancy in Asia, Taiwan and Singapore are both nurturing it. In Singapore, companies could rent laboratory space and equipment in the Incubator Unit of the Bioprocessing Technology Centre (BTC), run by the National Science and Technology Board (NSTB) at the Singapore Science Park II. It is one of the ways in which the Republic is building up its life sciences cluster, which comprises the pharmaceutical, biotechnology and health-care industries. Last year, this cluster grew by 10 per cent, with a total output of US$2.2b. The NSTB hopes that, by providing the basic infrastructure to cutting-edge research efforts, it can attract the sort of projects which will make Singapore a world leader in high value-added research and development.[3] Dr Lily Chan, the deputy director of BTC, said:

> Here, firms get the much-needed technology support services, an infrastructure, which [if they were] left on their own, small and medium-sized biotech companies cannot afford because of high start-up costs.

Infotech: Its Impact on the Economy

Information technology, infotech, is giving birth to a new economy where bits replace atoms as the primary building blocks.[4] The word 'infotech' primarily implies computing capabilities combined with telecommunications and networking; it also includes expert systems, imaging, automation, robotics, sensing, technologies, and mechatronics (microprocessors embedded in products, systems, and devices). These interconnected technologies are moving out of the office into our everyday lives, whether we work on a farm, in an office, a factory, a hospital or a classroom. Unfortunately, while infotech will bring about positive changes, including making many jobs more challenging and rewarding, it may also lead to job loss, a sense of depersonalization and boredom. It is already causing massive shifts in infrastructure, some believe greater than those of the industrial revolution.

An interesting example of how infotech can give you the competitive edge in marketing occurred with the launch of Netscape Navigator, an Internet browser. Instead of going through the traditional retail or reseller distribution channels, Netscape released the commercial version of Navigator on-line. Anyone interested could download an 'evaluation copy' at no charge, try it out and then decide whether to pay US$39 for the fully supported version. The entire downloading process only takes two minutes. Contrast this with most major software releases, where delays are common while thousands of trial copies are tested and feedback collected and analyzed (Netscape does this on its home page on the Web and feedback comes at the click of a mouse). Within four months of its release on the Internet, Netscape's success was apparent: with neither advertising nor sales in retail outlets, a stunning six million copies of Netscape Navigator were already in use.

What other revolutions can infotech bring about? The power of connectivity, speed and efficiency has the potential to redefine the way we live, learn and work. Infotech will be the driving force behind changes in lifestyle and organizational structure; it will not just make the world a borderless one, it will also erase boundaries between industries and change the kind of relationship we have with customers and colleagues. For example, it is very difficult to draw lines between the insurance, mutual fund and banking industries any more. But if we assume that high technology will take over completely, we are making a fatal mistake. As futurist John Naisbitt observed, 'Understanding the interplay between high tech and high touch, ie, the co-evolution of technology and culture, will hold the key to success for business in the information economy'.[5] The new economy born out of the changes wrought by technological revolution will also reinforce humanity's spiritual quest.

A new way of working

The content of traditional jobs has already changed. For example, farmers today use electronic sensors and controls to analyze soil condition, fertilizer mix and moisture content, and to check on plant health and the degree of ripeness of crops. Biotechnology is already producing new clones of fruits and vegetables, and whoever possess the best seeds calls the shots. Those who still think that farming is a very low-tech and labor-intensive occupation are in error.

Police and security officers in some advanced cities are now armed with on-the-spot information. They can plug in to a centralized database system, instead of, for example, having to search door to door. DNA samples are used extensively in evidence. Doctors and scientists can team up and work from different locations. Expert systems enhance the physician's skills by providing data during complicated procedures as well as routine diagnoses. Teachers and textbooks are no longer the sole sources of knowledge, now that students can access databases at the click of a mouse; in many cases, the teachers will be learning with the students. These days, the role of teacher is moving into the area of counsellor and motivator.

Needless to say, in manufacturing, more and more technology will be deployed. Just as an example, the number of people employed in manufacturing in the United States has dropped significantly (from some 65 per cent in the 1950s to around 11 per cent today). Instead of decreasing, however, the total value of manufacturing output has been increasing as the GDP grows, staying at around 22 per cent of GDP. Mastering technology and being computer literate also means being better organized. Everyone has to learn how to master modern tools if they are to be effective, productive and creative. For example, if you run a networked organization, you must have team members who are familiar and comfortable with computers and electronic technology such as e-mail and voice messaging; you don't need people who are still nervous of leaving messages on a machine.

Telecommuting is growing all over the world. It is estimated that, by the turn of the century, some 50 million people will be working from home in the western world. Asians who are currently devoting resources to building offices and other infrastructure to bring people together to work must study this trend carefully, as telecommuting has the potential to revolutionize their business. I visited IBM's office in Singapore and toured their flexi-office. While it can only accommodate 30 staff members at a time, it is serving up to 90 flexi-teleworkers. Imagine what this can do to overheads, productivity and the bottom line.

A bleak future for the unskilled

Industrial era skills rapidly become obsolete in the information age. This is one of the reasons for unemployment. The findings of a study carried out by Oren Levin-Waldman, an economist at Bard College in the United States, revealed that long-term unemployment was higher among people with college and postgraduate degrees.[6] While those who are educated generally have the ability to learn new skills, those with neither education nor skills are destined to be society's underclass. 'Even the domestic help today must know how to operate the high-tech household appliances in modern homes,' said an Asian executive. Another study carried out by *The Economist* suggests a widening wage gap between those with a college education and those who don't attend college. It reported:

> In 1979, the average American male college graduate earned 49 per cent more than a high-school graduate; by 1993, the gap had widened to 89 per cent. The lowest 10 per cent of American men have seen a drop in their real wages of almost 20 per cent since 1980; the top 10 per cent have enjoyed a real pay rise of around 10 per cent.'[7] The situation in Asia is little different. Low-skilled jobs are not just low-paying, they are the ones most vulnerable to displacement by technology.

Both studies clearly indicate that the skills required in the knowledge economy are very different from those offered by conventional education. Twenty years ago, hardly anyone worked in the area of computer software. Today, millions work in the software industry. If a young Malaysian chose a career in biotechnology in the early 1970s, employment opportunities were likely to be limited. But skills in biotechnology are much in demand now as Malaysia moves rapidly up the high-value technology ladder. The opening-up of the Asian economies means that young people have many choices: where they work and live, the type of career they want to train for and the people they want to work with. We are moving from a 'no choice' environment to one that has myriad possibilities. The unskilled, however, are heading for the dinosaur club, and those who are presently skilled but refuse to learn new skills, will soon join them.

For individuals as well as governments, it is important to identify the specialist fields of the future and to acquire the skills needed for leading-edge competency in them. The competition in Asia makes it all the more important for us to look to the future. Failure to anticipate the changing competitive patterns may result in wasted education and unemployment. Hong Kong did not pay enough attention to retraining as the manufacturing sector moved north. As a result, workers trained for the factory floor found themselves redundant in an economy based on information technology and service industry. Rraining and continuing education for the working population should be given emphasis, especially in the more developed Asia undergoing economic restructuring. Singapore is perhaps the region's most pro-learning and pro-active community: Singaporeans are keenly aware of the concept of lifetime employability and constantly update their skills and invest in personal development.

Discriminating Consumers

Consumers today want better products at a reasonable cost. With the huge range of products on the market today, it takes a lot of effort to retain customer loyalty. A product must at least equal its competitors in every respect to be given shelf space. People will not even buy products made in their own countries if they perceive them to be substandard. The fact remains that because world-class products are available everywhere, locally-made products must be of the same standard. That is the message for every employee and company in any part of the world, catering to either a domestic market or overseas markets. Asia's continued prosperity depends on its ability to create products and services the world wants to buy. Whether manufacturing an original product, finishing off an existing one, or providing a distributing and marketing service for the product, the future of Asia lies in its ability to satisfy the demands of today's discriminating consumers.

In some aspects of business, Asians have borrowed the technology from the Western corporation in making products. Workers never had to think or produce new ideas. As a quick way to generate profit, Asian companies just copy. Countless publishing houses in Asia are still lifting pictures and text and printing them as their own without regard to copyright.

Asians have to create in line with global standards. This means taking the best product in the world as a bench-mark and investing in research and development, not only to narrow the gap between their product and the bench-mark but to exceed it. The challenge to reach the top of the value chain means that good design, process engineering, creativity, innovation and diversity will become more important than volume, obedience and systems on the factory floor. It is in good ideas and even better ideas that Asia's hopes for growth in the next century lie.

Discovering needs

There is no point in making the best product of its kind in the world if it can't be sold. Identifying consumer needs and meeting them are equally important. Where and who are the consumers? Young people always create the latest popular culture and form the biggest market for new products and services. Women, who are gaining more and more independence and affluence, as well as retired people will be very important global markets. We need to know them, know what they think, and know how to reach them. Information about potential customers and their lifestyles is vital in the development of new products or services. For example, research into the needs of people traveling on business has led to alliances between the manufacturers of office equipment and hotel chains. Hotel rooms that feature outlets for power, phone jacks for modems, good working lights and ergonomic furniture are proliferating. And, in whichever city you happen to find yourself, there is sure to be at least one Internet cafe where you can surf the Net while sipping a cappuccino.

What would Generation X (those who were born between 1965 and 1981) need? Jay A Conger, executive director of the Leadership Institute of Southern California has been studying Generation X managers and found they share the following traits:[8]

- They need a balance between work and private life: they apparently want to build more traditional families and be more available to their children.
- They desire independence and mobility: X-ers believe you get better salaries and challenges not by waiting patiently to move up the ladder, but by moving between companies. 'The objective for each job is to use it to build skills that will create opportunities for the next job. Loyalty is only to yourself and your team-mates, not to the boss and the company.'
- Fluency with computers: they are the first generation to have grown up with computers and are the first true information-age managers.
- They have a need for the workplace to look like a community.

Free Markets Need Free Minds

The wars of the 20th century saw the creation of new lethal weapons: circumstances and sheer necessity were the driving forces behind their invention. In Asia, one often hears the question, 'Why reinvent the wheel?' which really does describe the state of affairs in the region. We may not have to reinvent the wheel to cope with the present, but we certainly have to participate in the continual search for knowledge to ensure our future survival. Free trade and free markets need free minds. Traditional businesses will have to be run in modern ways; we also need to discover new businesses.

Turning silicon into gold

Microsoft's Windows operating system probably runs on most of the world's personal computers. However, Microsoft is far from being the only winner of gold in the new digital economy: from 1983 to 1995, database company Oracle Corporation grew from 35 employees to 24,000 employees, with revenues to match. The success of Netscape's Navigator is also well-documented. In Silicon Valley, a large number of the world's biggest electronics and software companies have taken root. In 1996, 11 companies were established every week in the Valley, and every five days, a company went public. Many of these companies often began with little start-up capital. What really counts in Silicon Valley is how smart you are.

Taking risks

Back in 1938, Professor Frederick Terman of Stanford University loaned US$538 to two of his students, William Hewlett and David Packard, to produce an audio-oscillator. From there began Hewlett-Packard and a Valley legend. What is behind the success of Silicon Valley, which has a market value that is about the same as the whole of the French stock-market?

American romantic entrepreneurialism lends itself to taking risks, testing out ideas and, of course, creating wealth. Of course, one major advantage the Valley enjoys is the non-stop cross-fertilization of ideas. People exchange ideas and fund start-ups, always finding the best way to get things done. Computer experts and venture capitalists alike have to be daring. Successful enterprises are mainly the result of small start-ups by individuals and not by established big players. It was the venture capitalists who saw their potential and funded them.

Encouraging talent

In Silicon Valley, your talent matters most. It does not matter how old you are, where you come from or where your grandfather was born. Palo Alto is home to over 100,000 technologically competent Asians and Europeans. The way work is organized is democratic. 'It's a network, as opposed to a hierarchy,' said venture capitalist L John Doerr, 'and it's rooted in a terrific educational system'. Indeed, the Valley owes a lot to its neighboring universities, especially Stanford University, which attracts both domestic and foreign talent. At Stanford, technical excellence blends with entrepreneurship. It's commonplace for faculties or students to start up their own company.

Most Valley companies are generous with their share options. The options cost the company nothing in cash but when they are exercised, they are considered an expense according to the US tax code. However, for the technology companies, the idea is not to shelter income but to share wealth. Options are what attract and keep talented executives, engineers and salespeople, and many companies eventually extend options to all their staff. For those enterprises just starting out, it is a way to keep salary costs down and earnings up, because employees are willing to work at a lower salary if options are available. Another bonus is that realized options can fuel more start-ups and foster more economic growth.

A Paradigm Shift in Asia

For Asia to get even close to what is going on in Silicon Valley, a paradigm shift needs to take place. We have to define more accurately what we mean by labor; there must be recognition that labor is no longer a dispensable factor of production but a value-generating entity. Traditionally, human resources functions in most Asian companies are merely administrative. They cover recruitment, welfare, union matters, discipline, retirement and terminations, but they have not been recognized for the contribution they can make to the strategically important matter of training for the future. Hiring and training to meet future needs are pivotal to survival, let alone prosperity.

In December 1996, Leif Evindson, director of the Skandia Future Centre, told me about his company's plans for the future. The 140-year-old Swedish insurance company, Skandia Group, is planning its future strategies from a prosperous present; its 1995 revenues exceeded US$7b. Skandia has built a Future Centre in a sprawling villa some 40 minutes from Stockholm, where a carefully selected group of 30 people of all ages from around the world are gathered. These people, possessed of a great depth of knowledge, work in teams that investigate the five driving forces of the business environment, ie the European insurance market, demographics, technology, the world economy, organization and leadership. They then present their vision of the future to Skandia's corporate council, the company's 150 senior executives.

The human resources issue will move sharply into focus in the years ahead, not only as a response to the acute shortage of the skills Asia desperately needs, but also because of the urgent need to align technology upgrades and management reform with the existing work culture. If any significant advances are to occur, there must be a fundamental shift in mind-set, from a perception of labor as merely a factor of production to a perception that it is a source of intellectual capital. The implications of this change in mind-set are tremendous, as they will lead to the redesign of the compensation system, a redesigned working environment, new supervision and leadership styles, focused training and development and intellectual property protection. 'If people start to treat me as a human being and respect my profession, that will be progress,' said Asian-American architect Calvin Tsao. 'Hierarchy perpetuates the class mentality, and equality is not a value in traditional Asian practices. Even professionals are merely looked upon as hired hands, and not respected as human beings.'

Recognition is a basic human need. If Asian societies continue in the hierarchical old way of master and servant relationships, there is the danger that their creative energies will continue to flow to the West. I often wonder whether talented Asian-Americans like Calvin would be as creative if they were living and working in Asia. The working environment must allow talent; the United States especially allows the individual great freedom for creativity. While in the United States, freedom and respect for the individual are taken for granted, in China, the individual has until very recently been suppressed. Asians, especially the Chinese, don't talk about or celebrate their individual successes because they fear that the 'big tree draws in the wind'. Children are more often rebuked than praised for their creative endeavors. Modesty also holds people back.

An Educated Work-force

The determinant of success in the competitive community will be the educational system. Silicon Valley and Route 128 in Boston have become centres of excellence in the high-tech industries because of the high concentration of well-qualified people there. A review of the educational attainments of Asian countries indicates that tremendous work lies ahead. Current figures show that 7.2 per cent of university-age Malaysians are enrolled in local tertiary institutions, compared with 35.8 per cent from the same age group in Argentina, 54.8 per cent in South Korea and 79.7 per cent in the United States. Every country wants to increase the numbers of its citizens that are educated: Malaysia aims to have 40 per cent of its university-age citizens studying at tertiary level by 2020. While much of developed Asia has the education infrastructure in place, some 50,000 Malaysians, comprising 20 per cent of Malaysian tertiary students, studied overseas in 1995, at great cost to the country.

Education in Thailand already receives a huge resource allocation, which is set to increase further as the government extends compulsory education from six to nine years. Limited capacity is a problem in developing Asia; in Thailand, 200,000 high-school graduates competed for 20,000 places in the State-run universities.

Meeting the needs of industry

To catch up with the educational standards of the developed world, most East Asian economies, even Hong Kong and Singapore, will probably need several more decades. Education is not only about how to make learning more widespread, it is also about updating curriculum, changing the way things are taught and improving the thinking, judgement skills and confidence of students. School curriculum must be tailored to the needs of industry, taking into account changing global economic and technological trends. Parents, teachers and government planners need to examine the relevance of the skills and knowledge taught today in the future. Most Asian schools spend much time and resources on things past, dwelling on principles and static knowledge that students will find of little use later on. The learning method focuses on achieving excellent results in examinations, rather than producing students with imagination and analytic skills, needed by the information economy. We need to review the educational system.

Asia as a region seems to suffer from a mismatch of skills and economic opportunities. However, China and India have the highest number of skilled and technical personnel. China is in a position to dominate manufacturing in Asia due to the large numbers of technically and scientifically trained people in its work-force. The annual output from India's institutions of higher learning is staggering: it produced over 40,000 engineers in 1992, and annually it produces about 70,000 diploma-holders and 300,000 certificate-holders.

Miron Mushkat, chief economist for Asia Pacific at Lehman Brothers, pointed out that the Tigers of East Asia will start to face structural constraints if they don't educate their work-force better, start investing more in research and development and become more receptive to skilled foreign workers. Southeast Asia will be increasingly technologically constrained by the meagre output of its educational institutions and the consequent scarcity of skilled workers. Although Asian firms are acquiring Western technology companies, East Asia largely remains an importer of technology. While this has, so far, not adversely affected technological progress, such heavy dependence on outside sources for innovative ideas could present great difficulties in the future; there could be grave consequences for the development of domestic capabilities and local talent. Two conclusions can be drawn. First, countries that are driven by nationalist impulses and are reluctant to tap into the international pool of skilled workers will not fare well in the technological stakes. Second, a cavalier attitude towards intellectual property rights will have a detrimental effect on the growth of knowledge-intensive industries, because it reduces the incentive to invest in home-grown capabilities and talents.[9]

Learning, knowledge and skills

Teachers, entrusted with the task of imparting knowledge, were revered in traditional Asian societies. Today, some teachers have become so out of touch with the latest developments in their field because of the lack of training and poor compensation that there is simply no motivation for them to update their skills. A vicious circle is thus formed. The generation brought up on television and the Internet knows far more than its poor, inadequate teacher, who still relies on traditional teaching materials; respect for the teacher declines and the teacher becomes even more frustrated.

Teachers will have to assume a new role from the embodiment of knowledge to a guidance counselor. With more and more women going out to work, and more and more families living without the benefit of grandparents, the role of the teaching profession will become even more critical. A young Malaysian writer, Karim Raslan, wrote:

> I may be old-fashioned, but to my mind, the way we treat our educators, teachers and headmasters is a reflection of how we value education in the broader sense. Everyone grovels when the CEO of a public company or a political party

> chief walks in the room: the embodiments of money and power respectively. Nowadays, however, no-one is too concerned about a teacher, the embodiment of education and knowledge.
>
> The contribution of men and women teaching the present generation of schoolchildren is woefully neglected. Sadly, this is where we reveal our fatal weakness, because the education that we receive can only be as good as the people entrusted with that responsibility. Treating them like dirt will help no-one.[10]

The most important issue concerning teachers in the present system is how to create an environment whereby they can continue to develop themselves and to strengthen motivation so that they do not experience fatigue in teaching. Education for the next generation will have to be a partnership between government, businesses, parents and teachers. Everyone is responsible, and to do well, everyone must take an active role. If working parents, especially, could find time to be with students and take on some of the teaching load, their perspective and experiences in the real world would help to bring a sense of reality to the school curricula. If children spend all their learning time in a controlled and simulated environment, how can we expect them to cope in the real world?

If our objective is to have confident and creative children, we must encourage the young to regard the acquisition of knowledge and skills with a more appreciative eye; we need to encourage them to dig deep and not just focus on the money-making aspects of a particular skill. Asian parents are guilty of instilling this 'investment mentality' in their children. When kids are sent to music or painting classes, it is intended that the skills they learn will yield income later on in life. For example, girls are given piano lessons so they can give piano classes themselves after they get married and can remain at home to look after their children. Few Asian parents would invest in nurturing a painter or a musician, as in traditional Chinese societies, these professions are considered to be poverty traps. If one wishes to master a certain body of knowledge or a specific skill, it must be taken seriously, for only in this way can Asia accumulate its own stock of intellectual wealth.

Learning must also be entertaining. It must be a fun experience and not solely one long grind to get a paper qualification. Grading in the school system carries the risk of perpetuating a culture of denial and elimination; it is like telling the kids straight in their faces that the moment they do not measure up, they are finished. Those who are eliminated from higher education carry with them for life a stigma of 'poor performer', their self-esteem destroyed by the education process, instead of being enhanced by it. How can a society advance when the majority of its people are stamped 'poor performer'? The aim of education is not to create second-class citizens, but to help everyone find an opportunity to put their potential to good use. We need to rethink the way we grade our students. Education for the future must help strengthen children's resolve to express their views, to explore the world and share their comprehension of it.

If Asian institutions of learning cannot quickly respond with the appropriate reforms, there is the risk that, inadvertently, a class system will develop. 'Local Malaysian graduates are less expressive,' said Ariffin Mamat, human resources director at Texas Instruments Malaysia. 'If solicited, they come up with very good opinions. But they tend to agree with the person in charge.' Ariffin also commented that if encouraged, local graduates can come out of their shells; but that he takes pains to prod locally educated applicants to see what they have to offer. Perhaps, for example, the question Malaysia should ask is: why should it be left to multinational companies and foreign universities to unlock the creative potential of Malaysian youth?[11] There is also the fact that many Western-trained Malaysians have, upon their return, revert to the old conformist culture. It is a very frustrating and counter-productive experience for both the individual and the community.

A blend of Asian and Western modes will work best. There must be respect for education and teachers, but it should not inhibit curiosity and questioning. Nor should discipline override or suppress creativity and the need to nurture creativity. Above all, students should get more enjoyment out of their educational experiences. Dr Lee Yuen Tze, President of Academia Sineca, is at the forefront of Taiwan's education reforms. To meet the challenges thrown up by Taiwan's fast-restructuring economy, the education reform committee he headed came up with the following recommendations:

- Schools should be places where students find learning fun and enjoyable.
- There should be freedom of expression and an atmosphere of exchange of ideas and debate.

- Authority and control should be relaxed. The head teacher should be elected and not appointed by the ministry. Teachers should be selected by a committee made up of existing teaching staff, parents and administrators, and not be allocated by the central education ministry.
- The main task of teachers in the new education system is to help stimulate students' curiosity, help them to look up resources, analyse and discuss their findings.

Education and the business community

As mentioned, problem would arise if the education system churns out young people with skills and orientations that are not compatible with the needs of business. The only way to rectify this is for business itself to have greater involvement in education. In 1989, the United States government convened a 'Goals 2000' project, whereby each state governor will go to the annual education meeting accompanied by the chief executive of a major corporation from his or her state. IBM for instance, is a prime mover behind this meeting. In an editorial in 1996, *BusinessWeek* applauded the participation of business in the education system, and set out four reasons why businesses should throw their support behind public education.[12]

First, executives should actively help educators and state officials come up with clear and rigorous standards of excellence. If students don't know what's required of them, they won't be motivated to aim higher.

Second, executives should work hard to deflect opposition from political extremists to the adoption of standards.

Third, executives should compel school districts and states to strive for excellence by linking performance measures to hiring decisions.

Finally, companies should take active measures themselves to help finance reform, the adoption of technology, and teacher training through grants, products and volunteer work.

All over the world, businesses are increasingly involved with and supportive of institutions of learning. Their support is no longer confined to contribution of fundings—they are making their core competencies available. School curricula are being enriched by technological know-how and management skills. Staff selected for their business skills are delivering lectures and joining university committees. Stan Shih of Acer Group in Taiwan and Morris Chang, the founder of Taiwan Semi-Conductors (known in Taiwan as the father of semiconductors) are returning to their respective Alma Maters as lecturers. The American company Du Point collaborates with university staff in the development of curricula; Siemens collaborates in the running of educational programs; and Andersen Consulting is experimenting with a school of the future in-house, applying global best practices to the curriculum. In Japan, 47 universities have joined to create a research centre as a regular forum for discussions with academia and industry.

Asian companies are known for their generous financial support of education. Many Chinese entrepreneurs donate an entire school to the community, and businesses are building schools all over Asia. Although such financial support is important, of greater significance for the education of the next generation is the quality of the content of their curricula. Asians who make financial contributions would do well to dedicate some of their funds to the retraining of teachers, to the conduct of research into teaching methods, and to the reforms in education that such research indicates. Funding the software of education may be more important than just providing the physical infrastructure.

Forever a student

Asia is a region full of many rags-to-riches stories of self-made millionaires. Many entrepreneurs did not go to college; some may only have had a few years of primary education, but they are keen learners. School is not the only place to get an education, and if you do go to school, you should never stop learning once you leave. Learning must continue because the restructuring of our economies and the advent of newer technologies means the content of jobs changes. By the time university students graduate, 1/2 of what they learnt in their first year may be irrelevant in their chosen disciplines. In some industries, in five years' time, 1/2 of the blue-collar skills will no longer be needed due to new technology. Change is constant, and the only way to survive is to continue to learn.

In the United States today, continuing education for adults is the fastest growing segment, according to the US Association of Continuing Education. Nearly 1/4 of American adults attend school; approximately 20 million Americans participate in some kind of learning program, part-time, online, or through distance learning.[13] The countries that occupied the top ten places in the world in terms of income in the mid-1890s are more or less the same ones that occupy the top ten places now. One of the reasons is that they keep improving the level of education of their citizens. In many Western countries, large numbers of adults pursue some form of higher education: learning does not stop when you graduate at 22, it continues for life.

New ways of regarding labor, updating skills and retraining are not enough, nor is asking for more investment in our children's or our own education, whether the funding comes from parents, schools or government. Any expenditure on education or training or rehabilitation is purely speculative, there is no guarantee that the output will match the input. No pool of skilled human resources can be created without the personal decision of the individual to participate, work hard and develop skills and comprehension. We don't just need physical infrastructure: what is more important are people who are capable of independent thinking and who can assume responsibility for their own lives. A society that is tightly controlled from the top becomes dependent; people expect the government to look after them, and blame the government when things go wrong. Asian society must move towards a more trusting culture, where people are given the opportunity to decide for themselves and to take responsibility.

The World Loves an Artist

The global economic boom has allowed artists to indulge in their artistic passions as well as live a better life. While the world needs engineers to build machinery and tools, it also needs artists. In the coming century, there will be an explosion of artistic expression and creativity. Writers, musicians, singers, actors, painters, designers and other creative artists, each excelling in their art form and their culture, will find tremendous demand for their interpretations of life.

Sport and other recreational activities will increase in popularity all over the world. Already in Asia, sport is big business. Stadium attendances and television ratings for sporting events have soared, and corporate sponsors are falling over each in the rush to capitalize on the boom. In the Philippines, companies such as beer giant San Miguel and food group RFM have bought into basketball teams and pay between US$1.3m and US$1.9m a year. Each team gets around 48 hours of television exposure a year, and company logos feature prominently on players' shirts. The enthusiasm for sports extends into mainland China. Although still in its infancy, China's Marlboro League shows how much can be achieved in a short space of time. Teams like Jinan now show match receipts in the order of US$150,000 per game. Only a decade ago, Asian sports stars had to keep a day job in order to subsidize their sporting careers. Now, thanks to soaring salaries, generous bonuses and hefty endorsement deals, players like Singaporean footballer Fandi Ahmad and Indonesian badminton champion Susi Susanti can concentrate on staying at the top for as long as they can.[14]

Skills for the New Century

Globalization and technology advances make it necessary for all of us to secure our employment prospects. At certain stages of our lives, perhaps every couple of years, we need to examine where we are in terms of personal development. We need to be fairly ruthless in our self-examination. Our skills and abilities may be adequate for where we are now, but will they be adequate next year, or even next month? Look at yourself, develop your capabilities and market your uniqueness with the kind of intensity and emphasis that companies use to promote brands. I propose that we assemble the following set of personal attributes:

- Develop the skills of a CEO. You need to have the overall picture of the business you are in, and be able to see the wood for the trees. You also need to excel in the detail of your business or profession.
- Build up an enviable reputation. Have a strategy by which your achievements and credentials become known, and ensure that people recognize what you stand for.

- Know yourself. You must know your own strengths and weaknesses.
- Always give of your best. Be effective in everything you do.
- Never lose sight of your goal. Exercise discipline and stay focused.
- Don't follow the herd. Because something has always been done in a particular way doesn't mean it's set in concrete. Don't be afraid to be unconventional.
- Be better and be different. Better doesn't always mean working harder or longer, it means working smarter. If everyone competes at the same level, no-one moves ahead. Set yourself apart from the competition.
- Don't try to work in isolation. You need support, advice and expertise in areas that are important to your success. People who would be pleased to help you include business acquaintances, family, colleagues, mentors and friends.

For a good number of Asian companies, the stock of knowledge, intelligence and technology that they have acquired from the West will stand them in good stead, even if they spend nothing on research and development. However, they urgently need to establish a learning culture so that this expertise can filter downwards in their organizations. Companies that manufacture their own brand-name products for export will be competing globally, and their employees will have to compete with their opposite numbers working in companies in more advanced economies. To meet the global challenge, both organizations and individuals need to develop certain skills and attitudes.

Building trust

Building trust and relationships will take on added significance as we communicate with people we may never see, keeping in touch through cyberspace. Trust and relationships are fundamental to the sharing of ideas and perspectives and will, in fact, become more important as we use more technology in our lives. The freedom and liberation created by technology have not eliminated the human need for support and feedback.

Developing entrepreneurial skills

Whether you work for yourself or for others, you need to be entrepreneurial and take risks if you want the business to continue prospering and to keep your job. Being entrepreneurial means always looking out for new opportunities and ways to maximize value. For example, consider how an existing service or product can be represented or repackaged so that it acquires added value in the new information infrastructure. Also, consider the fact that publishers are cross-selling through multimedia presentation: powerful software allows text and images to be stored and repackaged for output in the form of print, CD-ROM or a Web page. With computers, it is also possible to produce material in more than one language by changing the text component at reasonably low cost.

Maximizing our use of resources

The Internet is a huge database, a huge store of knowledge from which to obtain information and to share research findings. Unlike a library, the Internet is always open. Now we need not go through the agony of acquiring knowledge that has no immediate application; we only need to know where to find it when we need it. It is enormously rewarding and productive to learn how to exploit the Internet: the networks one can belong to, and the many sites where specialized as well as general knowledge can be found. However, we must also develop new skills to handle the information we receive from different sources and in many formats. The way in which information is treated, formatted, presented, and quite possibly, the way consumers are affected by it is subject to distortion. For example, just as advertising has been accused of manipulating the perception of consumers, modern media can be equally guilty. Commenting on the effect that live coverage of the Gulf War was having on Americans, the media analyst Jeff Greenfield wrote in 1991:

> We watch almost hypnotically and yet we watch with a growing sense of frustration, a hunger to hear every fragment of information linked with the knowledge that much of what we learn we will unlearn in the next half hour.[15]

In the multimedia world, we take items from newspapers and magazines, which rely on linear thinking, and transmogrify them into what is essentially a non-linear video program, such as the CD-ROM format or the world wide web, complete with image and sound. Users simultaneously receive text, images and sound, and it is sometimes hard to distinguish between fact and fiction.

Choosing and discriminating

There is an information explosion out there. There is so much information yet so little time in which to absorb it. To be able to take just what we need, we must have a credible network of good information sources. Gathering information today is very expensive, and in time, only the very best will prosper in the market. For quality decision-making, one has to know and have access to sources of information of the highest quality.

Today, we need the ability to discriminate and to sort out the sheer mass of information to obtain what is useful to us. The new media forms will also affect traditional critical thinking skills. Before the advent of television, when the print media was the main vehicle for news, information and entertainment, we could read the assertions of writers and take time to evaluate them for their veracity. The same was true of print advertising: claims could be made and we could ponder their logic and decide whether or not to believe the message. Telling the difference between truth and untruth is not always easy, but it did seem easier when we had more time to consider. Now we are subject to a multitude of fleeting images that are on the screen for only seconds or even fractions of a second. It is now harder to tell the difference between lies and truth.

How can we educate ourselves so as not to be misled? When every form of important public discourse was a product of the printing press, it made sense to educate our students in logic, rhetoric and semantics. Today's world, however, is driven by the electronic media, and this earlier type of education, while still useful, is no longer adequate. We need to understand modern television techniques; we need to know how video images are made and how they can be altered to make us see things that do not really exist. We need to know how we absorb knowledge so we can better understand the ways in which moving images and sounds affect us, and how different these ways are from the way in which we absorb information presented in a purely linear way, as on the printed page. The new ways in which information is being presented—hotlinks in web sites are just one—add up to a new form of literacy.

If we are not to be illiterate, we must educate ourselves in the ways in which information is disseminated through the electronic media, and consider it with informed, critical minds. For example, in countries where election campaigns have immense television coverage, viewers tend to choose their candidates solely on the basis of how they present in front of the cameras. The carefully manipulated and edited visual imagery that appears on the television screen has a powerful effect. We owe it to ourselves to understand how the media control the form that information takes, and how that information is targeted and disseminated.

Developing expertise in language and culture

Mastering languages is an important skill for success in an open new Asia and the global village. If more than one major language is learned, it should be English. English is needed to sell and to learn from the world; it is the language of the Web and the official medium of the global economy. In the race to become the high technology centre of Asia, Taiwan may be disadvantaged compared to Singapore, the Philippines and India in terms of English language skills. Mandarin, however, is very useful not only in mainland China, but also in Southeast Asia. Mastering Mandarin will help to unlock the wisdom of an ancient civilization and is certainly worth the effort. It will certainly be very useful if you have the capacity to learn more Asian languages, as they will enhance your cultural skills.

If you want to be a mobile global worker, fluency in more than one language and culture is essential. Understanding culture, being sensitive and knowing when to be respectful is a prerequisite for someone who wishes to serve a global audience. People who are brought up in homogenous societies such as Taiwan may have to make greater adjustments compared to, say, Singapore, which is more heterogeneous and cosmopolitan.

Communicating effectively

The ability to communicate effectively can often mean the difference between success and failure. Effective communication today is no longer confined to print or voice. In this age of digital image and satellite television, the effective communicator must learn to work with different media and learn new skills in communication through electronic media. Malaysian fast-food chain Sugar Bun conducts staff training and corporate development using a series of humorous cartoons!

Business is a large rhetorical arena. From simple retail sales spiels to carefully controlled boardroom presentations, speech keeps the wheels of commerce turning. Good speakers make good impressions, and a good speaker is always in demand. Whether the event is a business convention or a presentation, the speaker who goes down well not only adds to the occasion, but also gains respect and credibility.

Working in teams

No one person can be skilled and experienced in every aspect of a business or an industry: The global economy is far too complex for that. Even though you can work very effectively on your own, the demand for specialized skills and the competition require that you work well with a first-class team.

Bill Miller, the head of research and development for the US-based office equipment company Steelcase, said:

> You need other people to know things. You have to share with other people. Two people, working together, learn things faster than individuals alone. Pairs solve problems faster than individuals can. That's why the office will persist and grow. Because knowledge aggregation is faster in groups. The office has shifted from a place to work as an individual to a place to work as a group.[16]

Working in networks is very productive: the benefits include better products of a higher quality, a faster time in getting the product to market, and higher returns on the balance sheet.

Breaking out of a confined mind

It is important that we learn to look at issues and things from a new perspective. Nowadays, it's not only the office that has a new look, people do, too. In the offices of some new age companies in the United States, a new dress code emerged; many corporate executives are abandoning their pin-stripped shirts and jackets for jeans and T-shirts. Most people know that Microsoft's headquarters is called 'the campus'. At Clifford Selbert Design Collaboration in Cambridge in the United States, astroturf covers the floor in the reception area. Along one wall is a golf practice area and a stack of clubs. Beans bags, neon, disco balls, CD racks and large splashes of red and yellow. The aim is to make the office a place that people can relate to, a place people want to go to and feel they are having fun while they work. Less colourful, perhaps, but equally impressive offices are found all over the world. Some companies have gone to great lengths to accommodate all their staff on the same floor, to make communications easier and to break down the physical and psychological barriers that occur when people are on different floors.

Being innovative

The first interactive museum devoted entirely to news, the Newseum, opened in Washington DC in the United States in April 1997. It occupies 72,000 square feet. Visitors of all ages can become reporters or editors through a computer game that sets up sources and settings for a story as well as the newsroom of *The Daily Mirror*. You can act out the role you selected, sports announcer or news anchor, and later buy the video of yourself in action. The concept of the Newseum was developed over five years of consultation between people involved in the media news executives, television producers, writers, editors, broadcasters and historians.

Museums have long peddled postcards, posters and books, usually in a small shop off the entrance lobby. Recently, in recognition of the public's appetite for art and culture, museums in New York and elsewhere have broadened their merchandising efforts. From developing and selling products based on the collection in the museum, they are expanding their retail spaces into stores elsewhere, and selling products wholesale to other outlets. The New York Metropolitan

Museum of Art, a pioneer in the successful coupling of art and commerce, has opened 14 stores in the United States in the last decade, and 19 more overseas through licensing agreements. As the merchandising departments of museums grow more sophisticated, they have begun to bring in staff who have backgrounds in retailing. The range of products is diverse, from scarves, neckties and jewellery to cocktail napkins, compact discs, tableware and toys. With museums showing strong sales growth, it was only a matter of time before the concept of art-inspired gifts crossed over to into the mainstream retail sector. The Museum Company, founded in 1989, began with a single store in Arlington, Virginia. Today, there are 78 stores, including nine in the New York area alone.

Use your Uniqueness as Leverage

You know you are unique. It is your uniqueness that makes you distinctive and sets you apart from others. Share that with the world—tell the world what you stand for and how can it benefit from what you and your company's network have to offer. In order to go from hands to minds, you must always ask yourself the question: 'What can I do to add more value and meaning to the community I am dedicated to?' If you subscribe to the belief that business exists to create a product or service for the satisfaction of its customers, and if you always have this belief as your guiding light, the investment in your own uniqueness will constantly reward you.

Part III

Good Governance

Chapter 8
From Powerful Leaders to Empowering Leadership

"Here lies a man who attracted better people
into his service than he was himself."

—Andrew Carnegie—
(the motto he wished to have on his tombstone)

Heroes influence the minds and lives of others. Great leaders help others in their search for truth and wisdom, and help them get it right. I like to view the heroes and great leaders of this world through this prism: leaders are men and women whose work has made a difference in the lives of humanity; heroes are those whose personalities and charm mesmerize us. Leaders can be heroes, but not all heroes make great leaders.

The rising expectations of the masses, combined with the complexities of today's world, are challenging the skills of many modern leaders. For centuries, a leader has always been regarded as one who radiates glory, power and omnipotence; one who always has the ideal solution. These days, the awe in which leaders have traditionally been held is vanishing—we have finally come to the realization that leaders don't necessarily have all the answers.

With this change in the public perception of leadership, men and women in traditional leadership positions will have to adjust. They will have to cope with an increasingly educated, information-rich and demanding public, clamoring for more autonomy and an environment that encourages creativity. In other words, powerful leaders need to be empowering; they must devolve responsibility to others, and distribute their power. For tomorrow's leaders, the more empowering they are, the more powerful they will become.

The transition from the old model of command-and-control to empowerment is in progress, although there are no alarm bells to show the happening of this bottom-up movement. Deng Xiaoping's leadership in mainland China was significant, and will probably go down in Chinese history as a landmark, the first break in leadership style from the 'powerful' to the 'empowering'. With the world moving to a new architecture defined by telecommunications, information, globalization, trade and open competition, top-down leadership will become obsolete.

The Story of the Paramount Leader

When China's paramount leader Deng Xiaoping came to power in 1978, China was desperately poor. Sixty per cent of its population lived on less than a dollar a day. Reform unleashed tremendous energy from the grassroots and launched China on a high growth curve. Between 1978 and 1995, China's foreign trade increased from US$36b to US$300b.[1] Per capita income doubled between 1978 and 1987, and doubled again between 1987 and 1996. Every nine years, income doubled, a rate almost unheard of in modern history. (By comparison, Britain took 60 years to double its per capita income; the United States, 50 years.) Deng lifted more than 200 million people out of poverty in just two decades.

Deng was already 74 when he finally assumed the leadership. In 1992, when he went on the famous *Nanxun* (tour of the south), he was 88. During the tour, commenting on the opposition to change put up by a number of elderly Party officials, he said that old age made people stubborn, and if such people could not show more flexibility and openness in their thinking, then they really ought to 'go to sleep'. In spite of the great turbulence of his political career, he stayed true to his belief that what matters most is the welfare of the majority of the people.

Deng Xiaoping died in February 1997, aged 93. President Jiang Zemin, in a moving eulogy, described Deng's 'three rises and three falls' as a metaphor for most of China's 20th century history. Repeated downfalls did not diminish the man's fervor for reform or shake his conviction that a new China must be built.

He was unconventional, ignoring the conflict of ideologies. 'Ideologically, I must confess that not only have I not raised high the banner of Mao Tse-tung thought, but I have not even lifted this banner up. Recent events have revealed me as an unreformed petite-bourgeois intellectual who failed to pass the tests posed by socialism.' He made this admission in October 1966 while under attack as a 'capitalist roader'.[2] He set China on course to create a capitalist economy within a communist political system and turn it into a major force in the global economy. 'If today we still do not set about the task of improving the socialist system, people will ask why it cannot solve problems which its capitalist counterparts can,' he said in a 1980 party speech.[3]

He was in favor of economic incentives. 'If they've acquired it through their own labor and not corruption, it's entirely appropriate. Those who are lazy and unenthusiastic should suffer.' He favored education and incentives over ideology and pressure. As long as the Party remained in control, whatever worked economically was more or less right with him. Results were what counted. Deng wanted to create a wealthy and powerful China, not a utopian or messianic paradise. It was a straightforward decision. 'I have two choices. I can distribute poverty or I can distribute wealth.' He had seen enough of the former under Chairman Mao.[4]

What was remarkable was when Deng finally passed away, neither a nervous Hong Kong, awaiting the handback to China, nor the economy on the Mainland, registered so much as a tremor. It was unprecedented in Chinese history that with the passing of a paramount leader at the end of a dynasty, the 'sky did not change'! Instead, Deng left behind in the hearts of the Chinese people a seed of hope, a promise that if each and every one of them collectively worked towards it, they could bring the good life to a people and a nation that, since the beginning of the Chou dynasty, had suffered some 2,917 years of war, civil strife, instability, poverty, impoverishment and humiliation.

Deng was an unusual man with unusual talent—he gave people what they wanted. A Shanghai newspaper reported a little-known fact that, while the young Deng was in Paris in the early 1920s, he opened a restaurant called the China Bean Curd Shop:

> The bean curd was good, the restaurant was a success, and Deng expanded his menu and his seating space. His early business experience had come to serve him well providing something of quality that people actually want to buy ... that melding, more or less, is just what Deng sought to accomplish during his two decades as China's paramount leader.[5]

An ordinary yet extraordinary man

Deng's life and leadership style had the effect of breaking many taboos, and introducing new concepts to the Chinese people. He boldly pointed out that 'Truth should only be sought from facts, and not shrouded by awe of the leader or tradition.' Deng's leadership style was characterized by two things: he never lost sight of the fact he was one of the people, and no matter what happened, he never deviated from his determination to get it done and do it right. His stature came from impeccable revolutionary credentials. He studied in France in his teens, where he became a communist and struck up a friendship with Zhou Enlai, who later became the Chinese premier. Back in China, Deng became a guerrilla leader in China's bloody civil war and participated in the Long March, and fought against the Nationalists and the Japanese occupation forces. After the founding of the People's Republic of China in 1949, Deng was summoned to the national leadership in 1952, and became a vice-premier two years later. After the failure of the Great Leap Forward, Deng and President Liu Shaoqi in 1961 devised a plan to revive the economy by introducing individual incentives. Unfortunately, this plan was ahead of its time. A power struggle was followed by the Cultural Revolution, which set China back one whole generation.

In the turmoil, Deng was purged and branded a 'capitalist roader'. He spent several years working in a tractor factory in Jiangxi province. In 1973, Deng was rehabilitated and returned to Beijing to resume the post of vice-premier. Mao viewed Deng as the only man capable of taking over the day-to-day affairs from Premier Zhou Enlai, who was ill and dying. But in 1976, when Zhou finally died, and as Mao's strength began to wane, a leftist group called the Gang of Four purged Deng once again. Only after Mao died in late 1976 and the Gang of Four was swept from power was the way clear for Deng's ascendancy.

Deng first changed the Party's priorities. Contrary to Mao's thoughts, Deng said that the class struggle was no longer a top priority: the most urgent problem was the design of the socialist system. Deng's slogan, 'No matter whether the cat is white or black, as long as it catches mice, it is a good cat', hinted at his adoption of some capitalist principles.[6] At first, he went slowly. Agricultural reforms that effectively disbanded collective farming were introduced, spurring vigorous cultivation and raising productivity. By the mid-1980s, Deng had turned his attention to industry. With roughly 2/3 of the manufacturing sector still owned by the State, changes were cautious. Reforms were initially trialed: a textile plant might be permitted to tie pay raises to profits, or a soap factory could reduce the influence of party cadres.[7] Deng also slowly opened China to the world, conscious that he needed foreign help to achieve economic reform. Politically, to allow foreign investment was a tricky move, but he persisted. Under Deng, the Sino-Japanese Friendship Treaty was signed and diplomatic relations with the United States were consolidated. China started to encourage foreign businessmen to invest, establishing several special economic zones (SEZs) around the coast of China. SEZs suffered relatively little from government red tape and attracted a lot of foreign capital.

The SEZs are a Dengist reform that have had a huge impact on the performance of China's economy and on the views of its people. The nation's first four SEZs were created in 1979—the Zhuhai, Shenzhen, Xiamen and Shantou SEZs—and were experiments in industrial reform. In 1984, Beijing extended to 14 coastal cities, including Shanghai and Tianjin, many of the same liberal, open policies that had hitherto been reserved for SEZs. The economy responded by soaring into runaway inflation. This situation was behind much of the popular discontent in 1989.[8]

A post-Tiananmen pall stalled growth for a while. Many foreign companies, especially American ones, reconsidered their involvement in China. To revive a stagnating economy, Deng introduced greater reforms in Shenzhen, Zhuhai and Shanghai. On a visit to each location, he called for 'bolder reforms' and 'more opening up'. Those who did not support reform, he said, must 'step down'. At first, his remarks were reported only in the Hong Kong press, but once the propaganda machine warmed up, the nation was electrified and economic reform had a new lease of life. From 1992 onwards, China's growth rates led the world.[9]

Leaders of like mind

'Leaders,' Deng once said, 'are men, not gods'. From the moment he assumed power in 1978, Deng was conscious of the need to groom not only a successor to his position, but a whole generation of successors for the country. Thus, he never assumed the top position, whether in the Party or the government. However, the result was to create an anomaly in China: a situation where the people who held power, primarily Party elders, did not carry corresponding titles.[10]

The Party's bureaucracy was his biggest enemy. The officials were too old and were experts only in 'class struggle'. They did not have the experience or the knowledge to be productive. Deng forced all middle and low-level government officials over 60 years old to retire, and replaced them with younger and better-educated people. In the early 1990s, Deng defused a national debate over 'socialism' and 'capitalism' by announcing that what was important was whether something worked, not whether it was ideologically correct. The decision for China to adopt a market economy was something that no other Chinese leader could make. Only Deng, with his enormous personal prestige, was not in danger of being denounced as a traitor to Marxism.

Deng opened China to the world, no simple task for a nation that had been cloaked in secrecy and isolation for three decades. By allowing some 60,000 of China's brightest young people to study in the West, he risked criticism from conservatives and political foes in respect of students who stayed abroad after their studies were completed. He knew that if they returned when conditions improved at home, the know-how they would bring with them would vindicate his decision.[11]

Building a new china

Based on the number of lives he improved, Deng far outdistanced any other leader at any time in history. During his leadership, hundreds of millions of Chinese escaped the bonds of destitution. The World Bank has estimated that in the first 12 years of reform alone, the poverty rate dropped from 28 per cent of the population to 8.6 per cent. Deng's particular outstanding success was in agriculture. After he allowed China's 800 million peasants to farm their own plots and sell their produce in free markets, the nation's agricultural output rocketed from US$90m in 1979 to US$190b 14 years later. During the same period, his industrial reforms reduced the State's control over the nation's enterprises from 80 per cent to 43 per cent.

Table 8.1: Nation on a Roll (China Indicators)

	1978	1995
GDP per capita (in RMB)	376	4,750
Exports (in US$billion)	9.8	149
Foreign investment (in US$billion)	1.7	91.3
Currency reserves (in US$ billion)	0.8	73.6
Steel production (in million tons)	32	96.21
Grain production (in million tons)	305	466.1
TV production (number of sets)	521,100	55,530,000
Cars per 1,000 population	1.4	8.0
Phones per 1,000 population	2	68.5
SOE's share of industrial output	77.6%	36.6%

Source: China Statistical Yearbook

The new-found wealth of ordinary Chinese, together with the economic opportunities created by the reforms, led to a substantial loosening of the Communist Party's control over people's lives. Xiao Zhuoji, a leading economist at Beijing University, said of Deng, 'He transformed the mind-sets of ordinary Chinese'. The world, and particularly neighbors in Asia, felt much more comfortable with Deng's pragmatism than with a leader motivated by radical ideology and the export of revolution.[12]

Though he overhauled his country's economy, Deng left its anachronistic political system virtually intact. Some observers think that Deng missed his biggest opportunity by not liberalizing the political landscape in tandem with the economy. It will be left to history to judge whether a gradualist approach was right and in the best interests of the situation that then prevailed in China.

Deng has been regularly reviled by the Western media as the man who ordered the killings at Tiananmen—the unforgivable ruthless dictator. He, could, however, be considered a great historical figure who saved 1,200 million people on the brink of disaster—what would have happened to China, and Asia, if the protests in Tiananmen Square had spread into chaos nation-wide? Many people in China and throughout Asia felt that if he had not dispersed the demonstrators, China would have plunged into a worse mess than the Soviet Union, thereby destabilizing the whole region and the entire world. This view is, of course, an interpretation of events through the lens of history and suffering. Deng had been through chaos and revolution and recognized the danger signs at Tiananmen. Gorbachev had never experienced a revolution and he did not recognize the signals of impending collapse. Because of Deng, China did not disintegrate. 'China now has the prospect of becoming a huge industrialized nation in 20 to 30 years,' Senior Minister Lee Kuan Yew of Singapore said in 1997.[13]

On Deng's death, power did not merely transfer to Jiang; rather, Communist China experienced a fundamental change in regime. For the first time in China's modern history, collective rule has replaced the strongman.[14] 'We used to complain about Mao and Deng,' says a young Chinese writer in the capital. 'Now we complain about "the Government"; that is the difference.' As historian Paul Johnson so eloquently wrote, 'Who is to judge? There is no logic nor justice in history, only chronology'.[15]

Strong leaders

There is a trap in limiting ourselves to choosing between two options, to making a decision that has an either/or outcome: experience should tell us that it need not be like this. The debate on leadership styles for Asia has in the past focused on a dichotomy authoritarian vs. democratic. Both styles have their strengths according to the context: the times, situations and circumstances of the people vary. When countries and societies are young, there is a greater need for strong direction, whereas when these societies develop, more and more of the responsibility can be shouldered by the community. It is too simplistic and dangerous to assume that all of Asia needs to loosen up immediately: such a course of action could spell disaster for those societies in transition. The important thing is to know when to retain control and when to let go. The Chinese have a saying about this paradox:

> Some leaders are made by the times and trends [such as the democratic leaders in Hong Kong], while others have the power to shape the trends and times [such as the nationalist leaders who fought for independence.

The style and effectiveness of leadership must be relevant to the times and situation of those being led. A number of strong and forceful leaders, dedicated to development, have brought about several decades of good government. Indeed, few Asians will disagree that in a diverse region confronting wide-ranging problems, the only way to harness and unite all this energy is to use an iron grip. Several East Asian countries that have successfully built a modern economy owe much to their strong leaders, whereas others are less fortunate and are still recovering from the damage inflicted on them. Thousands of Filipinos, unable to support their families at home, experience the pain of separation as they leave to work overseas—one of the legacies of the Marcos years.

East and South Asia each provide a contrasting backdrop to a study of leadership, history and culture in Asia. East Asia, often criticized in the West as authoritarian and oppressive, has in the last several decades managed to produce a good economic report card. But India, where 'a jubilee without joy' was celebrated in August 1997 to mark 50 years of independence, is a country still muddling through an archaic and inefficient economic structure. The 20th century has seen the rise and fall of egalitarian idealism embodied in communism and socialism. The information and technological revolution now under way is setting the stage for a new kind of society, one where individuals will have the ability to express themselves in a manner quite unprecedented. The world we are entering will be a very different one—John Naisbitt described it as a place 'Where the traditional dominance of "central mainframes" will give way to networks of powerful PCs'. This opportunity is arriving for the first time in Asia. We would do well to recognize this infrastructure shift and seize the opportunity to 'download' greater personal power to lead more fulfilling lives.

Those of us remaining in traditional leadership positions will feel we have lost control if we do not recognize that a very different role is now demanded of leaders. If we don't adapt, we risk becoming irrelevant. Greater international competition, a more educated and assertive work-force and rising expectations, all interacting in a more transparent environment, will change what people expect of their leaders. Adjustments need to be made on both sides of the leader-follower relationship. The results have the potential to be more stressful, as well as more exciting, than any other social change Asia has experienced.

The shifting base of power

No political, business or community leaders can afford to ignore what's happening in the world. Today's issues and forces are massive and global, be they economic, ethical or environmental. Leaders must have a holistic world-view in addition to the knowledge and expertise to deal with specifics. Because of the transparency created by the global media and by technology, very few political actions go undetected. The electorate at home and the international investing community are just two groups who demand almost immediate disclosure and accountability.

Malaysia's finance minister Tun Daim Zainuddin, said:

> Leaders today must at the outset realize that there are many global trends that are at work that will influence and impinge on their effectiveness and ability to turn their visions into reality ... Another global trend will be the increased consideration for the environment and quality of life, it can be logically expected that issues pertaining to the environment will be in the forefront of public discussion for a larger part of the 21st century ... The information revolution is a revolution in power. There has thus to be a constant and continuous process to acquire new and up-to-date knowledge so as to keep abreast with current developments.[16]

Traditionally, Asians have great reverence for scholars, looking to them to provide direction. However, the modern world is a lot more complicated. Indeed, no leader today has all the answers. Professor Ambrose King of the Chinese University of Hong Kong has said that the world is changing so fast that, to run it, we need to command a wide spectrum of knowledge. Leaders must know about science and technology, ethics and culture, and must also learn from cross-disciplines and from various sectors of the community, including business. Political leadership will subside in importance compared with what scientists and engineers can contribute. Entertainers and creative artists will also have greater influence.

David Ho, named 'Man of the Year' in 1996 by *Time* magazine for his breakthrough work in AIDS research, said:

> I did not realize that young people look upon me as a new role model. When I return to visit Taiwan [where Ho came from], young people say to me that they want to be like me.[17]

Ho's pioneering experiments and his insight set the stage for an enormously productive shift in the treatment of AIDS. In March 1997, the well-known Malaysian architect, Ken Yeang, described to me his innovative eco-friendly design work. He has been working for decades on integrating technology with climatic and cultural considerations in the design of the built environment. His research is helping us to achieve balanced living in Asia's climatic and cultural environment.

Public office: maintaining integrity

The Far Eastern Economic Review observed:

> Across the region, ambitious but ill-conceived privatization programs have attracted allegations of corruption. It doesn't help that the most visible products of reform are usually infrastructure projects such as power plants, roads and telecom services, all involving investments of billions of dollars. Their very scale, added to the often arbitrary manner in which the necessary licences are issued, makes them open to suspicion.[18]

It appears that in Asia, public life has been badly tarnished by corruption and scandal, so much so that many people think that those seeking public office are only trying to enrich themselves. The misconduct of public officials erodes confidence in their values. In a report on corruption, environmental activist and chairperson of the Citizens Party of Hong Kong, Christine Loh, shares the view that public life needs to be reinvigorated. The most effective leaders often come from other areas; for example, candidates who enter politics from business. These people may bring a different perspective with them, a broadness of empathy with different sectors of society, which is crucial. Will we see a different model of leadership in Hong Kong's first chief executive, Tung Chee Hwa. Tung was a reluctant candidate for the job of the chief executive, his personal success has already made him a distinguished member of Hong Kong society and a respected personality in the international community. Tung is widely acknowledged as a man of integrity, and most importantly, being a grandfather, he can be counted on to build a better tomorrow for future generations. Will this combination of motivation and character help bring dignity and nobility of purpose to public life in Asia?

Character is the key that will determine the greatness of tomorrow's leaders. Kanosuke Matsushita, the founder of the Matsushita Group of Companies who died in 1989, is a good example. Asians respected Matsushita for his noble purpose and selfless dedication to the community. Although he is not known for his innovations or spectacular breakthroughs, it was his philosophy that made him so endearing as a leader. The theme that ran throughout his life was growth as a human being, a business person, and a leader. Matsushita developed strategies that set him apart from the competition: he was obsessed with productivity and low costs, he developed innovative marketing techniques, and he introduced after-sales service. In bad times, he insisted on keeping all his employees and set about upgrading his business by placing more emphasis on recruitment standards. He recognized the benefits of having people work in small groups, and that dedication came from working in an entrepreneurial setting. In contrast to the general tendency for employees to lose commitment over time, many at Matsushita felt that they were associated with a noble and just cause. Matsushita's proclaimation that, 'The mission of a manufacturer should be to overcome poverty, to relieve society as a whole from misery, and bring it wealth' is well-known.

Matsushita devoted his great wealth not to the accumulation of villas in France but for the creation of a foundation similar to that established by Alfred Nobel. He also founded a school of government to reform Japan's political system and undertook a number of other civic projects. During his later years, he wrote books on philosophy, researched human nature and prodded his government to do more for its citizens.

Leaders do the 'right' thing

Fundamentally, leaders must do the 'right' thing, regardless of how the outcome will affect their place in history. Their character determines how ready they are in making 'right' but unpopular decisions, and how well they articulate the people's vision. The biggest challenge for future leaders is to help people understand that certain courses of action, though unpopular, are the right ones. It will be a difficult task to help people clarify what it is they really want. Debate will include such issues as what kind of lifestyle has less impact on the environment; how we can spend more time with the family; how we can achieve more community involvement—issues that will, in the end, bring greater meaning into our lives.

Ideas and Idealism

The ancient Chinese scholar Wen Tianxiang had great spirit. Frustrated at the continual oppression on the people and the emperor's rejection of his proposed reforms, he took his own life by jumping into a river. The Chinese revere him as one who was willing to die for his beliefs, and his moving poems are still being recited today. That admiration and respect stem more from their identification with Won than from a sense of helplessness to change the system. Young people do not think much of martyrdom. A young man in Singapore told me, 'If the leaders are effective, they don't even have to take us to war. He surely could have found a better solution to end the conflict than resorting to such a lose-lose strategy.' He is right. Leaders today are judged by results and not by their lofty idealism. The eloquence of John F Kennedy moved the hearts of many young men and women, East and West. The famous line, 'Ask not what your country can do for you, ask what you can do for your country. Ask not what America can do for the world, but what together we can do for mankind' symbolized the ideals of many starry-eyed, good-natured people. There is no denying the great power of worthy ideals, but people's interests today are more localized, more immediate, and more specific.

Li Lu, the young man who was deputy commander of the student demonstrations in Tiananmen Square in 1989, faced tanks and tear gas, and risked his own life. Now an entrepreneur who operates his own hedge fund in the United States, Li has a new perspective:

> Business, not politics, is the force driving social change ... business has become the ultimate expression of individuality. This generation may not have the

> power to change the government, but it has the power to change its own economic situation ... They are building a power base. In another 10 years, they will be in leadership roles in every aspect of Chinese society.[19]

Election platforms along the lines of 'Vote for the leader who can do the most for your pocket' will be the ones the villagers of China choose in the direct elections that are now taking place.

From Revolution to Reform

Taiwan's Vice Premier Lien Chien used to explain to the electorate:

> In the past, we had revolution, and that meant you chopped off the heads of those who disagreed with you. Today we are pushing for reforms, which means we need to persuade and communicate with those with a different point of view. We need to convince them and bring them into our fold.

The task is to communicate ideas and not force people into submission. Leaders must be in tune with the mood of the electorate, listen to people, have a blueprint for action, be able to persuade the masses to rally behind them, and then act. The world loves a good speaker, but needs a doer. For thousands of years, Chinese court officials were assiduous theoreticians, eloquent orators and sharp debaters. They were proud and aloof, and had little idea of what the real world looked like. Many blame China's backwardness on this elitist group that obstructed China's modernization.

Managing from the Middle

Watching the transfer of power from John Major to Tony Blair was a fascinating experience for Asians. It went smoothly, swiftly and without a hitch, all because Britain has a civil service that swears allegiance to the business of government, not a political strongman. The Hong Kong civil service demonstrated similar professionalism and independence both before and after the handback. The management of large companies is beginning to follow similar lines; in fact, some people are starting to say that CEOs are becoming irrelevant. First, if CEOs are at a distance from the operational side and the market, they are unable to appreciate and therefore assess whether the business, the industry or the corporation has a future. Second, if management is strong and decentralized, companies can function without them. I see a changed role for CEOs, where their main tasks will be to look to the future of the enterprise, steer it into ever-more profitable areas, plan strategy, and motivate the entire organization. Professional managers will have the foresight to ensure the system works efficiently and competitively.

Many Asian organizations are a long way from this. The top-down management culture makes the succession issue especially critical for those Asian companies that are run by family patriarchs. An urgent priority for Asian communities and organizations overall is to strengthen middle management and to gradually transfer power from the top to the middle echelons.

There are those who do not believe in autocracy and are not reluctant to share power. Malaysian billionaire, Robert Kuok, who is known as a great boss who takes care of his people, attributes the secret of leading a successful business to a strong middle-management network. He said:

> A business is like a tree. At the beginning, there are not many branches and leaves. As times passes, as the tree grows, it will get bigger and stronger. Business is the same. At the beginning, it is small; as a decision-maker, at this stage, you are able to have hands-on management in everything. When the business gets tremendously huge and wider in scope, it is impossible for you to handle everything by yourself. This is the time to delegate job responsibility to subordinates ... It is a matter of selecting capable people ... it also requires highly effective support staff for coordination and supplementary contribution.[20]

Key Tasks for Asian Leaders

Asia is facing a challenging time to seek a new formula to continue sustainable growth and development. There will be political, economic, social and international tensions in a region with rising expectations. Dr Robert Chia of RC Associates, a consultant on the region, said:

> Asia needs a new breed of leaders. They must be businessmen and professionals who can react swiftly to and exploit the series of tidal waves that are sweeping the region. They must embrace the fundamental change in philosophy required to deal with these challenges. They must be "Global-Asian" leaders.[21]

Downsizing the bureaucracy

The bureaucracies of many Asian countries must be reformed if modern political, economic and social lives are to be conducted efficiently. In the past, China has made many attempts to reduce its government bureaucracy, and has recently professed its renewed determination to carry out the dismantling process in line with accelerating reforms now being undertaken. Pressure is being applied to Japan's heavy bureaucratic system, and Hatoyama Yukio, 49, a three-term Diet member from Sakigake, is one of the reformers. He heeds the public clamor to be listened to, respected and served.[22] He said, 'We aim to become leaders of a type Japan has never seen. My plan is to form a party for a new breed of statesmen.' He hopes that 'The government restructuring will promote stronger leadership, a less self-serving bureaucracy, and efficient operations.'

Combining a background in traditional politics with a reform agenda, Hatoyama and his partner, Funada, probably personify the kind of change agent that Japan needs. Plainly, the nation should not completely abandon the old ways, which have served it well despite their flaws. Moreover, for reformers to make headway, they need to harness support from all quarters, including the establishment. With their backgrounds rooted in tradition, Hatoyama and Funada seem well-placed to build on the past, adjust to the present and move towards a better future for the nation.

Adjusting to change

Everywhere in the world, things are changing rapidly. Many of the changes that are taking place have no precedents. Thus, it is a key responsibility of a leader to help people understand these changes and assist them in adjusting to them. This is a very great challenge. Tough decisions need to be taken; there is the potential for socially and psychologically disruptive outcomes which, if not handled properly, could inflict great damage on the leadership.

Persuading Western societies that welfare is unsustainable is one example; the end of lifetime employment in Japan is another. After a brief upswing in 1996, Japan has slipped back into a near-comatose economic state. Japan must return to a decisive, tough government where the leadership of the day gets to govern, and not the bureaucrats. Leadership must encourage people to help themselves, to organize themselves so they can withstand the shocks of a fast-moving world.

Backing winners

Richard Branson, founder and chairman of the diversified Virgin Group, is an entrepreneur who encourages bottom-up creativity:

> It all comes down to people. There's nothing else that comes close. Motivating people, bringing in the best. The girl who opened what will be the best bridal shop in Europe was an air hostess. She came to me with an idea and I said, 'Go for it'... now it's Virgin Bride. By having the freedom to prove herself, she has excelled. Everyone you hire is as important. You assume that every switchboard operator will excel and they will ... Praise people ... value them and give them the opportunity to contribute in ways that excite them. Everything comes back to people. Nothing else. You get loyalty, enthusiasm, and great service for your customers.[23]

Michael Bloomberg is a banker turned information entrepreneur who seems to run his company like a benevolent dictator, albeit one who listens and who is as generous as he is demanding. When talking about his management style, he said, 'You got to make sure that even the most junior guy can tell you what's right. You got to give him plenty of opportunity to fight you and not step on him, because then he won't have the courage of his convictions. When managing a company, you need a decision; you can't do it by committee. You have to be consistent; consistency in management is terribly important.'

Keeping in tune

Leaders fail when they lose contact with their base. Leaders must always assimilate and reflect the aspirations of the group they're leading. The choice of timing is also very important because if you advocate an idea which is too advanced or controversial, then you find yourself without followers. Leaders should be one or two steps ahead, but not 20 steps ahead.

Promoting a learning society

Learning is not about piling up qualifications or becoming an eloquent writer. Learning is about knowing how to do something right, and applying one's skills for the greater good. Professor Warren Bennis pointed out that:

> The key competitive advantage in the 90s and beyond will be the capacity of top leadership to create a learning environment, an adaptive, agile, athletic, social architecture capable of generating intellectual capital. All the leaders I know are concerned with only three things, and they all pertain to resource allocation: people, dollars and ideas.[24]

A Chaordic Organization

The failure of the command-and-control model of organization has led many to contemplate a model that really works. Dee Ward Hock, founder of Visa International, suggests an alternative model—the chaordic organization—the synthesis of chaos and order in one structure, based on distributed power, diversity, competition and collaboration.

The card company operates in some 200 countries world-wide, serving half a billion card members and with an annual sales volume approaching US$1 trillion.[25] Hock had thought hard about an effective organizational model and finally concluded that the most effective one must follow the laws of nature, specifically the law of human nature. He observed that healthy, adaptive systems will always exhibit a kind of dynamic tension between chaos and order, and so arose the concept of the chaordic organization. The Visa system encourages as much competition and initiative as possible throughout the organization; chaos while building in mechanisms for co-operation, out of which comes order.

Visa International is different from the conventional business organization. It is a non-stock, profit-making corporation with ownership in the form of non-transferable rights of participation. Management roles such as authority, initiative and decision-making are pushed out to the periphery of the organization. Visa bylaws encourage members to compete and innovate as much as possible. This harmonious blend of co-operation and competition allows the system to expand world-wide across different currencies, languages, legal codes, customs, cultures and political philosophies. Visa has been called 'a corporation whose product is co-ordination'. It is effective without being centralized or coercive. Hock believes that an organization must be adaptable and responsive to changing conditions, while preserving overall cohesion and unity of purpose.

For a chaordic organization to work, Hock maintains that committed people are the key. On the subject of personnel, he advocates promotion be considered on six levels: first, on the basis of integrity; second, on motivation; third, on capacity; fourth, on understanding; fifth, on knowledge; and last, on experience.

> Never hire or promote in your image. It is foolish to replicate your strength. It is essential to employ, trust, and reward those whose perspective, ability, and judgment are radically different to yours. It is also rare, for it requires uncommon humanity, tolerance, and wisdom.

On leadership, he recommends:

> Invest at least 40 per cent of your time managing yourself—your ethics, character, principles, purpose, motivation, and conduct. Invest at least 30 per cent managing those with authority over you, and 15 per cent managing your peers. Use the remainder to induce those you "work for" to understand and practise the theory.

From Hock's observations and reading, he is convinced that the command-and-control model of organization that evolved to support the industrial revolution '... was not only archaic and increasingly irrelevant'. These organisations '...were becoming a public menace, antithetical to the human spirit and destructive of the biosphere. I was convinced we were on the brink of an epidemic of institutional failure'. Whenever Hock talks to people about chaordic organizations, someone always wants to know, 'Where is the plan? How do we implement it?' That's the wrong question.

All organizations are merely conceptual embodiments of a very old, very basic idea—the idea of community. They can be no more or less than the sum of the beliefs of the people drawn to them, of their character, judgements, acts and efforts. An organization's success has become enormously more to do with the clarity of a shared purpose, common principles and strength of belief in them than to assets, expertise, operating ability, or management competence, important as they may be.

As Hock explains it, this is the essence of a successful organization, organizing itself according to common goals, not according to a blueprint.

Power in the 21st Century

As technology turns the world into a global village, leaders are finding that their influence on people's lives is being eroded. The options people have today have also moved the base of power from the traditional 'command' position. People all over the world are driven by economic pragmatism; they care about the good life and when and how they can enjoy it. Fewer people adhere to principles of idealism. Leaders therefore have to prove themselves, they have to justify their existence. Young people today have a certain disdain for authority.

Jimmy Lai, the founder of *Apple Daily* in Hong Kong, said:

> The messianic approach of politics is very repulsive to me, because I think human beings have their own resources, intelligence and ability to interact equally with other human beings and to love a free life, if given a choice. Government is only needed where the market cannot function.

One thing is certain: power will come through trust and strong relationships and no longer through formal structures.

Effective leadership

A leader's main task is to organize people to support a mission. Strategy and tactics may change, but not the fundamentals. Management guru, Peter Drucker, maintains that an effective leader must know four simple things:

> The only definition of a leader is someone who has followers. Some people are thinkers; some are prophets. Both roles are important and badly needed, but without followers there can be no leaders.

An effective leader is not someone who is loved or admired. He or she is someone whose followers do the right thing. Popularity is not leadership; results are. Leaders are highly visible; they therefore set examples. Leadership is not rank, privilege, status or money; it is responsibility.

Having worked with and studied leaders for decades, Peter Drucker offers the following key qualities that make leaders effective:

> Leadership is a matter of how to be, not how to do. It is the quality and character of the individual that distinguishes great leaders.

> Leaders build bridges. The most important task for leaders is to build a cohesive community within and outside the organization, to invest in relationships and to communicate a vision that touches the hearts of their followers.

A main part of the leader's job today is to help people adjust to change, so leaders have to be healers and unifiers. True leaders at every level of an organization understand that a deteriorating, fragmented community is not going to provide the kind of engaged, energetic, high-performance work-force that competition, and their own mission and goals, demand.

Leaders understand, too, that in a world where no individual can possibly have all the answers, it is the inclusive organization that excels. Leaders of those organizations know they must disperse leadership across the organization, ban the hierarchical structure, and create more circular, flexible and fluid management systems based on collaborative relationships, the wise use of teams, and mutual respect.

Effective leaders are doers, not preachers. Peter Drucker recounted this story from his final high-school years. The history teacher, a war veteran who had been badly wounded, told his class to pick several books on the First World War, read them carefully and then write an essay on them. When these essays were discussed in class, one of his fellow students said, 'Every one of those books says that the Great War was a war of total military incompetence. Why was it?' His teacher did not hesitate a second but shot right back, 'Because not enough generals were killed; they stayed way behind the lines, and let others do the fighting and dying'. Drucker has said:

> Effective leaders delegate a good many things; they have to, or they drown in trivia. But they do not delegate the one thing that only they can do with excellence, the one thing that will make a difference, the one thing that will set standards, the one thing they want to be remembered for. They do it.[26]

Building bridges to people's hearts

Can we believe in leaders? Are leaders for real? How can leaders make themselves believable?

Today, there is a whole battalion of experts and spin doctors helping leaders look credible and convincing. Short of a polygraph examination, it is impossible to know what is genuine and what is not, so one might as well ascribe to Abraham Lincoln's dictum, 'One cannot fool all of the people all of the time.' However, there are countless people who have a golden heart and a passion to serve, but unfortunately their communication skills fail them. In a world where people are judged by their media image, the ability to communicate effectively is all-important.

Anand Panyarachun, a former prime minister of Thailand once said:

> Integrity is important, a relatively impeccable record, objectivity and being a good communicator. You have to listen well ... have a degree of detachment: you have to be able to stand back and look at things from a distance.[27]

A traditional view of leaders, especially in an Asia steeped in Confucian values, is that leaders are a moral force, symbolizing both the emperor and the father. They are there to take care of their subjects, and will only act in the best interests of the people. However, leaders do not necessarily have to be saintly. Indeed, their credibility may actually be enhanced if they have had an interesting past. So long as leaders openly admit their past and their behavior is consistent with their account of it, people will accept them. But if there are contradictions, leaders will be accused of hypocrisy and will lose support. Today, credibility is built on action as well as words. Leaders must not only speak of the kind of lives they believe in, their actions must demonstrate it.

Women Making a Difference

Laura Liswood is director of the Women's Leadership Project in the United States. The aim of this organisation is 'To encourage the vision of a woman as president of the United States'. Laura said:

> The world has got a number of presumptions about leaders. As generally perceived, a leader looks like a man. It's difficult to imagine, if you're not a man, yourself or your daughter as a leader. This is one of the most difficult things to overcome.

She advocates women moving on, from agitating for rights to asserting leadership by developing their capabilities, getting involved and demonstrating excellence in leadership roles. 'I don't really believe men or women have better or worse leadership skills. The best leaders are those with the greatest leadership skills.'

Laura added:

> Women coming to power feel they're scrutinized much more severely than men. Many felt that expectation levels were higher when they came to power, higher than they could meet, especially in Bangladesh and Pakistan ... In many cultures, women are not supposed to have power ... In many cases, voters are still reluctant to see women in political positions.[28]

Who are the heroines for Asian women? Is it the feisty, tough-talking Datuk Rafidah Aziz, the Trade Minister of Malaysia, or Madam Wu Yi, the former Minister of Foreign Trade of the People's Republic of China, who stood up to the American trade negotiators and told them they were robbers? Would it be Anson Chan, the Chief Secretary of Hong Kong, who gave the international investment community such confidence following the handback? What about the thousands of businesswomen who are helping to run Asia's economies? There are many women who do special things, who go out of their way to make a difference. Asian women will blossom into leaders in a wide range of professions, including careers in community service and government. By doing well in a career carved out amidst the changing dynamics of Asia's political, economic and social landscape, women will become role models, symbolizing the new face of leadership in Asia.

Everyone is a leader

Anyone seeking success must be self-motivated, self-organized and self-managed. In other words, people must be leaders in their own lives and in the lives of their families before they can extend their leadership into the community. Before we can become a leader, we have to become a better human being. *Sun Tzu's Art of War* advises leaders to cultivate five personal qualities: wisdom (*Zhi*), courage (*Yong*), trust (*Shin*), discipline (*Yan*) and compassion (*Ren*). Leaders can only be empowering if they are accomplished and continue to pursue personal growth.

Human nature is such that, no matter how independent we are, we need leaders who we can respect as guardians of the truth—accomplished people whose upright characters we can aspire to, and whose lives we can try to emulate. Those who occupy positions of leadership must be mindful that those positions are not permanent; they will be rejected if they do not play by the rules and act in the interests of their followers.

As George Mellon commented, in relation to the office of the American presidency and the law (and with particular reference to President Clinton's legal problems with Monica Lewinsky):

> It is important to keep in mind what is really at stake when a person in high office trespasses the law, law itself comes under threat. Laws, fashioned out of public debate and enacted by elected representatives of the people, are what bind democratic societies together. They are the only protection against degeneration into disorder, chaos and ultimately civil violence. The iron principle that no man can be above the law is vital to the preservation of a society where men and women can feel secure in both their persons and property against the threat of injustice and abuse of power. Holding the presidency of a great nation is not an entitlement; it must be earned every day. It seems that a lot of people, and presidents themselves, need to be reminded of that from time to time.[29]

These remarks echo the wisdom contained in the advice that the Chinese scholar Guan Zhong gave to rulers and leaders many thousands of years ago.[30]

Chapter 9
From Strong Government to Engaged Citizenry

"All politics is dreadful.
What really matters is good governance.
Governments must be sensitive to the populace.
A leader must not just insist on his own idea."

—Chang Yo Fah—
Chairman, Evergreen Group, Taiwan

Having suffered centuries of misrule and turbulence, it is understandable that Asians yearn for stability, even at the expense of democratic rule. In general, they seem to hold the view that, whatever the political system, what matters is good government that brings stability and economic growth. The experience in Asia for the last five decades has been that good government has more to do with the quality of leadership than it has with the institutional framework or system. Asian leaders maintain that economic and social achievements speak for themselves. The people seem to view democracy as secondary, to be sought only after the more basic needs in the Maslow's hierarchy have been met.

That strong leaders and powerful governments exist in a region that is still developing and struggling with economic and survival issues is understandable. Bearing in mind the ethnic, religious and cultural diversity of the region, the principal aim of government, planners and the citizenry is a peaceful, stable environment. To the average man and woman in the street, it is hard to see the connection between democracy and good government. 'People cannot see the relationship between components of democracy, such as greater legislative representation or participation in decision-making or the accountability of the executive, and making money. The women especially pleaded with me not to stir up trouble,' Emily Lau, a former legislative councilor of Hong Kong's now disbanded Legco, said to me. This would hold true for most countries in non-Japan Asia, apart from perhaps Taiwan, where the transition from strong government and leadership to democratic self-government is proceeding in a chaotic but steady manner. Recent electoral trends in Taiwan also suggest a possible shift of power from the ruling Kuomintang to the relatively new opposition party, the Democratic Progressive Party (DPP) which had a sweeping victory in the minor municipalities in the local elections of 1997.[1]

However, the changes in government in Thailand and South Korea following the financial crisis, and the traumatic experience of the Indonesians, have no doubt put in sharp focus the quality of governance and the need to have political institutions of integrity. The people will now demand a greater say in the running of their countries, and will expect their governments to be accountable to them in the conduct of public policy. The way in which political institutions deal with these expectations in Asia is as important as the economic restructuring that the region has to undertake to achieve sustainable growth.

The era of nationalism is coming to an end for the developing Asian communities. With the intensifying of economic restructuring and greater global competition, in the decades ahead, politics will evolve into a continuing debate over ideas and programs, and will perhaps be less preoccupied with factional interests. The nature of the social contract between the governed and the government will change as the region's population becomes more affluent and educated. While some Asian governments are guilty of nepotism, repression and corruption, a few, in the name of efficiency, are doing too much for the citizenry, which has made them dependent and complacent.

A challenge for the future is to find ways in which people can become engaged in the system of government, to become actively involved in sustaining progress and advancing the interests of their country. In this scenario, the citizenry moves from dependence on government to taking responsibility and participating in the formulation of public policies. Globalization has demonstrated the limitations of governments: no matter how good they are, and how competent their bureaucracies, they cannot cope with all the complexities of the global market-place. The future success of Asia will rest on the collective engagement of her people, and less on strong leaders or strong government.

Is it the End of History?

In his provocative work, *The End of History and the Last Man*, American writer Francis Fukuyama suggests that there is no viable, alternative political system to that of a liberal democracy. He wrote:

> The social changes that accompany advanced industrialization, in particular, universal education, appear to liberate a certain demand for recognition that did not exist among poorer and less educated people. As standards of living increase, as populations become more cosmopolitan and better educated, and as society as a whole achieves a greater equality of condition, people begin to demand not simply more wealth but recognition of their status. If people were nothing more than desire and reason, they would be content to live in market-oriented authoritarian states like Franco's Spain, or a South Korea, or Brazil under military rule. But they also have a thymotic pride in their own self-worth [an inner need for recognition], and this leads them to demand democratic governments that treat them like adults rather than children, recognizing their autonomy as free individuals. Communism is superseded by liberal democracy in our time because of the realization that the former provides a gravely defective form of recognition.[2]

There is a heightened consciousness among the educated, open-minded and pragmatic young leaders of Asia that a form of government that both encourages rapid growth and more holistic development must be developed. The idea of liberal democracy is attractive, but it is the 'how' and the consequences it has had in the West that pose the problem. Will, in a 100 years' time, the Asian system of ideal government resemble the liberal Western system? It is neither unlikely nor impossible for, at the moment, no-one has the full picture. Asians are very clear on their priorities given the unique circumstances of their communities, they would rather err on the side of caution. S Jayakumar, Singapore's minister of foreign affairs, said:

> In heterogeneous societies, populist policies could prove very dangerous and destabilizing, if mismanaged. As societies become differentiated and as the pace of change accelerates, the differences between rural and urban, between secular and traditional elite broaden, [and] this could set the stage for religious and ethnic fundamentalism. The experience of the more mature economies in Europe and elsewhere is instructive. Their experience has shown that with economic growth, politics becomes differentiated with multiple interest groups and parties. This makes the process of adaptation difficult. Yet greater

> independence and integration with the global economy makes rapid and constant change essential to sustained growth. If politically mismanaged, growth may make further growth limited. This is a paradox but is a reality in Southeast Asia ... and the consequences of slow or negative growth will be even more severe than elsewhere.[3]

Contemporary Asian Views on Government

I have heard two arguments which are in favor of strong government, and both are supported by the leadership and the citizens, including the elite.

The first argument is based on the efficiency theory so famously propounded by Senior Minister of Singapore, Mr Lee Kuan Yew and his team. This maintains that Asia's diversity and scarce resources warrant that discipline and single-minded pursuit of economic welfare must come first. Dissent destabilizes society and renders the system inefficient, and a small country like Singapore could not afford such a high price. Besides, Mr Lee suggests that, for Western-style democracy to work, it will take at least several more decades for the educational level of the region to catch up with the sophisticated levels of the West.

The second argument is based on the stability theory. East Asians are both obsessed with and proud of the stability in their societies. As there is a large gap in economic well-being between the various levels of society, and society is itself so diverse, communal politics are potentially explosive. A strong controlling hand is a guarantee of stability and national security. 'Father knows best, and knows what is best for you' is the unspoken but widely acknowledged norm. Stability is wanted by everyone and is deemed good for everyone. So, the citizenry surrenders itself to strong government. East Asian countries such as Malaysia, Indonesia, Singapore and China often use this argument to defend the strong stance taken by their governments and political leaders. On the other hand, weak political leadership in Japan is cited as the main reason for its policy paralysis. They also claim further proof of their legitimacy by pointing to the deficiencies of the democratic systems in the slower-growing economies of the Philippines and India.

Chinese leaders used to maintain that economic development must precede democratization, and they cite the recent history of South Korea, Taiwan , and other 'Asian tigers'. We know that the experiences of these nations convey a more complex lesson: promoting economic growth while monopolizing political power is an almost impossible balancing act over the long term, especially in a world increasingly made transparent by communications, travel and trade.[4]

It is hard to argue against strong government when those governments deliver. Their systems work, and work well in bringing about spectacular improvements in both the economic and the social conditions of the citizenry. While the citizenry is aware of wrongdoing and abuse of the system, the unspoken social contract means that as long as the government delivers growth, it is not challenged. However, since the financial crisis of 1997, when the extent of the mismanagement and corruption was exposed, this attitude has altered. Will disillusionment and economic hardship bring radical change?

Barry Wain, a long-time resident in Asia and editor-at-large for *The Asian Wall Street Journal*, observed:

> Political institutions, parties and personalities no doubt will come under pressure as marginalized groups feel the pinch and the newly emerged middle class contracts. But localized discontent is more likely to translate into adjustments to the system—for instance, greater transparency and a reduction in crony capitalism— rather than the overthrow of the system itself.[5]

There is also a third theory, advanced by Asian liberals and championed by Westerners. This theory holds that a system wherein the people become engaged is fundamental to sustainable growth. Opponents to this view charge that democracy would be potentially chaotic and incompatible with Asians' nature or culture. South Korea's new president, Kim Dae Jung, has defended this theory in response to Senior Minister Lee Kuan Yew's assertion in *Culture is Destiny*, and has argued that democracy is as Asian as Buddhism.[6] If one listens to the political rhetoric between East and West, one gets the impression that the West champions sovereignty of the people by fervently promoting democracy in Asia, and that the regimes in Asia hold down the masses under authoritarian rule. The fact is that, in many instances, the authoritarian rule cannot be called harsh, rather, it is benign. There is another very important cultural difference. The approach of Asian governments to the business of government is paternalistic, somewhat in the command-and-control style, but increasingly taking a reduced role in the economy. As a percentage of their gross domestic product (GDP), most Asian governments spend little by Western standards.

Confucius: 'People are Stupid'

Those Asians who do not believe that people can govern themselves subscribe to the Confucian view that 'people are stupid'.[7] How could the humanistic sage, Confucius, be anti-human? Could he be wrong about human nature in relation to democracy? During the May Fourth Movement, a political protest movement that started in China in 1919, efforts were made to discredit Confucianism because the sage's teaching, *min ke shi you zhi, bu ke shi zhi zhi*, was viewed as anti-democratic . The first part of the sentence is interpreted as, 'Just tell the people what to do. Give it to them as in a military order; point to the target, tell them the distance needed to cover and indicate clearly how much time they have to reach the target'. The second part of the sentence says, 'Never let them know the reason, demand absolute obedience'. Any way it is viewed, this is paternalism.[8]

Subsequently, Chinese intellectuals tried to reposition Confucius as a democrat by inserting punctuation marks: *min ke, shi you zhi, bu ke, shi, zhi zhi.*[9] The interpretation is, 'When the literacy and knowledge of the people has risen and they can make choices through elections, give them political freedom. When the people haven't reached this level, educate and train them, first give them knowledge'. Not everyone agrees with this; there is another interpretation, which is, *min ke, shi you zhi, bu ke, shi zhi zhi*. Translated, this says 'When you look at this society, the people are ready, give them self-rule. When people are not ready, educate them'. We may be playing with semantics, but the essence is the relevance of the system to the circumstances of the people, especially in terms of whether the system is compatible with human nature. Many of those who adhere to the teachings of Confucius believe, based on experience, that most people are only capable of doing certain things and are not capable of handling too much complexity. They believe that Confucius was right and that he was nothing if not humanistic, on the grounds that 'It is better to give people what works best for them, specific instructions, and not bother them with too many 'why's'. His defenders say that it is not anti-human to say 'people are stupid', as some critic had argued, but a true appreciation of human nature.

Freedom, self-determination and control over one's destiny are the aspirations of the liberal-minded. However, so far, freedom has meant freedom from external domination, not personal freedom. Sun Yat Sen of China, Jawaharlal Nehru of India, Tunku Abdul Rahman of Malaya (as it was then called), and other leaders of movements against colonialism fought hard to bring about self-rule. Freedom fighters also attempted to replace feudal rule with the rule of the people. Such were the objectives of many of the past political, nationalist movements in Asia. With few exceptions, most Asian societies still have not moved beyond that phase of making self-government a reality, a system and a culture. Some of the earlier attempts at democracy failed; eg, Dr Sun Yat Sen's republic failed because the social conditions in China at the time were too impoverished for it to stand a chance. Although the basic framework for economic development now exists in many countries in the region, much work needs to be done in building the institutions through which a liberal democracy works. It is not really a matter of leaders not allowing participation by the citizenry (although some loosening up would be helpful), but that, by and large, only a minority of people is interested. An advisor to the Environment Protection Society of Malaysia, Gurmit Singh, expressed his disappointment by what he sees as the selfish attitudes of local residents. 'They expect the non-government organizations to fight for them all the time, even petty issues, because they do not want any repercussions. They don't want to get into trouble.'

Western-style democracy, as it exists in the United Kingdom and the United States, has taken 200 years to evolve. However, Asia will not have the luxury of such a leisurely pace towards democratization. The varying levels of development within the region demand caution in following a 'one model fits all' process. Professor Daniel Bell of the University of Hong Kong made this observation:

> The task of extending democratic institutions to the non-Western world is less straightforward than optimists had supposed in the heady days after the collapse of communism in the Soviet Union. Brutal ethnic warfare, crippling poverty, environmental degradation, and pervasive corruption, to name some of the more obvious troubles afflicting the Third World, pose serious obstacles to the successful establishment and consolidation of democratic political ar-

> rangements. Ultimately more challenging to democrats with a belief in the universality of that form of government, however, is the view that non-democratic political regimes in modern East Asian societies can deliver social peace, economic success, and political stability. Perhaps most tempting of all, such regimes also promise to secure rich and fulfilling communal attachments instead of no-holds-barred individualism, rootlessness, alienation from the political process, and other phenomena related to the erosion of communal life in Western democracies.[10]

We can see many different styles: Singapore, Malaysia, Thailand and Taiwan, for example. To suit her current circumstances, China is eager to show that a market economy with Chinese characteristics works for mainland China; at the same time, the various forms of democratic government are being examined as China gets ready to introduce more political reforms. Singapore practises a form of communitarian socialism to achieve maximum efficiency from her resource-scarce city-state. Depending on the circumstances and the quality of its leadership, the citizenry of one Asian community may enjoy greater sovereignty than those of another. The entire region is in search of a workable system, and the momentum is accelerating. Those at a higher economic level and with a more mature, law-abiding culture and an educated populace will move at a faster pace; others will proceed more slowly. All will be propelled by the effects of internationalization, technological and economic forces, struggling at the grassroots and a change in attitude by the political leadership.

Evidence suggests that the Asian leadership itself is an active agent of democratization. The efforts of the late Chinese leader, Deng Xiaoping, to introduce mandatory retirement for China's politicians and the support some Asian governments give to non-governmental organizations is another. The limitations of a top-down government structure in a globalized environment are being increasingly felt. Any Asian leadership that stays oblivious to global trends will have to face social instability, economic setbacks and political chaos. Leadership in the future must face up to the realities of the world and help people take their place in society. Those leaders who persist in hiding behind a facade of grandiose, unattainable government programs, paid for by the taxpayer, are deluding themselves.

Democracy in India

Perhaps the greatest diversity in the world lies in India. Her 950 million people speak more than 1,000 languages and dialects. Her democratic system supports more than 20 political parties, and the 4,000-year-old Indian civilization is a mixture of Hindu, Islam, Buddhist, Christian, Sikh and modern secular influences. In addition, there are countless adherents of other faiths. In the absence of a common language, containing such diversity is no easy task, and coalition governments can only hang on in the face of religious strife, ethnic conflict and disparate interests.

Economic bankruptcy in India has forced the State to release its command of the economy, leaving its coffers with insufficient money for such things as education, health and nutrition that are vital for growth. Bankruptcy has, in one sense, produced some short-term gains—the private sector has become more dynamic and efficient. But in the long run, the private sector needs greater opportunity before it can thrive. This points to an urgent need for deregulation and for a sustained program of reforms.

Frustrated businessmen and reformers blame democracy for the chaos and slow progress. With the democratic process, it is difficult to make the hard-hitting decisions that are needed to put a reformed economic structure in place. However, democracy does have some self-correcting mechanisms that keep India's muddled consensus on the rails. First, by allowing all parties a chance of power, it forces them to grapple with the forces that produced liberalization in the first place. Second, the democracy that creates competition in populist giveaways is also the democracy that sets limits on the process.

Mahoman Singh, a former finance minister, argues that while India's political system may produce slower growth than some of the authoritarian countries of East Asia, democracy may in the long run provide a surer foundation for growth:

> Political pluralism is the wave of the future ... Political societies that are rigid and monolithic are like command economies. They can produce very rapid growth in the short term, but in the long run, it's not sustainable.[11]

India's embrace of democracy is more a historical legacy from Nehru than a true acknowledgement of the superiority of the democratic process as a solution to government in such a diverse country. Fareed Zakaria, editor of *Foreign Affairs*, observed that:

> It is often remarked that Nehru was the last Englishman to rule India. He was indeed a product of England's great institutions—Harrow, Cambridge, the London Bar. His conception of nationalism was entirely European, a product of Enlightenment ideas about self-determination, liberalism and rationalism in politics.[12]

However, taking into consideration the problems faced by Japan and South Korea, and some of the countries in the Association of South-East Asian Nations (ASEAN), particularly after the financial crisis, Asians may be more ready to do some serious thinking about taking greater responsibility. As an editorial in the 8 December 1997 edition of the Chinese-language magazine, *Yazhou Zhoukan*, said, 'Governance is not about taking command of power. It is about taking over the burden of responsibility.'

The View from the United States

In general, America's benign interference irritates and causes resentment in Asia. To properly understand the American passion for spreading democracy throughout the world, we must begin with an examination of the character of that nation. After touring and studying democracy in America, the French historian, Alexis de Tocqueville wrote:

> America is the only country in which the starting point of a great people has been clearly observable ... The foundation of New England was a novel spectacle, and all the circumstances attending it were singular and original. Nearly all colonies have been first inhabited either by men without education and without resources, driven by their poverty and their misconduct from the land which gave them birth, or by speculators and adventurers greedy of gain. Some settlements cannot even boast so honorable an origin; Santo Domingo was founded by buccaneers; and at the present day, the criminal courts of England supply the population of Australia.

The settlers who established themselves on the shores of New England all belonged to the more independent classes of their native country. Their union on the soil of America at once presented the singular phenomenon of a society containing neither lords nor common people, and we may almost say neither rich nor poor. These men possessed in proportion to their number, a greater mass of intelligence than is to be found in any European nation of our time. All, perhaps without a single exception, had received a good education, and many of them were known in Europe for their talents and their acquirements. The other colonies had been founded by adventurers without families. But the immigrants of New England brought with them the best elements of order and morality as they landed on the desert coast accompanied by their wives and children. But what especially distinguished them from all others was the aim of their undertaking. They had not been obliged by necessity to leave their country. The social position they abandoned was one to be regretted, and their means of subsistence was certain. Nor did they cross the Atlantic to improve their situation or to increase their wealth; it was purely intellectual craving that called them from the comforts of their former homes; and in facing the inevitable sufferings of exile their object was the triumph of an idea.[13]

Inspired by idealism and the universality of their beliefs, the Americans took upon themselves a global mission to spread democracy. Foreign policy has given the American presidency an extensive scope of influence, and successive American leaders have reiterated America's leadership role for the world. Beginning with Abraham Lincoln's inspiring Gettysburg address which Chinese President Jiang Zemin can recite from memory, American presidents have championed the cause of liberty and democracy. President Woodrow Wilson said in 1919, 'We set this nation up to make men free, and we did not confine our conception and purpose to America'. To what extent the American people identify with this Wilsonian vision is hard to tell, but American foreign policy, or at least its political rhetoric, shows that this idea of promoting democracy throughout the world has a powerful grip on the American psyche.

To date, Asians' efforts to respond to the West have been confined to rhetoric. If Asians want to demonstrate an alternative way, we need to take action to develop and strengthen our own institutions according to our own standards—standards that can deliver the same universally desired end results. Why should some Western organization run 'Human Rights Watch Asia', when we ourselves should be responsible for 'Human Rights Asian Watch'? Even more pertinent is the question: 'Why don't Asians start and run their own Human

Rights Watch organization?' It is not unreasonable to question the claim made by the West that what is good for one is good for all, and to condemn such a claim as ethnocentric and hegemonic—or even to remind the West that it does not have any credibility or high moral ground from which it can champion human rights. Given its record of colonialism and past excesses in Asia, the West indeed lacks moral authority. In April 1997, *The Economist* stated:

> It is hubristic to try to export Western ideas of freedom to places with different traditions and levels of development and assume that it is best for them. Attempts to introduce Western political models into poor countries have a habit of coming unstuck—just look at Africa or Cambodia. Besides, the experience in Western societies shows that their rights evolved over time; universal suffrage came to Britain only in 1832, racial segregation continued in parts of the United States until the 1960s.[14]

Democracy Today

In a true democracy, people govern themselves. They are engaged in the formulation of public policies and participate in the decisions that affect their well-being. In other words, when people are self-governed, they need very little government. 'It doesn't matter who is the president, America will still function,' said John Naisbitt. In a democratic country, the government and the leaders are servants of the people, they are there to facilitate and carry out the wishes of the people; for the most part, society can function without them. Talking about a world increasingly driven by economic considerations, Naisbitt said, 'We are, all over the Western world, in a "political crisis" because political leaders have ceased to be very important. It is almost a universal condition in the West. But take away politics, there is no crisis.'[15]

As one measure of the extent to which people in Asia are ready for democratic self-government, ask about succession. In how many Asian countries can people be unconcerned about who is at the helm? Which stock-market will not react to rumours of the death or declining health of the leader? Thailand has demonstrated its stability, but some said that can be attributed to its enlightened king. Would the Philippines, India, South Korea, Taiwan and Hong Kong, or even Singapore with a succession plan firmly in place, answer these questions with the confidence of Thailand? On this subject,

China surprised not a few. When Deng Xiaoping died, the Hong Kong stock-market did not miss a beat. (However, his death did cause the demise of the army of death-watchers that had grown up around the world!) As for the rest of the Asian countries, how much influence does the political leadership have? By and large, my conclusion is that government in Asian societies is still very much driven from the top, and this state of affairs will continue for some time, until people truly understand how democracy works.

Democracy is best described in Abraham Lincoln's words, as a system of government of the people, by the people and for the people. The major features of modern democracy include individual freedom, which entitles citizens to the liberty and responsibility of shaping their own careers and conducting their own affairs, equality before the law and universal suffrage. Basic to democracy is the rule of law, and a law-abiding culture where citizens have faith and ownership in the system of laws which they helped to frame.

In earlier times, there were direct democracies in the West, where everyone could speak and vote in assemblies, as epitomized by the New England town meetings. Representative government was unnecessary because of the small size of the communities. In modern democracies, the people elect officials to represent them in a parliament or senate, and these representatives are then responsible to their electorates. Equally, the people also have the power to throw out these elected officials.

Elections are Only the Beginning

The election process is only the beginning of democracy, but it is not democracy itself. In his article on democracy, Fareed Zakaria observed that:

> Elections are only a process for creating a fair and law-abiding government. They are not, by themselves, what freedom is all about. For almost a century in the West, democracy has meant liberal democracy not just free and fair elections, but also the sanctity of basic liberties, like free speech and assembly, private property and contracts, and the rule of law. But from Peru to the Palestinian Authority, from Slovakia to Sri Lanka, from Pakistan to the Philippines, we can see the rise of illiberal democracy ... plenty of elections, but few individual rights.

The democratic system all over the world has been marred by manipulation and subversion. Money, influence and control of the media sometimes speak louder than ideas, and upright leaders committed to doing good for the community have no guarantee of the chance to serve if elections are not fair.

The 1996 election in Thailand was marred by reports of widespread vote-buying, and in the past year, local and national politicians have been implicated in land scams, a banking scandal, and even a murder case. 'Thailand's democracy is taking a major ideological step: shifting from a purely parliamentarian system towards one bound to special courts and the judiciary. The argument is that the courts can tackle abuses such as vote-buying, patronage and corruption more effectively than the parliament,' observed Daniel Bell, political science lecturer at the University of Hong Kong.[16]

Although in any democracy some parties and candidates will always have more money than others, money and the exercise of influence should not be inevitably connected. Yet the overwhelming evidence from the world's champion of democracy, America, is that dollars now speak louder than ideas, that access is bought and sold, and that unless they have funds of their own, challengers and third parties are often drowned out.[17] In the United States in 1996, at least US$660m was spent by candidates and parties in search of seats in the Senate; spending in all elections is estimated at over US$3b. It has been calculated that, if campaigning for a seat in the Senate now averages US$4.5m, each senator must raise at least US$14,000 every week of his or her six-year term.[18]

If the costs of campaigning, the fees for political consultants, and the funds for expensive broadcast time are all added together, the total is enormous. *The Economist* observed that this state of affairs:

> ... suggests that candidates are not so much corrupt, as trapped; they dare not be outspent. Politicians, many think, are spending most of their working hours raising funds for the next campaign: governing America is done in their spare time.

Chasing public office is becoming immensely expensive, candidates have to work hard to get there and, once there, they have to work even harder to stay there. One can't help but speculate on the real motivation to achieve office. The same circus is observed in Canada, although the Conservatives were wiped out by the Liberals, despite heavily outspending them. More often than not, though, money helps. As a rule, incumbents in the United States enjoy a financial advantage over their opponents, and in most cases, those who spend more, win.

In the 1988 campaign in the United States, candidates discovered the delights of 'soft money', ie funds that could be given without limit to parties for grassroots 'party building'. For the 1996 election, soft money donations shot through the roof. The political parties raked in US$262m in soft money, tripling their 1992 'take'. According to Common Cause, a non-profit group that tracks donations of US$10,000 or more, corporations generated 93 per cent of the Republicans' war chest (or the 'Grand Old Party's' backdoor cash hoard) of US$138m, and 74 per cent of the Democrats' US$128m soft money cache.[19]

There are growing calls in the United States for campaign financing to be reformed. Many countries, such as Japan, Italy, France and Belgium, have experienced far more serious incidents involving political corruption, but no other developed country tolerates a money chase of this scale. Even in America, the cradle of liberal democracy, the democratic system is still evolving.

An Engaged Citizenry

The starting point of modern democracy is the belief that every sane adult is entitled to an equal say in the conduct of public affairs, and that the sovereignty of the people should be guarded against any encroachment by the state. Reality is somewhat different. As Brian Beedham wrote in *The Economist*, in most democracies, the citizenry is expected to stand quietly aside for periods of up to seven years while the parliamentarians do all the deciding. About the only time the voice of the people is heard is at election time. This, he called 'part-time democracy'.[20]

If democracy means rule by the people, then decision-making by referendum is a great deal closer to the original idea of democracy than is the usual pattern of voters going to the polls every few years. As Brian Beedham wrote:

> The world has changed radically since the time when it might have seemed plausible to think the voters' wishes needed to be filtered through the finer intelligence of those 'representatives'. The changes that have taken place since then have removed many of the differences between ordinary people and their representatives. They have also helped the people to discover that the representatives are not especially competent. As a result, what worked reasonably well in the 19th century will not work in the 21st century.

John Naisbitt predicted that information technology will usher in an era of 'direct' democracy, in which all eligible voters can vote directly on selected issues, leaving parliamentary representatives to deal with more mundane legislative matters.

While the prospect of direct democracy is becoming increasingly real, in the meantime, the respect accorded those in public office is vanishing. Voters no longer trust politicians to the extent they once did. Opinion polls in the United States, Britain, France and elsewhere all make the same point: people nowadays regard their representatives with disdain. Modern-day democracy is basically rule by a few, by a minority, who do not necessarily have the support of the majority. The question then is how to ensure this minority will act in the best interests of the majority, and if they do not, how can the majority throw them out? If they work against the interests of the majority, how can they be punished? Thanks to globalization and transparency, fund managers, currency traders and international investors have almost instant access to knowledge of government policies, and can register their approval or disapproval through the actions they take. The vote of the international finance community, reinforced by the international media, is turning out to be a new safeguard for the local citizenry and brings an end to any ideas that 'all politics are local'.

Equality in communication

Asians still lead a largely communal life, even with industrialization and urbanization. Their social lives follow a definite hierarchical pattern: the young are deferential to their elders, and the women are submissive to seniority and authority. Usually, the man at the helm of the household, village or particular social group, takes command. Communication travels vertically, and there is a distinct pecking order. This is still very much the order of things in Asia, and is particularly evident in the villages.

In the West, everyone has a point of view which they freely assert, whereas in Asia, only the leaders and elders talk; the rest sit quietly and must listen intently (or pretend to!). I once attended a dinner party for the head of a major business conglomerate in Kuala Lumpur and found a complete segregation of men and women; the wives of the senior executives were all seated at a separate table away from their husbands. Communicating horizontally has never been an Asian habit, and they are less skillful at doing it. The Chinese language is filled with 'You should do this' and 'You should do that', and not 'Would you mind doing this?' Listening to Chinese talking, one hears phrases like, 'The teacher says...', 'My mother says...', 'The boss says...'. But rarely 'I would like to...'.

Asians need to learn to discuss alternate viewpoints. In the provincial capital of Guangzhou in southern China, the Communist Party committee of the municipal government has joined the Guangzhou Television in the organization of street public forums on issues that involved the well-being of the people. Since 1992, 42 televised public forums have been held. Discussion panels have comprised government officials as well as members of the public; membership of the audience has been entirely open. During the visit to China by US President Bill Clinton at the end of June 1998, China television carried live a joint press conference between the US President and Chinese President Jiang Zemin. This was a ground-breaking event, especially for the people of China, who watched their leader debating policy in public and cordially disagreeing with his guest. This was for many an extraordinary experience, and an introduction to democracy.

Using the vote

In many parts of the world, more perceptibly in the developed world, the evidence is mounting that the citizenry is becoming disillusioned and increasingly uninterested in politics. In the developed democratic countries, especially, voter turn-out in major elections has been falling. For examples, in 1996, Bill Clinton was elected by 1/4 of the eligible registered voters; in Japan's national election in 1996, only

59.6 per cent of the voters bothered to vote, a post-war low; in Britain's 1997 election, which threw the Tories out after 18 years, just over 70 per cent of the voters turned out; and in Pakistan, the Pakistan Muslim League, led by Nawar Shariff, gained a landslide victory in February 1997, but the fact that fewer than 38 per cent of the voters turned out has weakened Mr Shariff's claim to a popular mandate.[21]

Elsewhere, however, the new democracies are more enthusiastic. In July 1996, more than 72 million citizens in Russia, that is over 67 per cent of the eligible voters, turned out at 96,000 polling places across 11 time zones. Such a high turn-out was particularly impressive given that 70 per cent of the Russian voters had already gone to the polls in the first round of the election two and a half weeks earlier. This figure was nearly as significant as the 14-point margin of Yeltsin's victory.[22] In June 1996, the Mongolians participated in their country's third democratic election. Over 92 per cent of those eligible cast ballots, many after travelling for hours on horseback; they handed an unexpected and overwhelming victory to the democratic opposition.

In Asian countries, the voter turn-out at the last general elections as a percentage of total registered voters is as follows: Japan (1996), 59 per cent of 97.9 million voters; Thailand (1996), 62.4 per cent of 38.6 million voters; South Korea (1996), 63.9 per cent of 31.5 million voters; the Philippines (1995), 70.7 per cent of 36.4 million voters; Malaysia (1995), 71.8 per cent of nine million voters; and Singapore (1997) 95.9 per cent of 800,000 voters.[23] In Singapore, voting is mandatory.

It can be concluded that, while elections are necessary, they are, in themselves, insufficient to ensure that democracy becomes a permanent feature of national life. What is there to stop an election winner who then suspends democracy and exploits his new power to suppress his opponents? Given the choice, though, most citizens would prefer to vote; after all, the democratic process is still better than many alternatives.

The role of intellectuals in public life

The business of government is becoming increasingly challenging. The remuneration of the people's representatives is often not attractive enough to entice the best people to serve. That being the case, how can we ensure high-quality input and commitment? The search for remedies is on. The colonial government of Hong Kong used a system of functional constituencies: professional bodies, such as those of bankers, engineers, doctors and lawyers, nominated their representatives for the legislature. Singapore has her nominated members of parliament, distinguished members of the community who are selected through public nominations. Candidates must be persons:

> ... who have rendered distinguished public service, or who have brought honor to the Republic, or who have distinguished themselves in the field of arts and letters, culture, the sciences, business, industry, the professions, social or community service or the labor movement; and in making any nomination, the Special Select Committee shall have regard to the need for Nominated Members to reflect as wide a range of independent and non-partisan views as possible.[24]

Professor Tu Weimeng advocates the idea of public intellectuals, that is, people of knowledge and expertise who are actively engaged in the process of shaping public policy through continuing dialogue. 'This way, although these public intellectuals are not directly involved in government, they contribute to the quality of government.' Daniel Bell, a professor of philosophy at the University of Hong Kong, has researched Confucianism and democracy and has suggested that, in order to reconcile the Confucian emphasis on rule by a wise and uncorrupted political elite with the democratic values of popular participation, accountability and transparency, government should be, 'A bicameral legislature with a democratically elected lower house and an upper house composed of representatives selected on the basis of competitive examinations'.[25] The proposal for a 'Confucian' upper house, ie 'House of Scholars' was first suggested by Huang Zongxi, a 17th-century Confucian scholar. Huang argued in his book, *Waiting for the Dawn: A Plan for the Prince*, that imperial power should be curbed by a 'school' of meritocratically chosen scholar officials. The school should engage in outspoken discussion of issues without fear of those in power, and the emperor should be questioned on the administration of the country. In Bell's view:

> A House of Scholars is more meritocratic, and no less democratic, than the House of Lords in the UK and the Senate in Canada. Deputies in the House of Scholars could be held accountable for abuses of power with term limits and stiff penalties for corruption, and political deliberations could be televised and transmitted directly to the public. It would also help to institutionalize checks on the decisions of the democratically elected majorities. At the very least, it could provide a group of talented and relatively disinterested individuals ready to act for the common good, for example, by sitting on commissions and independent bodies that evaluate policy and advise the government.

He maintains further that a House of Scholars which restrains democratic majorities could also have the paradoxical effect of securing a democratic system in East Asia. Instead of turning to a strongman who promises to restore national pride when things go wrong, the citizens can rely on a democratic system that incorporates an element of traditional political culture.

There is one concern with the concept of the house of scholars, and that is, how current are they with fast-changing social and economic conditions? One complaint about scholars is they are often locked away in ivory towers, aloof and distant from the masses. If that is indeed the case, how capable are they of representing the people? Would involving professional people, business entrepreneurs, corporate executives and scientists be part of the program? To support Tu and Bell's visions, the media takes on an especially important role.

The media as watchdog

A free and independent media is vital for a healthy and vibrant democracy. The media can ensure transparency in the formulation of public policies and decision-making, and hold politicians and public officials accountable. The robustness of public opinion reflects the involvement of the community, and is a good barometer of the level of freedom a community enjoys. Hong Kong, for example, has one of the highest and most informed newspaper readerships in Asia. The media, through its coverage and feedback from readers, provides a forum through which issues of public interest can be debated. It also provides a forum through which those in government can promote their policies. A truly independent media can, in the public interest, expose the activities of those who abuse their power to the detriment of the public good. Knowing this, public officials are more inclined to act with propriety.

Of course, the manipulative side of the media cannot be overlooked; but people can decide for themselves what to believe and what to ignore. We are now living in a multimedia world, where images are created that are perceived as real. The electronic media especially is a potent force in shaping opinion and can even tip the balance of power. Clever marketing and smart campaigns work on the premise that 'perception is reality'. They have the ability and the tools to actually shape values—it is said that the media actually creates the president that Americans want. The public persona of the president or any other public official can be very different from the real person. In the end, the citizenry must be able to filter out all the media influences, and think and act independently.

Asia's road to democracy must begin with the media. The region's press is more reactive than proactive. Newspapers in Tokyo, Seoul and New Delhi are saturated with stories about corruption and the misdemeanours of politicians and bureaucrats. Most, however, are not printing what they have found through investigative reporting, but are merely printing public releases. In the People's Republic of China, the scene is quite different. The press has taken on a more 'activist' role: it is investigating and reporting official misconduct and corruption, environmental pollution, and malpractice by private companies. It is also acting to heighten society's awareness of the issues of the day, expressing public concerns, rallying support for common causes, and providing solutions to problems that local governments seem incapable of resolving. For example, *Southern Weekend*, a popular newspaper in the southern city of Guangzhou, now has more scoops on social and political matters than any other newspaper—within the permitted parameters, of course. There is an intellectual fervor not seen since the heady days before the Tiananmen incident in 1989. While the government is beginning to feel the weight of public opinion, it is not discouraging debate. The book publishing industry is also getting bolder. For example, *Crossing Swords*, an account by two People's Daily reporters on China's two decades of ideological struggle, was a sensational bestseller that sold close to half a million copies nationwide. The translation of Austrian economist Friedrich von Hayek's *The Constitution of Liberty* has started a series of public forums on liberty and the market economy after becoming a bestseller among the nation's intellectuals.

Towards Representative Government

By and large, Asia is moving towards representative government. But to go beyond superficial appearances, such as elections, a democratic culture must be developed and the citizenry become more engaged. The world is watching the political transition in Indonesia; how a people used to strong one-party rule can come to govern themselves. There is a need to be realistic about the likely outcome of the Indonesian reforms: it will be a long time before they take on the look and energy of a liberal democracy. The fact remains that in Indonesia, a democratic culture is non-existent. It will not exist until the concept of democracy as a political system is taught and understood. Democracy will not be achieved through a top-down process; it must be bottom-up.

While Asian countries may have directly elected legislatures and systems of law, this does not automatically mean that a law-abiding culture exists among the people. To take an everyday example, there is widespread disregard for traffic regulations in Malaysia. In the capital of Kuala Lumpur, it is not uncommon to see two riders, sometimes even a family of four, illegally astride a motor cycle. Cars and trucks ignore pedestrians at zebra crossings and maneuver according to whim on highways. At one of the entrance of the general hospital, there is a large sign stating, 'For Emergencies Only', yet everyone uses it as a short cut. You probably understand why 'Everything is fine in Singapore': social engineering begins with such trivial personal habits as flushing toilets to issues like looking after parents. In spite of the government's efforts, Singaporeans still have difficulties adjusting to a rigid rules-based environment—in private, many tell you how they try to outwit the government by going around the rules.

Open and informed debate requires an educated, involved and critical electorate that respects the rules, otherwise it only leads to confusion. In Asia, when you ask some people what they want from their leaders, they often have no clue whatsoever. There is the danger that when they have economic and financial incentives dangled before them, they will give in to vote-buying by politicians. People must want to be involved.

Learning from America

The key to a successful and robust democracy is the voluntary involvement of the people. As many as 80 million Americans do voluntary work and are involved in some kind of public cause. If the experience in America is instructive, it is perhaps a useful reference for us. Alexis de Tocqueville, writing in *Democracy in America*, made the following observations on American society:

> It could be said that, compared to Europe in the 19th century, in America, the township was organized before the country, the country before the state, and the state before the union. Political and administrative life was conducted on three levels: the township was the primary focus, then the country, and lastly, the state. Great equality existed among the immigrants who settled on the shores of New England. It is not only their financial circumstances that were equal; even their accomplishments were of the same uniform standard.

De Tocqueville declared that he did not believe that:

> ... there was a country in the world where, in proportion to the population, there were so few ignorant and at the same time so few learned individuals. Primary instruction was within the reach of all, but few had received higher education. Almost all the Americans were in fortunate circumstances and had obtained a basic education.

Hereditary wealth was scarce; nearly all Americans had to take up a profession. Nowadays, every profession requires an apprenticeship. Learning is important, and Americans pursue degrees to equip themselves with greater skills and knowledge. We know that America has the greatest number of institutions of higher learning in the world, and some of the world's best. The percentage of the population with a university degree is also the highest in the world.

Most of the rich people in America were formerly poor; most of those who now enjoy leisure pursuits were involved in business when they were younger.

It is not the administrative but the political effects of decentralization that I most admire in America. In the United States, the interests of the country are everywhere kept in view; they are an object of solicitude to the entire nation, and all citizens are as warmly attached to them as if they were their own. They take pride in the glory of their nation; they boast of its successes, to which they believe they have themselves contributed, and they rejoice in the general prosperity by which they profit. The feelings they entertain towards the State are analogous to those which unite them to their families, and it is through a kind of selfishness that they interest themselves in the welfare of their country.

To the European, a public officer represents a superior force; to an American, he represents a right. In America, then, it may be said that no-one renders obedience to man, but to justice and to law. If the opinions that citizens have of themselves are exaggerated, they are at least salutary; they have complete faith in their own powers, which appear to them to be all-sufficient. When private individuals become involved in undertakings which are concerned with the common good, they never think of soliciting the co-operation of the government. They plan the undertakings, willingly execute them, seek the assistance of others and work to overcome obstacles. Undoubtedly, they are often less successful than the State might have been, but, in the end, the sum of these private undertakings far exceeds all that the government could ever have done.

Citizens of the United States are taught self-reliance from infancy, in order to resist the evils and difficulties of life. They mistrust social authority and turn to it for assistance only when they cannot do without it. This attitude is even seen in schools, where children establish their own rules for their games and punish misdemeanors which they have themselves defined. The same spirit pervades every act of social life.

In the United States, voluntary associations are established to promote the safety of the public, commerce, industry, morality and religion. An association consists simply of a number of individuals who all publicly support certain doctrines, and who agree to promote these doctrines in a certain manner. When a body of opinion is supported in such a way, it necessarily assumes a more exact and explicit form. The association brings together those who subscribe to its doctrines and engages them in its cause. They, for their part, become acquainted with one another, and their enthusiasm for their cause is increased as their numbers grow.

Independence of the press is the chief element of liberty. A nation that is determined to remain free is therefore right in demanding, at any price, the exercise of this independence.

I was surprised to find so much distinguished talent among the citizens and so little among the heads of the government. It is a constant fact that, at the present day, the ablest men in the United States are rarely placed as the head of affairs, and it must be acknowledged that such has been the result in proportion as democracy has exceeded all its former limits. The race of American statesmen has evidently dwindled most remarkably in the last fifty years.

Favorable conditions

History has shown that there are three essential ingredients for political reform, wherever it is carried out. These are: establishing the norms governing elite politics; the restructuring of basic institutions governing relations among parts of the state, such as the division of power among the government's different branches; and the strengthening of the institutions of political participation. Minxin Pei observed in *Foreign Affairs* in early 1998:

> The Chinese political system inherited by Deng Xiaoping in 1978 resembled a Hobbesian world. No norms governed elite politics. Its key government institutions, especially the legal system and the bureaucracy, had been seriously damaged by the economic and political turmoil of the Great Leap Forward of 1958 and the 1966–68 Cultural Revolution. There were no institutions of political participation under Mao Zedong, mass political campaigns and mob violence had been the main forms of participation. Deng was faced with rebuilding China's wrecked political system and reforming its backward economy at the same time.[26]

Donald Kagan, Professor of Classics at Yale, summarized the three necessary conditions for democracy: first, a set of good institutions; second, a body of citizens who possess a good understanding of the principles of democracy, or who have developed a character consistent with the democratic way of life; and third, a high quality of leadership, at least at critical moments.[27]

The Chairman of the Democratic Alliance of The People's Republic China, Yen Chia Chee, listed a step-by-step guide to the gradual evolution of democratic government in China:

1. Freedom of the press.
2. Reform of the nomination procedure of the representatives to the People's Congress.
3. Step-by-step amendments to the Chinese Constitution.
4. The Communist Party to abandon the management of civil servants by category of functions; the strict enforcement of the Civil Service Ordinance.
5. Direct election of representatives to the People's Congress to be expanded to the provinces.
6. The enactment of a freedom of association ordinance.
7. Transparency.
8. To abolish political and party executives within the military.
9. To enact legislation governing the military's involvement in politics.
10. To promote broad acceptance of the independence of the legislature, and reforms to the legislative system.
11. The emergence of political opposition.
12. Direct election of members of parliament.
13. Autonomy to Tibet, Sinkiang, Inner Mongolia, Liaxia and Kwangsi provinces.
14. Government-to-government dialogue between Beijing and Taipei on the reunification of China.
15. Election of representatives to the Constitutional Reform Congress.
16. Convening the Constitutional Reform Congress, Proclamation of the Peace and Reunification Constitution leading to the dawn of the 'Third Republic'.
17. Hold the first direct election of members of parliament based on the new Constitution; the formation of two houses of the legislative body.
18. Formation of the Cabinet led by the ruling political party.
19. Enactment of legislation to outlaw money and violence from interfering in the political process.
20. Install a mechanism in the Constitution to deal with possible conflicts between the power of the legislature and the executive.
21. Peaceful governance to be strengthened.[28]

Democratic principles will gain strength over time, through the events that take place and by legislation. In a true democracy, individuals answer only to themselves; they are owned by no-one, they bow to pressure from no-one, and no family or corporate influence can be perceived. To some extent, this phenomenon can be seen in the United States, where people enjoy great equality of opportunity; in other words, people there are more equal in terms of individual power than they are in any other country of the world or at any other time in history.

At the grassroots

Democracy is about decentralization and taking government to the people, ie, local government. Most countries hold elections at the local government level, and grassroots elections are a good place to begin the democratic transformation. Since 1988, there have been elections in over 80 per cent of the approximately 900,000 villages in China, home to perhaps 3/4 of the country's 1.3 billion people. These villages have elected, through universal suffrage and secret ballots, their own chiefs and village committees, who serve for terms of three years. By 1997, 95 per cent of villages will have held elections. Some of those elected are Communist Party members; but the majority are not.[29]

The Power of One

Chinese moves towards democracy, set in motion by paramount leader Deng Xiaoping, have been directed towards getting rid of the personality cult, and reforming the system to drive out stubborn adherence to power by one man or a small group. To the Chinese, putting an end to rule by man means a big cultural and attitudinal change, a significant step forward.

From rule of man to rule of law

In China's *hwa xia* culture, the emperor was said to have the mandate of heaven. There was a willingness to put one's trust in the leader, whether he is Emperor Wu of the Han dynasty or Mao Zedong of the People's Republic of China. Because of the assumption that all leaders are virtuous and saintly, it was unthinkable that they would not act in the best interests of the people. It was this belief that led to no safeguards being erected that would contain the power of the State. For the last 2,000 years, the accepted wisdom has been: if the leaders are good and if the 'good' is unambiguous, why the need for checks and balances? When leaders act irresponsibly, they automatically disqualify themselves as leaders and lose the mandate to govern. This must therefore be removed. This has happened many times in China's long history

To the Chinese, a hero, by definition, was good. His mistakes, if he made any, were likely to be tactical in nature. His intentions were good and he meant well. However, if rulers abuse the moral code, the people will revolt. The intuitive nature of the Chinese makes them disregard the need for forward planning, the need to provide for problems or contingencies. As the Chinese proverb says *zhuan dao qiao tou zi ran zhi*, (the ship will straighten its course as it is approaching the dock). This reflects that the Chinese simply deal with the consequences when they arise. I am afraid this is not very scientific or rational. The Chinese themselves have lamented this tendency as 'romantic' and hardly an efficient way of bringing about change! The assuring news is that change is in sight.

Change has come, especially in mainland China. China is rushing to enact laws to specifically define relationships and conduct. Minxin Pei, the Assistant Professor of Politics at Princeton University, noted in *Foreign Affairs* that The National People's Congress passed 175 laws between 1978 and 1994, and the local people's congresses enacted another 3,000. Although on paper, Chinese laws borrow extensively from Western legal doctrines, concepts, procedures, and terminology, '...undeterred by the poor enforcement of the law (only half the legal judgments in commercial disputes are enforced), an increasing number of Chinese citizens and business people have turned to the legal system to protect their property and personal rights,' wrote Minxin Pei. People are also increasingly assertive about their rights, as Chinese courts are finding out. The number of professionals in the legal community is expanding. The number of lawyers went from 31,000 in 1988 to 90,000 in 1995. Minxin Pei, who also wrote *From Reform to Revolution: The Demise of Communism in China and the Soviet Union*, said in *Foreign Affairs* that:

> The implementation of an extensive body of law has not only created an institutional legal framework but has benefited important groups private entrepreneurs, foreign investors, an expanding middle class who would likely resist any reversal of the trend, and the legal system is likely to become a critical arena in which the Chinese Communist Party's authority can be indirectly challenged and checked before the initiation of competitive reforms.

Mandatory retirement

History has taught us that no man must hang on to power for too long. Great leaders are greater if they retire at an opportune moment. The monopoly of power is dangerous, and the system must provide for rejuvenation at the top by the injection of fresh ideas and the addition of new personalities that gives the system its dynamism. Young people with new ideas must not wait too long to have their turn.

Paramount leader Deng Xiaoping introduced mandatory retirement for party and government officials to put an end to the perpetuation of individual power, complacency and nepotism, and accelerated the ascent of the next generation. President Jiang Zemin is continuing with this generational change in the central leadership. 'Although China's term limits have attracted little attention abroad, they have probably had the most far-reaching little effect of any reform on the composition and outlook of the ruling elite,' Minxin Pei concluded. According to Pei's research, at the beginning of 1982, the retirement age for ministers, provincial party secretaries, and governors was set at 65, and that of their deputies at 60. A two-term limit has also been imposed on all party and government positions. Until 1982, the average age of ministers and vice ministers in the State Council was 64; only 37 per cent of them were college-educated. After the reforms in late 1982, the average age of ministers and vice ministers dropped to 58, and 52 per cent were college-educated. The membership of the central committee also reflects this reform: in 15 years, the average age declined from 59 to 56, while the proportion of college-educated members increased from 55 to 92 per cent. The ruling elite at the provincial level also underwent the same dramatic change. In 1982, the average age of provincial party secretaries and governors was 62; it dropped to 55 in 1983 and has remained below 55 ever since. During the same period, the proportion of college-educated provincial leaders rose from 20 per cent in 1982 to 79 per cent in 1996. As Minxin Pei observed, 'Almost instantly, it transformed a ruling elite dominated by poorly educated, aging revolutionaries into one composed mostly of middle-aged technocrats'. The leadership in China today is the youngest and most educated in China's history.

Towards a united Chinese commonwealth

For a country with a huge population and vast territory, decentralized government is perhaps the most effective method of administration. The vision of a united Chinese commonwealth may help to resolve the remaining territorial and sovereignty issues that exist in the regions of China. With the Hong Kong question settled, the Taiwan issue and also the question of Tibet, Sinkiang and others have moved centre stage. Taiwan officially dismissed the validity of the 'one country, two systems' arrangement. 'We are not Hong Kong. Taiwan wants "one country, one good system" ', Taiwan premier, Lien Chien, said in a CNN interview immediately following the handback.

Under President Lee's new policies, Taiwan began pressing vigorously for admission to international organizations. Lee also made highly publicized trips to nations with which Taipei has formal ties. Even more impressive was Taipei's drive to develop intergovernmental relations with countries that had diplomatic relations with Beijing. Also, Taiwan's unofficial relations with the United States continued to improve, with the United States announcing an upgrading of its economic and cultural ties with Taiwan. In June 1995, Lee made a private visit to the United States and delivered a speech at Cornell University, his alma mater. This made him the first Taiwanese president to have set foot on US soil.

Lee himself has stressed the need to root policy in public opinion. Taiwan's ruling party, which he heads, must be transformed into a 'Kuomintang of the Taiwanese people'. In July 1994, his administration reaffirmed its preferred model, of 'one China, two [equal] political entities', in a white paper on relations with the Mainland. The document also formalized Taipei's rejection of China's 'one country, two systems' program for reunification. Many fear that the relationship between the Mainland and Taiwan could, if not handled well, deteriorate to a point where the world's leading nations could become embroiled. The consequences of this could destabilize the entire Asia-Pacific region, wreck China's economic reforms and shatter Asian dreams of prosperity. If Taiwan declares independence, some analysts predict that China will almost certainly mount military action against it, America and Japan would become involved, and the world would face the prospect of another major conflict.

In Taiwan, pressure grows for more attention to be given to Taiwan and less to China, yet the reality is that Taiwan's economic future lies with the Mainland. In spite of the politics, Taiwanese businesses continue to invest in China, and the business community, including leading businessmen such as Wang Yu Ching, Kao Ching Yuen and Chang Yo Fah, has criticized the government for not being realistic in its reunification policy. The Chinese leadership has increasingly demonstrated its willingness to accommodate a scenario of 'one country, many systems'; perhaps paving the way for China to move towards a commonwealth of states in the next century. In late 1997, the chairman of the Chinese representatives on the Cross-Straits Negotiation Committee, Wang Dao-han, gave a new interpretation of the 'one China policy': 'One China refers not to Taiwan, not to the Mainland—it refers to a unified China.'

The character of the leadership, both in Beijing and Taipei, is the most crucial and decisive factor in the reunification issue. Now the handback of Hong Kong is approaching its first anniversary, China's 'one country, two systems' appears to be on a good footing, which gives reason for hope for a new Asian way. Activists in the West would do well to let go of their narrow definition of democracy and remember the words of Robert L Bartley, editor of *The Wall Street Journal*. 'Americans ought to have faith in their own ideals. If the United States really believes that development engenders democracy, it should stipulate that China's rapid development is in America's own long-run national interest.[30]

Part IV

Cultivation of the Individual

Chapter 10
Winning Values

"The true test of civilization is not the census,
not the size of cities, not the crops,
but the kind of man the country turns out."

—Ralph Waldo Emerson—

Museums, art galleries, libraries and universities preserve the treasures of civilization. These treasures bear witness to the glory and failings of a civilization. However, they hardly represent the real essence of a people. The real essence, indeed, lies in the people's capabilities and mental outlook in responding to change, in their abilities to come to terms with past failings, cultural imperfections, and in their readiness to continue the pursuit of improvements.

One of the reasons why the soft power of America is spreading rapidly around the world, many would agree, is the optimism and promise that the American culture exudes. In contrast, the Chinese in particular, look back to the days when their civilization was great, when the Middle Kingdom was superior to the rest of the world. While the Americans seem to say that the best is yet to come, the Chinese habitually remind us the greatness of their past achievements. The country's economic backwardness and the humiliations inflicted by the Western powers and the Japanese have surely seared a strong scar on the psyche of these proud people. Debating history is, however, futile. The priority for China and elsewhere in Asia should be to nurture a new and modern culture which will enable progress.

In recent times, impressive growth has already been recorded and there have been vast improvements in the lives of millions of people. However, resentment against the West still exists all over Asia, and this has sometimes resulted in some ill-advised attempts to outdo the West, causing resources being devoted to extravagant projects which made little economic sense.

At the dawn of the 21st century, the question we have to honestly ask ourselves is whether we are ready to set aside the 'baggage' of history and start focusing on our future. In the world of the future, what values will help us succeed?

China Loosens the Bonds of History

Some scholars claim that Chinese recorded history can be traced back 7,000 years. Taiwan-based Chinese historian Po Yang has done some calculations and found that throughout this long history, there were only three golden periods: the Spring Autumn and Warring states (770–221BC); the Tang Dynasty (627–727) and the mid-Ching Dynasty (1660–1770).[1] During these periods, the emperor was humane, the rule just, the court friendly, and the people involved. Civil society was active, intellectual activity was vibrant and free, and everywhere the economy was prosperous. These were times when art and literature flourished. Today, when the Chinese talk about their glorious 5,000-year-old history, consciously or not, they are referring to these 750 years of extraordinary achievements.

The real obstacle to modernization in China, apart from the constraints imposed by its huge population and scarce resources, is the rigidity of its hierarchical structure. Almost 4,000 years of a social system that kept the people's energy in check and sealed the lid on creativity led to stagnation. Confucian thoughts were interpreted to mean that the most important goal in society was order and stability. The court mandarins (who we would call the bureaucracy today) were very powerful and corrupt; they sat at the apex of the social and political system, overseeing and controlling everything that went on.

A tight Confucian moral code that celebrates obedience and filial piety enveloped the Chinese mind and restrained the behavior of the people. Wealth creation was looked upon as immoral; man should instead strive to become gentle and moral. During the East Han dynasty, the government decreed that no intellectuals could write or say anything that was not within the boundary set by their teachers. It was against the law to defy this decree. One can imagine what damage this did over time; all creativity and lateral thinking was stifled. It is therefore not surprising that in the 4,000 years that followed Confucius, there were few thinkers in China. For generations, people have not only been obedient out of habit and fear of recrimination, they have even lost the ability to imitate, the courage to object, the curiosity to venture out and the self-confidence to create.

Weighed down by firm traditions and the power of the mandarins, no one dared to think about freedom. To survive, the Chinese had to be very careful and smart; they had to rely on the goodwill of people whose influence could save them should any unfortunate event occur. This is the famous Chinese *guanxi*, whereby people accumulate goodwill and do good deeds to each other as a kind of social insurance. Networks of personal relationships developed and the seeking and selling of favors became widespread. A corrupt bureaucratic culture lasts to the present day, a key obstacle to the Chinese government's efforts to modernize the country.

While the Mainland was bogged down in this repressive culture, the various overseas Chinese communities underwent a kind of modernization through influence from the West. Western ideas on governance, their celebration of materialism, the way of the free market, the rule of law and open communication provided a foundation for efficiency and gave the overseas Chinese the opportunity to use more of their potential. People in Hong Kong developed a culture of efficiency, professionalism, and respect for the law. The Taiwanese learnt industrial production from the Japanese and the West, and the intellectual community are also now enjoying open debate on democracy. Rationality was embraced as a central value, and the centuries-long disdain for commerce and wealth creation was replaced with an obsession to make money. When living standards in Hong Kong, Singapore, Taiwan and other overseas Chinese communities achieved developed-country status, self-confidence returned. People's attitudes gradually changed and their behavior modified.

Today, very few in these communities talk about being humiliated by the West or boast about China's ancient grandeur, except perhaps the older generation. While faith in the family system remains strong and deeply embedded, the clan and family are no longer exclusively important. The nature of *guanxi* is also changing. A young Chinese may say, 'I will call Arthur Andersen as well as the daughter-in-law of my wife's fifth uncle when I need tax advice. It is not because our uncle's daughter-in-law is our relative, but because I have heard that she is good. Even then, for a matter of great importance, I will still call a well-known professional for a second opinion.' Advice is now sought not only from the family, but from other networks, regardless of race, creed or nationality. Objectivity overrules *guanxi*.

A Cultural Morass

Asia's modernization has been driven by external forces, by Western influences. Western ways led to an environment where tremendous pent-up energy that had been suppressed by a repressive regime could be unleashed. In the developed regions, those with confidence recognized, celebrated and embraced the foreign influences and values that proved useful to their own progress. However, certain cultural habits die hard—condemnation of Western influences is still heard, particularly from the political and intellectual quarters, though not so much from the business sector. One of the most persistent criticisms of capitalism is that it is brutal and encourages inhuman Darwinian competition.

For people who are used to a culture of paternalism and dependence, it is not surprising that some are finding it hard to adjust. Recently, the government of the Hong Kong Special Administrative Region was criticized for not intervening in the economy during the financial crisis. Conservatives complained that, in spite of Hong Kong's vast foreign reserves, its 'savings for a rainy day', the government was not prepared to release much of it, although it was in the middle of a very severe storm. In this cultural shift, from paternalism to self-reliance, it will take some time for people to understand that competition, the price mechanism, the rule of law and the protection of private property are all handled very differently in a rule-based market economy. In the past, because of lawlessness and bad rulers, the Chinese practised a form of reluctant self-reliance. Now things are different; they must practise creative self-reliance. People must persevere in this if Asia is to emerge as a modern, progressive and prosperous region.

What are the unattractive traits that must be changed? Taiwan-based historian Po Yang is among the most critical: 'The Cultural Revolution and other turbulent events of the past have totally destroyed many good virtues upheld by the ancient Chinese people'. His discussion of the many flaws in the Chinese system in his best-selling book, *The Ugly Chinese*, landed him in jail in Taiwan. While it is not my intention to provide an in-depth analysis of the ugly side of the Chinese character here, what I aim to do in the next few paragraphs is to highlight some serious flaws in the value system that obstruct growth.

Contradictions in values

Conservatives waving the Confucian moralist flag insist that Asian civilization is far superior to that of the West. They claim that Asians are moral beings, and the goal is to be a gentleman (*jun zi*) and a saint (*sheng xian*). Reality, however, is rather different. Confucius probably overlooked the fact that it is difficult for the poor and hungry to be gentle or saintly. Some Chinese people are loud, greedy and unscrupulous (although such traits are not confined to the Chinese race alone). The prejudice towards wealth creation is misplaced. Wealth creation is not immoral; in fact, it is quite the contrary. If wealth is created in the service of mankind, it is highly moral and useful to the community; it results in more jobs, products and services that serve humanity.

Those Asians who moralize should remember that some of the worst violations of intellectual property rights and instances of corruption occur in Asia. Asians who buy videos of just-released movies for US$3 at the night market have total disregard for those who invested a great deal of money in making the movie. It is even more shameful that they show no remorse, some taking the view that they are outsmarting the foreigners. The West may have lost millions of dollars by such abuses of intellectual rights, but it is the Asians who have more to lose in the long run. These are self-defeating attitudes that will make Asia's own enterprising and creative minds go to the West, where their work will be valued and protected.

Many Chinese have little inclination for team-work. They describe this aspect of their behavior as resembling a tray of loose sand (*yi pa san sha*). The saying, 'One monk lives by carrying his own water; two monks live by sharing the load; and three monks together live without water' describes the lack of cohesion. There is also a certain narrowness in their attitude, they confine their relationships to those they know.

Every now and then, the echo of China's 5,000-year-old civilization and the utter conviction that the Chinese are the greatest people in the world are heard, to remind you. If any critical observations are made, the usual defence is that the points put forward by the critic are incompatible with Chinese culture or the actual circumstances. There is no concept of equality between people: one is either a master or a servant. Paradoxically, along with the superiority complex, there is also an undercurrent of anger that stems from feelings of inferiority. Little self-esteem is left when there has been prolonged repression. The need to keep 'face' is another psychological barrier to open and honest relationships.

Confucius had it that a husband must reward his wife's loyalty and obedience with faithfulness and responsibility towards the family. However, men with three wives and four mistresses were common. Only recently, we heard about the 'concubines village' in southern China created by Hong Kong businessmen. Asian society still harbors an attitude that tolerates, if not favors, male infidelity. To most Asians, US President Bill Clinton's sex scandal is merely a storm in a tea-cup.

Confucianism today

In all great societies and in the lives of successful individuals, there is an unyielding stubbornness to adhere to important ideals: former British prime minister Margaret Thatcher called it the power of conviction. Confucianism embodied philosophical ideals that are comprehensive. One criticism of Confucianism is that it has high ideals that, in theory, are great, but are not realistic or achievable. However, reinterpreting Confucius in the modern context can go some way towards resolving the conflict of morality and productivity. For example, it has been argued that wealth creation was immoral, and therefore being productive was immoral. But if we look at wealth creation as a form of value creation in the service of all, it is a way whereby the individual increases his usefulness (a central concept in Confucianism) for himself, his family and the community at large. The modern productive person is also a moral one.

The Confucian models of 'usefulness' (*nuo zhe*) are as follows:

- People who possess values (and skills) that make them self-reliant would not be a burden on society. Thus the first duty of any person is to be productive to the employer, and continue to be productive and keep up with relevant skills to stay employable. Achieving financial independence means not needing help from others financially.
- After achieving self-reliance, one cultivates additional intellectual, technological and organizational capacity to bring value to others. For example, when employees outgrow their jobs and develop valuable competencies, their employers ask them to become partners and to continue to work for them. In this way, the employers expand their enterprises, creating wealth and more jobs.
- When an entire community becomes a dynamic learning community, vigilant in maintaining their competitiveness, their prosperity is assured.
- When a local business develops into a global enterprise, useful products and services at affordable prices are made available to people all over the world. The enterprise is culturally attractive and environmentally friendly: it gives meaning to the lives of employees, shareholders, consumers and management.

Confucian values will flourish in the modern world if we apply the philosophy of a person's usefulness in the creation of wealth and have the motivation and strength of character to pursue our ideals.

Cultural values for the 21st Century

Po Yang's criticisms are hard-hitting. He has been trying to drive home the point that although Chinese civilization was great 4,000 years ago, that was in the past and the Chinese must now start anew to build a progressive culture.[2] Any discussion of the merits or faults of a civilization carries the risk of perpetuating prejudices that may hide the real gems of that civilization and do it an injustice. The fact of its survival demonstrates its amazing strength. The continuing modernization of Asia must focus on a fundamental reassessment of values; this will not be without its difficulties because the top-down culture is so ingrained. The good news is that not everyone is well-versed in Chinese history. Not all have experienced the cultural faults and know only the good aspects. Acer founder Stan Shih has remarked that he has no hang-ups on self-esteem and was brought up to believe that he had to find his own way. Asia has a young population—it is unlikely that many under 30 worry about historical errors.

Towards One World

The process of integrating with the rest of the world is well-advanced, especially in Asia's cities. Modern attitudes are also gaining wide acceptance, rapidly in some places and more slowly in others. A first-time visitor to an Asian city will find the sights, sounds and smells exhausting and confusing, but to an Asian, they are invigorating.

Watching Asian children in restaurants eat noodles with forks reminds one of foreign influences on Asian cultures. An English-speaking child brought up in an Anglicized home will wrap the noodles around the fork in the Western way; one brought up in an Asian home, be it Chinese or Thai, will either pick up a pair of chopsticks or use the fork like a pair of chopsticks. If one is interested enough, people-watching in Asia is a moving picture of history.

A blend of cultures

The really sophisticated and contemporary Asian knows all the latest fashion trends, both in the East and in the West. The most popular look for the modern Asian city woman in July 1997 was very short, closely cropped hair and completely natural make-up. There are platform shoes, cellular phones, and the smell of Calvin Klein's 'Just Be'. Few young overseas Chinese are conscious of their ethnic status: their identity is Taiwanese, a Hong Konger, a Singaporean or a Malaysian.

Teenagers put their baseball caps on backwards; they talk in bits and bytes, hook on to the Internet and keep electronic pets. Some rush home for piano and violin lessons, learn Mozart and Beethoven, and then go to a Spice Girls concert. This is not Western behavior; it is just how they conduct their lives in today's world.

The China Club in the old China Bank Building in Hong Kong sports a large portrait, done in the 'pop art' style, of Chairman Mao with Whitney Houston. Entrepreneur David Tang pays the gorgeous actress, Gong Li, huge sums to show the world that Chinese is chic. In stadiums that seat tens of thousands of near-hysterical audiences, laser-lit Canto-pop singers belt out Chinese versions of rap, pop and rock.[3] Thai-Chinese Singaporean classical violinist, Vanessa Mae, plays in a mini-skirt, rocking away on the stage. It is difficult to make out whether it is a Western or an Asian tune. The best Chinese restaurants in Asia recommend their guests to have white wine with their roast chicken. The Chinese cuisine and the Western wine blend perfectly to give the diners a memorable meal; they do not stop to think whether they are enjoying an Asian or a Western experience.

Popular culture is where modern trends first show up. Today, popular consumer culture is a vast system of interconnected global and local cultures—sushi bars and fast-food outlets, Issey Miyake and Ralph Lauren, the Spice Girls and Canto-pop. These are the cities of the new Asia, Asian ways in juxtaposition with Western tools, sometimes looking seamless, sometimes awkward. In 1996, I went to a contemporary art exhibition of the work of young Asian artists in New York City entitled 'Traditions/tensions'. Some artists were criticized for the lack of a distinct identity in their work. One comment was 'These expressions are neither here nor there, not Thai enough and not totally Western'. This remark encapsulates the state of Asia's urban culture. A new modern Asian culture is waiting to be born; the wait may not be too long.

Creative chaos

The reverence that some Asians have for their past and the paternalism that is deeply embedded in their cultures can make them uncomfortable with Western liberal ideas and what seems to them to be disorder. Bearing in mind China's stagnation, 'stability' and 'order' are not in themselves growth. Some degree of creative chaos is necessary for rejuvenation. How to get the leadership and society to accept chaos as creative is the first step.

A Modern Value System

To achieve things through one's own efforts is a universally celebrated mark of self-reliance. There appears to be no conflict between the Confucian or the Western definition of a productive person. The consensus everywhere is to achieve self-sufficiency and prosperity for the community through economic development, ie wealth creation. Values such as respect for learning, openness to new ideas, self-discipline, respect for others and honesty are indispensable for any society to survive. But as societies move up the ladder of competition, where greater intellectual capabilities and knowledge are needed, it is critically important to provide a climate where these qualities can be further developed and creativity encouraged. Hence, such things as personal freedom, the rights of the individual, and freedom of expression must be allowed to move centre-stage. The importance placed on values varies, not only between West and East but, as the following tables show, between Asians themselves.[4]

Table 10.1: Values most cherished by Asian societies

Japan	Harmony
Hong Kong	Orderly society and personal freedom
Singapore	Orderly society
Thailand	Personal financial success
South Korea	Thinking for oneself
Taiwan	Self-reliance

Source: Wirthlin Worldwide Research

Table 10.2: Values emphasized in Asia and North America

Importance	Asia	North America
1	Hard work	Freedom of personal expression
2	Emphasis on learning	Personal freedom
3	Honesty	Self-reliance
4	Openness to new ideas	Personal rights
5	Sense of responsibility	Hard work
6	Self-discipline	Personal achievement
7	Self-reliance	Thinking about oneself

Source: Wirthlin Worldwide Research

Values such as hard work, honesty and self-discipline are universal and span all cultures. However, the degree of emphasis on these values varies relative to the priorities of development and interpretation, but the outcome is the same. With increasing education, it is only natural that people seek to achieve more in their lives and demand greater room for individual expression. With competition coming from unexpected quarters, few in the world can claim to have a permanent edge over others. Many skilled software writers in the West have lost their jobs to well-educated Indians in Bangalore who will do the same work for perhaps 1/10 of what the Westerner is paid. Now the Africans are joining in the race. Becoming creative and productive is a daunting challenge as Asia moves up the value chain from assembling products to making them. Moving from a top-down culture to one of bottom-up initiatives is vital if Asian societies are to achieve economic self-reliance in a competitive global economy.

Until a uniquely Asian core value system evolves, values in Asia will be a blend of the best of East and West. Because modern societies are also open societies, undesirable elements are inevitable. For example, distasteful material that even Western societies abhor slips past television censors. Asian governments were protective; however, it is not the job of the government to decide what is desirable and what is not. It is the responsibility of each and every Asian to make that decision.

Getting priorities straight

Many people are so caught up with the wonders of modern technology that they seem to have neglected personal values. We are producing highly competent people, but sometimes, people with questionable moral codes. The moral in the movie *Titanic* is clear: the ship was technically unsinkable, but human arrogance and ambition drove it to the bottom. Many societies, families and individuals could suffer this fate if we continue to pay too little attention to our moral anchors.

Families used to be close; grandparents were there to help children see the difference between right and wrong. Today, less time is spent with the children, and even when families are together, the time is spent in front of the television or the computer. There is a need to get educational priorities straight and to concentrate on nurturing human beings with an ethical value system. With the right values, skills automatically follow.

In businesses today, managers are waking up to the cost of hiring people with the right values. Malaysian entrepreneur, Chew Poh Jin, has this to say of talent:

> If someone has 80 per cent talent, but wrong values and bad attitude, as an employer, you probably can get [out of him] half of that talent endowed in him. In contrast, a responsible and honorable man will give his best, and if he is only endowed with 50 per cent talent, he will give it all. I will hire the less talented guy.[5]

Overprotective Asian parents often retard the development of their offspring. Once, riding home in a taxi, I complained about parents spoiling their children by giving them material things whenever they ask for them, and not making them work to earn them. The driver disagreed. He said it was too risky to let teenage children go out to work where they come under undesirable influences. He said his father prevented his children from picking up gambling habits by making them stay at home. To make them obey, his father gambled with them with very small stakes! Such an attitude is almost beyond belief—so long as the kids are within sight, parents think they are in control. Maybe, but it doesn't help the children. Such an upbringing can never help prepare children for the real world. Anxieties are being expressed about the personalities of children who have no siblings. China's 'little emperors', the reputedly spoilt products of the one-child policy, are said to be having a revolutionary effect on Chinese society. Through infancy, youth and adolescence, this generation has never known the foundation that is essential to Chinese character-building—*chi ku* (eating bitter), a reference to the endurance of hardship. The parents have endured the Cultural Revolution, whereas their child has grown up in the most stable period in China's history. The parents were brought up on revolution, hardship, heroism and collectivism, but their only child has no knowledge of their difficult past and knows only pop culture. Many Chinese parents are concerned with their children's strength of character and worry about their capacity to withstand difficulties in their adult lives. These concerns are understandable, but it does suggest a certain hang-up with the past. Why should children not grow up being taught the right values in the modern context? Values such as courage, assertiveness, respect, tolerance and creativity are needed today, more so than the older values of frugality, submissiveness, excessive deference, and tolerance of repressive authority.

The goal is personal growth

Seeking personal growth should be more important than accumulating things, not that there is anything wrong with the latter. People who bring value to themselves become, in the process, better and more useful individuals. If each and everyone strives to become a better person—a better son or daughter, a better husband or wife, a better father or mother, a better friend, a more supportive boss or a more productive employee, further success will follow. If a society has a collective growth orientation, its future is assured.

There is a need to get managers to refocus through modern management training. Since 1983, Professor Chakraborty of the Indian Institute of Management in Calcutta has worked on an approach that focuses on values instead of skills and intellect.[6] He has put forward four categories into which members of an organization can fall: (1) values-weak, skills-weak; (2) values-strong, skills-weak; (3) values-strong, skills-strong; and (4) values-weak, skills-strong.

Seventy per cent or more of the participants in Professor Chakraborty's program say that people in the 'values-weak, skills-strong' group constitute the majority. The preferred combination of skills and values is always 'values-strong, skills-strong'. This is clear evidence of what Professor Chakraborty terms a 'values gap'. Yet current management training techniques almost completely focus on skills.

Universal Values

Regardless of colour, creed or religion, the important values of self-reliance, efficiency, openness, a global mind-set and a preoccupation with excellence have served people and the community well throughout the world.

Self-reliance

Someone who is self-sufficient would not be a burden to others, and as such, would have discharged his basic duty as a member of society. And for one to become self-sufficient, wealth creation is fundamental. Altruistic young people talk about their concern for growing inequalities and the widening gap between the haves and the have-nots. But when asked for the answers to these problems, most tend to look to the state. It is ironical that people can still place so much faith in the state, when the state has a record of failure. What has been proved, time and again, is that people can only be helped to help themselves. You can only help someone by giving them the skills to fish, not by giving them the fish. It is more important that a society has the power to create and grow a bigger and better pie, than devoting its energies to dividing up the existing one.

Efficiency

This is about maximizing the use of scarce resources, the basis of all value creation. Being productive and efficient means continually stretching the individual's ingenuity in solving problems, overcoming obstacles and innovating, as well as staying abreast of what is relevant and current. Competition may be brutal, but it has a positive effect on the individual—it pushes the individual towards growth and does not allow complacency to take hold. This is why monopolies are bad for everyone concerned.

Openness

One of modern Asia's strengths is in its openness to ideas, products and foreign concepts, especially in the area of technology. Asians enthusiastically embrace Western science and technology without thinking about their cultural origins. In June 1997, Professor Wu Chai Wei, President of the University of Science and Technology in Hong Kong, said to me, 'Only a very confident people are not afraid of culturally being engulfed by foreign influences. If the indigenous culture is superior, it will not give way to foreign influences; the impacts are only temporary'. Take Chinese food as an example: it only got more popular with the arrival of MacDonalds and KFC. Openness to information and new cultures helps to stimulate new ways of thinking, and will turn out to have an enriching effect on both the student and the teacher.

A global mind-set

Because urban Asia has been very open to foreign influences, its societies could develop a truly global mind-set before any of the more ethnocentric Western communities do. A global mind-set rests on a foundation of openness; it celebrates the best in a culture, recognizing that flaws are inevitable anywhere. People with a global outlook understand the different value systems, different norms of behavior and different assumptions. They can accept and even celebrate differences. They accept diversity and heterogeneity as natural, and as sources of opportunity rather than inconveniences. One of their most valuable traits is their flexibility, and their ability to see things from another person's point of view.

The face of urban Asia has many shades, reflecting Asia's spiritual traditions and modern lifestyles. While each shade remains very distinct, it shows the influence of the others. In Malaysia, Vision 2020 wants to build a 'Bangsa Malaysia' (a Malaysian race). Perhaps a Malaysian culture is possible, not a Malaysian race. By 2020, the Chinese will still remain distinctively Chinese, the Indians will still be Indians, and the Malays will still be Malays. However, new common cultural habits will inevitably form among Malaysians through a kind of osmosis, as a result of a long period of living together. While there may be a long way to go to achieve complete unity, the new Asian way is about living with and celebrating these differences now.

Excellence

Being the best is both worthy and profitable, and the only way to survive in today's world. Asians in general, and the Chinese in particular, need to reorient themselves and regard excellence as a worthy goal in itself. Money must never be the first and last motivation in pursuing knowledge, nor should knowledge be pursued for purely romantic reasons. The Japanese pursue excellence and embrace *kaisen*, constant improvement. *Kaisen* has almost become a religion among the Japanese. There is no similar insistence on standards among the Chinese, an attitude that threatens to make dinosaurs of Asian companies. The Chinese are known for their *ma fu* and Malays for their *tidak apa* attitude. These attitudes must change.[7] Asians must invest more resources if the quality of their products and services are to be world-class.

The lack of systematic organization and an unwillingness to share knowledge have been a major cultural weakness. Whereas the Japanese are creative imitators, most Asians are lazy copycats. We would do well to change our mind-set from the short term to the long term, and devote more time to studying and learning about quality and excellence. Greater effort, greater Asian-ness and greater creativity and originality are required in all fields, including science, technology and management. We must focus on overcoming Asia's daunting challenges, such as environmental degradation and population pressure. We need to have a better understanding and mastery of the physical environment, the technologies to combat disease, and learn how to deal with new management and cultural challenges.

Hong Kong investment banker Tam Siu Cheung has a collection of 2,000 antique maps. According to Tam, they display a distorted view of the world, inviting reflection on China's current backwardness in science and research. Tam hopes to promote a greater awareness of cartography and the physical world among the Chinese people. He saw greater significance in the US landing on Mars than in the 1997 handback:

> While China celebrates the redressing of a past event, the Americans are mapping Mars. How many more years will China take to acquire that kind of technology?...So many Westerners are saying "China is strong", that the Chinese are starting to believe in it. The truth is, China is no longer weak, but it's far from strong.[8]

Concern over China's backwardness dates back to1923. Dr Sun Yat Sen minced no words when he said:

> I compared Heungshan [a mainland township] with Hong Kong and, although they are only 50 miles apart, the difference of the government impressed me very much. Afterwards I saw the outside world and began to wonder how it was that foreigners, the Englishmen, could do so much as they had done, for example, with the barren rock of Hong Kong within 70 or 80 years, while in 4,000 years, China had no place like Hong Kong.[9]

Promoting Cultural Pursuits

Wealth is not the be-all and end-all of existence; the cultural dimension is important in any civilization. In Kuala Lumpur in 1997, the Brazilian Ambassador to Malaysia, Sergio Barcellos Telles, said to me, 'At one point, Americans built lots of museums and public libraries to counter the obsessive wave of materialism. Asians are too obsessed with money. No-one sends me a thank-you note after I send them books. You only talk money. Show me your great literatures, your music and your painters. Don't tell me that you are poor and you can only afford to invest in culture after you are rich.' I had to run for cover. The ambassador had a very important point: where is our soul?

Fortunately, the Shanghai Museum will help to dispel the perception that Asians only love money. Ma Chengyuan and Wang Qingzheng were the driving force behind a new, modern museum in the heart of China's great metropolis of Shanghai, and have created a showcase of treasures from China's past.[10] Ma and Wang worked relentlessly to build what many consider to be the finest modern museum of Chinese art. The high-tech lighting, good design and the spectacular collection have set a new standard for Asia, and perhaps the world. Now the fight for finding donors for the project is over, the next challenge is to make more Shanghainese and Chinese visitors interested in their own culture. Most of the adults who visit the museum are parents with only one child, who claim that they are too busy and uninterested to visit the museum themselves, but they want their son or daughter to understand their history.

It is hoped that the Shanghai Museum will inspire other Asian countries and galvanize them into taking similar action. We must remember that culture is not just hardware; software is in fact more important. People must be interested enough to get involved, whether as the audience or as the artist. Asia needs more philanthropic efforts to build libraries and museums, and to invest in better collections and better management of them, rather than investing in the construction of prestige projects or more high rise buildings. We need friendly and more interesting places where young people can get motivated to explore and discover for themselves.

The Damaging Effects of Paternalism

During the election campaign in Thailand's Buri Ram province, a rice farmer admitted he did not know who he would be voting for, 'The village leaders have not told us yet'. Paternalism breeds a culture of dependence, and now it is proving to be a burden. In good times, the people listen to the ruling class; in bad times, they expect the government to help them through. But to think for yourself is an individual responsibility and is not something the government or the family can do for you. To blame the rat-race or Western television programs for lowering morals is an abdication of personal responsibility. Whenever someone complains about 'decadent' television programs, I do not hesitate to remind them that the solution is to get up and press the button. Paternalism has replaced intelligence with dependence; people are not thinking and expect someone else to press the button for them.

It has been said that people in Malaysia read very little. Some Malaysians describe themselves as a watching nation: watching football matches, watching the crowd at the bus stop, and now, with 20 channels of television, there will be even more watching. If people choose to watch and believe, and not think or analyze, they risk living their lives from the outside in. The consequences can be very unhappy. Singapore's paternalistic ways are as famous as the good service on board Singapore Airlines. But Singapore is not alone in its strong paternalism. Other Asian countries have it too, though they have not institutionalized it and enforced it as strictly as Singapore does.

Patrick Teoh, Malaysia's popular radio deejay, says:

> In the months that I have been doing this program, it is very evident that a lot of these listeners know how to complain but don't know how to discuss and communicate. [They will phone up to complain about an issue], but when you try to draw them into a discussion, they can't. They just want to know, 'What are you going to do for me?' always standing there for a hand-out. Complain, complain, complain...give me, give me, give me. That's one of the problems.[11]

Creativity cannot be created by official decree; it only happens when individuals are free and not afraid to explore. In a special report on 'Value Judgments', conducted by the *Far Eastern Economic Review*, a hefty 47 per cent of Singaporeans either did not care or felt 'neutral' about human rights issues. The people of the Lion City broke rank with almost everyone else in Asia by voting against freedom of expression.[12] In a conversation with me in Kuala Lumpur in 1997, Calvin Tsao, a Hong Kong architect and designer, whose father is property developer, Frank Tsao, said, 'My father complains that they [the staff] always run back to him and ask, ' What should I do?' He gets very irritated...'. This type of behavior is hardly surprising. Young Asians are told what to learn and what to think, and are never encouraged to speak up.

A Two-way Revolution

The existing culture is that direction comes from the top. Those below just respond to orders, looking up to the leader for cues. The demands of the new century, the need for speed and new ways of doing things, require people to respond fast, to take risks and assume responsibility. A two-way revolution in mind-set and habits is needed. This is the creative chaos Asia needs: if executed well, the process may have dramatic and liberating consequences, unlike the Cultural Revolution in China in the 1960s. First to go must be the hierarchies in our minds— the hierarchies that define boundaries. There is a big difference between respect and subservience: modern Asians must know how to show respect but the days of servile dependence are over. Those at the top must be prepared to distribute power and let go; those being ruled must know that they have to take responsibility for their own well-being. The millions of workers in China, South Korea and Japan who have been promised lifetime employment may feel betrayed. No matter how difficult it is to accomplish this change in attitude, we need to begin now. Through education and supportive communities, we will see a new generation that is more spontaneous, more creative and more self-reliant.

The Balance of 'Qing', 'Li' and 'Fa'

The complicated web of human relationships, the lack of respect for the rule of law and an over-emphasis on personal feelings, has often clouded judgment. Asians, being very used to lives revolving around relationships, must be able to balance relationships, rationality and respect for the law. Traditional Asian societies put relationships at the top, followed by rationality; respect for the law comes last. Another model is to put equal emphasis on relationships and respect for the law, and whenever conflict arises, reasonableness or rationality prevails. Asians are often under the impression that Westerners are cold and not relationship-driven; that they almost always rely on the law to guide their behavior. This view is flawed. It has been reported that when the shooting of the film *Titanic* went over budget, and its backers were beginning to worry that they had a financial disaster, director James Cameron offered to waive his contractual profit-sharing to help the backers recoup their investment. As it turned out, *Titanic* was a huge financial success, and it had been reported that the studio would do the right thing by sharing the success with Cameron and members of the cast. This is an example of human interaction where relationship, reasonableness and the law all came into play, and where reasonableness was the guiding value.

'Qing': the value in relationships

Qing is at the foundation of fruitful and lasting relationships that Asians are accustomed to, whether they are between individuals, families or businesses. Effective leaders use *qing* to reinforce their decisions with their staff and in their business dealings. In a Chinese enterprise, no-one would normally discharge an employee as a form of disciplinary action because of the belief that, in taking action, one should consider *qing* before the punishment. Sometimes, over-emphasis on *qing* creates inefficiency. *Qing* is also used to expand business networks and gain the confidence and support of customers as well as other businessmen. Stan Shih of Acer was quoted as saying that losses incurred by staff members should be looked upon as 'tuition fees'. This is an example of using *qing* to cement loyalty and obtain the full commitment of staff members. In difficult times, he falls back on *qing* to obtain assistance from others.

'Li': rational and reasonable behavior

A reasonable person never pursues a goal they cannot achieve by their own efforts. They want to earn their goals. If they undertake to do something that requires the co-operation of a number of people, they never count on anything but their own ability to persuade them and to obtain their agreement voluntarily. Worth and respect have to be earned. Someone's position will not automatically bring them respect or love and it is not rational to believe otherwise.

Some people seem confused about the services others can provide, and expect unconditional hand-outs. Many wish to be rich, but never bother to find out what is needed to acquire wealth. If they don't become wealthy, they blame society and others for not giving them the opportunity; it does not occur to them that opportunity is self-created. Similarly, a young woman wishes to be loved, but never thinks of discovering what love is, what values it requires, and whether she possesses any lovable attributes. Love, she feels, should be given automatically, just because she is the daughter, the wife or the sister.

As Ayn Rand said:

> Their son (daughter) does not love them, and who, simultaneously, ignore, oppose or attempt to destroy everything they know of their son's convictions, values and goals, never thinking of the connection between these two considerations, never making an attempt to understand their son. The world they never made and dare not challenge, has told them that children love parents automatically. There is the man who wants a job, but never thinks of discovering what qualifications the job requires or what constitutes doing one's work well. Who is to judge? He never made the world. Somebody owes him a living. How? Somehow.[13]

Many of us Asians are particularly vulnerable to this kind of weakness. For some, just because there is a blood or marriage relationship, they expect to be loved; they fail to recognize that love works both ways. There is no denying that the universal goal is to be happy. However, happiness is a goal, not an entitlement. The question therefore is, 'Who is responsible for one's happiness and who should make the effort?' The idealistic think that there should be fairness and justice for all, and some higher force such as the government should ensure equality for all. This was what led to the welfare state and communism. In shedding one's responsibility for one's own life, one drops the responsibility of ever having to consider the interests and lives of those who are, somehow, to provide the satisfaction of one's desires. In communist theory, everyone is equal and is responsible for everyone else, but in practice, it turns out that no-one is responsible for anyone.

'Shou fa': respect for the law

Once we accept that we need to observe certain standards and behave ethically and rationally in order to achieve our goals in life, we respect the law. The law defines the boundaries within which individual freedoms may be exercised and defines the conduct for living within a community. Only when we respect the rights of others will our own rights be respected. Freedom does not mean one is free to do anything: it is always defined in the context of what kind of behavior between individuals or groups is acceptable and what is not. Maintaining a balance between *qing, li* and *fa* is essential for the success of a community as well as for an individual.

Making Morality Cool

As pointed out earlier, Asian elders tell the younger generation what they should do, whereas popular culture tells them to do what they want. This is the difference that divides the generations within Asian societies and between East and West. We have to find an image for ethical behavior that appeals to young people; an image that morality can be cool. We must find a way to persuade people that leading a moral life is not difficult; it is an ordinary, everyday way of life that is rewarding and attractive. Perhaps we can take a lesson from Mickey Mouse. Why is Mickey every Asian child's best friend? Barry Hing of Singapore wrote that 'Mickey has a touch that is intensely human and humorous'. How did Mickey carry the day?

Mickey is irresistible because he directly appeals to our basic quest for enjoyment. He helps us realize that we belong to a common humanity because, when we react to his antics, we discover we share identical feelings and emotions, no matter what our background may be. Mickey doesn't need any particular language to achieve this, nor does he see any need to take himself seriously. Mickey Mouse and popular culture are a no frills-package, free of pretension and show.[14]

In Asia, traditional religions are being repackaged: the modern way of spreading the word is through marketing and seminars, or even religious rock concerts. When Master Sing Yun spread the teachings of Buddha in Hong Kong and Kuala Lumpur, popular Canto-pop singers, soberly dressed, joined him in singing hymns.

While these new ways do not sit comfortably with traditionalists, they signal that change is under way. Religious leaders recognize that they must find contemporary ways to reach people and need to modernize their communication strategies.

A Market-driven Renaissance

The lessons of Asia's past convey a very clear message: self-reliance is essential if there is to be progress and development. Society must be de-institutionalized, with the driving force coming from the bottom. The much-discussed Asian renaissance has to be market-driven, led by private business and a critical but free media. A supportive government can be an asset if it helps accelerate the process; the important thing is that it doesn't impede progress.

Talent and the Competitive Edge

The renaissance of each Asian country will depend on the strength of its culture. This needs to be a powerful blend of traditional values and new attitudes developed to take on the challenges of the 21st century. The competitive tools of the future are to be found in a strong culture and in the attractiveness of the cultural character of a community, not purely in technology. Asian businesses will benefit if they work hard to create and build modern images, and create new art forms that give their products a strong identity and a competitive edge. Ultimately, it is culture that decides who the winner is. Consumers buy the value in the product, the culture it represents.

Talented people want to immerse themselves in a vibrant, stimulating culture. In a world where their talents give that extra, deciding edge to the competitiveness of a business or community, the culture and strength of that community will determine whether the talented people stay or move on.

Gordon Wu of Hong Kong has pledged US$100m to his alma mater, Princeton University in the United States. When commended for his generosity, he said, 'I was grateful to have the opportunity to benefit from an American education. At that time, perhaps by giving me a place, someone else had to be denied. I am simply giving back to where the money will be most efficiently deployed.' The renaissance of the 21st century will be global. It will have no precise geographical location. Those people and places with the best ideas will always attract money and talent, and really talented people will always succeed in finding support. The modern Asian global mind-set must acknowledge the fact that it is the culture and the trust it engenders that decide where resources go.

Satisfying the consumer

Jimmy Lai is popular in Asia: young people talk about his drive and express their admiration of him. Lai's determination and unconventional approach have made him controversial. He has taken a number of products, such as Giordano, *Next* magazine and *Apple Daily*, packaged them and positioned them in a highly competitive market. The success of these products shows that Lai correctly identified changing lifestyles, reflecting changing demographics and thinking. Sadly, many still refuse to put away those old spectacles.

Consumers buy the value they perceive to be in the brand; they don't really care whether it's Asian or Western. Asians are buying Western brands because many Western brands communicate the values they desire: quality, modernity and trendiness. If a business is to survive, it must learn to adapt. Successful modern products communicate a contemporary 'new Asia' image, not replacing the old, exotic Asia but endowing it with a cool and modern persona.

The Fish has Finally Discovered Water

Asian self-esteem has been weakened in the face of Western superiority, and there is little solace to be found in indigenous cultures. Many Asians today are still doubtful about their own great cultural heritage. Karim Raslan, a young writer in Malaysia, described the contradictions that beset the Asian mind:

> In the past, we in Asia would have looked to Plato, de Tocqueville, Marx and Milton Friedman for guidance in the belief that everything that came out of the citadels of Europe and America had to be right because they the Mat Sallehs were taller, whiter and had bigger noses. Nowadays, it's become just as fashionable to decry the West and disparage the writings we once adulated because the same people are suddenly lazier, stupider (because they've got big noses) and more barbaric than we at first realized.[15]

For close to two decades now, I have been working with people from both East and West who run businesses and thought leaders who shape management and business trends. My experience with Asian audiences (perhaps with the exception of those in Hong Kong) is that they almost always find a Caucasian speaker more credible. A social critic, Marshall McLuhan, reminded us that it wasn't fish who discovered water. It is often a Westerner's admiration and appreciation of Asian culture that gives Asians their first appreciation of it. It is interesting to note that the majority of those Asians who wave the 'Asian values' flag have spent time abroad and worked closely with Westerners. They have a good understanding of the kind of challenges that Asia faces in the future and the predicament of Western societies today.

This is food for thought; if we take food as an example, we find an amazing propensity among Asians to blindly imitate. Many Western fast-food products are neither attractive on nutritional grounds nor part of a warm dining experience. Famous American cooking doyenne, Julie Child, has chided the unsophisticated way most Americans eat, and made a career popularizing French cooking in America. When Westerners dine out, the dishes are usually served on an individual basis. In fast-food restaurants, everyone has their own burger and drink. Eastern dining habits, on the other hand, revolve around the community. Dining in a circle where one can serve others before serving oneself is an opportunity to show hospitality and concern for one's guests. Blind adoption of Western dining habits could destroy a wonderful interactive social custom that has been with us for thousands of years. It takes tremendous discipline and will-power to retain these valuable traditions. The choice is ours.

It is useful for young Asians to learn about history of Asia and the world. The young people who are growing up with television have no idea of their heritage and they know very little of their own culture. 'I'm Chinese. I may live in Shanghai later. I refuse to emigrate to soulless places like Canada. I travel more through the East than through Europe,' says Cheong-leen, a successful dancer and designer with a British Guyana Chinese father. Cheong-leen went to an English school, studied ballet and became the first Chinese dancer in the Royal Ballet. Recalling her experiences at the Royal Ballet, she said, 'They wanted me to be English. They wanted me to change my nose, my lashes, my hair. They wanted me to change my name! I couldn't live like that.' Cheong-leen wants to play a part in Asia, or at least China's modernization. She will have taken revenge on the China of 'dark people looking darkly' during the Cultural Revolution when she launches her new line of clothes based on Chinese fashions. 'In my kind of China, the line is bright, easy, with thrilling colours. It's based on the kind of China that I have always imagined. And now my personal imagination can reinvent my own heritage.'

Filipino novelist F. Sionil Jose urged fellow writers not to limit themselves to readers in their own countries, but to compete against the very best writers in the English language. Although he is not saying that the West is the best, he believes Asians must get rid of their inferiority complexes if they are to find out how far their talents will carry them. In mainland China, one of the most successful and most discussed films in 1995 was *Red Cherries*. Its success was a turning point for China's film industry. *Red Cherries* was produced by the Beijing Film Academy Youth Studio and combined high production standards and poignant story-telling with an unusual international backdrop. It is a tale of a group of Russian schoolchildren who resist the Nazi invasion of Moscow. *Red Cherries* was mostly shot abroad, with no special effects, million-dollar movie stars or state-of-the-art animation. And yet it turned out to be one of the year's biggest and most passionately discussed hits.

Values Matter Most

Values indeed make the person. We must take care not to get our priorities wrong. Whether the world is a good or a bad place to live in depends on our own conduct; each and everyone of us must take the responsibility for making it a better place.

Chapter 11
From Public Institutions
to
Self-support Communities

"Among the laws that rule human societies,
there is one that seems more precise and clear than all others.
If men are to remain civilized or become so,
the art of associating together must grow and improve
in the same ratio in which the equality of condition is increased."

—Alexis de Tocqueville—
Democracy in America

With the end of the Cold War and global acceptance of the free market as the model for economic development, there is at last the prospect of a lasting peace. However, the reduction in military threats is fast being replaced with new security threats that could change the status quo in the developed and developing worlds alike. These threats are referred to as 'soft' threats—they do not require governments to deploy their military nor are they location-specific.

New Threats to World Security

'Soft' threats have developed and are still developing on a global scale, leading to a redefinition of the word 'security'. World security is now seen in the context of the way people go about their daily lives. Security lies in their ability to access food, shelter, health care and employment opportunities in a safe environment.

Increasing urbanization

The urban component of the global population is growing faster than that of the world population as a whole. According to a report by the

United Nations Fund for Population Activities (UNFPA), within 10 years, over three billion of the world's population of 6.59 billion will live in the cities. Many of the new urban dwellers, particularly women and their children, will be among the poorest people in the world. It is expected that the greatest increases will be found in developing countries. In some Asian countries, such as Bangladesh, India and Indonesia, a large percentage of the urban population lives in slum or squatter settlements. In a number of major cities, the slum population, as a percentage of the total population, is already huge—84 per cent in Cairo, 34 per cent in Rio de Janeiro and 57 per cent in Bombay. In several other cities, millions live below the poverty line.

The rich can no longer live in isolation without attracting envy from the poor. The global media, especially television, are making people question the inequalities. The question of how to manage rising expectations must be urgently addressed by governments in the developing world; it is not just a question of creating more jobs, but of providing better-paying jobs. Economies need to deregulate faster, greater opportunities must be created and access to education and skills training increased at faster rates. People all over the world are crying out for empowerment programs, not hand-outs.

Environmental degradation

The world environment is experiencing stress from the pressure of increasing population and careless development. The rapidly growing middle class is adopting a high-consumption lifestyle, and a growing number of people are depleting natural resources and so degrading the environment in an effort to survive. Since the end of the Second World War, world population and industrial production have increased threefold. Today, the earth is threatened in almost every respect. Because of the acute pollution of the world's rivers, the World Bank predicts that competition for clean water could become a source of open conflict between nations.[1] Every year, the forests of the world disappear at a rate equivalent to the entire area of England, and with them, go wildlife. Our careless and sometimes mindless activities and lifestyles are destroying our environment. Much more education and a more disciplined, bottom-up approach are needed to prevent the continued erosion of the ecological systems.

The pension crisis

Planners in the West are becoming increasingly alarmed of the costs of taking care of the aged. Western pension schemes that are based on a pay-as-you-earn system funded by taxes levied on those still working will be in serious deficit as the aged population increases. Tax increases of over 30 per cent, to fund just pensions, are projected. America's much-vaunted public retirement system will be in crisis by the year 2015 if the social security system cannot finance its obligations. With an increasingly graying population, the ratio of workers to retirees will shrink, thus jeopardizing the ability of the work-force to support its pensioners. In 1955, the ratio was 8.6 workers to every retiree; in 1995, the ratio dropped to 3.3 workers; and by 2040, the projected ratio is two workers for every retiree.[2]

Although Asia may have no immediate problem, it will also face similar problems in time to come. At the heart of the problem is the shrinking base of current workers needed to support the pay-as-you-earn pension system. There is urgent need to de-institutionalize the way we look after ourselves when we grow old. Not only are revenues from taxes not enough, the returns on pension funds are not large enough to meet our obligations for self-funded retirement. Rates of interest in Asia can be in as low a range as three to four per cent per annum.

Other emerging concerns

When cultures, peoples and communities come into contact with each other using modern tools of communication, new situations arise. It is not so much that there will be a 'clash of civilizations' (as described by Professor Samuel Huntington of Harvard University), but differences in values between the East and West will mean that differences in attitude will clash at first contact. Such clashes will be common when people equipped with a low understanding of other cultural traditions increasingly encounter those traditions. My concern is, do we have the right mind-set and skills to deal with each other in the new global village created by technology and globalization? How do we deal with ethnocentricity? Even within a culture, there are people who are good at certain things and weak in others. People are not equal in their own cultures, so getting them to recognize ethnic differences and deal with them sensitively will take time. However, 'cultural sensitivity' skills will be essential for global interpersonal and intercommunity relations. Developed societies in both East and West must discard long-held attitude of superiority when they encounter people whom they have hitherto regarded as being of less important than themselves and 'backward'. Citizens of the world must start to treat their fellow human beings with respect. Added to that, we must begin to understand that ethnic and cultural heterogeneity will become a way of life. We must therefore start to seriously study other cultures to ensure success in the global village.

The world today is shifting its attention from maintaining the supremacy and power of nation-states to providing the necessary conditions for ordinary citizens to achieve their economic and emotional well-being. Even in America, the land that celebrates idealism, elections are won, not on America's role in the international arena, but on measures that enhance the well-being of its people. This is a significant departure from the mood that prevailed during the Cold War, when military and political domination was of great concern to Americans. Today, it is the bread-and-butter issues concerning minimum wage, paid leave, medical care, and education that have moved to centre-stage.

Many of us feel that we lack the power to do anything that could solve the huge problems, ie the threats to world security, that I have outlined above. However, we know from experience that leaving such important issues to the government to solve will get us nowhere. With governments, it is always a case of 'too little, too late'. It is for this reason that people and communities all over the world have learned to stop complaining about the inertia of public institutions and starting to build self-support communities to address issues that ineffective and inefficient bureaucrats cannot managed. Citizens are seeking to bypass government and public bodies, wherever and whenever they are unresponsive, while enlightened governments are learning to harness the growing energy and influence of the citizens' action groups, power from the bottom up.

Cleaning up Sweden

Dr Karl-Henrik Robert, a leading cancer researcher in Sweden, noted in 1989 that:

> Much of the debate over the environment has had the character of monkey chatter amidst the withering leaves of a dying tree the leaves representing specific, isolated problems. In the midst of all this chatter, very few of us have been paying attention to the environment's trunk and branches. We must learn to deal with the environmental problems at the systemic level; if we heal the trunk and the branches, the benefits for the leaves will follow naturally.[3]

A framework for action

Despairing over the quality and focus of the environment debate, Dr Robert decided to do something about it. He wrote a draft discussion paper on the core issues of the debate to form the basic document for effective, nation-wide action. The draft was circulated to leading scientists, asking for their input, and was then revised and circulated again. The process was repeated 21 times, always asking, listening and revising, never defending a point of view. The result was not only national consensus, but also a clear exposition of the biological science that underlies environmental problems. An extract from the final document appears below:

> Presentations of the consensus knowledge can start with the living cell, which is our common to each other and to the rest of nature. Plant cells are also engines of production in the biosphere and the foundation of our economic activities.
>
> Material value is produced by concentrating and structuring matter into useful forms. Yet due to the law of nature that 'everything disperses' (the second law of thermodynamics) all productive activities will always cause greater dispersal and disruption elsewhere. Plant cells are the engine of creating value in the biosphere since only they can oppose the tide of constant decay by using energy from the sun. The other law of nature, 'nothing disappears' (the law of conservation of matter) shows how every atom has only two choices: it either becomes new resources or accumulating junk.

Over the past three and a half billion years, living cells have processed matter in natural cycles, transforming the original toxic stew into a clean, diverse biosphere. However, for the last hundred years, human societies have been processing resources in a linear direction, into visible and molecular rubbish which is accumulating. This is evolution in reverse. Adapting our societies to cyclical processes is a non-negotiable requirement if we want to keep our health and prosperity.

In all areas of activity, we need positive models showing practical steps towards a cyclic sustainable society. To provide an attractive role, these good examples should be economically and ecologically sound, and capable of being further developed.

There are four ecological system conditions for a good example:

1. Stored deposits: less use of underground mineral deposits.
2. Alien compounds: less use of persistent artificial substances.
3. Eco-systems: greater diversity and capacity.
4. Metabolism: reduced need for energy and materials.[4]

This framework provides a clear, practical approach that cuts right through the technical and political debate.

The value of education

The final document became the basis of an educational pack on environmental issues. The information was produced in the form of an illustrated booklet with an accompanying audio-cassette, and over four million copies were mailed to every household and school in Sweden. Surprisingly, the initial impetus for this educational campaign was provided by 10 large Swedish corporations, which funded the initial mail-out. Large corporations are not generally known to be sympathetic towards the environment. The high cost of making environmental-friendly products is given as a reason, an excuse, for not doing anything.

Dr Robert was able to persuade these companies to support the campaign on the grounds that they were in the best position to find solutions to environmental problems. The companies can pool their considerable resources and thus reduce the prices of products. For example, Gripen, a conglomerate that produces floor products, has struck a deal with Scandic Hotels, one of Europe's largest hotel groups, to discontinue the use of plastic materials in floors. Gradually, wooden floors will be laid in hotels all over Europe. This will drive down the price of Gripen's wooden floors, making them affordable to the general public. Because all things have repercussions, the plastics industry must now adjust and stop using non-degradable compounds in its products.

In Dr Robert's view, the catalyst to come up with environmental solutions does not come from the government but from people who apply their skills for the betterment of all; the best way to foster a culture of sustainability is for good examples to be set. Once companies adopt a culture of environmental sustainability, the morale of their workers will rise. After all, who wants to work in a polluting industry?

With wide backing and the support of the king of Sweden, the Natural Step organization was founded in April 1989. Natural Step focuses on raising environmental awareness through education. Measures to improve the environment must accord with four fundamental ecological principles.[5] Do the measures:

- Reduce finite mineral resources?
- Reduce the use of synthetic products or molecules that have long lives?
- Preserve or increase natural diversity and the capacity of ecocycles?
- Reduce the consumption of energy and other resources?

Seventeen local governments have declared themselves 'eco-municipalities'. They are among dozens of local governments setting themselves environmental goals and reaching agreement with residents, retailers and manufacturers to help meet those goals. For example, to reduce the load on municipal water treatment systems, residents are encouraged to shop for cleaning products that generate fewer toxins, while retailers encourage their suppliers to come up with cleaner products. These measures complement the environmental education of the business community, which in turn complements traditional environmental regulations. Today, visitors to Sweden marvel at its pristine environment.

The Conscience of Taiwan

When I alighted from a small propeller plane at Hualien, on the eastern seaboard of Taiwan, I had no idea of what I was going to see. It was October 1995, and I was visiting the Tzu Chi Compassionate Foundation, founded in 1966 by Master Cheng Yen. It is described by the mass media in Taiwan as 'the other Taiwan miracle' and 'the conscience of Taiwan', references to the famous economic miracle that first transformed the island into a powerful industrialized nation, and the fact that the Foundation is a strong moral force in Taiwanese society.

The Tzu Chi Compassionate Foundation is a voluntary organization of some four million people whose primary mission is to perform charitable and disaster relief work. It was founded by Master Cheng Yen, a Buddhist nun. She describes Tzu Chi as an organization driven by compassion and motivated by love. Its members, 90 per cent of whom are women, raise some US$150m annually through voluntary donations, and this money funds an 800-bed hospital employing 140 full-time doctors, 500 nurses and 900 staff members, as well as a nursing college, a medical school and a publishing house. Tzu Chi plays a significant role in disaster relief, educational and community counseling, and self-help activities, both at home and abroad.

In 1996, a typhoon ravaged an area to the north of Taipei. Phone calls mobilized 10,000 volunteers, of which the first were from Tzu Chi. These volunteers immediately organized the purchase of water and food, and in less than two hours, were passing out hot meals. A few days later, they lined the streets of Taipei and raised US$9m for the typhoon victims. The local media lauded the efforts of these 'thousand-hand Buddhas', as they are called. Tzu Chi volunteers are always present at large and small disasters and accidents in Taiwan. Their resources are extensive, not only in the number of people they can mobilize, but also in terms of the material resources they can command. Funds for emergency relief can be used to purchase land and build new homes for victims. Over US$15m was raised in 1995 for emergency relief purposes and in the same year, funds for international relief touched US$5m.[6] What is behind this phenomenal outpouring of compassion and voluntary effort? What motivates these people?

A network of buddhas

There are thousands of charitable organizations in Taiwan, so how is it that Tzu Chi can mobilize so much grassroots support and exert such widespread influence? Volunteers come from all over the island, as well as from mainland China, the Philippines, Outer Mongolia and even Africa. Observers attribute Tzu Chi's influence to its flexible organization. Nearly four million volunteers are organized in networks within networks. The 6,000 full-time voluntary committee members, an all-female middle group, have established their own mini-networks of at least 100 members; some have over a thousand. In other words, 6,000 committee members have given rise to 6,000 networks. Master Cheng Yen's original aim to recruit 1,000 volunteers, has, to her delight, multiplied into tens of thousands.

'The holding power within the Tzu Chi organization, the convergence of its members' power, comes from the dedication and living-by-example leadership of the Master,' said the Chairman of Taipei-based Community Group 'Six Cycle', Cheng Pei Yuen. Master Cheng Yen does not perform religious rites, neither does she build temples. She leads a life that is totally separate financially from the Foundation. All funds collected by the Tzu Chi members are carefully accounted for and go to support the hospital, nursing and medical colleges. Master Cheng Yen believes that the bottom-up power of Tzu Chi does not come from any organizational or management theories, but rather from the energy and commitment of its members. She said, 'Tzu Chi members learn to be Buddha; they are not learning Buddhism, they are living Buddhas'. Tzu Chi members do not expect anything in return for their efforts. 'Anything the organization does is carried out with the utmost pleasure and gratitude. We are thankful to those who give us the opportunity to cultivate and refine ourselves.'

The joy of giving

Tzu Chi gives its members the opportunity to find out about themselves, and their capacity to love and to express that love in compassion towards strangers and people in distress. Getting involved in Tzu Chi's activities is a self-development, personal growth venture. In a conversation with the author, Master Cheng Yen said:

> The compassion demonstrated by Tzu Chi members cannot be expressed in words, but we have to look at it through the lens of gratitude. Everyone possesses this ability to love, it is not expressed because there is simply no opportunity. The Tzu Chi members have simply discovered that they are capable of loving. This is very pure and innocent. They do not only understand the phi-

> losophy, they have acted out the beliefs.
>
> The intentions are not altruistic, not in the least. All positive efforts and energies stem from self-interest. People want a chance to display and act out the better side of themselves. They want to feel good about doing good. We are simply creating a channel for that need to be fulfilled.

At a time when there is low credibility and trust in the government of Taiwan and people are frustrated with their leaders, Tzu Chi brings hope to the community. 'Disaster relief and community support are traditionally the domain of the government, but they are so ineffective and corrupt. The government itself generates disasters,' said Professor Wang Guang Kuo of the National Taiwan University. 'Tzu Chi steps in to fill the void, to do the cleaning up.'

The Tzu Chi family

The structure adopted by Tzu Chi could be described as 'maternal'. Members believe in 'the mother hen guiding the little chicks' and address each other according to seniority in age and length of association with the movement. Even in the American branch of Tzu Chi, the same culture is in force. Tzu Chi practises a mentoring and learning-by-doing approach: this and its self-organizing basis are the reasons for its rapid expansion. Membership grows at the rate of 20 to 30 per cent a year. Such rapid growth has not slowed the organization down; instead, it has become even more efficient, more responsive and more powerful.

Asked to comment on the tremendous organizational power in Tzu Chi, Master Cheng Yen replied, 'Actually, I do not know about organization. Why do all of you always talk about organization and management? Isn't it very troublesome? My fundamental belief is: I hope everyone becomes self-managed.' To the Master, the Tzu Chi voluntary team developed naturally.

In its October 1996 issue, *Commonwealth Magazine* commented, 'Small government, powerful people. Self-help is the ideal of a society of the people. The Tzu Chi Foundation has taken the first step, it has rekindled the light of idealism.'

The Chinese Independent Schools in Malaysia

By standing on its own feet is how the Chinese community in Malaysia has managed to maintain an independent school system for almost half a century. The Chinese education system in Malaysia is closely entwined with the history of the Chinese immigrants who came to Malaysia (known then as Malaya) in the 19th century at the invitation of the British colonial government to serve primarily as laborers in the booming tin mining industry. The Chinese brought with them their culture, of which education is a central plank. The Chinese education system in Malaya up to1904 was modelled on the traditional one that emphasized rote learning of the Confucian classics along with the abacus and calligraphy. In 1904, the Chinese government replaced the traditional Chinese curriculum with a modern one. Apart from studying classical Confucian texts, pupils were now taught modern subjects such as history, geography, arithmetic and drawing.[7]

Until independence in 1956, the Chinese education system was essentially left alone by the British colonial government, although it did legislate Acts such as the Registration of Schools Ordinance of 1920 and the Education Ordinance of 1952, which gave it some control over the Chinese schools. The most important development before 1956 was the formation of the United Chinese School Teacher's Association of Malaya (UCSTAM) in 1951 and the United Chinese School Committees Association of Malaya (UCSCAM) in 1954. They formed the backbone of the Chinese education movement. Both organizations were jointly called 'Dong Jio Zong' in Mandarin, a term that means they were at the pinnacle of those championing Chinese education.

The fight for the Chinese language

Changes began when Malaysia was granted independence in 1956. Chinese schools, which previously had enjoyed a great deal of autonomy, now came under the scrutiny of the Malaysian government as it considered how the Chinese education system could be absorbed into the mainstream. Chinese schools, especially those outside the national system, came increasingly under pressure to conform to the national policy on education where the national language, Bahasa

Malaysia, was the main medium of instruction. Politics centred on Chinese education intensified in the 1970s and 1980s. The Chinese primary schools were eventually absorbed into the mainstream education system, retaining the Chinese language as the medium of instruction. Those secondary schools that did not want to be absorbed became independent schools. In 1962, out of the 114 Chinese private secondary schools established in Malaya, 54 Chinese schools accepted the government's offer while 60 rejected it and became independent. That situation remains today.

A great source of friction between the government and the Chinese community over the issue of education was the proposal to establish an institution of higher learning that would use Mandarin as the medium of instruction. The independent Chinese schools followed a curriculum similar to that of the mainstream schools, using the Chinese language as the medium of instruction and making Malay and English compulsory subjects. Since 1975, UCSCAM has conducted an examination for graduates of secondary schools that is not recognized by the Malaysian government but which is recognized by institutions of higher learning overseas for purposes of entry. Successful graduates were therefore denied entry to local universities, and many went to Taiwan to continue their higher education. To date, about 30,000 Malaysian Chinese have received university education in Taiwan, but their degrees are generally not recognized in Malaysia.

In an effort to alter this unsatisfactory state of affairs, and to give graduates an opportunity for higher learning in Malaysia, in 1967, UCSTAM proposed the setting-up of a university (known as Merdeka University) that would use Mandarin as its medium of instruction. The Chinese community in Malaysia came out in full support of this project, and it was widely endorsed by various guilds and associations. A starting fund of a quarter of a million dollars was raised almost immediately. However, the project had to receive the blessing of both the King and the Malaysian Parliament. This it failed to get, on the issue of the language of instruction. Negotiations continued over the years. Finally, in 1997, the Malaysian government relaxed its language policy and approved the setting up of the New Century Institute, using the original funding and concepts of the Merdeka University project. English, Chinese or Malay may be used as the medium of instruction.

Preserving a Rich Cultural Heritage

The Chinese community has been very persistent in preserving its education system, and is determined to pass on its cultural heritage to subsequent generations. Between 1983 and 1992, there was an upsurge in student enrolments in independent Chinese secondary schools from 45,000 in 1983 to 60,000 in 1992 representing a growth of roughly 31 per cent (see table 11.1 below).

Table 11.1: Student enrolment in independent Chinese secondary schools

Malaysian State	No. of schools	1983	1992
Johore	8	12,269	15,056
N Sembilan	2	2,531	3,433
Malacca	1	1,353	1,921
Selangor	4	2,651	4,285
Federal Territory	4	6,230	8,558
Perak	9	5,727	7,564
Kedah	3	650	1,732
Penang	5	4,534	3,691
Sabah	9	4,890	5,968
Sarawak	14	3,821	5,781
Kelantan	1	NA	376
Total	60	44,656	58,365

Source: Yap Sin Tian, *The Chinese Schools of Malaysia: Towards the Year 2000*, United Chinese School Committees Association of Malaysia, K.L. p.105.

This independent education system is an expression of the self-reliance of the overseas Chinese community in Malaysia. Besides paying fees for the students' tuition, the community contributes some US$20m annually to support the schools.

The Rise of Citizen Group Initiatives

All these and many other similar initiatives show that the world is moving towards self-support communities. The single phenomenon that will best characterize the 21st century will be empowerment. People the world over are no longer sitting back, waiting for their leaders to determine their future, especially in places where political leadership is uncertain, social conditions unstable and governments cannot provide even the most basic conditions for a decent living. Citizen groups are becoming more assertive: they are organizing and mobilizing resources in a multitude of areas that previously were the sole province of the state. Lester M Salamon, Director of the Institute for Policy Studies at John Hopkins University, predicts that this phenomenon 'may prove to be as significant to the latter twentieth century as the rise of the nation-state was to the latter nineteenth'. Calling it an 'associational revolution', he said:

> The upshot is a global third sector, a massive array of self-governing private organizations, not dedicated to distributing profits to shareholders or directors, pursuing public purposes outside the formal apparatus of the state. The proliferation of these groups may be permanently altering the relationship between states and citizens, with an impact extending beyond the material services they provide.[8]

At the same time, Professor Salamon observed that, 'the growth of this phenomenon is all the more striking given the simultaneous decline in the more traditional forms of political participation, such as voting, party affiliation and union membership'.

Citizen action groups fit in with John Naisbitt's global paradox—the larger the world economy, the more powerful would be its smallest players. They are small in scale, flexible and as energetic as the communities they represent. The number of citizen action groups and non-government organizations (NGOs) is growing at a remarkable speed. Today, NGOs deliver more official development assistance than the entire United Nations system, excluding the World Bank and the International Monetary Fund.[9] In the developed countries, a 1982 survey of non-profit human services organizations in 16 American communities showed that 65 per cent had been created since 1960. The number of private associations has similarly skyrocketed in France, with more than 54,000 formed in 1987 alone, compared to about 11,000 per year in the 1960s. This phenomenon is even more dramatic in the developing world. Already there are 4,600 Western voluntary organizations actively working with some 20,000 indigenous NGOs. In Bangladesh, there are 10,000 registered NGOs; in Sri Lanka, the Sarvodala Shramadana movement has organized more than 8,000 villages to produce small-scale improvement projects; and similar developments are evident in other parts of Asia, Latin America, Eastern Europe and the former USSR.

The rise of citizen action groups is a direct result of people recognizing that they have to take responsibility for their own lives. Of course, it also reflects the inability of governments to respond effectively to human needs.

Trends in Asia

It is impossible to accurately gauge the number of citizen action groups or NGOs, as they are also called, that exist in the world. Published figures can mislead. There are certainly millions of them, from the tiniest village association to international groups like Amnesty International and Greenpeace. It is impossible to get an exact picture of what's happening in Asia due to the sparse studies done on such organizations in this region; nonetheless, we can sketch an outline of the trend. Saddled with probably the worst bureaucratic government, the frustrated Japanese are losing patience. It is therefore not surprising that Japan is experiencing rapid growth in NGOs. A Directory of Japanese Non-Governmental Organizations Active in International Cooperation, 1994, was compiled by the Japanese NGO Center for International Cooperation, and mapped progress over a series of periods.[10]

Table 11.2: The Growth of NGOs in Japan

Term	Number
through 1969	10
1970-1974	12
1975-1979	21
1980-1984	46
1985-1989	69
1990-1992	12
Total	186

Source: Toshihiro Menju & Takako Aoki (1995), p.145.

As Table 11.2 illustrates, new Japanese NGOs established between 1970 and 1992 recorded a growth rate that almost doubled every five years. Such rapid proliferation has also taken place in Thailand and Singapore. In 1989, Thailand had approved the formation of 8,408 general non-profit associations and 2,699 foundations, almost half of them focused on funding cultural and education activities.[11] By early 1994, about 4,562 registered societies were listed with the Singapore government.[12]

What has caused this phenomenon? Professor Lester M Salamon explained the pressure as 'coming from three sources: from "below" in the form of spontaneous grassroots energies, from the "outside" through the actions of various public and private institutions, and from "above" in the form of government policies'.

The desire for self-determination

Self-determination is a major factor, and one that can explain the so-called Asian economic miracle. People have come to the realization that, among other things, self-reliance is more effective in improving their lives than are efforts to improve and enforce basic rights. Self-reliance has contributed to the spectacular success of the overseas Chinese in Southeast Asia. When their children were denied jobs in the civil service because of affirmative action, they became entrepreneurs and built businesses. When faced with limited access to the public education system, they created and supported a fully self-funded education system. For China itself, the real story of the new Chinese economy is that people are free to innovate and work towards their well-being.

Rising affluence, high expectations

The global economic boom has given rise to a growing middle class who will not sit around waiting for things to improve. The growth in the world economy has brought vast material improvements in people's lives, and has also engendered rising expectations. As the middle class expands, so does their dissatisfaction with the existing organizational channels of social and political participation through elections, political parties and labor unions. Citizen action groups are seeking more direct routes in shaping their world.[13]

A place in Asian societies

The dissatisfaction felt by the middle class and the proliferation of NGOs in developing countries have their roots in the inability of

Asian governments to bring about equitable economic development. Many NGOs consider their role to be that of reflecting concerns about the economically and socially disadvantaged, and putting them on the national political agenda. With growing pluralism in society and the limited ability of governments to satisfy these concerns, there is an increasing awareness among Asians of the need to develop a 'civil society' in their countries.[14] In Bangladesh, NGOs have become such a strong force for development that they have become known as 'the other government'.

While NGOs alone cannot solve Asia's social problems, they are showing what can be done. Policy-makers should take note. Initially, many governments in Asia felt that NGOs were a hindrance to development, but since the early 1990s, signs of change are appearing. Many government leaders have been giving explicit or, at least, tacit acknowledgment of the useful functions of the NGOs in their countries. For example, the Malaysian government invited moderate organizations, such as the Federation of Malaysia's Consumers' Association (FOMCA) and the National Council of Women's Organizations (NCWO), to participate in national economic consultation and to provide input for the national economic policy, the socio-economic blueprint of Malaysia. Former President of the Philippines, Fidel Ramos, had proved adept at using NGOs to build popular support for economic reforms. To get the economy moving, he reduced the power of the monopolies that stifled the country's economic potential; the NGOs provided him with the necessary political cover. The Bangladesh Rural Advancement Committee, possibly the world's largest NGO with 17,000 full-time staff and an annual budget of US$88m, steps in where the government lacks the resources. In 1990, the Minister of Community Development of Singapore expressed the view that individuals and community groups should be given a chance to contribute to welfare services, while the government's role should be that of a catalyst, providing the basics funding. Such recognition accelerates the growth of NGOs.

A role for women and young people

New ideas and new technology are bringing new talent to public affairs. Women are playing a dominant role in NGOs. The Beijing

Women's Conference held in December 1995 saw some 30,000 participants from various women's organizations throughout the world engaged in discussions on issues related to women and development. Women are an important and a rising voice in the activities of NGOs and citizen action groups. Young people are also becoming very socially conscious. They take to heart social and environmental causes, and many tell me that they want to have careers that help people.

Citizens united by technology

Information and communication technologies are spreading the news about the activities of self-support communities across the globe. The world is more and more like a village, and governments can no longer act without first thinking of how their own citizens and the international community might react. Media organizations are becoming more and more powerful; global coverage makes them the new watchdog for local communities. In every sphere of activity, instant access to information and the ability to use it increases the number of significant players and reduces the power of those in authority. Distance is no longer a barrier. Fax machines, satellite hook-ups and the Internet connect people across physical and cultural borders. Technology, in one sense a powerful, globalizing force, can also be the agent for political and social fragmentation by enabling more and more organizations that share a common goal and which are scattered around the globe to coalesce and thrive.

Above all, information technologies disrupt hierarchies, spreading power among more people and groups. Literacy and the interconnectivity of the world, powered by telecommunications, means people of similar interests and with common goals and convictions can come together. Individuals or groups can plan joint action without having to build any physical or formal presence. Networks have no person at the top and no centre. Instead, they have multiple nodes where collections of individuals or groups interact for different purposes. Governments, on the other hand, are quintessential hierarchies, wedded to an organizational form that is incompatible with that of networks.

Building a Civil Society

The relationship between the governor and the governed is changing. Increasingly impatient communities want to work in partnership with the authorities to accelerate the development of and improvement in their conditions; they want a larger role in shaping the outcome of issues directly affecting their quality of life. However, self-support communities must be more than activist organizations; they must also develop and propose viable alternatives. Governments still have a very important role to play in maintaining law and order and in ensuring stability, peace and security, including the protection of citizens' rights. Governments must also create conditions that are conducive to the well-being and prosperity of its citizens; it is against these benchmarks that the success of today's government are measured.

Red tape and corruption

It is true that corrupt and inefficient governments are an obstacle to development. While red tape, bureaucracy and inefficiency plague development efforts, far more damaging is corruption. Asia is riddled with corruption. An over-regulated society almost inevitably leads to corruption within the government. Countries such as India and Japan are good examples. The LDP in Japan and the Congress Party of India, political parties that ruled their respective countries for decades, were thrown out of power in the early 1990s because of corruption. A former prime minister of India was recently indicted on charges of bribing the opposition to vote for his government. In the aftermath of the Hanbo scandal in South Korea in 1997, eight senior politicians and bankers have been charged with channelling billions of dollars from state-controlled banks into the construction of a steel mill, and of accepting in return, from the Hanbo Group's owner, boxes stuffed with cash.

In addition to corruption, an over-regulated government is also an inefficient one. A glaring example of Japanese government inefficiency was seen in the Kobe earthquake disaster. Although the government had for a long time been warned of the threat of an earthquake in the Central Pacific region, it had relaxed vigilance in the western part of Japan. While in Tokyo, both army and civilian groups conducted annual drills, military officials admitted that in the Kobe area they did not. The result was a deadly confusion that seemed to paralyze every level of government.

Gary S Becker, who in 1992 won the Nobel Prize for economics, has said:

> Every regulation, law and public program, whether it's a government contract or an export subsidy, can be manipulated to favor particular interests. Companies try to influence these decisions through legitimate lobbying and by arguing their case for government help. But some are also tempted by the huge sums involved to bribe and use other unlawful means to influence the outcome ... Much smaller, democratic and business-like governments would help [reduce corruption] a lot.[15]

Community involvement

It is heartening to note that in the wake of the Kobe earthquake, spontaneous offers of help came from over a million people. Many of the volunteers were students, who rushed to the aid of people who were hurt or made homeless. At its peak, Kobe had two volunteers for every distressed inhabitant. It is sad that we need a major earthquake to make us realize that government authorities are not infallible and that in times of crisis, people have to rely on themselves for survival.

There are fundamental reasons why government, as an institution, is flawed. First of all, citizens lose confidence in a government that seems incapable of appreciating their needs. This is due largely to the type of people who make up what could be called 'the ruling class'. The ruling class are often the elite in society, and many have minimal understanding of the kind of problems the bulk of the population is experiencing. How can they be expected to understand and be sensitive to other people's needs and priorities? Secondly, there is reason to believe that the 21st century will see the decline, if not the total disappearance of, inter-state armed conflict. Since the end of the Cold War, nearly all armed conflict has been intra-state. Many conflicts start because of governments that act against the interests of their own citizens, through violence, corruption or sheer incompetence. In an effort to promote greater understanding amongst the various ethnic communities and to build greater cohesion, several NGOs, staffed by volunteers, have a presence in volatile areas.

Signs of change are everywhere. The pressure is coming from the bottom up. According to Kengo Ingue, a writer living in Japan:

> Local authorities sometimes have been ahead of the central government in enacting new freedom of information laws. New citizen groups took advantage of these laws to check government documents minutely. They have thus learned, for example, that in many prefectures, local government officials have been entertaining themselves on a huge scale at public expense. Disturbed by what they themselves have wrought, many local governments have tried to stem the tide of citizen investigations. Fortunately, their efforts have been in vain. Some latter-day mandarins have argued, and lost, cases in courts. Governor Sasaki of Akita, for one, had to resign for saying that he would like the people of his prefecture to waive the right to know.[16]

Centrally directed institutions are less effective than the voluntary efforts of citizens such as those of the NGOs because the motivation of most bureaucrats is different. Salaried executives are working to build a career. Volunteers come together because of passionate beliefs; they participate because they want to and not because they have to. Large agencies, including many in the United Nations, tend to spend more time in meetings than actually doing work. The so-called experts have a low level of understanding of the reality on the ground. I was told of a situation where aid officers sent some machinery to developing regions and later found that it was lying idle because the electrical power needed to operate it was non-existent there. Sometimes, corruption and self-interest actually prevent projects being undertaken.

The leadership for NGOs often comes from ethical and moral principles. People respond spontaneously to causes which help them bring out their better qualities.

The complexity of some issues is sometimes beyond the capacity of government. The responsibility of governance is simply beyond the resources and capabilities of most modern governments, who work to a timetable set by the date of the next election.

Government recognition

There are some enlightened governments, however, to show the way. The growth of NGOs has been encouraged by progressive government leaderships that recognize the need for them and value a partnership with citizens' groups. In Western societies, examples include the conservative governments of Ronald Reagan and Margaret Thatcher, which made support for the voluntary sector a central part of their strategies to reduce government social spending. Other governments are learning to engage NGOs in the business of government and development. While some Asian governments still view NGOs as groups of activists, this attitude is fast changing. In 1990, for the first time in Japan, a law permitting corporations to deduct charitable contributions was passed. Some Asian governments have been instrumental in sponsoring mutual aid and grassroots organizations, especially in the rural sector, either by design or by default. In China, the embryonic non-profit sector has had official encouragement for a reform process to tap individual initiative and creativity in Chinese society.

Who Can Stop Moral Decadence?

The rat-race, excessive materialism and what seems to be widespread confusion in society about what makes life fulfilling, lead, in the end, to all kinds of illicit activities, resulting in increase crime and violence. While one would have thought crime and violence are more likely to occur in poor countries, the opposite is true. Affluent societies suffer greater stress and chaos of the human spirit. Taiwan, for example, has been plagued with violent crimes, gangsterism and teenage prostitution; it has more social problems now, with a per capita gross domestic product of US$10,000, than it had when the economy was much poorer.

For decades, we have had unrealistic expectations about the abilities of governments. The challenges nations and governments face today are enormous, and are compounded by the threats to national, and global, harmony posed by the teeming masses in the cities and environmental degradation. If not resolved, the new security threats could also have a serious effect on a country's competitiveness. Governments have to learn to deal with intensifying economic competition between regions; they have to grapple with the fact that transnational companies can switch their operations elsewhere, with serious consequences for the economy. Elements vital to the maintenance of a competitive edge, such as skills and adequate infrastructure, must become the focus of attention. Keeping the skills of a country's work-force current requires more than government directives. While the government must provide training programs and tools, one has to do the learning oneself. To expect our governments to be entirely responsible for our lives and our future is asking too much; the complexities of the modern world are such that it is an impossible task. Since there are limitations on the power of the state, people working in networks, including business networks, will have more and more influence.

Many people blame the government for its ineffectiveness in maintaining order and security; some even blame it for being unable to instil a sense of morality in the community. This blame is not only misdirected, the mind-set behind it totally misjudges what the government can and cannot do. Matters of morality and conscience are not within the powers or the realm of government. It is individuals and families who have to decide what kind of community they want to live in, and it is the community that needs to do more in promoting and enforcing a moral code. If a father does not think that having dinner at home is a priority, no amount of public campaigning can change it. If Asians are serious about a holistic outcome to development, they will have to refocus and re-order their priorities. Each and everyone of us has to make these decisions, and stick to them.

Chapter 12
The New Asian Way

"Ask not what sacrifices people can make,
But ask them what they can do to become their best."

—Foong Wai Fong—

The quest for improvement and a perfect living condition for mankind has consumed our energies and occupied our minds since time immemorial. This has resulted in the birth of various philopsophers and thinkers, ranging from Aristotle, Confucius, Karl Marx, John Maynard Keynes, to modern days political leaders, think-tanks, and economists. As we reflect on human history, we recognize the triumphs and follies of the various ideologies. Undoubtedly, human ways have to differ because of physical, social and cultural conditions, but basically, the goals are the same. Depending on where people are and their circumstances, some have to take a longer and more winding route, while others may have the audacity to take a short cut.

The Americans had a fresh start in building a new society. Those who fled repressive institutions and cultures left their past behind by becoming immigrants to the United States. Although they did not know exactly what new institutions they would build, they had a clear idea of the kind of outcome they desired. America therefore embarked in a straightforward manner on experiments to develop a new way of life. The same kind of outlook was shared by the people of Hong Kong. As refugees running away from suffering, they were open and eager to try anything that would work for them.

This attitude cannot be said of many other Asian communities who are weighed down by emotional and cultural baggage. A long history and a mind-set that accommodates both superiority and inferiority complexes have resulted in a mixed response to modernization. Asia therefore presents a confusing picture of a region welcoming the icons of the new (such as technology and democracy) and, at the same time, showing unwillingness to relinquish the old. Although eager to say goodbye to the past, many Asians are still very reluctant to let go of the glories of their much earlier civilization; some still harbor resentment towards what they perceive as the injustices done to them by Western colonialism.

From Ideology to Realistic Idealism

It is submitted that the New Asian Way could be the new global way, suitable for anyone who seeks success in the world of the 21st century. When I shared my idea of this book with Professor Tu Weimeng, the distinguished scholar on Chinese classics at Harvard, he immediately asserted, 'The New Asian Way ought to be the normal way'.

The politicization of East-West relations has unfortunately put the East and the West at odds with each other. This shows the human-ness, or, if you like, the tribalism and inner yearning in every one of us to be different, to want to appear exceptional. For example, the measures we took to achieve high economic growth and the mistakes that we made that resulted in the recent financial crisis: our reactions and responses to each other over our successes, challenges and shortcomings have been interpreted through that prism—hollow and meaningless, counter-productive and even childish. If an idea is good or a technique is excellent, it knows no East-West distinction. Given the fact that some people understand things better, execute things better, have less emotional baggage, the outcomes will inevitably be very different.

Additional factors are timing and conditions: no matter how strong our determination, brilliant ideas can be premature if a community does not have the right conditions to give it the opportunity to flourish. An example is the concept of liberal democracy: no matter how strong the yearning for freedom and liberal values, if the rest of the community does not fully appreciate democracy as a way of life, rather than solely a system of government, to try and impose democracy in that community is doomed to failure. People need to realize that the ideal, true democracy, needs no government; according to this ideal, people govern themselves and only elect representatives to implement their wishes. Even in the West, a lot more work needs to be done to make the idealism of true democracy a reality. It would be futile to bring in true democracy before its time. This argument is akin to concluding, when an idea doesn't work, that it wasn't a good idea. A good idea is a good idea: the only difference is whether it is a good idea for everyone involved, and whether it is a good idea at the time. Community building means we have to work towards making that good idea a good idea for everyone, at the same time and at the same place.

'I don't have to be right, as long as we get it right,' describes the true sense of 'we'. It is in this sense that progress can be made from ideology to realistic idealism. This is the new mind-set we need for the New Asian Way.

The Fatal Conceit in History

A lot needs to be done to unwrap preconceptions, unlearn prejudices and undo old ways. Human progress is a journey towards making an ideal a good idea, not just because its proponent thinks so, but because the people for whom the idea is intended think so. From time to time, people succumb to the passion of one person to the point that it becomes the focus of their lives, influencing their attitudes, their values and priorities. That was how humanity made big leaps in history, put a man on the moon, built communism and subsequently dismantled it. The results have been mixed; the world is both a happier and sadder place. The most influential and greatest leaders in the next century will be those who not only know and can articulate what is in people's hearts, but those who can also help people reach those goals on their own. No one should try to do for individuals what they can do better themselves: that should be one of the guiding principles for the way ahead.

In my research, I learned a fallacy about success, whether it be success at an individual, community or state level. It is that a formal structure, ie institutionalization, is ineffective. Nevertheless, most leaders, and their followers, believe it. No doubt institutionalization emphasizes the importance of a certain value, such as filial piety, but one wonders about it when the state sanctions a law allowing parents in Singapore to sue their sons. Such institutionalization may not have the desired outcome, but of course, one could argue that it could be worse without it. The problem with it is that it encourages a 'Let me do it for you, because I know what is best for you' mentality on the part of some leaders, and on the part of the public, an attitude of 'It's the government's job to look after us'. Fortunately, this mentality is not so widespread in Asia as it is in some parts of the West, at least not yet.

Humanity's quest for utopia led to socialism, a miserable failure. We now know how illogical and wrong was the belief that equality among all would be created by combining people into one single mass. Friedrich von Hayek described as the 'fatal conceit' the idea that 'man is able to shape the world around him through central planning, ie the top-down approach'. The concern over Asia's future is not so much that collectivism or socialism might make a comeback as communism has been thoroughly discredited. The concern is that, with greater democratization, responsibility is removed from the individual and given to some faceless and impersonal institution. Interventionist governments need to reconsider their roles in the economy; they need to withdraw and let the private sector take over. Such governments are not exclusive to socialist societies; they exist in different shades in so-called liberal, capitalist democracies, where they are much given to introducing big spending packages 'to stimulate the economy'.

While it may be cynical to doubt the nobility of the intentions of our leaders and their commitment to improving the lives of the people they serve, the 'fatal conceit' unfortunately means that many well-intentioned actions end up in disastrous outcomes. A good case in point is Mao Zedong's experiments with communism, which had tragic consequences for millions of people. In revealing to the world the horrors of the Great Leap Forward, Hong Kong-based writer, Jasper Becker, wrote in *Hungry Ghosts*:

> Mao had won power by espousing a philosophy based on rationalism and modern Western thought. In place of the millennia of feudal emperor-worship, he promised democratic and scientific Marxism-Leninism. He was genuinely convinced that scientific farming and collectivization could transform both Chinese agriculture, the basis of the country's economy, and the lives of the vast majority of Chinese.
>
> Mao was impressed by what communism had done for Russia, and China was desperate for a doctrine to help her out of her deplorable conditions. "After all, in the Soviet Union, Lenin and Stalin had used the same meth-

> ods and had created a superpower, which had defeated Nazi Germany, built the nuclear bomb and, in the 1950s, launched the first satellite into space. It was strong and disciplined, modern and scientific: China could be the same.[1]

The Great Leap forward was a vast tragedy. Extreme violence and misery were unleashed; it is estimated that during Mao's reign, at least 30 million people starved to death. Jasper Becker wrote:

> Mao could not accept that his peasants would not behave as he thought they ought to if the country was to jettison its legacy of feudal habits and beliefs. Mao wanted to modernize China but could not grasp the basis of modern thought, the scientific method: that the way in which the natural universe behaves can be proved or disproved by objective tests, independent of ideology or individual will.

So instead of becoming 'new men,' Mao and his followers lapsed into a pattern of behavior established 2,000 years earlier by the first emperor, Qinshihuangdi, perhaps the greatest tyrant in Chinese history.[2]

The Search for an Asian Identity

So far in history, it seems that Asia has been responding to the West while still searching for an identity. It seems almost forgotten that people in both the East and the West share the same aspirations and yearnings, the same needs and wants. The chief concern of a middle-class couple, whether in Kuala Lumpur or in Kansas City, is that their family stays healthy and safe. The couple are also concerned with making enough to pay for the mortgage, to send the kids to college, and to have enough for retirement. They have the same sense of pride when their kids graduate from college, make headway in their careers and finally settle down to raise a family themselves.

In this search for an identity, it is much harder for Asians because, through their English-language ability, they know so much of what is going on in the West. The West also shares its values with the world through a network of very effective media, in contrast with Asian reticence. The result is many Asians end up knowing a lot more about the West than they do about themselves. Those Asians who are brought up to speak English are learning about themselves in a foreign language. This partly explains the identity crisis apparent in Asian societies. Does anyone hear a voice asking, 'Tell me, how do

I look? What does it really mean to be a modern Asian?' Does anyone care? A Hong Kong friend points out to me that this debate is a total waste of time. 'Nobody thinks too much about that any more; the world is very global today.'

The world is converging

When a song is good, it is popular everywhere. When a really good movie becomes a blockbuster in one place, it is likely to be a blockbuster everywhere. If you think it strange that *The Bridges of Madison County* could have such an impact on Japanese housewives, then you don't understand the predicament of housewives everywhere. Princess Diana was immensely popular all over the world as an icon of glamor and beauty. Billions of people stayed glued to their television sets to watch her fairy-tale wedding and also her tragic departure. Whatever it is that strikes an emotional chord in people, it is universal. We are the same deep within our hearts, whether we are yellow, white, black or brown outside. Tiger Wood comes to mind. Called 'the global hero', he is far more than just an exceptional golfer he is an American to the Americans, a Thai to the Thais, and a black to the African-American. This wholesome boy next door is universally admired; he represents an ideal eagerly embraced, enthusiastically promoted and welcomed by all.

Asians have long sought answers from the outside, partly because of their fascination with the progress made by the West, but largely through frustration with the backwardness of their own communities. The problems that Western experiments have run into are lessons for Asia, but we must be keenly aware that the search for a better way is still far from over.

For the last 50 years, the focus has been on feeding Asia's millions. It still is, even more acutely. However, Asia must now seriously consider its options in its selection of political, economic and social systems. Without the right choices and the right values, we cannot hope to meet the rising expectations of a growing number of people and proceed with modernization. We must stop observing and start thinking and experimenting at all levels, be it at the individual, the company, the community or political level. Our own complacency and failure to be creative and to take risks may mean we end up as mere copies of the West; there may even be the danger that we end up as copies of models the West is starting to discard. Neither East nor West has all the answers. In searching for the New Asian Way, we know that we are not alone—the West is walking beside us. Let us focus again on those fundamental questions: What makes individuals successful? What makes families strong? What makes societies modern?

A modern society

Diane Ying, the respected publisher and editor of Taipei-based *Commonwealth* Magazine and winner of the Magsaysay Award, wrote, 'Modernization is defined as continuously adjusting and responding to an ever-changing world.'[3] Professor Dr Tu Weimeng, suggested the following as the defining characteristics of a modern society: a market economy, democratic government and individualism. To restate the essence of what I have written on what constitute a modern society, a modern society is one where:

- each individual is accorded respect, is treated equally and with dignity; and is offered opportunities for their potential to blossom;
- there is equality of opportunity, but no attempt to make individuals equal through centrally directed or redistribution programs;
- there is sufficient material well-being, delivered by the liberating and invisible hands of the free market; where people and private businesses are left to run the social and economic systems; where competition and trade take place, freely allowing co-operation among individuals and groups; and where governments facilitate, not obstruct, the flourishing of private enterprise;
- the political system encourages people to be involved in decisions affecting their lives, and where there are peaceful and stable mechanisms to express the people's wishes in a culture that accepts conflicting and even confronting points of view;
- the aspirations of the community are met, and the limitations of both the physical and cultural environments of the community are addressed;
- there exist the attitudes and competencies to deal with change, to reinvent itself when necessary, always vigilant in preserving its

guiding values and keeping its development goals on track, and knowing that growth is not just a process, but a goal in itself;

- each and every community in this diverse region of 3.2 billion people finds its own way of development, a unique fulfilment of their needs and aspirations; and
- the values it possesses are compatible with the changing global political, economic and social conditions of the times, in recognition of the fact that change is the only constant.

There is no predictability for human development: what works for one region and one culture at a particular time may spell disaster for another at a different time in history. For example, some Chinese intellectuals today are asking, given the low level of material well-being, whether China at the end of the Qin Dynasty was ready for Dr Sun Yat Sen's idea of liberal democracy.

A new mind-set

Within Asia, there are two of the oldest civilizations in the world, the Indian and the Chinese. Chinese civilization, especially, could give many lessons to guide us to the future. The world's great museums are testament to the grandeur of Asia's past glories. The Tang, Han and Song dynasties were periods of great prosperity, when the arts flourished; Asia also had its share of great thinkers. Some scholars have tried to prove that Asia's economic gains can be attributed to cultural factors. The rebuttal to this line of argument has been: if culture was the determining factor, why has it only been in the last half century that East Asian economies have taken off? Those who are familiar with the ups and downs of Chinese history know that the culture itself has been the very reason for its decline and decay.

Undoubtedly, the Chinese civilization derived its strength from a very long history—a culture that existed for thousands of years must have been resilient. As Czech President Vaclav Havel said, 'The only societies alive today are those that have a history'. Unfortunately, Chinese culture has also harbored a certain arrogance that defied modernization. Past glories made the Chinese proud, causing the culture to be conservative and resistant to change. Deep humiliation at defeat by foreign powers drove China into isolation, cutting herself off from the outside world. China failed to modernize in keeping with the global environment and changing domestic circumstances. In other words, China failed to reinvent herself. Throughout China's recent history, there seems to be a paradox in her people's thinking: both East and West are best.

When Asian societies first encountered the Western maritime powers, many of their leaders were mesmerized with the technological superiority and material progress the West had achieved since the Industrial Revolution. These leaders, including those in China and Southeast Asia, abandoned their own cultural traditions to remake themselves in the image of the West. Looking overseas for ideas and answers was not a new strategy: Asian history abounds with such examples. Running in parallel with this admiration of things Western, however, was a deep conviction of the superiority of ancient Asian civilizations. Past glories bred a tremendous pride and politicians, remote and out of touch with the realities of the day, delighted in expounding ancient doctrines and engaging in intellectual discourse. Not turning to practical things, they never did what really needed to be done.

Do it yourself

If you can accept that what is good for society must be good for the individual, then it must follow that what is good for the individual must be good for society. This is so because society is made up of individuals. To give society dynamism, individuals and communities must be involved and take responsibility for their well-being and prosperity. In the words of Friedrich von Hayek, 'A social order resting on the general recognition of certain principles [is preferred] to a system in which order is created by direct commands'.[4]

It is the voluntary effort of individuals and communities that gives society its dynamism and flexibility, not formal commands by institutions. British author Samuel Smiles wrote so eloquently 150 years ago in *Self-Help*:

> No laws, no matter how stringent, can make the idle industrious, the thriftless provident, or the drunken sober. Such reforms can only be effected by means of individual actions, economy, and self-denial, by better habits, rather than by greater rights.

Even the best institutions can give a man no active help. Perhaps the most they can do is to leave him free to develop himself and improve his individual condition. But in all times, men have been prone to believe that their happiness and well-being were to be secured by means of institutions rather than by their own conduct. Hence the value of legislation as an agent in human advancement has usually been much over-estimated.[5]

Above all, develop values

Values make a culture and characterize the civilization. On a personal level, values make the person, giving him or her the distinctiveness of character that will determine how far they can advance. In a world that places too much emphasis on technology and technological skills, we tend to overlook the importance of values. Values are the key to the continuing dynamism of a community, and the right values make success last. Unfortunately, many of us, individuals and communities, have our priorities backwards.

It is useful for us to look deep into the values of our cultures for guidance and inspiration. From my reading of both ancient and recent Asian history, I am convinced that the values for winners, the one fundamental set of values that will make the New Asian Way, are embodied in the philosophy of self-reliance and community. Self-reliance and community have helped many Asians, as well as other successful communities in other parts of the world, to build a new life and a new world, for themselves and those associated with them. The overseas Chinese communities world-wide have benefited greatly from these values. When paramount leader Deng Xiaoping returned to China after his visit abroad, he made a very poignant remark, 'The most successful Chinese are those outside China.'

Many people blame their own failure and helplessness on the system and the government, not recognizing that it is they themselves and the decisions they make every day that constitute the success or failure of their lives.

Self-reliance and community

Museum treasures and rare antiquities are cherished by cultured people and command enormous prices at auctions. However, the true treasures of a civilization are not found in museums or great works of literature, which few can appreciate, but in a superior set of ethics. Ethics must have the power to affect humanity, to shape behavior, to restore balance and bring fulfilment. The greatness of a civilization should be written on the faces of its people and displayed in the conduct of all men and women, boys and girls.

People's actions and behavior are influenced, if not guided, by ethics. Ethics are not a mystic fantasy, a social convention, or some subjective intellectual discourse only academics and scholars engage in. Ethics are not what the government says, nor what his neighbors think and say. They comprise the science of morals, his guiding light that tells him what is best for him and his loved ones. Ethics guide people in their pursuit of the common good.

In November 1991, Taipei-based *Commonwealth* magazine made a comparative study of modern Taiwan and Japan. It highlighted the impact a book had on young Japanese at a time when Japan was learning from the outside world.[6] The book was *Self-Help* by Samuel Smiles. The Japanese translation, published in 1871, was reported to have sold more than a million copies. It was keenly promoted during the Meiji Restoration, when its contents were adapted and used in the Japanese school curriculum.[7] In June 1996, *Self-Help* was republished in the United Kingdom. Joe Rogaly wrote in *The Financial Times*:

> Samuel Smiles is alive and well and available to lead us into the next decade. The Victorian moralist's universal bestseller, *Self-Help*, is a better guide to the prevailing political and economic orthodoxy than the incomprehensive texts of that other 19th century thinker, Karl Marx. Granted, *Das Kapital* has influenced the behavior of most people for most of the present century, but is now safely buried under the rubble of the destruction it caused.[8]

Ayn Rand, the American philosopher and the famed author of such works as *The Fountainhead* and *Atlas Shrugged*, has stated that:

> The potential is a superlative machine, his consciousness; but it is a machine without a spark plug, the self-starter and the driver; he has to discover how to use it and he has to keep it in constant action. The material is the whole of the universe, with no limits set to the knowledge he can acquire and to the enjoyment of life he can achieve. But everything he needs or desires has to be learned, discovered and produced by him by his own choice, by his own effort, by his own mind.[9]

Yes, it is self-reliance and community that bring universal success, and which initially built the Western world and the ancient societies of the Orient. While these values were gradually eroded in some Western societies, the Asia of today was built on them. Self-reliance and community make a winning value system that will deliver universal well-being in the 21st century we must return to nurture them.

Service above self

It is difficult to establish exactly when people began to regard service to others as virtuous and moral. That others benefit is a fundamental tenet of altruism. Altruism declares that:

> Any action taken for the benefit of others is good, and any action taken for one's own benefit is evil. Thus the beneficiary of an action is the only criterion of moral value and so long as that beneficiary is anybody other than oneself, anything goes.[10]

In Asian societies, people involved in commerce and trade were generally regarded as immoral and unscrupulous, caring only for profits. As their actions only benefited themselves, they were perceived as exploitative on society. Accordingly, the Chinese put the merchant class at the bottom of the social hierarchy. In contrast, conduct that addresses the good of the community is considered heroic and sacrificial. Anyone who puts community and family above self is a true hero and a role model.

Confucian tradition holds that a young man will never leave home if he has ageing parents. If he were to leave his family and village behind to pursue his goals, he would immediately be condemned as unfilial, ungrateful and selfish. The whole clan could disown him as a deterrent to other young men. The same goes for any son or daughter who refused to inherit the father's business or to marry someone of their parents' choice. However, if a young girl stayed at home to care for her ageing parents and gave up her own chance of marriage or career, she was cherished as virtuous and pious, respected for the sacrifices she made.

Although today's women in urban Asia are becoming more and more assertive, many know stories of young widows who were expected to mourn for the rest of their lives to prove their fidelity. Such behavior was considered of high moral value. However, to a modern, liberal-minded person, this kind of morality has very negative overtones. There is nothing to be gained from it, only self-sacrifice.

The self-inflicted loss, self-inflicted pain and the gray, debilitating pall of an incomprehensible duty is all that one can expect. One may hope that others might occasionally sacrifice themselves for him, but he knows that the relationship will bring mutual resentment, not pleasure and that, morally, their pursuit of values will be like an exchange of unwanted, un-chosen New Year presents, which neither is permitted to buy for himself![11]

If this philosophy is so counter to the needs of the individual, how is it that it has been so widely accepted? We were all taught not to be selfish, and we teach our children the same. We are supposed to feel virtuous when we make sacrifices for others, not resentful that our own interests have been sidelined. How can this be a sustainable and happy set of ethics, and how has this philosophy helped the world?

Not much, I'm afraid. We constantly hear about the increasing disparities between the haves and the have-nots, and that rich people and rich countries have an obligation to help the poor. I have often wondered how did the rich get there in the first place, and who helped them? And, if the rich got there by the sweat of their own brow, by their wit and ingenuity, how can the rest of the world impose a surcharge on them? Perhaps inherent in this is the suspicion that the rich got rich through or at the expense of the community, and that their subsequent philanthropy is both repentance and a way to clear their conscience. Many Chinese hold that view of the philanthropic acts of merchants.

Many young people harbor great ideals and want to change the world through public office. While interviewing young people for jobs, I have often witnessed an outpouring of passion, ideals about reaching out to help the poor, the homeless and the underprivileged. The almost instant response from these young people was that the government '... is not doing enough' there must be greater redistribution of resources, more affirmative action and more unconditional aid.

The world seems to be running on altruism, which is one reason why many people opt for political life instead of business. In spite of the millions of dollars spent on aid and the thousands of hours spent in summit meetings, misery, disease, hunger and strife are still rampant. What is wrong here? The altruist says: 'I know better. I sacrifice for you. If you send me to political office, I will create the institutions to serve you.' Such are the political manifestos everywhere, Asia included. But people must be told the reality, that it is they themselves who have to do it.

In the last 50 years, a distinct pattern has emerged in Asia: while the politicians were struggling with ideological issues and were busy holding on to power, millions of people went about improving their lot, on their own. In the 1960s, anyone coming to Asia would have dismissed the region as a basket-case. Back then, countries in Africa and South America had greater prospects than war-plagued and disease-ridden Asia. But since 1974, in almost every measurable area, life expectancy, trade and education, impressive progress has been made. The now-famous World Bank report, *The East Asian Miracle*, said, 'If growth were randomly distributed, there is only one chance in 10,000 that success would have been so regionally concentrated.'[12] What had happened was self-reliance at work.

It really is not about asking people to make sacrifices; it is really about asking people to do their best. In doing their best, giving their best, becoming their best, they benefit others.

Reinterpreting Individualism and Self-interest

Dictionary definitions of individualism range from 'self-reliant individual action' to 'social theory favoring free action of individuals'. Taking individualism to the limit is to push one's potential to the utmost to benefit not only oneself but others also. In economic terms, individualism suggests pursuing productivity and not consumption. This is an important distinction. Many Asians are wary of the excessive consumption so evident in the West, and blame individualism for its destructive effect on the community. By and large, this view is accurate. However, truly successful individuals in the West both produce and consume, a behavior pattern that is consistent with a prosperous economy maximizing output and supply.

Promoting self-interest is different from being selfish. Selfishness is negative and antagonizes, but caring for one's self-interest is far from being selfish. A selfish person is one who would go to any lengths, use any means to achieve the desired result, who cares for no living being and pursues nothing but instant gratification. Such a person has no understanding of respecting self and cherishing self. It must also be pointed out that living in harmony with others does not imply altruism.

A very old and widely understood Chinese adage comes to mind: 'If one does not put one's self-interest first, heaven will condemn and earth will destroy.' In Confucian thinking, heaven is the ultimate authority and the final judge. So, if you don't care for yourself, heaven will judge that you are irrelevant and therefore the earth must eliminate you. When this adage is repeated among the Chinese, they usually react with a matter-of-fact shrug, which acknowledges its legitimacy. This adage advocates the same 'rational selfishness' propounded by Ayn Rand.

The starting point of almost all human endeavor begins with self. It is only in this way he can assure the benefit of himself and others. Man needs a moral code that deals with his own interest and that man must be the beneficiary of his own moral actions.[13]

Why not look at self-interest this way: it is one's appreciation of one's potential and one's basic duty to oneself to make full use of that potential. This is positive, creative and immensely powerful and productive. It is not about being self-centred, as the only way to acquire any worth for the individual is to be of value to others.

So what goals should people pursue? What values does prosperity require, and what form should relationships with others take? 'Man must choose his actions, values and goals by the standard of that which is proper to man in order to achieve, maintain, fulfil and enjoy that ultimate value, that end in itself, which is his own life,' said Ayn Rand. The basic social principle in the objective ethics that Ayn Rand advocated is that:

> Just as life is an end in itself, so every living human being is an end in himself, not the means to the ends or the welfare of others and, therefore, that man must live for his own sake, neither sacrificing himself to others nor sacrificing others to himself. To live for his own sake means that the achievement of his own happiness is man's highest moral purpose.[14]

And to do that, he needs the cooperation of others, he needs other to move in concert with him. Balance between the individual and the community represents the finest art in successful modern living.

Incentive and Motivation

Let us examine how self-interest could stimulate efforts and bring productive results. It has been said that when money is left in the hands of its owner, it will be frugally and wisely deployed; if left with someone who has not as much interest in it, it will probably not be used so well. Professional fund managers will object, but unfortunately that is the norm rather than the exception. The thesis is that ownership and control must be combined in order to assure optimal deployment; control without ownership carries the risk of abuse and wastage, and the opportunity for gain is usually not maximized.

You are the spender

The spending patterns of economist Milton Friedman and his wife, Rose, help to explain this thesis. According to them, there are four categories of spending.

- Category 1 is where you spend your own money on yourself. When you shop in the supermarket, for example, you have a strong incentive both to economize and to get as much for your dollar as you can.
- Category 2 is where you spend your own money on someone else. You have the same incentive to economize, but not the same incentive to get value for money, as the purchase is determined by the preferences of the recipient. You will, of course, want to get something the recipient will like provided that it also makes the right impression and does not take too much time and effort. As the Friedmans put it, 'If, indeed, your main objective were to enable the recipient to get as much value as possible per dollar, you would give him money instead and the recipient can spend it as in category 1.'
- Category 3 is where you spend someone else's money on yourself. Lunching on an expense account, for example. You have no strong incentive to keep down the cost of the lunch, but you do have a strong incentive to get your money's worth.
- Category 4 is where you spend someone else's money on still another person. You are paying for someone else's lunch out of an

> expense account. You have little incentive either to economize or try to get your guest the lunch that he will value most highly. However, if you are having lunch with him, that lunch becomes a mixture of category 3 and category 4, and you do have a strong incentive to satisfy your own tastes at the expense of his, if necessary.

Of the troubled welfare system in the West, the Friedmans pointed out that:

> All welfare programs fall into either category 3 for example, social security which involves cash payments that the recipient is free to spend as he wishes or category 4, for example, public housing, except that even category 4 programs share one feature of category 3, namely, that the bureaucrats administering the program partake of the lunch, and all category 3 programs have bureaucrats among their recipients.[15]

'In our opinion, these characteristics of welfare spending are the main source of their defects,' wrote Milton and Rose Friedman.

Hong Kong entrepreneur Jimmy Lai succinctly sums up self-interest in money matters. Commenting on Hong Kong's tax system and small government in a meeting with the author, he said:

> When you vote with your own money, you are voting with your future, your family and your children's future you better be sure you do a good job of it. Also if the government only represents eight per cent of your life, and you are responsible for the larger 92 per cent, there is very little mischief the government can do.

Family support

The family enlarges the self-interest of the individual. It embodies an environment where consideration for an individual's welfare is inspired by love and hope; in other words, the basis of relationships is unconditional. The family has been central to the lives of Asians, and is likely to remain central in the future because it has been the most resilient and effective social economic unit. Fortunes have been built on family strength. As the basic unit in organizing and regulating political, social and economic activities, the family has withstood the test of time, and as the basic support unit for the individual, it does a more efficient job, economically, socially and psychologically, than government-directed efforts. Individuals do their best to meet family or community expectations of them. They are encouraged to excel by the support and recognition they receive and they are motivated by a sense of gratitude and indebtedness to do well to repay the goodwill one enjoys. In the family setting, members do not rate each other according to each other's usefulness. People are bound by ties of duty, need and love, hence the willingness and patience to work differences out.

The traditional Asian marriage is a case in point. When the romance of the relationship fades over time, the form and appearance of marriage is kept, not just for the sake of the children and their future, but because couples feel a sense of duty towards each other and they feel they are a role model for the young. The Chinese express it as 'From *qing* (love) to *yi* (duty).' This value system has long held marriages together, although it cannot be denied that couples have been trapped in loveless and unfulfilling marriages.

Reinventing the Family

Of course, the family unit in Asia is not always a bed of roses. There can be great strains on the various relationships that exist within it, brought about by the demands of modernization and changing interpretations of the moral code. As more and more women go out to work and more people live in cities, the institution of the traditional family is beginning to show signs of decay. This weakening in family cohesion is due in part to affluence, leading to the assertion of individual rights and a misguided notion of entitlement. Many people take things for granted, not realizing that to keep something of value requires constant effort. It is therefore very important to understand that the sanctity of the family is not solely the concern of those who take the moral high ground, or of academics looking for a subject to research and deliberate on. The family is the most efficient social and economic mechanism by which an individual can achieve success and happiness. It is therefore in that individual's interests to preserve it, to work on reinventing it and to redefine the relationships within it in the context of modern living. 'If there is peace at home, everything else under the sun will take care of itself.' My grandmother's recital of the Chinese adage still rings in my ears.

Senior Minister Lee Kuan Yew of Singapore has this to say about the family:

> History in China is of dynasties which have risen and fallen, of waxing and waning societies. And through all that turbulence, the family, the extended family, the clan, has provided a kind of survival raft for the individual. Civilizations have collapsed, dynasties have been swept away by conquering hordes, but this life-raft enables civilization to carry on and get to its next phase.[16]

The community is a network of families

Society cannot function well if its people are self-centred and selfish; a code of discipline is needed to ensure harmony and balance. This code should take the form of clearly defined rules and moral values. They must not be viewed as restraints, however, although they are intended to restrain undesirable activities and behavior, but as necessary defining conditions which provide the basis for a community to function and under which we can each seek happiness. Individuals find material and psychological gratification in the support and recognition of their communities. A cohesive community will support individuals if the state infringes their rights; it will also work to uphold the community's moral code itself rather than resort to state-enforced law.

Pot luck parties

Man derives tremendous benefits from community living because it facilitates the exchange of trade and knowledge. There is now a vast store of knowledge available to mankind, far greater than any one person could acquire in a single lifetime; everyone benefits from the discoveries of others as this store of knowledge is passed on from generation to generation. There is mutual benefit; each of us adds value to the lives of others.

Another great benefit of community is the division of labor. Everyone can devote their efforts to a particular field of work in which they excel and trade with those who provide the products and services they need. This form of co-operation allows all who take part in it the opportunity to acquire greater knowledge, skill and productive return from their efforts than they could if each had to produce everything.

These community benefits define what kind of person can be of value to others and in what kind of society. However, as Ayn Rand puts it, 'Only rational, productive, independent men in a rational, productive, free society are desirable. Parasites, moochers, looters, brutes and thugs are of no value to a human being.'[17] No society can be of value if people must surrender their right to live their lives as they wish, but it is also important to understand that no society can function unless most of its members 'behave'. By this is meant people voluntarily heeding their moral commitments and social responsibilities. Man and community should be in a symbiotic, win-win relationship. For example, if everyone keeps to the rules, let's say, maintains the beauty and quality of the neighbourhood, the environment will become pleasant and attractive; property values may even be enhanced.

'Community' is a much misunderstood concept, often implying the curbing of individual liberty. Instead of thinking in terms of the rights of the individual or the rights of the community, let us consider how each of us can work for the benefit of all. In other words, what kind of relationships will benefit all parties. To begin with, nobody owes anybody anything. If people, or peoples, do come together, there must be an exchange of value, each must have something the other wants. For example, although *guanxi* has no precise translation, it refers to the Chinese concept of 'relationships' with people who can help you, not necessarily in a material sense. An unspoken but well-understood request is 'Please give me face'. The Chinese believe that favors and respect are granted by another person; there are no such things as rights, only goodwill. It is interesting to note how powerful the moral voice in a community can be, and how individuals are moved to get involved. When the community appreciates, praises, recognizes, celebrates and toasts those who serve them, many will come forward. This reminds me of the time in Malaysia when an appeal was made for donations for a Chinese school. In many fund-raising events for schools, if one donates $1,000, one is honored as a very important guest and gets to participate in the ribbon-cutting ceremony. Apparently, the response was overwhelming. Over 2,000 individuals donated this amount. As the school hall turned out to be too small to accommodate so many, the organizers had to quickly innovate. So these kind-hearted philanthropic individuals found themselves gathered in the school football field, formed into circles so that everyone felt equal (very important in

Asia), where each released a balloon so that they could officially be part of the ceremony. What a sight!

Trust the Process

Professor Tu Weimeng suggests that new development models are emerging in Asia. One that is Confucian-based is emerging in industrial East Asia. He has said, 'From the historical viewpoint, Confucian influence has permeated many Asian societies for a long time: at least 800 years in China, 200 years in Japan, 500 years in Vietnam, and at least 400 years in Korea.'[18] He has also predicted that the Confucian values of the 21st century will be modern Confucian values.

Many new ways will emerge: some will feel good and comfortable; some will seem provocative, but only initially. These alternative directions will come and go, until finally a distinct one will arrive. Asian society needs an attitude of openness and trust in the process—we need to be proactive and encourage change, rather than have change forced upon us. In the midst of all the confusions in the new millennium, it seems clear to me that the value that would serve Asia and the world very well is self-reliance. For example, the overseas Chinese, 55 million people of ethnic Chinese origin, operating in vastly different political, economic and social environments, with little or no support from the state apart from political stability, have, in less than five decades, built the third-largest economy in the world. That is no mean feat. There is no central government to unite the members of these communities: in fact, they are often described as 'a tray of loose sand', a reflection of how separate they are. While credit must be given to the favorable global conditions that made Asia's rise possible, the 'Asian miracle' is in fact the sum total of millions of personal and family enterprises.

Many of us have forgotten the formula for early success. Isn't it amazing that an economy such as Taiwan's, with no political recognition or diplomatic ties with her major trading partners, could have built a foreign reserve that ranks among the highest in the world? How did those young men and women of ethnic Chinese origin, returning to Malaysia after obtaining recognized degrees in Taiwan yet with no prospect of getting jobs in the civil service, build businesses that are now worth millions? How do millions of poor people in

Bangladesh working with micro-loans meagre US$50 and US$100 loans manage to break out of poverty? Perhaps the most dramatic story is China's, where, for the first time, millions of townships and village enterprises have control and ownership of the fruits of their labors and have begun, it is no exaggeration to say, the most dramatic transformation in world economic history. Already 400 million people in Asia have been lifted out of poverty in the last 50 years; millions more will follow if they can continue to rely on themselves and community support.

These rags-to-riches stories are inspiring. The New Asian Way will be built by a combination of self-reliance and entrepreneurial verve, enhanced by family and community support and discipline, and a sense of responsibility and commitment. Such attitudes will also influence the region's political, economic and social agendas. There will be a range of models, developed by Muslims, Hindus and other indigenous Asians as they each find their way to modernize their societies in ways that are compatible with their aspirations, needs and cultures. Each group will have its own interpretation of the values of self-reliance and community.

Asians must look at individualism with fresh eyes. It is not in conflict with the community, it is about doing justice to yourself, making the most of your potential and stretching it to the limit. The pursuit of self-interest can be balanced by a commitment to the community, without requiring us to lead a life of austerity, altruism, or self-sacrifice. Self-interest is positive and constructive when it is given the right social and economic opportunities; under such conditions, it can be expressed as ambition and creativity, not greed.

What a journey. Throughout this book, I have shared my strong belief in the sufficiency of individual and promoted it almost like a crusade. I hope it will challenge you to know yourself, trust your instincts and recognize your own genius. What remains to be done is a collective determination to remove the remaining political, economic and social restraints that can stifle our creativity. But first, break down any psychological barriers and doubts you may still have about yourself. Become strong and challenge yourself to become better than the best every day. Bon voyage.

Endnotes

Introduction

1. John Kenneth Galbraith, the well-known Professor of Economics at Harvard University, spoke at the Triglav Circle Meeting hosted by the Yenching Institute of Harvard University on April 4th, 1998.
2. "A Celebration in Time", *Time*, March, 16th 1998, p.4.
3. Malcolm Fraser, a former Prime Minister of Australia, chairs the Inter Action Group. Members include former American president, Jimmy Carter, former Canadian Prime Minister, Pierre Elliott Trudeau, and Senior Minister Lee Kuan Yew of Singapore.

Chapter 1

1. Alexis de Tocqueville, *Democracy in America*, Amereon House, Amereon Limited, PO Box 1200 Mattituck, New York, 1835.
2. "The Power of Invention", *Newsweek Extra 2000*, winter 1997–98.
3. "Man of the Year 1997", *Time*, December 30th, 1996/January 1997.
4. Lin Yutang, *My Country and My People, Lin Yutang on China*, Heinemann Asia Singapore, 1936, p.82.
5. Esther Dyson, *Release 2.0, A Design for Living in theDigital Age*, Broadway Books, a division of Bantam Doubleday Dell Publishing Company, 1997.
6. "Taking its Place in the Pantheon", *BusinessWeek*. The market capitalization of the high-tech industries of Silicon Valley stands at US$452b; Wall Street's financial services stand at US$405b; Detroit's automobile industries at US$113b; and Hollywood's entertainment industry at US$56b, August 25th, 1997, p.58.
7. Frank Ching, "End To Strongmen", *Far Eastern Economic Review*, June 4th, 1998.
8. Alexis de Tocqueville, *Democracy in America*, p. 94.
9. Daniel Yergin and Joseph Stanislaw, *The Commanding Heights: The Battle between Government and the Marketplace that is Remaking the Modern World*, Simon & Schuster, New York, 1998.
10. "American Opinion", *The Wall Street Journal*, December 12th, 1997.
11. "The Decade of Greed that wasn't", *Forbes*, November 3rd, 1997.
12. Interview with the author.
13. Friedrich von Hayek, *The Fatal Conceit: The Errors of Socialism*, ed. W.W. Bartley III, The University of Chicago Press, 1998, p. 49.
14. Adam Smith, *The Theory of Moral Sentiments*, 1759.
15. Martin Wolf (Martinwolf@FT.com), "What Price Welfare?", *The Financial Times*.
16. "A Continent at Breaking Point", *BusinessWeek*, February 14th, 1997, p. 24.
17. "The World Economy Survey", *The Economist*, September 20th, 1997, p. 11.
18. Paul Craig Roberts, "Welfare: Maybe the states can figure out what works", *BusinessWeek*, December 4th, 1995, p. 10.
19. "The World in 1997", *The Economist*.

20. *Dow Jones Guide to the World Stock Market*, ed. Dow Jones & Co in association with Morningstar, Prentice Hall, New Jersey, 1996,
21. "France: Special Survey", *The Economist*, November 25th, 1995.
22. "Budget Deficits", *The Economist*, January 31st, 1998.
23. Gary S. Becker and Guity Nashat Becker, *The Economics of Life*, McGraw Hill, 1997, pp. 274-6.
24. "The No-work Culture", *Newsweek*, January 26th, 1998.
25. Ibid.
26. Supra n23, p. 265.
27. Supra n18.
28. Louis Kraar, "A Blunt Talk with Singapore's Lee Kuan Yew", *Fortune*, July 21st, 1997.
29. Jusuf Wanandi, "A Lesson for ASEAN", *Far Eastern Economic Review*, July 14th, 1997.
30. "A Suitable Target for Foreign Policy", *The Economist*, April 21st, 1997.
31. "The Task for Asians: To Discover Their Own Political Morality For Human Rights", paper by Joseph Chan, Department of Politics and Public Administration, University of Hong Kong, delivered on December 4–5th, 1995 in Hong Kong at the conference, "The Contest for Asia".
32. Ibid.
33. Sali Tripathi, "Who Needs Stanford", *Asia Inc*, September 1996.

Chapter 2

1. Angus Maddison, *Monitoring the World Economy, 1820-1992*, OECD Development Centre, quoted in 1997 *Index of Economic Freedom*, The Heritage Foundation and *The Wall Street Journal*.
2. Robert L.Bartley (foreword), 1997 *Index of Economic Freedom*, The Heritage Foundation and *The Wall Street Journal*, November 1996, p x.
3. Ibid, p. xi.
4. "Asia's share of FDI shrinks as growth in supply slows", *Asian Wall Street Journal*, September 22nd, 1997.
5. *China 2020, Development Challenges in the New Century*, World Bank, 1997.
6. "The World Economic Outlook in 1998, A Year of Cyclical Recovery and Structural Shock", paper presented by David D. Hale, Chief economist of the Zurich Group in Chicago, Fourth Pacific Dialogue, Kuala Lumpur, January 1998.
7. "Some Like it Hot: The Mahathir–Soros Complex", *Far Eastern Economic Review*, July 16th, 1998.
8. "Malaysia's No-nonsense Reformer", *International Herald Tribune*, December 6th, 1997.
9. "Global Capital Flows", *The Economist*, September 27th, 1997.
10. Robert Wade and Frank Veneroso, "The Asian Crisis: The High Debt Model vs. The Wall Street-Treasury-IMF Complex", IMF2, The Russell Sage Foundation, March 2nd, 1998 (http://epn.org/sage/imf24.html).
11. Joe Quinlan, "FDI: Asia's Crisis and the Impact on Global FDI Flows", Global Economic Forum, New York

(http://www.ms.com/GDFdata/digests/971203-wed.html#xtocid149375).

12. Ibid.
13. Joe Quinlan, "Trade: Devaluations, Deficits and the End of Globalization", New York.(http://www.ms.com/FEFdata/digests/971222-mon.html#xtocid236652).
14. Ibid.
15. One billion people, mostly from the 10 emerging markets of China, India, Indonesia, Mexico, Poland, South Korea, Turkey, South Africa, Argentina and Brazil are expected to join the global economy. Jeffrey E. Garten, *Who Are The Big Ten Emerging Markets?*, Basic Books, (a division of Harper Collins Publishers Inc, 1997), p.21.
16. Lester Thurow, *Head to Head, The Coming Battle Among Japan, Europe and America*, William Morrow & Company Inc, 1992.
17. Ibid.
18. Ibid.
19. Ibid.
20. Gordon Redding, "China's School of Business", *The Economist*.
21. "The Tax Man Returneth, Japan's LDP to Raise Consumption Levy", *The Far Eastern Economic Review*, December 26th, 1996 and January 2nd, 1997, Editorial.
22. Karen Gullo and Vivian Marine, "American Consumers Sink Into a Black Hole of Debt", New York, *Business Times,* March 20th, 1996.
23. Daniel Yergin and Joseph Stainlow, *Commanding Heights: The Battle between Government and the Marketplace*, Simon & Schuster, 1998.
24. "The Withering Away of the State", *The Economist*, April 6th, 1996.
25. "The Global Salon: Don't Leave the Politicians Behind", *The Far Eastern Economic Review*, February 6th, 1997, Editorial.
26. Ibid.
27. *International Herald Tribune*.
28. *The Far Eastern Economic Review*, November 8th, 1996, Editorial.
29 Quote from Lee Kuan Yew
30. James Gwartney, Robert Lawson and Walter Block, *Economic Freedom of the World: 1975-1995*. Co-publishers include the Fraser Institute in Vancouver, the Cato Institute in Washington D.C. and the Institute of Economic Affairs in London, *The Economist*, January 31st, 1996 and *Business Week*, May 6th, 1996.
31. "The Numbers Tell the Story: Economic Freedom Spurs Growth", *Business Week*, May 6th, 1996.
32. Lim King Hong is a self-made millionaire in Malaysia. He started Kanzen, a publicly listed mattress-manufacturing business, on his own.
33. "Are you Paid Enough?" *Asiaweek*, November 29th, 1996.
34. Gary Becker, *Business Week*, Economic viewpoint.

Chapter 3

1. "Hong Kong: The City of Survivors: What Does the Future Hold ?" *Newsweek*, Special Commemorative Edition, May-July 1997.
2. "Bottomline", *Asiaweek*, 26 May 1997, p. 69.

3. "Hong Kong: Post Colonialism and Political Conflict", Lo Shiu-Hing in *The New Rich of Asia*, edited by Richard Robinson and David S G Goodman.
4. Ibid.
5. *Autobiography of Jin Yong*, Ming Pao Publishers, December, 1994.
6. "Picking the Right Straw", *Newsweek Special Issue*, May-July 1997, p. 60.
7. Victor K Fung, "Hong Kong Offers Value For Money", *Asian Wall Street Journal*, 14 September 1997
8. Conversation with author in Cambridge, MA.on 31 December 1997.
9. Conversation with author in Kuala Lumpur on 15 October 1997.
10. Conversation with author in Kuala Lumpur on 15 October 1997.
11. "Bottomline", *Asiaweek*, May 16, 1997 p. 69.
12. Gary Rodan,"Class Transformation and Political Tensions in Singapore's Development", in *The New Rich of Asia*, ed Richard Robinson and David S.G. Goodman, Routledge, London, 1996.
13. Ibid.
14 Figures on private tutoring in Singapore.
15. Supra n12.
16. "Singapore to Loosen up on Finance", *The Financial Times*, 10 December 1997.
17. *Business Times Singapore* and *Far Eastern Economic Review.*
18. "Indonesia's Chinese Fear for Their Future", *Asian Wall Street Journal,* 6 June 1997.
19. Ibid.
20. Ibid.
21. *The Economist*, 8 March 1997
22. *China 2020*, The World Bank Report, 1997.
23. Free competition among China's regional economies, *Yazhou Zhoukan*, 13 October 1997.
24. "China Survey", *The Economist*, 8 March 1997,
25. Abdurrahman Wahid, "Future Shock", *Far Eastern Economic Review*, p. 38, 1 May 1997.
26. Prime Minister Dr Mahathir Mohamed's speech at Vision 2020 6th Anniversary, 29-30 April 1997
27. "Developing the Bumiputra Middle Class", Datuk Salleh Majid, *Business Times*, 31 March 1997
28. Ibid.
29. Supra n18.
30. Richard Robinson and David S.G. Goodman, "The Middle Class and the Bourgeoisie in Indonesia", in *The New Rich of Asia*, Routledge, p. 96.
31. "What Price Legitimacy", *Far Eastern Economic Review*, April 3rd, 1997, Editorial.
32. *The Far Eastern Economic Review*, April 3rd, 1997, Editorial
33. "Department of Connections ", *Far Eastern Economic Review*, 16 October 1997,
34. Ibid.
35. *The Far Eastern Economic Review*, April 3rd, 1997, Editorial.

36. Barun Mitra, "India's Weak Government Bonds", *The Asian Wall Street Journal*, May 21st, 1998.
37. *The Economist*, February 22nd, 1997.
38. "India: Open for Business", *Fortune*, 10 August 1992, pp 20-25
39. Michael Pinches, "The Philippines New Rich: Capitalist Transformation amidst Economic Gloom", in *The New Rich of Asia*, ed Richard Robinson and David S.G. Goodman, Routledge, 1996.
40. *Megatrends Asia*, Chapter 1, 1995.
41. *Newsweek*, June 1998.
42. John Plender, "Can Japan Reflate?", *The Financial Times*, June 11th, 1998.
43. Gillian Tett, *"Pension Failures add to the Japanese sense of Economic Malaise", The Financial Times*, June 17, 1998.
44. Ibid.
45. Supra n 42.
46. Robert Edelstein and Jean-Michael Paul, "Japan's Broken Employment Escalator", *The Asian Wall Street 7ournal*, June 19th, 1998.
47. "The Japan that Can Say Yes", *The Asian Wall Street Journal*, June 11th, 1998, Editorial.
48. Jeffrey Young, "Springing Japan's Liquidity Trap", *The Asian Wall Street Journal*, June 11th, 1998.
49. "Japan's Economic Plight: Fallen Idol", *The Economist*, June 20th, 1998, p. 19.
50. Takatoshi Ito, "Springing Japan's Liquidity Trap", *The Asian Wall Street Journal*, June 11th, 1998 (on the dangers of easing monetary policy).
51. Robert Edelstein and Jean-Michael Paul, "Japan's Broken Employment Escalator", *The Asian Wall Street Journal*, June 19th, 1998.
52. Richard Robinson and David S. G. Goodman, eds (1996) The New Rich of Asia, Routledge, London.
53. "Thailand's New Song", *The New York Times*, 15 December 1997.
54. "Korea's Crisis", *Business Week*, 24 November 1997.
55. "Bitter Medicine Could Heal Peninsula's Rift", *The Financial Times*, 24 November 1997.
56. "Bailout or Not, Korea Needs Change", *Asian Wall Street Journal*, 24 November 1997.

Chapter 4

1. *Global Views* Magazine, November 15th, 1992, Editorial.
2. "World Bank to Redouble Efforts to Reduce Poverty", World Bank, News Release 96/74s, The World Bank Group Homepage: www.worldbank.org; March 22nd, 1997, pp. 1-2.
3. *1997 Index of Economic Freedom*, The Heritage Foundation, *Washington D.C. p15.*
4. *1997 Index of Economic Freedom*, The Heritage Foundation, Washington D.C. p.16.
5. Ibid. pp. 16-17.

6. Muhammad Yunus, Plenary Address at the World Summit for Social Development, March 9th, 1995, The Grameen Bank Homepage: titsoc.soc.titech.ac.jp/titsoc/higuchi-lab/icm/grammen-info.html; February 21st, 1997.
7. Paul Dietrich, " Is WHO Terminally Ill?" *New Straits Times*, March 4th, 1997.
8. "Features of Grameen's Credit Delivery System", The Grameen Bank Homepage: titsoc.soc.titech.ac.jp/titsoc/higuchi-lab/icm/grammen-info.html-february 24th, 1997.
9. Alan Jolis, "The Good Banker", *The Independent*, March 5th, 1996, from The Grameen Bank Homepage: titsoc.soc.titech.ac.jp/titsoc/higuchi-lab/icm/grammen-info.html-March 21st, 1997.
10. Shahid Khander, Baqui Khality, Zahed Khan, "Is Grameen Bank Sustainable?" The World Bank Group Homepage: www.worldbank.org; March 18th, 1997, p. 3.
11. Ibid. See also David Bornstein , *The Price of A Dream*, Simon & Schuster, 1996 Chapters 11&12, pp.92-108.
12. USD 1 is equivalent to Taka 43.2. The foreign exchange rate is based on *The Asian Wall Street Journal*'s exchange rate on March 21st, 1997.
13. Shahid Khander, Baqui Khality, Zahed Khan, "Is Grameen Bank Sustainable?" The World Bank Group Homepage: www.worldbank.org; March 18th, 1997, p. 3.
14. Originally the Grameen Bank started as an experiment with the intention of being handed over to the commercial sector within two years. However, it was decided by the Bangladesh government in the mid-1983 to let the bank become an independent entity with the government owning 60 percent of the shares while its members 40 percent. Also see David Bornstein, *The Price Of A Dream*, Simon & Schuster 1996: pp.128-129.
15. "Lender with a mission" The Grameen Bank Homepage:titsoc.soc.titech.ac.jp/titsoc/higuchi-lab/icm/grammen-info.html; February 24th, 1997).
16. Shahid Khander, Baqui Khality, Zahed Khan, "Is Grameen Bank Sustainable?" The World Bank Group Homepage: www.worldbank.org, March 18th, 1997, pp.5.
17. David Bornstein, *The Price of A Dream*, Simon & Schuster, New York, 1996 p.19.
18. Shahid Khander, Baqui Khality, Zahed Khan, "Is Grameen Bank Sustainable?" The World Bank Group Homepage: www.worldbank.org; March 18th, 1997, pp.2.
19. Ibid. p.6.
20. Ibid. p.6.
21. Ibid. p.6.
22. Ibid. pp.6-7. Note: The Paper made a reference to Chen, M. "Impact of Grameen Bank's Credit Operations on its Members: Past and Future Research", (Mimeo).
23. Ibid. p. 7.
24. Ibid. p. 7.
25. Supra n 12.
26. Ibid. pp. 13-15.
27. "Lender with a Mission", http://titsoc.soc.titech.ac.jp.80, February 24th, 1997. See also David Bornstein, *The Price of A Dream*, Simon & Schuster,1996, pp.139-140, on the fate of women born in poverty in Bangladesh and the positive effect

Grameen Bank has on them. The World Bank study reported the recovery rate of the Grameen Bank is about 98 percent. Interestingly, the study noted that the recovery rate for men is lower than for women—Shahid Khander, Baqui Khality, Zahed Khan (1994), "Is Grameen Bank Sustainable?" The World Bank Group Homepage: www.worldbank.org; March 18th, 1997, p.11.

28. "Star at Conference on Women: Banker who lends to the Poor", *The New York Times*, September 14th, 1995.
29. The Consultative Group to Assist the Poorest (CGAP), Focus Note No.2, Oct, 1995. "Maximising the Outreach of Microenterprises Finance: The emerging lessons of successful programs", which is a summary of the same title prepared by USAID's centrre of Development Information and Evaluation, The World Bank Group Homepage-www.worldbank.org; March 19th, 1997. The study concentrated on outreach and financial sustainability of the microcredit enterprises. Outreach refers to the central purpose of microcredit institutionsùto provide large numbers of poor people while financial sustainability refers to the institutions ability to become independent of donor or government subsidies. The eleven institutions studied were Agence de Credit pour l'Enterprise Privee (ACEP) of Senegal, La Asociacion Dominicana para el Desarrollo de la Mujer(ADOPEM) of the Dominican Republic, Banco Solidario S.A. (BancoSol) of Bolivia, Badan Kredit Desa(BKD) of Indonesia, the Unit Desa System of the Bank Rakyat Indonesia (BRI), Banking Raya Karkara of CARE (BRK) of Niger, Corporacion de Accion Solidario (CorpoSol) of Costa Rica, the Grammen Bank of Bangladesh, Kenya Rural Enterprise Programee (KO-REP), and Lembaga Perkreditan Desas (LPDs) of Indonesia.
30. "Microcredit Lending is Growing Strongly", *Asian Wall Street Journal*, June 18th, 1997.
31. Trickle Up Program Overview, Trickle up Program; Homepage: www.vita.org/trickle; March 20th, 1997.
32. Ibid.
33. "Tales of Trickle–America, Trickle up Program".
    Homepage: www.vita.org/trickle; March 20th, 1997.
34. Trickle Up Program 1995 Annual Report.
35. Ibid.
36. "The Trickle Up Program in Guizhou Province, China: A people-centered approach to poverty alleviation and conservation"; http: www.vita.org/trickle, March 20th, 1997.
37. Muhammad Yunus, " Does the Capitalist System Have to be the Handmaiden of the Rich?" keynote address at 85th Rotary International Convention held in Taipei, June 12-15th, 1994, The Grameen Bank Homepage: titsoc.soc.titech.ac.jp/titsoc/higuchi-lab/icm/grammen-info.html; March 21st, 1997.
38. Ibid.
39. "Uncovering the Cover-up", Asiaweek , Oct 1995. The Internet March 25th, 1997. See also "A Blown Billion", *Times*, October 9th, 1995; Financial Scandals Homepage: www.ex.ac.uk/%7ERDavies/arian/scandals.html; March 21st, 1997.

40. Muhammad Yunus, "Does the Capitalist System Have to be the Handmaiden of the Rich?" extracts from the keynote address at 85th Rotary International Convention held in Taipei, June 12-15th, 1994, The Grameen Bank Homepage: titsoc.soc.titech.ac.jp/titsoc/higuchi-lab/icm/grammen-info.html; March 21st, 1997.
41. Peter Montagnon, *Credit Where Credit Is Due: Bringing Microfinance into the Mainstream*, Center for the Study of Financial Innovation.
42. "Microcredit Lending is Growing Strongly", *Asian Wall Street Journal*, June 18th, 1997.
43. "Death of Foreign Aid", *Fortune*, September 29th, 1997.

Chapter 5

1. Conversation with author in Singapore on April 4th, 1997.
2. "Bottom Line", *Asiaweek*, January 3rd, 1997, p.88.
3. "The Discreet Charm of Provincial Asia", *The Economist*, April 27th, 1996, p. 86.
4. "Emulate HK Business Spirit", *Business Times*, March 10th, 1997.
5. I.M.Salleh and L.Rahim, *Enhancing Intra-Industry Linkages: The Role of Small and Medium Scale Industries*, ISIS, Malaysia, 1992, p. 7.
6. Fabulous and Fables, *The Economist*, March 29th, 1997, p. 81.
7. "India and Its Small Enterprises", National Small Industries Corporation (India).
8. A.T. Cheng and S. Tripathi, "Survival of the Fastest", *Asia.Inc*, October 1996, p. 46.
9. V. Bredow, "France's Small-Business Owners Fight Back", *The Wall Street Journal*, December 5th, 1995.
10. Supra n5, p. 131.
11. Z. Abdullah, "German SMIs Keen to Set Up Partnerships," *New Straits Times*, March 25th, 1997.
12. Department of Commerce, United States.
13. "Global M &A set to hit US$1 trillion", *The Business Times*, June 28th, 1996.
14. "Making Companies Efficient–The Year Downsizing Grew Up", *The Economist*, December 21st, 1995, pp. 93-95.
15. L. Richardson, "Thinking Global, Thinking Small", *Asian Business*, February, 1995 p. 58.
16. Conversation with Prof. Dr. Zhao Chujun, Deputy Dean of School of Economics & Management, Tsinghua University, June 25th, 1998.
17. H. Katayama, "Japan: The Next 50 Years", *Asia.Inc*, December, 1995, p. 38.
18. M. Schumann and N. Cho, "Korea's Conglomerates Make Diet Plans: High Debts and Low Profits Force Chaebol to Consider Tough Measures", *The Asian Wall Street Journal*, March 18th, 1997.
19. R. Ajello and L. Nakami, "Is the Economic Miracle Over?" *Asiaweek*, March 14th, 1997, p.43.
20. Sumantra Ghosal & Donald Sull, "The Courage Dream", *Financial Times*, March 4th, 1998.
21. Lee, C.S. "Out Of Tune", *Far Eastern Economic Review*, January 16th, 1997.
22. Ibid.

23. U.S. International Trade Commission, Office of Economics "Reform of China's Industrial Enterprises", *International Economic Review*, November 1995.
24. N. Chanda, "Withering State: The End Is Near", *Far Eastern Economic Review*, February 23rd,1995, pp. 48-54.
25. "China's Inventory Problem", *The Asian Wall Street Journal*, April 9th, 1997, Editorial.
26. K. Chen, "Jiang Moves China Toward Privatization", *Asian Wall Street Journal*, April 7th, 1997.
27. "Asia Pacific Daily Briefs of Oxford Analytica, Reform of China's State-Owned Enterprises", A Progress Report of Oxford Analytica (http:// ftp.worldbank.org), March 27th, 1997.
28. Interview with the author. Dr Yang Mu, a Mainland Chinese national, advised on the economic reforms and served as head of two of China's SOEs and TVEs as well as for Swiss Banker UBS. Dr Yang Mu now operates his own investment company based out of Singapore. He was trained both in China and America.
29. Supra n24, pp. 48-54.
30. "Balancing Act: China's New Economic Plan Gets It about Right", *Asiaweek*, October 20th,1995, pp. 20-21.
31. "Where Russia and China Meet", *The Economist*, September 3rd, 1994, pp. 16-17.
32. Yatsko, P. (1996) "Urge to Merge: China Pins Hope on Mergers to Save State Firms", *Far Eastern Economic Review*, May 23rd,1996, pp. 56-57.
33. "State Business: Privatization Fever Sweeps Asia", *Far Eastern Economic Review,* February 23rd,1995, p. 5, Editorial.
34. L. Ning, "Privatization the Chinese Way", *The Business Times*, February 4th, 1997.
35. *The Economist*, November 26th, 1996.
36. J. Wong, R. Ma, and M. Yang, *China's Rural Enterprises–Ten Case Studies*, Times Academic Press, Singapore, 1995, p. 22.
37. Ibid. pp. 38-39.
38. Ibid. p. 48.
39. Ibid. p. 21.
40. Ibid. pp. 26-27.
41. U.S. International Trade Commission, Office of Economics, "Reform of China's Industrial Enterprises", *International Economic Review*, November 1995.
42. Supra n36, pp. 43-44.
43. Ibid. p. 49.
44. Ibid. p. 17.

Chapter 6

1. Acer homepage: http://www.acer.com
2. G.W. Wang, *The Culture of Chinese Merchants in China and the Chinese Overseas*, Times Academic Press, 1991, pp. 181-197.
3. "Overseas Chinese Businessmen and the Global Century", Ronnie Chan, based on a speech delivered in Los Angeles, U.S.A. on October 2nd, 1996.

4. John Micklethwait & Adrian Wooldridge, "Witch Doctors: Making Sense of the Management Guru's", Times Books, February 1998.
5. "Banking on Buddies", *Far Eastern Economic Review*, November 13th, 1997.
6. "Taiwan's Giant: Manufactured in the Netherlands, Designed in the US, The Global Company", *Financial Times*, October 24th, 1997.
7. "Who's Who of Businesses in Asia", *Asia Inc Special Edition*, February 1997.
8. *Why Do They Succeed? Leadership, Strategy and Culture: The Acer Group*, Commonwealth Publishing, Taiwan.
9. Alan Rugman,"Multinationals are Regional Flagships", in *Mastering Global Business, Financial Times*, January 30th, 1998.
10. In the Confucian order, everyone has a defined role. The father's role is to be responsible; the son's, filial. There should be a responsible elder brother and a respectful younger brother; a committed husband and an obedient wife. The senior one is virtuous; the younger is deferential: the emperor is humane, and the court loyal. Relationships in the Confucian order are reciprocal.
11. "Managing: Ideas and Solutions", *Fortune*, September 18th, 1996.
12. Supra n8.
13. Theprestigious Peking University in Beijing is also known as Beida to the Chinese.
14. Mar Ballon, *"Campus Inc", Inc Magazine*, March 1998.

Chapter 7

1. Ian Morrison, "The Second Curve: Managing the Velocity of Change", Nichols Breadley Publishing, London 1996, p. 15.
2. "The Biotech Century", *BusinessWeek*, March 10th, 1997.
3. "Towards Making Singapore a World Leader in R&D", *The Strait Times*, February 20th, 1997.
4. Bits, compressed digital signals will distinguish the new economy from the old one of atoms of bricks and mortar, explained by Nicholas Negroponte in *Being Digital*, Alfred A. Knopf New York, 1995.
5. John Naisbitt, *High Tech/High Touch: The Biggest Idea In Business*, to be published in 1999.
6. "Egghead Blues", *Fortune*, January 13th, 1997.
7. Survey of the World Economy, *The Economist*, September 28th, 1996.
8. "Summers, Diane, Generation X Comes of Age", *Financial Times*, February 16th, 1998.
9. "The Tigers' problem is cyclical, for the moment", *The Asian Wall Street Journal*, November 5th, 1996.
10. Karim Raslan wrote in *A Salutary Lessons: Ceritalah 3*, December 1994.
11. "Silence of the Lambs", *Far Eastern Economic Review*, November 14th, 1996, pp. 25-26.
12. *BusinessWeek*, April 1996, Editorial.
13. *The Wave of Self-Development*, Commonwealth Publishing, February 1st, 1998, p.76.
14. "Kick Off, Cash In", *Far Eastern Economic Review*, January 16th, 1997.

15. Jim Willis, "The Age of Multimedia and Turbonews", in *Exploting Your Future, Living, Learning and Working in the Information Age*, edited by Edward Cornish, World Future Society, 1996.
16. Charles Fishman, "The Future of Work", Fast Company, January 1997.

Chapter 8

1. Daniel Yergin and Joseph Stanislaw, *The Commanding Heights: The battle between government and the marketplace that is remaking the world*, Simon &Schuster, 1998.
2. http://www.times.com/deng/leaders/html
3. Ibid.
4. Daniel Yergin and Joseph Stanislaw, *The Commanding Heights: The battle between government and the marketplace that is remaking the world*, Simon & Schuster, 1998.
5. Ibid.
6. Pujie Zheng, The Freeman (file:///Ai/D1.htm).
7. "To Get Rich Is Glorious", *Asiaweek*, March 7th, 1997, p.27.
8. Ibid. p. 28.
9. Ibid. p. 31.
10. "Deng Legacy: A China At Peace", *Far Eastern Economic Review*, March 6th, p.39,1997.
11. "To Get Rich Is Glorious", *Asiaweek*, March 7th, 1997, p.32.
12. Ibid. p. 33.
13. "Lee Kuan Yew's Obituary Note", *The Business Times*, February 21st, 1997.
14. "After The Patriarch", *Far Eastern Economic Review*, March 6th, 1997, p.14.
15. "A History of the American People", Paul Johnson, Harper Collins, p.744.
16. Opening Keynote Address: "Entrepreneurial Leadership", Tun Daim Zainuddin, September 18th, 1996.
17. "The Disease Detective", *Time*, December 30th, 1996/January 6th, 1997.
18. "Reform's Dark Side", *Far Easter Economic Review*, March 20th, 1997.
19. Li Lu, "He's the voice of the Tiananmen Generation", Fast Company, August 15th, 1997, http://www.fastcompany.com
20. "Who's Who Of Business", The Asia Inc: vol.6, no.2, February 1997, pp.33-34.
21. "The New Leaders that Asia Needs", *Asian Business,* September 1995, pp.56-58.
22. "The Struggle to Reinvent Japan", *Asiaweek*, May 31st, 1996, pp.47-49.
23. "Richard Branson", *Forbes ASAP*, February 24th, 1997, pp.95-102.
24. Warren Bennis, "Across The Board: People, Dollars and Ideas", *Fortune*, Sept 1993.
25. "The Trillion Dollar Vision of Dee Hock", Fast Company. Archive at http://www.fastcompany.com.
26. Foreword, "The Leader of the Future", The Drucker Foundation, Jossey Bass Publishers, San Francisco, 1996.
27. "Asian Leadership-Anand Panyarachun", *Asiaweek*, October 20th, 1995, pp.38-39.
28. "Women In Positions Of National Power", *Business Times*, September 25th, 1995.

29. George Melloan, "Clinton's Nature and the Nature of Politics", *Asian Wall Street Journal*, August 1998.
30. Guan Zhong, the Chinese Scholar said, "A wise ruler follows the law, not intellect. He relies on decided policy, not mere rhetorics. He respects the public desire, and not private wishes. He relies on the fundamental principles of governance and disregards all trivialities". *Quotations of Guan Zhong*, published by Hong Kong Educational Publishers, 1996.

Chapter 9

1. "Confident Taiwan", *Wall Street Journal*, December 1st, 1997, Editorial.
2. Francis Fukuyama, "By Way of Introduction", in *The End Up History and the Last Man*, The Free Press, 1992, pp. xviii-xvi.
3. S. Jayakumar, "Grow We Must", Singapore's Minister of Foreign Affairs in a speech delivered in April at George Town University, Washington, published in the *Far Eastern Economic Review*, May 30th, 1996.
4. Strobe Talbott, "Democracy and the National Interest", *Foreign Affairs*, 75.6 Nov/Dec 1996, p. 57.
5. *Asian Walls Street Journal*, January 12, 1998.
6. "Culture Is Destiny: A Conversation with Lee Kuan Yew" Fareed Zakaria, *Foreign Affairs*, vol.73, no.2, March/April 1994. Kim Dae Jung responded in "Kim Dae Jung" on the Asian Values that never were, Kim's Response to "Culture Is Destiny", *Foreign Affairs*, November/December 1994, vol.73, no.6.
7. People are stupid policy, *Yu Min Zheng Ce* is an assertion of Confucius. People are born with certain orientations. Some people are born to lead, while others are born followers. Some people even if given the chance cannot decide for themselves, so why ask them. This is a very elitist view underlying the basic assumption of strong government in contemporary Asian thinking.
8. Translated from *New Interpretations of the Analects of Confucius*. Nan Huai Chin, Lao Ku Culture Foundation Inc., p. 339.
9. The Chinese language is ambiguous, it has no tenses, one word can have many different meanings, and shifting punctuation marks can change the meaning of the entire sentence. While interpreting in the Chinese language, the context is very important. A word interpreted in the wrong context can mean different things. Because of the long history of this civilization, there is no clear distinction between disciplines, for example, history blends with literature and mixed with philosophy. Imagine how confusing this can be to a rational, analytical and structured-minded person used to western culture clearly defined branches of knowledge.
10. Daniel A. Bel, "A Communitarian Critique of Authoritarianism: The Case of Singapore", *Political Theory*, vol.25, no.1, February 1997, Sage Publications Inc.
11. "India: Tiger or Tortoise?" *The Economist*, April 27th, 1996.
12. Fared Zakaria, "From the Old to the New", *Newsweek*, August 4th, 1997.
13. Alexis de Tocqueville, *Democracy in America*, Amereon House, US, 1840 and 1935.
14. "A Suitable Target for Foreign Policy?" *The Economist*, April 1997.

15. John Naisbitt, *Global Paradox*, William Morrow & Co, Inc, 1994 p. 44.
16. *Far Eastern Economic Review*, April 3rd, 1997.
17. "How to Cut the Cost of Politics", *The Economist*, February 8th, 1997.
18. "Politicians for Rent", *The Economist*, February 8th, 1997, p. 23.
19. "The Backlash against Soft Money", *BusinessWeek*, March 31st, 1997, p. 32.
20. Brain Beedham, "Full Democracy", *The Economist*, December 21st, 1996, p.3, & British Broadcasting Corporation: http://www.bbc.org.
21. *The Economist*, February 8th, 1997, p 29.
22. Indicators on voter turnout at last general elections as percentage of total registered voters, *Far Eastern Economic Review*, July 31st, 1997.
23. Ibid
24. "Choosing Representatives: Singapore does it her way", *in The People's Representatives: Electoral Systems in the Asia-Pacific Region*, ed Graham Hassell and Cheryl Saunders, p.45.
25. Daniel A. Bell, "An Asian Democracy for the 21st Century", *The Asian Wall Street Journal*, March 13th, 1997.
26. Minxin Pei, "Is China Democratizing? Foreign Affairs", vol. 77, no.1, January/February 1998.
27. Strobe Talbott, "Democracy and the National Interest", *Foreign Affairs*, November/December 1996, p.57.
28. Yen Chia Chee, *How Can Democracy Come To China?* Yuen Li Publishing, Taipei, 1996 (Chinese Edition).
29. "China's Grassroots Democracy", *The Economist*, November 2nd, 1996.
30. "Middle Kingdom Requires A Middle Way", *The Asian Wall Street Journal*, April 1st, 1997.
30. Robert L. Bartley, "China: Taking a Long View", *The Asian Wall Street Journal*, June 11th, 1997.

Chapter 10

1. Po Yang, *The Ugly Chinese*, Lie Pie Publishing, Taiwan, August 15th, 1985, p. 81.
2. Po Yang, "Honest Look at History, Pragmatic about the Present", Translated from *Commonwealth* Magazine interview, Jan 1st, 1998 p. 394.
3. Canto-pop is Cantonese popular music. This is Hong Kong's equivalent of Western pop music. Singers combined elaborate stage showmanship complete with laser, props and sometimes high tech stunts to give audiences an involved experience. Canto-pop is immensely popular in all the Chinese-based communities, including many parts of the mainland. To expand their market, some Canto-pop singers are singing mandarin versions of their songs.
4. "Values as Asia's Winning Tool", *Commonwealth* Magazine, April 1st, 1996, p. 97.
5. Conversation with Angeline Ch'ng, who formerly worked with Chew Poh Jin. Sept 15th, 1998.
6. S.G. Atterhed, "Sustainability of the Inner and Outer Worlds", Paper prepared for The ForeSight Group, Sweden 1996 for circulation to its global network.

7. 'Ma fu' in Chinese refers to a careless and compromising attitude to accepting standards. 'Tidak apa' refers to the same kind of attitude to finishing a task of maintaining a high standard of excellence.
8. Jesse Wong, "Collector Charts China's View of the World", *Asian Wall Street Journal*, July 28th, 1997.
9. "The Face of China's Future", *Far Eastern Economic Review*, July 10th, 1997, Editorial .
10. "Shanghai Surprize, Two Art Lovers Confront China's Money Culture", *Far Eastern Economic Review*, November 7th, 1996.
11. T. Fong and M.Y. Tee, "Discourse: Duck-Off! Patrick Teoh on being Patrick Teoh" *Journal One*, May 1996, p. 10.
12. Asian Lifestyles: Special Report, *Far Eastern Economic Review*, August 8th, 1996.
13. Ayn Rand, *Virtues of Selfishness*, The New American Library, 1961, p. 54.
14. Barry Hing, "Mickey Mouse Deserves a Prize", *Asian Wall Street Journal*, January 7th, 1997.
15. Karim Raslan, *Ceritalah: Malaysia in Transition*, "Ruling with Aplomb", 1996, Times Books International, p. 55.

Chapter 11

1. "The Dawning of the Green Century", *Commonwealth* Magazine, June 1996.
2. Peter G. Peterson (1996), " Will America Grow Up before it Grows Old?" Random House Inc, New York, p. 24.
3. Gil Friend, "The Natural Step (1): From Linear to Cyclical Economy", April 25th, 1997, http://www.igc.apc.org/eco-ops/nbl/nbl.3.12.html
4. Ibid.
5. Gil Friend, "The Natural Step (2): An Industrialized Country Learns Common Sense" March 4th, 1997, http://www.igc.apc.org/eco-ops/nbl/nbl3.12.html
6. Information on the work of Tzu Chi drawn from *Commonwealth* Magazine, October 1st, 1996.
7. Details on the history of Chinese independent schools in Malaysia drawn from Yap Sin Tian, "The Chinese Schools of Malaysia: Towards the year 2000", United Chinese School Committees Association of Malaysia, K.L., p. 17.
8. Lester M. Salamon, "The Rise of the Non Profit Sector", Foreign Affairs, vol.73, no.4, July/August 1994, p.109.
9. Jessica T. Mathews, " Power Shift", Foreign Affairs vol.76, no.1, January/February 1997, p. 53.
10. Toshihiro Menju & Takako Aoki, "The Evolution of Japanese NGOs in the Asia Pacific Context", in *Emerging Civil Society in the Asia Pacific Community*, ed. Tadashi Yamamoto, Japan Center for International Exchange and The Institute of Southeast Asian Studies, Singapore, 1995, p. 145.
11. Amara Pongsapich , "Non-governmental Organizations in Thailand". The Evolution of Japanese NGOS in the Asia Pacific Context", Emerging Civil Society in the Asia Pacific Community, ed. Tadashi Yamamoto, Japan Center for International Exchange and The Institute of Southeast Asian Studies, Singapore, 1995, p. 248.

12. Chan Tse Chueen, "Non governmental Organizations in Singapore", The Evolution of Japanese NGOS in the Asia Pacific Context", Emerging Civil Society in the Asia Pacific Community, ed. Tadashi Yamamoto, Japan Center for International Exchange and The Institute of Southeast Asian Studies, Singapore, 1995, p. 221.
13. Yoichi Funabashi, "NGOs as a Force for Civilian Power: How the 'Associational Revolution' is changing the world", in *The Role of Non-State Actors in International Affairs: A Japanese Perspective*, ed. Tadashi Yamamoto & Yoichi Funabashi, The Japan Center for International Exchange, Japan, 1995, pp. 68-69.
14. Tadashi Yamamoto, "Integrative Report", in *Emerging Civil Society in the Asia Pacific Community*, ed. Tadashi Yamamoto, The Institute of Southeast Asian Study and The Japan Center for International Exchange, Singapore, pp. 11-12.
15. Gary S. Becker, "If you Want to Cut Corruption, Cut Government", *Business Week*, December 11th, 1995.
16. Kengo Inoue, "Japan's Fight Against Elitism", *Asian Wall Street Journal*, April 7th, 1997.

Chapter 12

1. Jasper Becker, *Hungry Ghosts: China's Secret Famine*, John Murray (Publishers) Ltd, 1996, pp. 307-8.
2. Ibid.
3. *Commonwealth* magazine, November 18th, 1991, Taipei.
4. Friedrich von Hayek, *Individualism and Economic Order*, p. 1.
5. Samuel Smiles, *Self-Help*, John Murray, London, 1867, p. 2.
6. Ibid.
7. *Commonwealth* magazine, November 1991.
8. Joe Rogaly, "A Self-help slogan for the 90s: How looking back a century can help us look to the future", *Financial Times*, June 29th, 1996.
9. Ayn Rand, *The Virtue of Selfishness: A New Concept of Egoism*, The New American Library Inc, 1961.
10. Ibid, p.viii.
11. Ibid.
12. *Far Eastern Economic Review*, November 24th, 1994.
13. Ayn Rand, *The Virtue of Selfishness: A New Concept of Egoism*, The New American Library Inc, 1961.
14. Ibid, p.27.
15. Milton & Rose Friedman, *Free to Choose: A Personal Statement*, A Harvest Book, published by Harcourt Brace & Company, 1980.
16. Quote from Lee Kuan Yew.
17. Ayn Rand, *The Virtue of Selfishness: A New Concept of Egoism*, The New American Library Inc, 1961.
18. Author's conversation with Professor Tu Weimeng, Director of Yencheng Institute, Harvard University.

Bibliography

Becker, Gary & Guity Nashat. *The Economics of Life*. McGraw-Hill Companies Inc, New York, 1997.

Becker, Jasper and John Murray. *Hungry Ghosts, China's Secret Famine*, 1996.

Cheng Yen, *Still Thoughts*, ed Hsin-Chiang Kao, trans Chia Hui Lin. Tzu Chi Culture Publications, Taiwan, 1993.

de Tocqueville, Alexis. *Democracy in America*. American House, Amereon Ltd, New York, 1835.

Friedman, Milton and Rose. *Free to Choose: A Personal Statement*. Harcourt Brace & Company, 1979.

Fukuyama, Francis. *The End of History and the Last Man*. Avon with arrangement with The Free Press, 1992.

Hassal, Graham, and Cheryl Saunders eds. *The People's Representatives; Electoral Systems in the Asia Pacific Region*. Allen & Unwin Pty Ltd, Sydney, 1997.

Holmes, Kim R, Bryan T Johnson and Melanie Kirkpatrick, eds, *1997 Index of Economic Freedom*, The Heritage Foundation and The Wall Street Journal, 1997.

Koh, Tommy TB. *Conflict and Cooperation: The United States and East Asia*. Times Academic Press, Singapore 1995

Lin Yu-tang. *My Country and My People, Lin Yu-tang on China*. Heinemann Asia Singapore.

Morrison, Ian. *The Second Curve, Managing The Velocity Of Change*. Nicholas Bradley Publishing, London, 1996.

Rand, Ayn. *The Virtues of Selfishness, A New Concept of Egoism*, contrib Nathaniel Branden. Signet Books, New American Library, Times Mirror, 1961.

Robinson, Richard and David S.G Goodman, eds. *The New Rich in Asia*. Routledge, London, 1996.

Samuelson, Robert J. *The Good Life and Its Discontents: The American Dream In The Age of Entitlement 1945-1995*. Times Books, United States, 1995.

Smiles, Samuel. *Self Help; with illustrations of Character, Conduct and Perseverance*, 1867.

Smith, Adam. *An Inquiry into the Nature and Causes of the Wealth of Nations*. University of Chicago Press, 1776.

Thurow, Lester. *Head to Head: The coming economic battle among Japan, Europe and America*. William Morrow and Company In, New York, 1992.

von Hayek, Friedrich. *Individualism and Economic Order*. University of Chicago Press, 1948.

von Hayek, Friedrich. *The Fatal Conceit: The Errors of Socialism*, ed W.W. Bartley. University of Chicago Press, 1988.

Yergin, Daniel and Joseph Stanislaw. *Commanding Heights, The battle between government and the marketplace that is remaking the world*. Simon & Schuster, 1998.

Chinese books

Po Yang. *The Ugly Chinese.* Lin Bei Publishing House, Taiwan, 1987.

Chan, Hong Chi. *The Salt and Steel Debate.* Zi Pao Cultural Publishing Company, 1997.

Yen, Chia Chee. *The Road to Democracy*.

Glossary of Chinese Words

Acer Group	宏基集团
Alan Chan	陈幼坚
Ambrose King	金耀基
Apple Daily	苹果日报
Asian Wall Street Journal	亚洲华尔街日报
Asiaweek	英文亚洲周刊
Bai jia zheng ming, bai hua qi kai	百家争鸣,百花齐放
Beida	北大
Business Week	商业周刊
Cang fu yu min, Bu yu min zheng	昌福于民,不于民争
Caohai Nature Province	高海自然保护区
Chen Mai Guang	陈袁光
Chi ku	吃苦
Chong Yo Fah	张荣发
Christine Loh	陆恭蕙
Chung Ting-yiu	钟庭跃
Commonwealth Magazine	天下杂志
Dau bu tong, bu sia wei mou	道不同, 不下为谋
David Ho	何大一
David Tang	邓永将
Democratic Progressive Party	民进党
Deng Xiaoping	邓小平
Dianne Ying	殷充芃
Dong Jiao Zong	董教总
Dr Emilia Roxas	郑绵绵
Dr Sun Yat Sen	孙中山
Dr Tommy Koh	许通美
Dr Yang Mu	杨沐
Emily Lau	刘慧卿
Evergreen Group	长荣集团
Far Eastern Economic Review	远东经济评论
Faye Wong	王菲
Foong Wai Fong	冯久玲

Founder Group	北大方正
Goh Chok Tong	吴作栋
Gordan Wu	胡应潮
GuanXi	关系
Guan Zhong	管仲
Guizhou Province	贵州县
Guo ke	过客
Han	汉
Hao nan bu dang bing	好男不当兵
Hu Xue Yan	胡雪严
Hwa xia	华夏
Jia feng li sheng cun	夹缝里生春
Jiang Zemin	江泽民
Jiao Tong Da Xue	交通大学
Jimmy Lai	黎智英
Jin Yong	金庸
Jun zi	君子
Jup sang	执生
Kao Ching Yuen	高清愿
Kiasu	怕输
Kim Dae Jung	金大中
KT Li	李国鼎
Kuomintang	国民党
Kwok Leng Beng	郭令明
Lao Tze	老子
Lee Hsien Loong	李显龙
Lee Kuan Yew	李光耀
Lee Teng Hui	李登辉
Lee Yuen Tze	李远哲
Li & Fung	利丰
Li Ka Shing	李嘉诚
Li Lu	李禄
Lian Chan	连战
Liberation Daily	解放日报
Lim Goh Tong	林梧桐
Liem Sioe Liong	林绍良

Lin Yutang	林语堂
Liu Shao Qi	刘少其
Lok Ma Chau	落马洲
Louis Cha	查良镛
Ma Cheng Yuan	马承远
Ma fu	马虎
Man Kam To	文锦渡
Mao Zedong	毛泽东
Martin Lee	李柱铭
Master Chen Yen	澄严法师
Michael Yu Ming Yih	吴明毅
Michelle Yeoh	扬紫琼
Min ke shi you zhi, bu ke shi zhi zhi	民可使由之, 不可使知之.
Min ke, shi you zhi, bu ke, shi zhi zhi	民可,使由之,不可, 使知之
Ming Pao	明报
Nan xun	南巡
Neoh Kuao Cheng	梁国祯
Next Magazine	壹周刊
Ning wei ji shou, bu wei niu hou	宁为鸡首, 不为牛后
Nuo zhe	懦者
People's Daily	人民日报
Po yang	柏扬
Qi pao	旗袍
Qi Quo	齐国
Qin Shi Huang Di	秦始皇帝
Qing chao	清朝
Qing, li, fa	情理法
Richard Li	李泽楷
Robert Kwok	郭鹤年
San qi si qie	三妻四妾
Sha Tau Kok	沙头角
Shanghai	上海
Shantou	山头
Sheng xian	圣贤

Shengyang	省阳
Shenzen	深圳
Shi cheng	师承
Shi nong gong shang	士农工商
Shou fa	守法
Song	宋
Stan Shih	施振荣
Sun Tzu	孙子
Tam Siu Cheung	谭兆宗
Tan Dun	谭盾
Tang	唐
Tao Zhu Gong	陶朱公
Tian xia da tong	天下大同
Tianjin	天津
Tong Kooi Ong	童贵安
Tseng Shih Chiang	曾仕强
Ṭsinghua University	清华大学
Tu Wei Ming	杜维明
Tung Chee Hwa	董建华
Tzu Chi Charitable Foundation	慈济功德会
Victor Fung	冯国经
Wang Gung Wu	王赓武
Wang Tao Han	王道涵
Wang Xuan	王宣
Wang Yung Ching	王永庆
Wang Zuo Rong	王作荣
Weining County	惠宁省
Wen Tianxiang	文天祥
Wu Chai Wei	吴家玮
Wu Yi	胡仪
Xiamen	厦门
Xin yi	信义
Ya men ba zi kai, you li wu qian mo jin lai	衙门八字开,有理无钱莫进来
Ya Zhou Zhou Kan	亚洲周刊
Yap Sin Tian	叶新田

Yazhou zhoukan	中文亚洲周刊
Yen Chia Chee	严家其
Yi ge he shang dan shui chi	一个和尚担水喝
Liang ge he shang tai shui chi	两个和尚抬水喝
San ge he shang mei shui chi	三个和尚没水喝
Yi pan san sha	一盘散沙
Ying xiong bu wen chu shen di	英雄不问出身低
Yo Yo Ma	马友友
Yong Teck Lee	杨德利
Zai seng	再生
Zhao Chujun	赵纯均
Zhi, yong, xin, yan, ren	智,勇,信,严,仁
Zhou En Lai	周恩来
Zhu Cheng	诸城
Zhu Hai	珠海
Zhu Rongji	朱镕基
Zhuan dao qiao tou zi ran zhi	船到桥头自然直
Zuo chi shan beng	坐吃山崩

Index

"Wai Fong has brilliantly demonstrated the inter-relationships between society, politics and economy in Asia's development experience. Her vision of progress and reform has tremendous reference value for a developing society like China. We should pay serious attention to the insights expressed in this book."

Mao Yushi, Director, Unirule Institute, Beijing.

"*The New Asian Way* is an important book about Asia's modernization. It provides a useful framework for us to reflect on our own development experiences."

Chang Yen, Scholar of International Studies,
Chinese Academy of Social Science.

"It is about time an Asian who hasn't got a government line to plug writes about Asia and the problems and opportunities facing us. It is also about time for Asians to admit that they too live in a multicultural world. Life is what we make of it. There is no point looking for an excuse or a conspiracy theory that the West wants to keep us down."

Christine Loh, Chair, Citizen Party,
Legislative Councillor, Hong Kong.

"The most valuable part of the *New Asian Way* is its wake up call to us Asians to let go of our imagined glory from the past, and focus on building the future. Outstanding woman writers are commonplace, but a woman thinker in the field of human development is rare. We are proud of Wai Fong. She has filled an important void."

Loh Chow, History Scholar,
The Chinese Academy of Social Sciences, Beijing.

"I strongly recommend *The New Asian Way* to anyone interested in success. Its core philosophy of initiative, awareness and self-reliance is fundamental to human progress. I hope Wai Fong's work will provide an impetus to many related work from Asia's very own thinkers."

Chen Caihong, Deputy General Manager,
China Construction Bank, Beijing.